W9-BZP-432

THE PURSUIT OF
FAIRNESS

Also by Terry H. Anderson

The Sixties

The Movement and the Sixties

A Flying Tiger's Diary (with pilot Charles R. Bond Jr.)

The United States, Great Britain and the Cold War, 1944–1947

THE PURSUIT OF
FAIRNESS

A History of Affirmative Action

Terry H. Anderson

OXFORD
UNIVERSITY PRESS

OXFORD
UNIVERSITY PRESS

Oxford University Press, Inc., publishes works that further
Oxford University's objective of excellence
in research, scholarship, and education.

Oxford New York
Auckland Cape Town Dar es Salaam Hong Kong Karachi
Kuala Lumpur Madrid Melbourne Mexico City Nairobi
New Delhi Shanghai Taipei Toronto

With offices in
Argentina Austria Brazil Chile Czech Republic France Greece
Guatemala Hungary Italy Japan Poland Portugal Singapore
South Korea Switzerland Thailand Turkey Ukraine Vietnam

First published by Oxford University Press, Inc., 2004
198 Madison Avenue, New York, New York 10016
www.oup.com

First issued as an Oxford University Press paperback, 2005
ISBN-13: 978-019-518245-3   ISBN-10: 0-19-518245-6

Oxford is a registered trademark of Oxford University Press

The Library of Congress has cataloged the cloth edition as follows:
Anderson, Terry H., 1946–
The pursuit of fairness : a history of affirmative action / by Terry H. Anderson
p. cm.
Includes bibliographical references.
ISBN-13: 978-019-515764-2 ISBN-10: 0-19-515764-8
1. Affirmative action programs—United States—History. I. Title.
HF5549.5.A34 A53 2004 331.13'3'0973—dc22 2003024637

9 8 7 6 5 4 3 2 1
Printed in the United States of America on acid-free paper

For Emily and Howard,

and for Rose

contents

| preface

As the nine robed justices listened to the arguments in the cases against the University of Michigan in April 2003, several thousand rallied outside on the steps of the U.S. Supreme Court Building. They had come from many universities, including Harvard, Penn State, U.C. Berkeley, Howard, Georgetown, and especially, Michigan. Most were black, some whites and Hispanics, and many held signs as they listened to speakers Al Sharpton, Martin Luther King III, and the Rev. Jesse Jackson. "We must fight this fight," Jackson declared, and then the crowd joined him in chanting, "The struggle is not over."

Others hoped it was over, including two white women. Jennifer Gratz had applied to become an undergraduate at the university, and Barbara Grutter had sought acceptance into the law school. Denied admission, the two women sued in separate cases, claiming that the university's policy violated their rights under the 1964 Civil Rights Act and the equal protection clause of the Fourteenth Amendment of the U.S. Constitution.

That policy was affirmative action. The university had used race as one of the many criteria for admission.

Ten weeks later, in June, the Supreme Court issued its decisions, the most crucial ones concerning higher education since the late 1970s. By a narrow 5 to 4 majority, the Court again found affirmative action constitutional. Writing for the majority, Justice Sandra Day O'Connor declared, "We expect that 25 years from now, the use of racial preferences will no longer be necessary."

The response was immediate and expected. "The court's decision is a great victory for American higher education," declared the former

University of Michigan president, Lee C. Bollinger, "and for the nation as a whole." Not so, wrote African American conservative Thomas Sowell. The majority opinion made "a mockery of the law. . . . This decision provoked not only dissent from four other justices but also sarcasm and disgust—as it should have."

Affirmative action. It has been a public policy for four decades, perhaps it will be for 25 more years, and it always raises emotions, contentious debate, and all too often charges of racism. Both sides claim moral superiority. Supporters declare themselves the champions of racial justice, protectors of Martin Luther King's Dream, while opponents see themselves as the defenders of merit, of colorblind equal protection enshrined in the U.S. Constitution. One thing is clear: the arguments of both sides have merit and are legitimate, and that in itself makes affirmative action an American dilemma.

The battle over affirmative action has led not to clarity but to confusion. Over the decades opinion polls have demonstrated that many citizens think the federal government mandates that all employers have quotas to help minorities and women. Fathers often are convinced that their sons cannot get into an elite college or professional school because he is not the right race or gender. Whites often think that affirmative action simply means reverse discrimination or quotas.

By the twenty-first century, pundits, lawyers, journalists, and academics had written dozens of books and thousands of articles on affirmative action. Unfortunately, many of these only added to the confusion. Most of the books were polemics, some were confessions of "affirmative action babies," while historians wrote studies that focused only on one aspect of the topic, such as the *Bakke* case, or one era, such as the 1960s.

This book is unique—the first history of affirmative action that traces the development of the policy from its genesis in the Great Depression and World War II era to the University of Michigan cases in 2003. It defines affirmative action during various presidential administrations and will demonstrate how its definition and rationale have changed significantly during the last half century. It examines how and why various presidential administrations established, expanded, and then diminished the policy, and how the U.S. Supreme Court changed affirmative action since its first ruling on it in 1971.

Affirmative action holds the keys to success in the United States—higher education, employment, business—and by examining the policy, this book will explore topics fundamental to citizens: equality, preference, and fairness. Who is admitted into the finest colleges and professional programs? Which applicant is hired or promoted? What business wins the federal contract?

Ultimately, affirmative action concerns fairness: What is fair in America? Examining the historical record will show the answer to that question has changed dramatically since the presidency of Franklin D. Roosevelt.

During the 1990s I was writing about social movements in the 1960s, and it was difficult to find a lucid text explaining affirmative action. That is my aim here. I place the development of the policy within the contours of American history. Naturally, a book this size cannot be a history of federal agencies or judicial cases, a detailed survey of the changing status of minorities or women, a dissertation on ideas of equality or theories of social science, or an exploration of other civil rights issues such as school integration, busing, or Title IX. When I told a friend what I was writing he blurted out, "What a bore!" Indeed, most books on this topic are laden with jargon, theories, legalese, and frankly, they are dull. They shouldn't be. After all, affirmative action is about people, their education, work, and what they think is fair.

As for terms, I use words and labels that conform to the historical era. In an attempt to be as neutral as possible, I avoid suggestive terms, such as "quota" when a president labeled his policy "goals and timetables." Using their own statements, I allow the actors of each era to define the debate.

Finally, a personal note: I was hired in 1979 as an assistant professor at Texas A&M University with the mandate to interview former students who fought in World War II and became general officers in the U.S. military, a specialized position that probably did not attract women or minority applicants. Since then I have published extensively and have been promoted through the ranks, enjoying life in Texas. Thus, to my knowledge, affirmative action has not had an impact on my career. That being the case, I have no ax to grind, no agenda, just a fascination at how this contentious policy developed and changed over the years.

We do not need another polemic. As the demonstrations and debate over the Michigan cases revealed, this nation needs a balanced history of affirmative action. Hopefully, that will result in a more enlightened discussion of a policy that affects—and divides—so many Americans.

Terry Anderson
College Station, Texas
November 2003

| acknowledgments

I owe a debt to those scholars who have written the best books on one aspect or one era of affirmative action. Their labor and research in presidential libraries paved the way for this study and although their books appear in the notes and bibliography, they deserve special attention: Gareth Davies, Paul D. Moreno, John David Skrentny, Dean Kotlowski, Nicholas Laham, and especially the late Hugh Davis Graham. Their research pinpointed key documents at various presidential libraries and allowed me to make quick visits or simply order the appropriate primary documents.

I would like to thank those archivists who were helpful. Allen Fisher at the Lyndon B. Johnson Presidential Library, Kelly D. Barton at the Ronald Reagan Library, and Robert Holzweiss and Stephanie Orial at the George H. W. Bush Presidential Library.

I would also like to thank those friends and scholars who read individual chapters of the manuscript: Dean Kotlowski and John David Skrentny. Hugh Gordon educated me on the Lockheed Corporation and other business practices. My friend and colleague Al Broussard read the entire manuscript keeping me on track on African American history, and as usual so did my finest critic, Rose Eder.

To help in this endeavor I hired my finest senior history majors to scramble over to the library and locate several thousand articles. Those research assistants included Kristie Smedsrud, Trish Rohde, Mike Police, and especially Steve Smith, who even supplied me with vital documents while I was teaching in Ireland as the Mary Ball Washington Professor of American History. Steve and Mike also read the entire manuscript, forcing revisions for clarity.

The Texas A&M University Association of Former Students generously funded a semester leave, which allowed me to finish the manuscript on time.

At Oxford University Press, Peter Ginna listened to my plans, encouraged them, sent a fine contract and, along with Catherine Humphries and Laura Stickney, kept the publication process moving in high gear.

As usual, my brothers, Steve and Jeff, and their wives, Ginny and Moey, provided great cheer, while my tennis buddies, David Ogden and Joe Golsan, tried to keep my line calls fair while observing my immature antics on the court.

This book is dedicated to three people. My late mother, Emily, my father, Howard, who struggled to teach me the meaning of fairness while I was growing up, and my companion, Rose, who doesn't know if she has won or lost that struggle, taught me her definition of "equal rights."

THE PURSUIT OF
FAIRNESS

one | Genesis of Affirmative Action

September 1940, with war clouds on the horizon, A. Philip Randolph contemplated his meeting with the president of the United States, Franklin D. Roosevelt. As the African American leader of the Brotherhood of Sleeping Car Porters entered the White House, Randolph was well aware of the power of his argument. In Europe, Nazi Germany had deemed itself the "master race" and was conducting a brutal war against its neighbors. In the Far East, Imperial Japan was maiming, raping, killing its way across China in its savage attempt to become the ruler of Asia.

Randolph held firm views on the war. As a Socialist he had opposed America's entrance in World War I, but by 1940 he had quit that party and criticized its neutral policy, aware of what he called the "fury and fire, death and destruction of Nazism."

The president, of course, was well aware of the international threat, and in a fireside chat he discussed the dictatorships, declaring that their aims were to "enslave the human race," labeling them the "oldest and worst tyranny. In that there is no liberty, no religion, no hope."

Thus, after the Third Reich overwhelmed and conquered France earlier in June, the commander in chief asked Congress to pass an act to increase troop strength. That autumn Congress established selective service—the first peacetime draft. Many volunteered, and during 1940 and the next year blacks comprised more than 16 percent of enlistments.

African American men changed from working clothes to army uniforms, but they were assigned to segregated units, usually as laborers. They were restricted from service schools, and in the Navy they were assigned to be messmen or officers' stewards. In 1940 blacks were not even allowed to enlist in the Army Air Corps and Signal Corps or into the Coast Guard or the Marines.

The president and Congress that year also greatly increased funds for the nation's defense industries. After the lean years of the Great Depression, jobs finally became available, and unemployment began to shrink. Yet, as men formed lines at the factories, it soon became clear that almost all of the defense plants would hire only white men. An executive for Vultee Aircraft stated to a congressional committee, "We do not believe it advisable to include colored people in our regular working force," and the president of North American Aviation added, "It is against the company policy to employ them as mechanics or aircraft workers." When blacks asked to join the union so they could work at Boeing Aircraft in Seattle, the labor leader remarked that they had "been called upon to make many sacrifices for defense and has made them gladly, but this is asking too much."[1]

American fairness in 1940: discrimination was tradition, and in some states it was law. As a grandson of slaves, Randolph was well aware of these customs and of the laws that during his lifetime had established a system based on race—Jim Crow.

Born in 1889 in Florida, young Randolph was raised during the end of a century that witnessed the passage of many laws in southern and border states which, in effect, challenged those amendments to the U.S. Constitution that states had ratified during Reconstruction following the Civil War. The Fourteenth Amendment had forbidden states to deny "equal protection" of the laws to any resident, which now included numerous new black citizens, and the Fifteenth had given black men the right to vote. By the 1880s, however, states were passing laws that restricted those rights, laws that were based on race and supported by people who agreed with Henry W. Grady, editor of the *Atlanta Constitution*. "The supremacy of the white race of the South must be maintained forever," he declared in the 1880s, "because the white race is the superior race." The Civil War had changed the U.S. Constitution but not the customs nor the feelings. "If anything would make me kill my children," a white woman said, "it would be the possibility that niggers might sometime eat at the same table and associate with them as equals."

The most educated and refined black, thus, was not equal to the most illiterate and indecent white, and to ensure that status, southern states passed Jim Crow laws. After the turn of the century, seventeen southern and border states had passed laws that established segregated schools, hospitals, jails, and homes for the indigent, elderly, deaf—even for the blind. They restricted blacks to the backs of streetcars, to separate train coaches and waiting rooms. Cities enacted local ordinances, so that after sunset entire neighborhoods could be "off limits" to blacks. In Atlanta, white and black court witnesses could not swear on the same Bible. In Florida and North Carolina public schools, textbooks used by white and black students had to be kept separate, while a Louisiana ordinance stipulated that the white and black lines to buy tickets for the circus had to be 25 feet apart. In Kentucky whites and blacks had to live on separate sides of the street, while Alabama forbade them from playing checkers together. In New Orleans, officials segregated prostitutes and red-light districts; Atlanta confined them to separate blocks, while Nashville brothels placed white girls upstairs and black ones in the basement.

In 1900 the Richmond *Times* demanded that strict segregation "be applied in every relation of Southern life" because "God Almighty drew the color line and it cannot be obliterated." White businesses such as hotels, boarding houses, and restaurants did not serve blacks. Signs were hung in public places, over entrances and exits, ticket windows, waiting rooms, water fountains, and toilets, designating "Whites Only" or "Colored." Blacks were either restricted from, or segregated at, public facilities such as libraries, theaters, sports arenas, parks, and beaches. Some recreational areas had signs: "Negroes and Dogs Not Allowed."

Southern fairness: Although blacks paid taxes that contributed to public buildings and spaces, they were not allowed equal access. When the automobile became available in the second decade of the century, some communities even restricted black motorists on public streets. Although blacks paid taxes that in turn paid the salaries of public officials, there was not one black policeman or judge in the South.

Naturally, African Americans fought back. In 1896 Homer Plessy's case reached the Supreme Court. In *Plessy v. Ferguson* he challenged a Louisiana law that forbade a railroad passenger to enter "a coach or compartment to which by race he does not belong." Plessy felt that the law violated his Fourteenth Amendment rights of due process and equal protection of the law. The Court voted 8 to 1 against Plessy. The one dissenter was Justice John Marshall Harlan, who wrote a prescient statement: "Our Constitution is color-blind, and neither knows nor tolerates classes among citizens. In respect to civil rights, all citizens are equal before the law." Six decades would pass before a majority of the Court would agree with Harlan, for in 1896 the majority agreed with Justice Henry Brown, who wrote that equal rights did not require "an enforced commingling of the two races. . . . If one race be inferior to the other socially, the Constitution of the United States cannot put them upon the same plane." Thus, the accepted notion of the day was that man-made laws were "powerless to eradicate social instincts or to abolish distinctions based upon physical differences." That being the case, the Court allowed "separate but equal" public facilities for the two races, which were always separate but never equal: in 1910 eleven southern states spent over nine dollars on each white public school student and less than three on each black one. All the while, other court rulings continued to deny blacks rights guaranteed by the Constitution.

Southern states also restricted black voting rights, although black men had been given the vote during Reconstruction by the Fifteenth Amendment. This was particularly troublesome to whites in the Deep South, since in 1880 African Americans were a majority in Mississippi, South Carolina, Louisiana, and made up about 40 percent of the populations of Alabama, Florida, Georgia, and Virginia. To white Southerners, the black vote had to be overturned; otherwise the assumption of white superiority was contradicted as they stood equally at the polls. Moreover, whites assumed that as long as blacks participated in the suffrage, they would aspire to social equality. And there was a darker fear. "To the ignorant and brutal young Negro" scribed a white novelist in 1904, social equality "signifies but one thing: the opportunity to enjoy, equally with white men, the privilege of cohabiting with white women." Thus, as historian Leon Litwack wrote, "To bar the black man from the polling place was to bar him from the bedroom. If blacks voted with whites as equals, they would insist on living and sleeping with whites as equals, and no Southerner could contemplate such degradation."[2]

The aim in the South, said one South Carolinian, was to assure the "permanent establishment of White supremacy," and to achieve that they took back the vote. As early as the 1870s Georgia and Virginia passed poll taxes, and by the next decade Mississippi, Florida, and the Carolinas had passed confusing election codes that made registration and voting more complicated and cut the number of semiliterate voters, most of whom were black. Virginia and other states gerrymandered their voting districts many times, which basically nullified the black electorate. Later, states began to amend their constitutions. Mississippi was first in 1890, and most southern states followed during the next two decades. Mississippi's population was more than half black, and its constitutional convention adopted a measure that did not mention race; technically, then, it did not challenge the Fifteenth Amendment. It required voters to be able to read or provide "a reasonable interpretation" of any section of the state constitution. The interpretation loophole was in place for illiterate whites, and the problem for African Americans was that the registrars were white and would judge that few blacks were able to provide an adequate interpretation. These literacy and understanding tests were followed by "good character" clauses, land requirements, and white primaries, which basically disfranchised most blacks in every southern state. Five years after Alabama's 1901 convention, only about 2 percent of blacks in the state were registered to vote, and within the next few years there were numerous counties across the South which had a majority of black residents but not one black voter. As one white wrote about Mississippi, the blacks had been removed from politics "as if the negro had been deported to Liberia."

By the turn of the century race relations had sunk to low tide. The "rights of the Negroes are at a lower ebb than at any time during the thirty-five years of their freedom," wrote a black novelist, "and the race prejudice more intense and uncompromising."

That seemed to be the case. After assuming the presidency in 1901 Theodore Roosevelt asked the most moderate black leader in the nation, Booker T. Washington, to dine with him at the White House. Washington had been the author of the "Atlanta Compromise," which advocated that blacks should end their demands for political equality in exchange for whites supporting black educational and economic advancement. The appropriate type of education for the blacks, Washington stated, would make them "humble, simple, and of service to the community." The president naturally thought that by inviting Washington he would be promoting him as the spokesman for his race, instead of the more demanding African Americans who were outspoken against the Atlanta Compromise, such as W.E.B. Du Bois. Roosevelt was mistaken. After the dinner, the Richmond *Times* declared that the event meant that Roosevelt wanted blacks to "mingle freely in social circles—that white women may receive attentions from negro men," and a Memphis paper labeled the president's action "the most damnable outrage ever perpetrated by any citizen of the United States."

Such feelings degenerated into slurs, which were common not only in the South but throughout the nation. The dominant Anglo-Saxon society seemed intolerant to anything different: Mexicans were labeled greasers or wetbacks; Puerto Ricans were spicks; Italians were dagos; Asians were chinks; and Jews were sheeney, kikes, yids, or jewboys. This bigotry transcended race and reached down into class, as elites labeled poor whites "trash," "rednecks," or "crackers."

The result of this hatred was limitations based on race. Harvard and many private colleges had quotas to drastically limit the number of Jewish students, but the system was harsher if one was black. By "the time I was 6," Rosa Parks recalled, "I was old enough to realize that we were not actually free." Similarly, by 15 Albon Holsey had become aware of his opportunities in the Land of the Free: "I was beaten and knew it. I knew then that I could never aspire to be President of the United States, nor Governor of my State, nor mayor of my city.... I had bumped into the color line and knew that so far as white people were concerned, I was just another nigger."[3]

If blacks didn't learn the racial difference, or "their place," then whites often discharged rigorous enforcement. Concerning race, the South was lawless. Whites owned the law, police, courts, press, and government. If a black brought charges against a white, it demonstrated disrespect to the superior race. Typical was a case in Mississippi in which a black woman in 1897 charged a white man with having beaten her with an ax handle. The justice of the peace dismissed the case, remarking that there was "no law to punish a white man for beating a negro woman." Some 20 years later in Texas a white man was accused of killing a Mexican. Judge Roy Bean went to his legal books and reported that he could find no law against killing a Mexican: case dismissed!

Nor was there punishment for lynching a black man. In 1892 Governor Ben Tillman of South Carolina declared that he would "willingly lead a mob in lynching a Negro who had committed an assault upon a white woman." As the governor said, the black man "must remain subordinate or be exterminated."

Thousands were exterminated, most often by lynching. In 1899 a black Georgia farm worker named Sam Hose asked his white boss for wages and permission to visit his ill mother. The boss refused and the next day started an argument with Hose, drew his gun, and threatened to shoot him. In self-defense, Hose threw an ax, striking the owner and killing him. The papers reported a much different version: Hose sneaked up on his boss during dinner, buried the ax in his head, and then dragged his wife in front of the dying man and repeatedly raped her. Hose's fate was sealed. After he was captured, some two thousand citizens witnessed his lynching in Newman, Georgia. The self-appointed executioners stripped him, chained him to a tree, and then cut off his ears, fingers, genitals, and skinned his face. Then they soaked him in oil and applied the torch. "Oh, my God! Oh, Jesus," were Hose's last words as his veins ruptured from the heat, and his blood hissed on the fire. The horror continued in Waco, Texas. In 1916 a young black farm hand named Jesse Washington confessed to sexually assaulting and murdering a white woman. In the subsequent court case the jury deliberated for four minutes and returned the death penalty. Suddenly, a white spectator yelled, "Get the nigger!" The judge had a revolver in his desk but made no move to stop the mob as they dragged Washington out to the street. While ten thousand people watched and cheered, the men slashed a struggling Washington with knives, cut off his ears, fingers, genitals, until a journalist noted "his body was a solid color of red." They hoisted him into a tree with a chain around his neck, and then let him down into the flames. After the execution, they tied his charred remains to a horse and dragged them through the streets. Cheerful boys pulled out his teeth and sold the "souvenirs" for five dollars each. The mayor and police chief watched it all and took no action against the lynchers, nor did the state government.

The NAACP's *Crisis* magazine labeled the lynching "The Waco Horror," and its editor W.E.B. Du Bois wrote that "any talk of the triumph of Christianity, or the spread of human culture, is twaddle so long as the Waco lynching is possible in the United States of America." It was very possible. From the decade of Randolph's birth in the 1880s to his meeting with FDR in 1940, there were almost 3,500 lynchings *that were reported*—all but about a hundred of them in the South. No one knows how many went uncounted. The worst decade was the 1890s with more than 1,100 of these executions, and the monstrous record was in 1892 with 161 blacks murdered by the mob.[4]

Consider the impact of these murders, the constant terror that African Americans felt living in the South, always knowing that an unusual look at a white person might mean a violent death.

The federal government did not intervene in the states and stop the killings; on the contrary, it had completely abandoned African Americans by the presidency of Woodrow Wilson. Somewhat ironically, the Democrat who became known for advocating "self-determination" for all colonial peoples throughout the world was much less concerned about black citizens in America. Wilson supported and implemented segregation in the federal workforce, and his administration dismissed hundreds of black federal workers. The president claimed that nothing could be done to improve the status of blacks, refused to denounce lynchings, and claimed that the appointment of black officials in the South was a "social blunder of the worst kind."

After Wilson asked Congress to declare war on Germany in 1917, his administration continued to discriminate against black Americans. The government drafted them into the military, others volunteered, but they were placed in segregated units—usually as laborers, ammunition handlers, or stevedores with little or no military training. Few ever saw combat. When the army was asked to explain this policy, the generals stated that African Americans lacked the natural attributes to fight courageously. An Army War College report a few years later declared: "The cranial capacity of the negro is smaller than whites," the "psychology of the negro . . . is one from which we cannot expect to draw leadership material." As for physical courage, the black man "falls well back of whites. . . . He cannot control himself in fear or danger."

At home, black troops were harassed. Because of police brutality in Houston, one unit rioted. The army tried and sentenced thirteen blacks to hang for murder and mutiny, carrying out the executions even before the cases could be reviewed. After the war black troops were discharged; when they returned home they were often greeted by bloody riots. As historian Harvard Sitkoff noted, "Some twenty-five race riots broke out," in 1919, "and at least seventy Negroes were lynched, some of them still wearing their military uniforms."

The Republican presidents of the 1920s had no interest in minorities, even though lynchings continued and there were race riots in many cities, including Chicago, Omaha, and Washington, D.C. President Warren G. Harding revealed his views when he spoke in a segregated park in Birmingham, Alabama, emphasizing the "fundamental, eternal, and inescapable differences" dividing the races and calling on citizens to "stand uncompromisingly against every suggestion of social equality." Nor did most blacks benefit from the prosperity of the 1920s, for most of them still lived as sharecroppers or tenant farmers in the South. Those who did escape the cotton fields and headed north were met with racism in cities such as Detroit, Chicago, Cleveland, Pittsburgh, and New York, where they were restricted to ghettos. Regardless of an individual's wealth, local ordinances restricted almost all minorities to the worst parts of town.

Minorities in the 1920s also were victimized by the Ku Klux Klan. The Klan was energized by black migration, the "foreign" influence brought back from the war, and the fear of radicalism and communism resulting from the Russian revolution. The KKK extended its activities into the North and Midwest, gaining social and political acceptance as it broadened its attacks from blacks to foreigners, radicals, Catholics, and Jews, or anyone the Klan felt was not "100 percent American." By 1924 the KKK was so strong that the Democratic convention failed to pass a resolution censoring the organization, and Republican President and nominee Calvin Coolidge decided to avoid the race issue altogether. In fact, during the 1920s the presidents of the Party of Lincoln seemed oblivious to minority needs. Harding and Coolidge would not support a federal bill aimed at prohibiting lynchings, nor would Herbert Hoover. His Presidential Commission on Law Enforcement refused to investigate those murders, along with disfranchisement and discrimination in public accommodations. As he left the White House, the federal government contracted some 4,000 workers to build the massive Boulder Dam at Lake Mead in the Nevada desert. Not one worker was black, and after the NAACP protested, a dozen were hired, only to be humiliated on the job by regulations that stipulated that they must drink water out of separate buckets.

During these Republican years white Americans profited, many getting rich buying stocks and gambling their money on the Bull Market.

Yet the economic bonanza came to an abrupt halt with the Crash of 1929 and the subsequent Great Depression—events that resulted in a political revolution that the 1932 Democratic nominee for president, Franklin D. Roosevelt, labeled the New Deal.

Most citizens, especially those with limited incomes or out of work in the Depression, were optimistic when FDR established the New Deal, but blacks were much more cautious. They were uneasy with the new Democratic president, fearing another Wilson administration. Moreover, Roosevelt never had made any statements supporting civil rights; he seemed more interested in avoiding the topic and keeping the "Solid South" Democratic. Southern Democrats were a powerful force in Congress, and they controlled many committees. People like Sam Rayburn of Texas, James Byrnes of South Carolina, Byron "Pat" Harrison of Mississippi, or William Bankhead of Alabama did not want any president to become interested in what they considered a local issue, and they had the power. Because of their seniority, the "Southerners . . . rule in Congress," the president said to NAACP's Walter White. "If I come out for the anti-lynching bill now, they will block every bill I ask Congress to pass to keep America from collapsing. I just can't take the risk."

FDR had to get the economy moving again, and blacks supported that because their situation was desperate. During the 1930s, three-fourths of all African Americans lived in the South, the poorest people in the poorest region. That same percentage had not finished high school, and one out of ten had no schooling at all. Thus, most black men were sharecroppers or unskilled laborers, and most black women were farmhands or domestic servants. Nationally, blacks earned less than 40 percent of what whites earned, and when hard times arrived they became the "surplus man," wrote a black sociologist, "the last to be hired and the first to be fired." When the economy slumped blacks faced stiffer competition for jobs than usual, especially in the South. In Atlanta, unemployed whites organized in 1930 with the slogan "No Jobs for Niggers Until Every White Man Has a Job!" It worked: five years later 65 percent of blacks there were unemployed, some 80 percent in Norfolk. In many southern cities charities often refused aid to African Americans. "At no time in the history of the Negro since slavery," proclaimed Urban League leader T. Arnold Hill, had their "economic and social outlook seemed so discouraging." By 1932 one half of all African Americans in southern cities could not find employment, and the next year the percentage nationally of black males unemployed and on relief was about twice that of whites. In Chicago, a third of blacks were on welfare, three times more than whites, similar to the situation in Philadelphia, Baltimore, Detroit, and St. Louis. Those figures in Cleveland and Pittsburgh were over forty percent, while in the nation's capital, for every one white man out of work there were nine blacks.[5]

With such poverty, leftist political parties such as the Socialist and Communist attracted new adherents, as did a new labor organization, the Congress of Industrial Organizations, the CIO. These organizations were especially popular on liberal college campuses and in major cities during the Depression. Unlike other unions, including the American Federation of Labor, the CIO accepted nonwhites as members as they promoted labor with the rallying cry, "Unionism is Americanism." The Communist Party agreed. They crusaded against fascism, demanded fair labor wages, and campaigned for racial equality, all topics that excited many who were not Anglo-Saxon Protestants, such as left-leaning Catholics, Jews, immigrants, and African Americans. "The communists," declared NAACP official Charles Houston, "have made it impossible for any aspirant to Negro leadership to advocate less than full economic, political, and social equality."

This "popular front," as the left was called, also put pressure on the Democrats to ensure that their New Deal policies helped all impoverished Americans, regardless of race. This contributed to a realignment of the political parties, and as public works programs began to employ blacks, they began to shift their allegiance from the Party of Lincoln to the Democrats. This was a slow process, but it began after FDR took office and Congress began to pass legislation, including the 1933 Unemployment Relief Act, which for the first time announced the principle of equal job opportunity in federal employment: "no discrimination shall be made on account of race, color, or creed," a clause that appeared in many New Deal programs. African Americans took note, especially when FDR made a few cabinet appointments of men known to be sympathetic to civil rights. Important was the man who became Interior Secretary, Harold L. Ickes.

Prior to coming to Washington, Ickes had been involved in race relations and, as a white man, had been president briefly of the Chicago chapter of the NAACP. Moreover, Ickes appointed a black economist,

Robert C. Weaver, and a liberal white Georgian, Clark Foreman, as aides on Negro affairs. After assuming office the secretary desegregated the facilities at the Interior Department, prompting other agency heads to follow his lead.

More significant, however, were Ickes' actions heading the Public Works Administration. In September 1933 he issued a remarkable order—one that seems to be the first attempt to establish a form of equal opportunity: the order prohibited discrimination in Public Works Administration projects. Henceforth, PWA contracts would include a nondiscrimination clause. The following year, Weaver and Foreman devised a forerunner to affirmative action. Based on the 1930 census, contractors in cities with an "appreciable Negro population" were required to employ a fixed percentage of skilled black workers—basically, a quota. Public housing was made the "guinea pig for experimenting with developing techniques for assuring the employment of . . . Negro labor on public financed projects." Contracts would have a clause stating that failure to pay black workers a percentage of the total payroll would be evidence of discrimination; that ratio was put at about one-half of their percentage in the local labor force. Thus, in Atlanta, where the census showed that about 24 percent of skilled workers were black, contractors who accepted federal funds to build public housing were required to pay at least 12 percent of their payroll to skilled blacks.

Why Ickes developed this precursor to affirmative action seems to be a mystery. Although this married man kept a detailed secret diary, one that even disclosed his long affair with a female in Washington, D.C., he never mentioned his rationale for instituting a new policy that started the federal government's involvement in desegregating the nation's workplace. He simply wrote that segregation at the Interior Department was "a thing of the past" and added that "Congress intended this program to be carried out without discrimination," which was questionable since that body was filled with bigots. Ickes probably was aware of the policy Henry Ford implemented after World War I, which might have been the first attempt at representational employment in business: "Negroes should make up the same proportion of the workers as corresponded to their proportion in the population of Detroit." Perhaps the secretary was aware of some local black groups that were advocating such employment policies during the Depression. While the NAACP did not favor quotas, it had asked President Hoover to ensure that "a just proportion" of public works funds be spent on black labor. Most likely, Ickes began the policy because of his long interest in civil rights and his previous affiliation with the NAACP.

Yet implementing nondiscrimination and proportional employment was difficult. Some contractors complied and hired blacks, since there were few jobs and the federal government controlled the money for a project. But more often the policy failed. The PWA was a temporary program, its enforcement was weak, and the PWA's proportional employment goals were very low compared to the black population. One project in Harlem, for example, mandated only 3 percent black workers. Moreover, racist employers, trade unions, and city and state officials often ignored the nondiscriminatory rules announced in Washington D.C. This was particularly true in the South. In many southern cities black carpenters were hired to conform with PWA regulations, only to be fired after the funding appeared. In other cities they were given temporary union memberships, good for one job only. In Miami the PWA goal for one project, 6 percent for black skilled workers, was not filled because the city segregated black mechanics to "their part" of town, and the project was located in the white districts. This discrimination not only appeared with the PWA but with many New Deal programs, even though they banned discrimination. In Georgia the governor refused to follow federal guidelines on equal relief for whites and blacks; Atlanta gave out monthly checks of more than $32 to whites, and only $19 to black recipients. Weaver admitted that he had tried to open new job opportunities for blacks, but that it was "most unrealistic to have attempted to secure significant occupational gains for a minority group in a period when there was mass unemployment."[6]

Nevertheless, blacks did benefit from some New Deal programs. African Americans were included in other programs besides the PWA, such as the Civilian Conservation Corps. They also received farm subsidies and loans, unemployment compensation, and eventually all citizens were paid the same minimum wage and received equal social security benefits. The Interior Department supplied funds for public housing for both whites and blacks, and because of Ickes' policies, some white labor unions were forced to hire black men at good wages. Moreover, directors of the U.S. Housing Authority and the Federal Works Authority adopted Ickes' plan, and they also pressured contractors to desegregate.

Not only did Ickes begin to change employment practices during the New Deal, but so did Harry Hopkins. A colleague described Hopkins as having a "mind like a razor, a tongue like a skinning knife, a temper like a Tartar and a sufficient vocabulary of parlor profanity . . . to make a mule-skinner jealous." FDR appointed him the administrator of the Works Progress Administration when it was established in 1935. The WPA was designed to be the key agency in the government's entire works program, which eventually included some 40 federal agencies, lasted for the next eight years, and employed nine million citizens, including one million African Americans. The WPA's education program taught a million blacks to read and write, the theater program staged dramas about Nat Turner and Harriet Tubman, and the writers' project published the first works by Ralph Ellison and Richard Wright.

At one of the first staff meetings about how to implement the WPA, Hopkins raised a significant question about women. The Depression had tossed millions of women out of work, and in 1932 Congress passed and President Hoover signed a bill that resulted in firing most wives from federal government jobs if their husbands were employed, setting a precedent for similar policies adopted by states, cities, and companies. That was considered fair. Most women agreed with a single San Antonio clerical worker when her company fired all working wives, "I ain't sorry, for I certainly am not in favor of married women working unless they have to; there are too many unmarried ones without jobs." And most would add, too many unemployed male breadwinners.

In summer 1935, Hopkins asked his staff if the WPA should pay women and men the same wages. The men, traditionally, said no. Yet one member, Aubrey Williams, disagreed, stating that both should be paid equally. "What makes you think you could get away with it?" Hopkins asked. Williams said that he didn't care if he could get away with it, but that it was the right thing to do. Hopkins countered, "Do you know who disagrees with you? The secretary of labor—a woman!" Hopkins was right; the first female cabinet member, "Madame Secretary" Frances Perkins favored tradition. But Williams responded, "Pay 'em the same!"

Hopkins did. Women who went to work for the WPA earned the same wages as the men, but few women did similar skilled or professional work. Instead, females generally worked at jobs aimed at improving their homemaking skills, such as food service, sewing, or housekeeping. Moreover, women seeking certification for WPA employment had to prove that their families included no able-bodied males.

The same year, 1935, marked an early appearance of the term "affirmative action." New York's Democratic Senator Robert Wagner pushed through Congress the National Labor Relations Act, more commonly called the Wagner Act, which allowed workers to organize unions and collectively bargain with their bosses. It prohibited employers from using "unfair labor practices," such as refusing to bargain or firing union members. If managers discriminated in any way against labor, then the bosses were to take "affirmative action" to put victims at a salary level or in positions where they would have been without the discrimination.

Obviously, the original use of affirmative action was markedly different from what it would later symbolize, but the concept was appropriate for the New Deal. The federal government was increasing its protection of some citizens, and during the Great Depression one of those groups was workers.

Another group was youth. That summer the president's wife, Eleanor, approached Harry Hopkins and Aubrey Williams. She recommended a plan in which young people who did not physically qualify for the Civilian Conservation Corps, especially women between the ages of 16 and 25, would receive relief and employment. Hopkins and Williams hesitated, thinking that political opponents might see the program as an attempt to organize youth, like Hitler was doing in Germany. Eleanor took her idea to the president late one evening, and FDR responded, "I doubt if our youth can be regimented in this way or in any other way." A few days later, he issued an executive order establishing the National Youth Administration, directed by Aubrey Williams.

Williams put youth to work across the nation, generally regardless of race. In Texas, for example, the state's NYA administrator, 26-year-old Lyndon Baines Johnson, not only helped 18,000 students continue their education while working for 35 cents an hour but also employed 12,000 other youngsters on public works. In New York City, the NYA put to work almost 100,000 young people, while kids in Massachusetts restocked fish hatcheries, Native Americans built camps on their reservations, black Georgians were trained in homemaking and farming, and black New Orleans girls helped at local hospitals.[7]

Eleanor Roosevelt also helped African Americans. An outspoken woman, one national columnist listed her among the "Ten Most Powerful People in Washington," labeling her the "cabinet member without portfolio." During her husband's first term Mrs. Roosevelt met and became personal friends with many influential blacks, including NAACP officials Walter White and Roy Wilkins, and Mary McLeod Bethune, president of the National Council of Negro Women, who later was appointed as Director of Negro Affairs at the NYA. As early as 1934 Eleanor declared, "we must learn to work together, all of us, regardless of race or creed or color." By the second Roosevelt administration the black community perceived Eleanor as symbolizing New Deal attempts to bring about racial justice and equality. She talked about abolishing the poll tax and spoke out in favor of a federal anti-lynching law, which northern senators introduced but failed to pass in the Senate in 1938. The next year, when the Daughters of the American Revolution refused to permit the famous African American singer, Marian Anderson, to perform in their Constitution Hall, Mrs. Roosevelt not only publicly resigned from the DAR but arranged for the Department of the Interior to make the Lincoln Memorial available for an outside concert on Easter Sunday. The First Lady attended and Secretary Ickes presided, as an interracial crowd of 75,000 heard the singer open with "America" and close appropriately with "Nobody Knows the Trouble I've Seen." Two months later, Mrs. Roosevelt presented Anderson with the Spingarn medal at the 1940 conference of the NAACP. "Democracy is never safe," she declared that year, "when it isn't safe for all citizens."[8]

The same summer Congress debated selective service, the peacetime draft. During these discussions, race relations within the military was a natural topic. Not one black man had attended Annapolis, and the entire regular army had only five black officers, three of whom were chaplains. Military officials noted that bases were segregated, not just in the South but usually in the North. At Fort Leavenworth, Kansas, black soldiers and their families could not use swimming pools, clubs, and a restaurant; all were for whites only. At the post theater blacks had to use latrines across the street. Moreover, the War Department left the racial composition of the National Guard up to the states. Consequently, less than 2 percent of the combined strength of the Army Reserves and National Guard was African American. "We can take no pride in our armed forces," a black New Yorker complained bitterly. "We can become no more than flunkies in the army and kitchen boys in the navy." Others were more militant. John P. Davis of the National Negro Congress declared, "the American Negro will not fight abroad; he will fight for his survival here at home."

Such statements concerned black leaders. Randolph and his Brotherhood of Sleeping Car Porters passed a resolution that called on the president and Congress "to see to it that no discrimination is practiced against American citizens entering all departments of the Army, Navy and Air Corps on account of race or color." Mary McLeod Bethune met with Mrs. Roosevelt and gave her a memorandum declaring "grave apprehension among Negroes" over the "existing inadequate representation and training of colored persons in the armed forces." Bethune urged that Secretary of War Henry L. Stimson name an outstanding African American as his aide to ensure fair treatment.[9]

Randolph was well aware of his aims as he walked into the White House on September 27, 1940, to meet President Roosevelt. He and other black leaders had asked for a meeting with the commander in chief and his Pentagon generals to discuss "the rights of Negroes . . . to participate in the whole structure of national defense, but particularly the Army and Navy." Randolph was accompanied by Walter White of the NAACP and T. Arnold Hill of the National Urban League. The men discussed the situation and submitted a memorandum calling for the immediate integration of, and "equitable participation" in, all defense preparations, increased opportunities for training black servicemen, adding blacks to local draft boards, and appointing African American advisers to the War and Navy Departments. Although Eleanor had been supportive, and New Dealers such as Ickes and Hopkins had made gestures toward equality, the president himself had usually avoided public statements on racial issues. Randolph felt the time had come.

The result of the session was not even mentioned in the *New York Times* or *Washington Post*. That was not unusual for a time when there were no national newspapers; in Jim Crow America whites and blacks read their own local publications. In fact, the most influential papers did not cover news about minorities unless it concerned something sensational, such as a frightful lynching or a deadly race riot. That being the case, white liberals who might be interested in minority affairs were often unaware of black needs or demands. After Pearl Harbor, for example, David E. Lilienthal, the man Roosevelt appointed to run the Tennessee Valley Authority, wrote down his thoughts on the possible social gains due to the New Deal and the war. He discussed bringing electric-ity to all homes and farms, collective bargaining, improved nourishment, even "better teeth." He did not even mention the plight of minorities—job discrimination, racism, the Jim Crow army. To most white Americans, a black was what novelist Ralph Ellison later would call an "invisible man."

Thus, on October 9, 1940, two weeks after Randolph's meeting with FDR, press secretary Stephen Early stated that the president had met with "Walter White and, I think, two other Negro leaders." As a result, he continued, the War Department had drafted a statement that affirmed the "balanced force" principle: since the nation's population was composed of a little more than 10 percent African Americans, then the same ratio should be allowed into the army. After a couple other vague promises the War Department's statement went on to say that the policy was "not to intermingle colored and white enlisted personnel," which reaffirmed the segregation policy.

The black leaders were outraged, for they had understood from the meeting that the president would modify, if not end, segregation in the armed forces. They felt misrepresented, especially when some black papers began to question if they had "sold out." On October 25 the president clarified his position in a private letter to the three men. After regretting "so much misinterpretation" of the War Department's statement, he wrote that the plan "on which we are all agreed is that Negroes will be put into all branches of the service, combatant as well as supply. Arrangements are now being made to give, without delay, training in aviation to Negroes. Negro reserve officers will be called to active service and given appropriate commands. Negroes will be given the same opportunity to qualify for officers' commissions as will be given to others."

All of that was fine, but the president's letter failed to mention the two main issues: integrating the armed forces and ending job discrimination in the defense industry. During an election year, these issues were too volatile for a president running for an unprecedented third term.

Two weeks later FDR won reelection, this time with additional help from northern blacks who showed up at the polls. Before the election the NAACP noted that the New Deal was addressing black and white poverty, and *The Crisis* added that "the most important contribution of the Roosevelt administration to the age-old color line problem in America has been its doctrine that Negroes are part of the country as a whole. . . . For the first time in their lives government has taken on meaning and substance for the Negro masses." Blacks continued to shift their allegiance from the Republican to the Democratic party. An analysis of fifteen black wards in nine northern cities showed that FDR captured only four in 1932, but he won nine in 1936 and fourteen in 1940.

One month after the election, A. Philip Randolph was on a train with his colleague Milton Webster. The two labor leaders were leaving Washington and heading south to organize for the Brotherhood of Sleeping Car Porters. After a long silence, Randolph turned and said, "You know, Web, calling on the president and holding those conferences are not going to get us anywhere." Webster remained silent, listening as Randolph continued. "We are going to have to do something about it. I think we ought to get 10,000 Negroes to march on Washington in protest, march down Pennsylvania Avenue. What do you think of that?" Webster wondered, "Where are you going to get 10,000 Negroes?"

On their first stop in Savannah, Georgia, the leaders called a meeting to announce that they were "gathering 10,000 Negroes to march on Washington to demand jobs in the defense industry." The idea struck horror in the minds of southern blacks. They were too aware of the possible consequences of confronting white authorities. After one local leader introduced Webster, he ran off the stage and left the meeting hall. Nevertheless, Randolph and Webster continued on to Jacksonville, Tampa, Miami, spreading the word, as did the black press. By the time they returned to New York the idea was circulating throughout the black community.

Sensing the time was right, on January 15, 1941, Randolph issued a dramatic statement:

> Negro America must bring its power and pressure to bear upon the agencies and representatives of the Federal Government to exact their rights in National Defense employment and the armed forces of the country. . . . I suggest that TEN THOUSAND Negroes march on Washington, D.C. . . . with the slogan: WE LOYAL NEGRO AMERICAN CITIZENS DEMAND THE RIGHT TO WORK AND FIGHT FOR OUR COUNTRY.

Randolph then attempted to enlist help from Lester Granger of the National Urban League and Walter White of the NAACP. These men were more conservative and not as enthusiastic about confronting a popular and reelected president with a march on Washington. Moreover, an African American march on the nation's capital never had been attempted—what if it failed? What if no one showed up, or if thousands did appear and there was no change in Roosevelt's policies? The largest black newspaper, the *Pittsburgh Courier*, became sarcastic, calling it a "crackpot proposal," while the *Chicago Defender* reminded readers that it had "not been possible to get them to march in protest against lynching, against peonage and poll tax. . . . To get 10,000 Negroes assembled in one spot . . . would be the miracle of the century." Nevertheless, Granger and White supported the goals of the demonstration, mostly by supplying funds, because their membership had great respect for Randolph.

Randolph hit the streets. In New York he walked up and down avenues and into bars, shops, beauty parlors, pool rooms, and restaurants. He spoke out on corners, in parks, and in theater lobbies. He asked integrated unions for money, and black workers and businessmen eventually raised $50,000 to hire buses and trains to transport his invading army to Washington. He declared, "Mass power can cause President Roosevelt to issue an Executive Order abolishing discrimination," and he set the date: July 1, 1941.

FDR had other things on his mind during the first months of 1941. He was preparing the nation for war. He proclaimed his Four Freedoms, which included freedom of speech and from economic want, and he and British Prime Minister Winston Churchill made a press release that became known as The Atlantic Charter, which included the right of all people to choose their own form of government. Freedom was the key, and in his State of the Union message Roosevelt pledged to democratic allies, "We are putting forth our energies, our resources and our organizing powers to give you the strength to regain and maintain the free world. We shall send you in ever increasing numbers, ships, planes, tanks, and guns. That is our purpose and our pledge."

The nation began to go back to work, but not all the nation. The black press noted that more than 250,000 jobs were closed to blacks in defense plants, and of the 100,000 workers making warplanes, only 240 were black. The president of the Standard Steel Company in Kansas City stated the views of most employers: "We have not had a Negro worker in twenty-five years, and we do not plan to start now."

FDR also began discussing national unity. He appealed to the public that spring, asking them "to consider the needs of our nation at this hour and to put aside all personal differences until our victory is won. There will be no divisions of party or section or race or nationality or religion. There is not one among us who does not have a stake in the outcome of the effort in which we are now engaged."

Yet to many African Americans, Roosevelt's statements seemed ironic. *The Crisis* asked its readers to consider "whether there is a great deal of difference between the code for Negroes under Hitler and the code for Negroes under the United States of America." Roy Wilkins added that, with the war on in Europe "it sounds pretty foolish to be *against* park benches marked 'Jude' in Berlin, but to be *for* park benches marked 'Colored' in Tallahassee."

Randolph shifted into high gear in May—and raised the ante: "When 100,000 Negroes march on Washington, it will wake up Negro as well as white America. . . . Let the Negro masses march! Let the Negro masses speak!"

That alarmed the Roosevelt administration. Eleanor wrote Randolph that the demonstration would be a "very grave mistake" and that it would "set back the progress which is being made" in the New Deal. The administration asked New York City mayor Fiorello La Guardia, a personal friend of Randolph, to use his persuasive powers to stop the march. La Guardia and Mrs. Roosevelt met with Randolph. The First Lady reminded the activist that the capital's police force were white southerners, that there might be violence, and then asked where the demonstrators would eat and sleep in Jim Crow Washington? Randolph responded that he did not see a problem: "The demonstrators would simply march into the hotels and restaurants, and order food and shelter." There would be no violence unless her husband "ordered the police to crack black heads." Randolph would not budge, and Eleanor arranged a meeting with her husband.

On June 18, 1941, Randolph again walked into the White House. He was with Walter White, and FDR greeted him with a few officials, including Mayor La Guardia, Secretary of War Stimson, and Secretary of Navy Frank Knox. As usual, Roosevelt began with his charm: "Hello, Phil, which class were you in at Harvard?" But it fell flat when Randolph answered coldly, "I never went to Harvard, Mr. President." FDR shifted to some other small talk, and after a couple of minutes Randolph broke in, "Mr. President, time is running on," and reminded him of the topic of the meeting: "jobs for Negroes in defense industries." The president said that he would call the heads of defense plants and ask them to hire Negro workers. "We want you to do more than that," Randolph said. "Mr. President, we want you to issue an executive order making it mandatory that Negroes be permitted to work in these plants." FDR hedged. If he issued such an order for Negroes, then there would be no end to other groups asking for such orders. In any event, he continued, he couldn't do anything unless Randolph called off the march. "Questions like this can't be settled with a sledge hammer."

"I'm sorry, Mr. President," Randolph replied, "the march cannot be called off." FDR showed alarm, "You can't bring 100,000 Negroes to Washington. Somebody might get killed." Randolph responded that a death was unlikely, especially if the president addressed the crowd. "Call it off!" Roosevelt demanded. Randolph again said no, and FDR stated that it was not his policy to be ruled by threats, with a gun at his head. "Gentlemen," Mayor La Guardia said, "it is clear that Mr. Randolph is not going to call off the march, and I suggest we all begin to seek a formula."[10]

The formula was announced on June 25, which satisfied Randolph who called off the march. FDR issued Executive Order 8802. It declared that there "shall be no discrimination in the employment of workers in *defense industries* or *government* because of race, creed, color, or national origins." It was the duty of governmental agencies, employers, and labor organizations "to provide for the full and equitable participation of all workers." To enforce the order FDR created a temporary Fair Employment Practices Committee (FEPC) and named two blacks to the five-member committee, one being Milton Webster. Two years later, the commander in chief used his wartime powers to expand his original order to eliminate discrimination in a broader range of "war industries," including "union membership," and authorized the FEPC to "conduct hearings" with an expanded staff of 120 in 15 field offices across the nation.

Roosevelt's executive order was a significant event in American history and some blacks labeled it the "Second Emancipation Proclamation." For the previous seven decades, since Reconstruction, the federal government had abandoned African American citizens, refusing even to uphold their rights as guaranteed by the Constitution. Now, a man with a mission, threatening a march as the nation prepared for war, had "persuaded" a reluctant liberal president to use his power to begin changing employment practices in the Arsenal of Democracy.

As far as African Americans were concerned, the rationale for a new national policy was as old as the American Revolution—taxation without representation. In 1776, of course, most blacks were slaves, but they received their freedom and citizenship with the Thirteenth and Fourteenth Amendments during Reconstruction. After that, they were taxed, but unlike whites they did not receive most benefits. Although their taxes helped pay for public facilities, they were not admitted to those facilities throughout the South. Although their taxes supported the government, they did not receive equal employment opportunities in their local and state public agencies, in the federal government or the military, or in the tax-supported private sector, such as defense industries. During the military buildup of 1940, aviator Jimmy Peck, a black combat veteran of the Spanish Civil War in 1937, noted that "colored Americans . . . are helping to pay for this air expansion" but were barred from flying in the Army Air Corps. When Negroes were given the right to become pilots in the Corps, he declared, "we will . . . get our just representation as taxpayers." *The Crisis* agreed in an article appropriately titled, "Warplanes—Negro Americans may not build them, repair them, or fly them, but they must help pay for them." Later, the magazine editorialized about the Navy, "Our taxes help keep up the Naval Academy at Annapolis where our boys may not attend. They help to maintain the numerous naval bases, navy yards, and naval air bases from which we are excluded." The Navy's "health care . . . the travel and education—all at the expense of the taxpayers—are for whites only!"

Most whites considered that fair. Traditionally, public and private employers had the right to hire whomever they wanted for a position, regardless of who paid for the final product. But in June 1941 the Roosevelt administration began changing the rules—and laying another foundation for affirmative action. The chief executive ordered all federal agencies and defense industries to end discrimination based on race or religion when hiring workers. The idea was simple: if you were an agency or a defense company that accepted a government contract—

taxpayers funds—then you must hire all the taxpayers. And that included African Americans.

Up to that moment, wrote historian Lerone Bennett Jr., the dominant issues facing African Americans were poll taxes, lynchings, segregated schools, and white primaries. But after the executive order in 1941, "Negro strategy" would be to place "unrelenting pressure" on Washington to ensure "decisive intervention by the federal government." Indeed, the federal government began opening its own doors and those of defense contractors to all workers.

Six months after FDR's order, in December 1941, the Japanese attacked Pearl Harbor, Germany and Italy declared war, and the United States was at war in Asia and Europe. "Your ancestors came to America on the Mayflower while mine came here on a slave ship," declared Walter White. "But we're all in the same boat now!"

But, for the most part, they were not in the same defense plant, for the FEPC had a checkered record during the war. Typical for the times, most white newspapers did not even report the executive order, or if they did, they tucked it away in the middle of the paper where few noticed it; fewer understood its implications. The FEPC was a temporary wartime agency without much popular or congressional support; it had a small staff and lacked enforcement power. Thus, some government agencies and contractors complied, while most dragged their feet. The ratio of blacks in shipbuilding almost doubled to more than 9 percent of the workforce, but the aircraft industry hired only a small number, usually as janitors. In fact, most jobs for blacks were unskilled, and most unions maintained segregation. As one southern teamster leader declared, "any Negro, any white man, or Chinaman or anybody else that would step forth and say they want social equality and intermingling of races . . . would be denying everything God intended to be." Enforcement always was a problem, for the FEPC had little power. It only could request that a defense contract be canceled, but that might seem unpatriotic and could impede the war effort. Thus, during the war the agency did not cancel one contract. Moreover, cases that complicated foreign relations were off limits. When the FEPC scheduled public hearings in El Paso, Texas, on discrimination against Mexican Americans in the Southwest, the State Department blocked the investigations, stating that a public inquiry would be used by the enemy for propaganda.

Most Southerners, of course, vehemently opposed the FEPC. Alabama whites formed the League to Maintain White Supremacy, the governor declared that he would refuse to sign a contract that would force him to abandon segregation, while the city council of Atlanta passed a resolution ordering the FEPC administrator to leave town. A Louisiana congressman declared the agency heralded the "beginning of a communistic dictatorship. . . . They want to dictate to you who shall work in your factory, who shall work on your farm, who shall work in your office, who shall go to your schools, and who shall eat at your table, or intermarry with your children." A congressman from Alabama added that "our people would rather be dead than have to put up with negro men giving our white women orders."[11]

After a series of hearings in 1942, the FEPC chairman stated that on the West Coast "company after company admitted that it did not employ Negroes, or persons of Oriental background, regardless of their fitness for the job. Here, in the midst of around-the-clock appeals for national unity and for an all-out effort to build our instruments for defense, we found unfair employment practices only slightly removed from the Hitler pattern." In fact, the committee found that some defense contractors refused to hire Jews, Catholics, Seventh-Day Adventists, Jehovah's Witnesses, and of course, Mexican and Native Americans.

Job discrimination continued throughout the nation. Writing *Manpower for Victory* in 1943, John Corson noted that the reason for the wartime labor shortage was simple: 13 million American Negroes were "not employed in numbers proportionate to the employment of whites; they are often refused skilled positions . . . are barred from certain occupations," while obstacles are "placed in the way of their full contribution to the war effort." In the South the result was absurd. Instead of employing numerous local blacks in war industries, managers recruited whites from other parts of the country, and this resulted in housing shortages and overburdened schools, transportation, and sanitation facilities. In the "event of an epidemic," Corson concluded, "the effect would be disastrous."

Jim Crow, of course, also continued in wartime America. In one of the most race-based actions in American history, the federal government simply ordered all 120,000 people of Japanese descent on the West Coast to internment centers far inland from their homes and property; two-thirds of them were American citizens. At the camps "One of our basic subjects was American history," one internee later recalled. "They talked about freedom all the time." African Americans who were eager to contribute to the Red Cross blood program were turned away, despite the fact that white and black blood are biologically identical. When citizens of southern cities, including the nation's capital, considered building air-raid shelters, they proposed separate shelters for whites and blacks. And as blacks were lured out of the South to fill jobs during the war they were met with racism. "We Want White Neighbors," read a sign at a Detroit federal housing project named after the famous African American Sojourner Truth. Tensions soared in that city until July 1943 when it erupted in the worst race riot in America since the post–World War I era—34 dead, 700 injured, and 1,300 arrested. Detroit was not alone. Riots ensued in Beaumont and El Paso, Texas, in Springfield, Massachusetts, and in New York City, while Anglos and Mexican Americans clashed in Los Angeles.[12]

Nevertheless, in many other parts of the country the war slowly began to change race relations. Liberals were appalled by the race riots, claiming that they only aided the enemy: "Americans infected with the spirit of fascism have attacked our fighting forces in the rear," editorialized The Nation. "We cannot fight fascism abroad while turning a blind eye to fascism at home." Wartime labor shortages meant more jobs, and the FEPC had some success in persuading contractors to accept black workers and convincing newspapers to discontinue discriminatory want ads. Unions such as the CIO worked alongside the federal government in integrating their workforce, and in a few cases the CIO even fired white workers who protested being on the same assembly line with African Americans.

Black employment increased dramatically, mostly because of manpower shortages. By the end of 1944 nearly two million blacks were employed in defense plants, which was more than 8 percent of such workers. During the war the number of African Americans working for the federal government more than doubled, reaching almost 20 percent of personnel in Washington, D.C.

On the assembly line, traditional racial views decreased but only marginally, since most white workers were busy at skilled jobs while blacks were usually unskilled laborers. The Opinion Research Corporation surveyed white workers in 1944, asking a number of questions: "Would it be all right if your employer put a Negro to work next to you?" Only 41 percent answered yes, and just a third supported integrated work stations. "Should a Negro be your foreman or supervisor?" Only 14 percent thought that was acceptable. And a question concerning fairness: "Do you think Negroes should have as good a chance as white people to get any kind of job, or do you think white people should have the first chance at any kind of job?" Only 44 percent thought that blacks should have an equal opportunity.

The wartime economy also affected women. "In some communities," FDR declared in 1942, "employers dislike to employ women. In others they are reluctant to hire Negroes. . . . We can no longer afford to indulge such prejudices or practices." Labor shortages that year resulted in "Rosie the Riveter" campaigns to get females on the job. Although statistics vary, it appeared that approximately three million women entered the war economy, about two million of them in defense plants. Because of the war, most Americans supported this change in tradition. Two months after Pearl Harbor a poll reported that 68 percent of the public and 73 percent of women favored drafting single women between the ages of 21 and 35 for training in war jobs. The key word in the survey was "single," for the society—male and female—overwhelmingly disapproved of mothers picking up the riveting gun or the welding torch. While the federal government and some plants built day-care nurseries, most of the female workers were just out of high school and unattached. Nationally, females were never more than 10 percent of defense plant employees, and those who did work at those factories usually were quickly trained as low-skilled welders or had office jobs as secretaries. A Gallup poll at that time also asked a question concerning fairness: "If women replace men in industry should they be paid the same wages as men?" Just over 70 percent of men said yes, 85 percent of women, and the Roosevelt administration also supported the idea. The War Labor Board ordered equal wages for women who performed "comparable quality and quantity of work" as men.[13]

Roosevelt's executive order, thus, began to change the workplace and lay the foundation for affirmative action, but for Randolph and his colleagues the order was only a partial victory. It did not mention their other concern—integration of the armed forces.

Total war forced African Americans to walk a thin line. Randolph and a few other leaders decided not to press the federal government too hard over segregation in the armed forces, since they did not want to arouse feelings that blacks were hurting the war effort, but others were more brazen. "NOW IS NOT THE TIME TO BE SILENT," demanded *The Crisis* in January 1942, "the fight against Hitlerism begins in Washington, D.C., the capital of our nation where black Americans have a status only slightly above that of Jews in Berlin." Most black leaders supported the "Double V for Victory" campaign—fighting fascism abroad and racism at home—while the NAACP declared its "two front" policy: "A Jim Crow army cannot fight for a free world."

Yet it was going to be a Jim Crow army. In September 1940 Congress passed the Selective Service Act, which declared a ban on discrimination on account of "race or color," but nothing really changed. The majority of citizens did not support desegregation, and most would have agreed with Secretary of War Stimson when he wrote in his diary, "Leadership is not imbedded in the negro race yet and to try to make commissioned officers to lead men into battle—colored men—is only to work disaster to both." The Marine Corps commandant agreed publicly, proclaiming in front of a congressional committee, "If it were a question of having a Marine Corps of 5,000 whites or 250,000 Negroes, I would rather have the whites."

Stimson was irritated that "these foolish leaders of the colored race" were seeking "social equality" while the nation was at war, but the commander in chief was more concerned about mobilizing the entire nation. He attempted to appease African Americans by appointing William H. Hastie, a former law school dean and the first black federal judge, as assistant to the Secretary of War. Hastie informed Stimson that the army was not utilizing black soldiers, and feared that it had adopted the "traditional mores of the South." Hastie urged that black units be integrated with white ones and African Americans be assigned to all new military battalions. Stimson asked Army Chief of Staff General George Marshall to respond. The general noted that Jim Crow existed, segregation was a custom, the educational level of Negroes was below that of whites, and that the military should not have to solve a "social problem that has perplexed the American people throughout the history of this nation. . . . The Army is not a sociological laboratory." Moreover, "experiments within the Army in the solution of social problems are fraught with danger to efficiency, discipline, and morale."

Thus, the top brass rejected any experiments with the military, and that included the way the nation raised the army, selective service. Hastie and other African Americans complained about racism in the selection process, but the administration responded that the draft was a local issue, the "responsibility of the Governor of each state." The NAACP asked the governor of Tennessee to appoint some black members to the state's draft board, and his response was typical: "This is a white man's country." None were appointed. Three years into the war only three southern border states had any African Americans on their draft boards; there were none in the Deep South. In fact, views that blacks could not perform in combat meant that many local boards would not draft African Americans. By the beginning of 1943, at a time when blacks comprised more than 10 percent of the population, they made up only 5 percent of the army. Hence, while some 300,000 single black males were eligible at that time, they were not drafted, while boards selected white married men for the battlefields. That caused resentment in the South. Mississippi Senator Theodore Bilbo bitterly complained that the army was "taking all the whites to meet the quota and leaving the great majority of Negroes at home." Rumors ran rampant in the South. Supposedly, blacks were purchasing ice picks and storing guns, waiting for a wartime blackout, so they could massacre whites. And always the continual fear—after white men go off to war "every Negro man will have a white girl."[14]

American fairness during the first years of the war: The United States was fighting a total war against the two most racist nations on earth, but federal authorities left the draft up to the states, who selected men based on local prejudice, usually resulting in whites going off to war and blacks remaining at home—which in turn irritated white bigots. This Jim Crow draft also had legal implications. Some three decades before the famous *Bakke* affirmative action or "reserve discrimination" case in 1978, the chairman of the War Manpower Commission wrote to the secretaries of War and the Navy that as white "husbands and fathers" become inductees, and "while single Negro registrants who are physically fit remain uninducted," there could be "grave implications should the issue be taken into the courts, especially by a white registrant." Fortunately for the federal government, none did.

Besides racism, another reason that the armed services were reluctant to draft African Americans was a legacy of Jim Crow education—

blacks generally scored low on educational achievement tests. Only 17 percent of blacks inducted into the army, compared with 41 percent of whites, had graduated from high school. The Army General Classification Test was divided into five grades, of which the top three were supposed to produce officers, airmen, and skilled technicians, while the lower two grades were deemed appropriate for infantry, semiskilled workers, or laborers. The AGCT was not an I.Q. test, the army claimed; it measured educational achievement only. Whites scored in all five categories, with a third of them in the lowest two grades, but 84 percent of black soldiers scored in those two bottom categories. In some black units, a third were illiterate. Military efficiency demanded literate soldiers, and so by the end of the war the army had taught over 150,000 black recruits to read and write.

During the first two years of the war the armed forces continued to discriminate against African Americans. Army units remained segregated, and almost all blacks were assigned as laborers. In the spring of 1943 fewer than 80,000 African Americans of more than 500,000 in the armed forces had been sent overseas. Even those trained in combat were being converted to labor units. "Snow Cleaners," the Pittsburgh *Courier* charged, "Cotton Pickers." The army's 555 Parachute Battalion was trained to jump into battle but was sent to Oregon where the only fighting they did was against forest fires. Moreover, army regulations stipulated that no black officer in any unit was to outrank or command a white officer, and one commander even shunned military protocol by claiming that on his post a white lieutenant was superior to a black captain! Most of the officers who led black units were white Southerners, and they were particularly hard on black enlisted men, many of whom came from the North. Officers in a unit stationed in Pennsylvania issued an order: "Any association between the colored soldiers and white women, whether voluntary or not, would be considered rape." The penalty was death. The Medical Corps had 11 percent black troops, but practically all were assigned to sanitation duty; there were no white sanitation companies. The Army Air Corps trained only one Negro squadron of pilots, the 99th Fighter Squadron, and the Marine Corps trained only one battalion. The first black marine officer was not commissioned until after the war.[15]

Navy ships had black sailors, but they lived in segregated quarters and virtually all served in the Steward's Branch—cooks, messmen, or officers' servants—regardless of their education or skills. A revealing case was that of messman Dorie Miller. Stationed at Pearl Harbor on December 7, 1941, Japanese fighters attacked his battleship, the USS *West Virginia*. Miller dashed to the bridge, dragged the wounded captain out of the line of fire, and without any training manned the machine gun and destroyed at least four attacking planes before the ship had to be abandoned. Nevertheless, the navy refused to allow Miller to become a gunners mate, and he continued serving as messman. It took a year before the admirals awarded the sharecropper's son the Navy Cross.

Segregation was not just for men. As one black soldier wrote, the army had "two types of segregation—race and sex." Eventually 350,000 women joined the Women's Army Corps or WACs, the navy's WAVES, the air corp's WASPS, or the coast guard's SPARS. Almost all were white, and those services usually avoided sending black servicewomen to technical schools to learn skilled jobs. Like the black men, they were placed in jobs such as cooks, bakers, laundry attendants, or postal workers. The Army Nurse Corps limited the number of black nurses it accepted, totaling only 1 percent; of 11,000 navy nurses only four were black. With rare exceptions, black nurses were assigned to hospitals that served only black servicemen. Eventually, this system proved impossible, and later in the war the army sent some black nurses to Britain. Since there were very few black soldiers in combat, and wounded, the nurses were ordered to care only for German prisoners of war, a policy that caused so much resentment that the chief surgeon ordered the nurses to aid all troops.

The Jim Crow army startled many northern white Americans. White and black recruits were confronted with segregation as soon as they arrived at training camps. A sign at one post listed religious services: "Catholics, Jews, Protestants, and Negroes." A white private at Camp Upton, New York, wrote that officers ordered men not to "drink with niggers or shake hands." He continued, "Negro draftees are segregated from the minute they come into the camp. . . . The whole picture is a very raw and ugly one. It looks, smells, and tastes like Fascism."

Nevertheless, most Americans thought the treatment of African Americans was fair. The Office of War Information took opinion polls, finding in 1942 that 60 percent of whites felt that blacks were satisfied with their status and were receiving all the opportunities they deserved. A majority of whites outside of the South believed there should be separate schools, restaurants, and neighborhoods, and that the reason blacks had a lower social status was a result of their own racial short-comings, rather than the laws passed and traditions practiced by whites. Army polls demonstrated that while a majority of black soldiers opposed segregated military units, almost 90 percent of white soldiers favored them. That seemed to confirm the army's contention that Jim Crow was necessary to uphold the morale of 90 percent of its troops. "Separate-but-equal was not achieved in the armed forces during the first years of the war," wrote historian Richard Dalfiume, "because the thinking behind military policy was focused on the *separate* to such an extent that efficiency, supposedly the major goal of the military, was always subordinated to the goal of segregation."[16]

By 1943, however, the armed forces suffered from an acute manpower shortage, and it became obvious that Hastie was correct—the Jim Crow army was too inefficient, thus hampering the nation's ability to achieve victory. Since the War Department refused to end Jim Crow, Hastie resigned, and as a result the administration ordered the Army Air Corps to expand skilled training for black troops and the military to promote more African American officers.

The break for African American troops came in 1944. It was an election year, and the Republican Party began making bids for the black vote in the North, talking about investigating how African American troops were being treated in the armed forces. But more important was that the War Department prepared to invade Hitler's Fortress Europa. The administration reviewed the "Negro Problem." A committee declared that the military must be "more affirmative about the use of our Negro troops," and they recommended "that colored units . . . be introduced in combat at the earliest practicable moment." Secretary Stimson had reluctantly arrived at the same conclusion, "We have got to use the colored race to help us in this fight." Consequently, the army ordered the African American Ninety-second and Ninety-third divisions into combat in the European and Pacific Theaters. The navy sent black sailors who had been trained in other ratings besides messmen to 25 auxiliary ships and announced that, for the first time, it would accept black women in the ranks and black men for commission to officers.

It was the need for manpower in a total war that wounded Jim Crow. In December 1944 the Germans launched a counterattack, the Battle of the Bulge, in the Ardennes region of France. The blitzkrieg killed or maimed 50,000 Americans in the first week, and in a month the fighting and harsh winter conditions resulted in more than 125,000 casualties. Stunned, the Supreme Allied Commander, General Dwight D. Eisenhower, allowed blacks assigned to his labor or service units to volunteer for combat training, and they did in droves, so many that Ike had to limit the number to 2,500. After six weeks of training more than 50 black platoons were ready to fight alongside white platoons—and these temporarily integrated infantry companies invaded Germany, crushing the Third Reich.

General Eisenhower praised the troops, and significantly, army polls demonstrated a new opinion of black soldiers. Only a third of white troops had expressed a favorable opinion of black soldiers before fighting with them, but after combat about 80 percent said they had a more favorable view of the African Americans. So did the War Department, stating that blacks had "established themselves as fighting men no less courageous or aggressive than their white comrades."

By the end of the war more than a million black men had been inducted and another 80,000 volunteered, meaning that the portion of African Americans in the armed forces reached their percentage in the population, over 10 percent. Ironically, this was the "balanced force" that the Pentagon had recommended at the beginning of the war—a proportional racial goal. To maintain this balance, the army initiated a recruiting campaign immediately after V-J Day. Surprisingly, thousands of black soldiers volunteered, and they reenlisted at a much higher rate than whites. The army's response again raised the fairness issue: in order to maintain a racial balance, the service branch in 1946 restricted enlistments to only those African Americans who scored 99 or better on the Army General Classification Test. Whites were accepted with a score of 70. Many black taxpayers who had fought for the nation in war were not allowed to continue defending it in peace.

Given their treatment in the military, one might wonder why African Americans would want to reenlist. A journalist answered the question by observing that the black soldier "loves Jim Crow military life more, but Jim Crow civilian America less," and that was a "penetrating comment on America's homecoming welcome to the Negro service man."[17]

When black Johnny came marching home, the welcome could be rude, violent, even deadly. In the industrial North there were racial problems as whites returned and demanded their prewar jobs, laying off blacks. Small riots erupted in Chicago, New York, and Gary, Indiana. Border states witnessed the reemergence of the KKK. In Columbia, Tennessee, an altercation between a white man and James Stephenson, a black navy veteran, erupted into a feud. When local police invaded the black business district, four men were wounded, prompting the Highway Patrol to invade the area, where they beat and arrested more than a hundred black citizens. Two blacks were murdered while waiting to be released from jail.

The South was worse. When Jesse Jackson's father came home to South Carolina, a proud veteran of the European Theater, he was ordered to sit in the back of the bus—behind defeated German POWs. When some black veterans attempted to register to vote in Mississippi they were beaten, and Senator Theodore Bilbo called on all "red-blooded Anglo Saxon" men to use "any means" to prevent blacks from gaining the vote. In Georgia, white racists shot and killed veteran Macio Snipes, the only black registered to vote in his district, and in another town a white mob dragged two veterans and their wives from a car, lined them up, and pumped sixty bullets into their bodies. The grisly tale made national headlines.

Even more egregious, some thought, was the treatment many black servicemen received while they were still *in uniform*, as in the case of Sergeant Isaac Woodard of the U.S. Army. After three years of duty and fifteen months in the South Pacific, Woodard received his separation papers and boarded a bus at Fort Gordon, Georgia, for the trip home to North Carolina. After the bus reached South Carolina, the driver cursed at Woodard for taking too much time in the "colored only" rest room and had the sergeant arrested for drunkenness, even though Woodard did not drink. The police beat their prisoner, rammed a nightstick into his eyes, and locked him in a cell. By the time Woodard could get medical attention at a military hospital, he was permanently blind.

This outrage also received national attention. Actors such as Orson Welles denounced the atrocity, and a black academic wrote to the new president of the United States, Harry S Truman, "to 'gouge out the eyesight' of a man who had used his eyes to safeguard the freedom of our country is surely a disgrace unheard of in any other country in the world." Truman, himself a veteran of World War I, established the President's Committee on Civil Rights to examine the violence and recommend appropriate federal legislation. Upon hearing of the incident, he turned to NAACP leader Walter White and declared, "My God! I had no idea it was as terrible as that. We've got to do something."[18]

Truman's words were prophetic. He would do a lot, but it would be difficult, as demonstrated by two events toward the end of the war that exhibited a challenge to, and defense of, Jim Crow.

First, the Supreme Court, which now held seven of FDR's appointments, ruled on *Smith v. Allwright*. Like many southern states, the Texas legislature had enacted a law erecting the white primary, which basically declared the Democratic Party a private organization that could determine its own membership and thus exclude black Texans. Dr. Lonnie Smith, a Houston dentist, was refused a ballot by election official S.E. Allwright. Smith sued, assisted by attorneys William Hastie and Thurgood Marshall. In 1944 Justice Stanley Reed wrote for the majority, 8 to 1, that the party was not a private organization but an agent of the state, and that being the case, Texas was violating the Fifteenth Amendment. The white primary was declared unconstitutional. This ruling was important because it demonstrated an increasing Court interest in unfair voting practices. But little changed in the South, for whites resisted the black vote by controlling the electorate. They continued to restrict registration with such gimmicks as poll taxes and especially literacy and understanding tests.

The battle to maintain Jim Crow also was demonstrated when the first Mexican American elected to the U.S. Senate, Democrat Dennis Chavez of New Mexico, introduced a bill in 1945 to change the wartime temporary Fair Employment Practices Committee into a permanent federal commission. A new FEPC would have a role in *peacetime* employment practices, and that was anathema to many conservative pro-business members of Congress, especially those from the South. Mississippi's Senator Bilbo led the attack. If the FEPC was made permanent, he declared, then "hell is going to break loose" when the federal government tells businessmen whom they should hire, a chore that would require "an army." He condemned the wartime FEPC as discriminatory, since only a few whites were on it with "66 Negroes, 12 Jews, a few gentiles, and two Japs." During the lengthy debate that followed, Bilbo maintained that the real purpose of the FEPC was "to break down the color line in order to aid the day of miscegenation and mongrelization between the races"; he could not understand how his colleagues could "sacrifice their white blood and their white race." Those who supported such "unAmerican and unconstitutional legislative monstrosities" were "pinkish, communistic, off-brand minority pressure groups."

Debate over the FEPC caused an uproar. Most Southerners rallied behind Bilbo. A Georgian wrote to the senator that if the FEPC continued, Americans would have to "acknowledge the Negro and the Communists, and Jews, as the master of the destiny of America." Meanwhile, newspapers in the region made wild claims about the legislation—that the FEPC would tell businesses, schools, and churches who to hire, resulting in firing white employees and hiring black ones; that it would nationalize all jobs; even that it would force private companies to make public their secret formula used in manufacturing products such as Coca-Cola. Most businesses joined the opposition, and the chairman of the Conference of American Small Business Organizations declared the bill "one of the most vicious pieces of legislation ever proposed."

Yet many liberals, union men, teachers, and northern journalists fought back. They especially were appalled by Senator Bilbo, claiming that he "preached Hitler fascism and racism." Some critics sent Bilbo copies of Hitler's *Mein Kampf,* and four veterans sent him a gag, a Nazi "Military Cross for Distinguished Service" with a fake citation signed by Hitler.

A permanent FEPC became "a symbol," wrote historian Robert Bailey, "for two philosophies of government and life." Senator Chavez represented liberals who felt that the federal government could, and should, legislate to end inequality and correct social injustice. Bilbo represented conservatives who felt that Jim Crow was a fact of life and that the federal government should not legislate against local traditions.[19]

President Truman supported a permanent FEPC, but early in 1946 Senator Bilbo began a filibuster of Chavez's bill, one that lasted 24 days. It was the longest filibuster since 1938, when southern senators talked the federal anti-lynching bill to death in 30 days. Chavez withdrew his bill. For now, the FEPC was dead. The federal government would no longer try to maintain jobs for minority taxpayers—even for federal contracts.

Yet the precedent had been started, and the fight would be continued, for America in 1945 was a different nation than it had been in 1941. African Americans came out of World War II with an enhanced sense of pride and a greater desire to win the Double Victory. "World War II has immeasurably magnified the Negro's awareness of the disparity between the American profession and practice of democracy," wrote the NAACP's Walter White. Black sociologist E. Franklin Frazier agreed, penning that the "Negro was no longer willing to accept discrimination . . . without protest."

The war laid the foundation for the future Civil Rights movement. African American military experience wounded Jim Crow. The "master race" had lost the war, which discredited the idea of racial superiority, especially as allied soldiers liberated German concentration camps, and magazines published photographs of emaciated Jews and other prisoners. The release of film footage of the Holocaust, and the subsequent war crimes trials at Nuremberg had a profound impact on most Americans. To prevent such crimes and work for a peaceful future, the Allies established the United Nations, which declared the concept of "universal human rights." Moreover, in Asia the British and French had not been able to "protect" their nonwhite colonies against Japanese aggression. Consequently, the next decade would witness independence movements in Asia, and this rise of nationalism would spread to African colonies. Politically, the war stimulated a great migration of southern blacks to cities in the industrial North, East, and West. This meant that blacks who had gained the vote would be able to influence elections in important electoral states such as New York, Pennsylvania, Michigan, Illinois, and California. In foreign affairs, by 1947 the United States was engaged in a struggle with a new enemy—the communist menace, the Soviet Union. Truman announced his doctrine that the nation must shoulder the burden of helping "all freedom-loving peoples" to fight against the "surge of expansion of Communist tyranny." America's domestic "race problem" now took on a new international dimension, for Washington battled Moscow in influencing and attracting allies throughout the world, especially the peoples of Asia and Africa. The Soviet Union appealed to those nonwhite nations by proclaiming that for black Americans there was no democracy or freedom. The Truman administration understood this diplomatic problem, and Secretary of State George Marshall stated that the "moral influence of the United States is weakened to the extent that the civil rights proclaimed by our Constitution are not fully confirmed in actual practice." Finally, a number of white liberals concluded that it was time for the nation to uphold the equal rights guaranteed by its Constitution for all citizens, and one of those was Harry S. Truman.

Truman had been reared in the border state of Missouri. The "Show Me" state had some Jim Crow laws but allowed blacks the right to vote, and Truman surely realized the potential of having the state's 130,000 black voters punching his name on election day. "In giving Negroes the rights that are theirs," he declared in his 1940 campaign for the Senate, "we are only acting in accord with ideas of true democracy." Yet Truman also had displayed some ambivalence toward African Americans. He hated the KKK and had stood up publicly against the organization; yet privately he had been known to use the term "nigger" to describe a man he disliked. He also disliked social mixing with blacks, especially inter-marrying; yet he was troubled by legal or political prohibitions against any citizen. He was appalled by the incarceration of Japanese Americans on the West Coast during the war, labeling it "disgraceful" and writing that "a lot of our Americans have a streak of Nazi in them." Moreover, he was an outspoken advocate of equal opportunity for all Americans. To Truman, a man who had been raised in fairly modest circumstances and had worked hard to become an important senator, opportunity was simply an issue of fairness.

When he moved into the White House in 1945, Truman was a man ahead of his times on race relations. He wrote to a friend about the vio-lence against black veterans in the South and decried that in Georgia "mob gangs can take four people out and shoot them in the back," and maintained that when "a Mayor and a City Marshal can take a Negro Sergeant off a bus in South Carolina, beat him up and put out one of his eyes, and nothing is done about it by the State Authorities, something is radically wrong with the system." The president might have erred on the details of the Isaac Woodard affair, but he understood the problem in Dixie: Southerners are "living eighty years behind the times. . . . I am not asking for social equality, because no such thing exists, but I am ask-ing for equality of opportunity for all human beings and, as long as I stay here, I am going to continue that fight."[20]

The president supported a federal anti-lynching law, a permanent FEPC, and because he was offended by the postwar mob violence, he established a committee on civil rights. In 1947 the committee published its findings, *To Secure These Rights*. The book was widely read, influential, and considered utopian for the times: "In our land men are equal, but they are free to be different. From these very differences among our people has come the great human and national strength of America." The report discussed and demonstrated racial discrimination in basic freedoms, education, public facilities, personal safety, and employment opportunities. The committee was disturbed by the state of race relations, and that included the evacuation of Americans of Japanese descent during the war "made without a trial or any sort of hearing. . . . Fundamental to our whole system of law is the belief that guilt is personal and not a matter of heredity or association." The recommendations were radical, calling for federal policies and laws to end racial discrimination and bring about equality: "We can tolerate no restrictions upon the individual which depend upon irrelevant factors such as his race, his color, his religion or the social position to which he is born." *To Secure These Rights* set the liberal legislative agenda for the next generation, that eventually would be signed into law by Lyndon Baines Johnson.

To Secure These Rights also called for desegregation of the armed forces. "Prejudice in any area is an ugly, undemocratic phenomenon, but in the armed services, where all men run the risk of death, it is especially repugnant." The rationale was fairness. "When an individual enters the service of the country, he necessarily surrenders some of the rights and privileges which inhere in American citizenship." In return, the government "undertakes to protect his integrity as an individual." Yet that was not possible in the Jim Crow army since "any discrimination which . . . prevents members of minority groups from rendering full military service in defense of their country is for them a humiliating badge of inferiority." Thus, the report called for an end to "all discrimination and segregation based on race, color, creed, or national origins in . . . all branches of the Armed Forces."

Truman agreed, and during the same year he also realized the need for a strong postwar military to confront the Soviet Union. Thus, in 1947 he and his advisers came up with a plan for a large standing military, Universal Military Training, and presented it to Congress. What was amazing about the plan was that the administration opposed all segregation in the new postwar armed forces: "Nothing could be more tragic for the future attitude of our people, and for the unity of our nation" than a citizens' military that emphasized "class or racial difference."

In June, Truman became the first president to address the NAACP. His speech was a significant departure from traditional race relations in the United States. In front of a crowd of 10,000 at the Lincoln Memorial, the president left no doubt how he stood on civil rights: America had "reached a turning point in the long history of our country's efforts to guarantee freedom and equality to all our citizens. . . . Each man must be guaranteed equality of opportunity." He then proposed what black citizens had been calling for—an enhanced role of the federal authority vis-à-vis the states. "We must make the Federal government a friendly, vigilant defender of the rights and equalities of all Americans. And again I mean all Americans." After the speech the president turned to the NAACP's White and declared, "I said what I did because I mean every word of it—and I am going to prove that I do mean it."[21]

Truman began proving it. A few months later his administration proposed the abolition of all state poll taxes, passage of federal anti-lynching and voting rights acts, desegregation of the armed forces, and enlargement of the federal government to include a permanent Fair Employment Practices Committee, a civil rights division in the Justice Department, and a Commission on Civil Rights. In February 1948 the president sent his civil rights legislation to Congress, but a Gallup poll demonstrated strong resistance. Most people were unaware of Truman's proposals, and of those who were, 56 percent disapproved and only 6 percent supported such legislation. Almost two-thirds favored continued segregation in the military. As for Truman's presidential approval rating, it plunged to just 36 percent at the beginning of the election year.

The 1948 election race was on, and although there were many issues, the future status of minorities was one of the most important. The eventual Republican candidate, Governor Thomas E. Dewey of New York, had a good record on civil rights, signing a law establishing a state FEPC and banning discrimination in employment. He was interested in bringing the northern black vote back to the Party of Lincoln, and he presented a formidable ticket by picking as his running mate the popular governor of California, Earl Warren. The Democratic Party was in tatters. The former Democratic vice president, Henry A. Wallace, declared that he would run for the presidency. Knowing that he would not be able to wrestle his party's nomination away from a sitting president, the liberal Wallace declared a run on the Progressive Party ticket. This, of course, gave Truman more incentive to keep African Americans in the Democratic fold by speaking out in favor of civil rights, which naturally outraged southern Democrats. They reminded the president that since Reconstruction no Democrat had been elected without the Solid South. After Truman's civil rights speech, a Virginia politician telegraphed the president "I really believe that you have ruined the Democratic party in the South," and one from Florida added that if his plans are "carried out you won't be elected dogcatcher in 1948."

Southern politicians also were concerned about the future of the armed forces, especially since so many military bases were on their soil. Congress had failed to enact Universal Military Training, which forced Truman to propose a resumption of selective service. Congress held hearings that spring, and the Senate Armed Services Committee called A. Philip Randolph: "This time Negroes will not take a Jim Crow draft lying down," he declared. "I personally pledge myself to counsel, aid and abet youth both white and Negro to quarantine any Jim Crow conscription.... I shall call upon all veterans to join this civil disobedience movement." Randolph threatened that passage of a discriminatory draft could result in "mass civil disobedience." That provoked controversy. The *Pittsburgh Courier* called Randolph's views extreme, writing that "the Negro has never produced any traitors," but a poll in Harlem found that more than 70 percent of blacks supported refusing induction into a Jim Crow army. *Newsweek* reported "strong sympathy and support for Randolph," while the *Chicago Defender* demanded "an American Army, not a Confederate Army."

General Eisenhower presented the army's position: "There is race prejudice in this country. When you pass a law to get somebody to like someone, you have trouble." Senator Richard Russell of Georgia favored an amendment to the draft bill that would allow enlisted men to request service in units of their own race, and a South Carolina senator declared that the "wars of this country have been won by white soldiers."[22]

Congress passed a selective service bill in June. Eisenhower had been too influential; his testimony won the day. The act did not mention integrating the armed forces. Under pressure to increase the size of the military to confront the Soviet Union, Truman signed the bill into law.

But conservatives won a Pyrrhic victory. Republicans who were eager to bring African Americans back to their party for the 1948 elections adopted a platform that opposed segregation in the military. Wallace's Progressive Party demanded a "Presidential proclamation ending segregation and all forms of discrimination in the armed services." Liberal Democrats responded at their convention. The mayor of Minneapolis, Hubert H. Humphrey, who was running for the U.S. Senate, declared that "the time has arrived for the Democratic party to get out of the shadow of states rights and walk into the bright sunshine of human rights." He proposed, and the party adopted, a platform calling for "equal treatment in the service and defense of our nation." Symbolically at least, the national Democratic Party now stood for civil rights, and that was too much for southern Democrats. "We bid you good-bye," declared an Alabama delegate, and many Southerners marched out of the convention and formed the States Rights' Democratic party, or Dixiecrats. They nominated South Carolina's Governor J. Strom Thurmond for their presidential candidate, who ran for the "segregation of the races" and against the "totalitarian government" in Washington, D.C.

Truman had won his party's nomination but was faced with major political problems. The Dixiecrats were running on their own ticket, Wallace was calling for integration, Randolph was advocating black draft resistance, and the Republicans had nominated Dewey and Warren, the popular governors of New York and California.

Thus, after the convention the president issued two significant executive orders. On July 26, he mandated the end of hiring and employment discrimination in the federal government, reaffirming FDR's order of 1941. Although some departments had been integrated, Truman's order meant that all federal agencies must end segregation and open jobs to minority taxpayers across the nation, a task that began slowly. Second, the commander in chief directed the implementation of "equality of treatment and opportunity" in the armed services without regard to race, color, religion, or national origin. Truman established two commissions to study the practices of the government and the military. He selected Charles Fahy, a liberal Georgia New Dealer, to head the armed forces committee, and appointed two black members to the Fahy Committee, Lester Granger of the Urban League and John Sengstacke, publisher of the Chicago *Defender*.

A. Philip Randolph called off his plans for draft resistance and wired congratulations, praising Truman's "high order of statesmanship and courage" as the president began his "whistle-stop" campaign. The train swept into small towns across the nation, where Truman spoke from the rear platform to ordinary folks who had never seen a president and had only heard the prepared speeches on radio. Truman immediately put them at ease, introducing his wife, Bess, as "the Boss" and his daughter, Margaret, as "the Boss's Boss," before talking about the domestic and foreign problems of the day. He was plain-speaking Harry, reeling off Democratic accomplishments during the Depression and war, mentioning the Soviet challenge, and declaring that his form of Democratic politics was the best course for the nation, not that of the Republicans and their "special privilege boys." Truman labeled Republicans "gluttons of privilege" before turning on the Republican-controlled 80th Congress, lambasting them as the "good-for-nothing" and "do-nothing" Congress. As prices for corn dropped in the Midwest, Harry shouted that the "Republican Congress has already stuck a pitchfork in the farmer's back!" As inflation cut into wages he declared that "big-business Republicans have begun to nail the American consumer to the wall with spikes of greed." He laid it on, revving up the audience, and soon supporters were yelling "Give'em Hell Harry!" He did with gusto, pledging a continuation of the New Deal, not its destruction, which he claimed was the aim of Republicans. Crowds grew, and in Los Angeles some 80,000 cheered him on while black supporters held a sign: "Thanks for the Civil Rights Program."

The whistle-stop crusade energized New Deal Democrats, while Dewey conducted a lackluster, overconfident campaign, mentioning few specifics for the future course of the nation. Although all polling organizations predicted a Dewey victory, on election day Truman was able to rebuild the old Democratic coalition of workers, farmers, and minorities that had supported FDR. By midnight HST was ahead by a million votes; by four A.M. it was two million, and by 10 A.M. Dewey conceded. African Americans had voted in record numbers outside of the South, and they gave Truman his slender margin of victory in California, Illinois, and Ohio, which handed him the victory. In Washington, D.C., Margaret Truman remembered, "bands, official and impromptu, seemed to be playing 'I'm Just Wild About Harry' on every corner." Congratulatory letters poured in, and perhaps the one the president cherished the most was from General Eisenhower, who wrote that at no point in American political history was there "a greater accomplishment than yours," and that was "traced so clearly to the stark courage and fighting heart of a single man."

Two months after his victory, in January 1949, Truman met with Fahy and the secretaries of the Army, Navy, Air Force, and Defense at the White House. The commander in chief was characteristically blunt, telling the secretaries that he wanted "concrete results" on desegregating the armed forces. "I want the job done," he ordered, also saying that he hoped that he would not have to "knock somebody's ears down," but if necessary, he would do that to integrate the military.

Throughout the first half of 1949 the Fahy Committee held hearings and investigations, helped by the appointment of a new secretary of Defense, Louis Johnson. The committee discovered many disturbing facts. The navy was attempting to integrate, but about two-thirds of its black sailors remained in the steward's branch. The admirals pledged to accept more blacks for officer candidate school, open other occupations, and integrate their basic training. The marines did the same for basic training, but they too had a long way to go. That branch had more than 8,000 officers and only one was black; only 2 percent of enlisted marines were black, and all were in labor or service units. The new air force, now separated from the army, responded the most quickly, integrating their units and pilots into the entire force.

The service with the most southern traditions, the army, naturally put up the most resistance. It had about 500 job specialties open to whites, but blacks could work in only about 180, mostly the unskilled occupations, and less than 20 percent of its service school courses were open to African Americans. The brass maintained a quota system—only 10 percent of the army could be black. Secretary of the Army Kenneth Royall again stated that his service was "not an instrument for social evolution"; blacks were not qualified for combat but were "peculiarly qualified" for manual labor. The generals wrote to Defense Secretary Johnson, complaining that "we are weakening to a dangerous degree the combat efficiency of the Army. These officers are familiar with the combat performance of Negro troops during war and feel that we have already gone too far in inserting colored organizations in white combat units." Thus, a year after the commander in chief's direct order, A. Philip Randolph wrote in the *New York Times* that "the Army does not intend to abolish its racist quota system or its segregation. . . . the bitter reality remains that Jim Crow in the Army is still with us and going strong."

Yet this time the commander in chief and his defense secretary were prepared for combat with the army. In April Secretary Johnson declared that the new policy for the armed forces would be one of equality of treatment and opportunity, and that personnel would be considered "on the basis of individual merit and ability" for enlistment and commissions, promotion, assignments, and admission to service schools. The new policy, he demanded, was that "qualified Negro personnel shall be assigned to fill any type of position . . . without regard to race." The generals complained, dragged their feet, and by summer Secretary Royall resigned and was replaced by Gordon Gray. The president intervened, publicly announcing again that his goal was desegregation. That autumn the army slowly began to follow orders, and by the spring of 1950 the generals agreed to abolish its quota.[23]

The army had agreed to integrate, but in practice segregation remained. As in World War II, it would take a manpower shortage to change the system, and that occurred after June 1950 when communist North Korea attacked U.S. ally South Korea. Soon Truman was raising an army for war, this time drafting men and placing them in integrated units. Others enlisted. Without a quota, just one month after war erupted, a fourth of all enlistments were black. By the end of 1951 all American units in Korea had been integrated. The rest of the services took longer. The air force abolished its last black unit in 1952, as did the marines. That corps was comprised of almost 75,000 troops just before the Korean War, with only a thousand blacks, half of whom were stewards, but by the armistice in 1953 there were almost 15,000 black marines, 6 percent of the total, integrated into combat arms. The number of black units in the army dropped from 385 in June 1950 to 88 in August 1953, and the last one was integrated in October 1954, the same year that the Defense Department integrated its civilian facilities at army and navy bases throughout the South.

The result of desegregation was stated in May 1951 by Brigadier General John H. Michaelis, who had a reputation as one of the finest commanders in Korea. He testified that white soldiers had no problem serving under black sergeants in combat. Discussing his command, he stated that "Negroes were integrated down to the lowest tactical unit, the squad, and in this capacity have proven satisfactory. Some have been promoted, others have been decorated. I mention this to point out that there is NO color line in a foxhole." A marine platoon leader agreed, stating that in combat "it didn't make any difference if you are white, red, black, green or turquoise," and a white southern infantryman added, "If a man can fire a rifle and knows his job, he's my buddy. I don't give a damn what color his skin happens to be."

In the long run, conservatives and Southerners had been wrong about desegregating the armed forces. They had stated that African Americans did not have the racial temperament or characteristics to fight in combat, but six of seven officers in Korea felt that white and black troops fought about the same. They had predicted racial strife in an integrated military, but while there were some hard feelings there were no violent conflicts, no riots in the new armed forces. They had declared that desegregation would hamper military effectiveness, but by the end of the Korean conflict the generals were stating that integration actually had improved effectiveness. They had stated that white troops would not accept working alongside black soldiers, but integration was accepted as standard operating procedure in the U.S. armed forces. Desegregation was, as the *New York Times* declared, "one of the biggest stories of the twentieth century . . . it warrants no lesser description."[24]

The genesis of affirmative action began during the Roosevelt and Truman administrations: beginning in 1933 Harold Ickes issued an order to prohibit discrimination in Public Works Administration projects, and the next year his assistants devised a proportional hiring system aimed at employing a fixed percentage of skilled black workers. The order and the system were neglected by most contractors and ineffectual, but other New Deal programs such as the minimum wage and social security granted benefits regardless of race or gender, and women who performed the same jobs as men were paid the same wages by the Works Progress Administration. More important, FDR established the temporary Fair Employment Practices Committee, which advanced the idea that public agencies and private contractors who accepted federal funds should employ all taxpayers regardless of race.

By 1941 the federal government had become involved with a new issue—hiring practices. With few exceptions, such as child labor, the government had left hiring up to employers and had not mandated that a business hire any particular race. The Roosevelt administration began to change that tradition. During a war against racist enemies many liberals came to believe that the federal government should promote employment free of discrimination throughout the nation. FDR's executive order not only laid the foundation for the antidiscrimination Title VII of the landmark 1964 Civil Rights Act but also had an impact on progressive states. By 1945, more than 20 states had passed laws barring discrimination in government employment, with half of these laws mentioning race and religion, and it became more common for states to have antidiscrimination clauses in their contracts with private businesses. That same year New York passed the first equal opportunity law establishing a state FEPC to regulate *private* hiring and promotions. By 1964 half of the states had set up their own commissions with jurisdiction over both public and private employment.

Harry Truman also changed tradition with his executive order desegregating the U.S. armed forces. By the early 1950s federal officials and the generals had accepted the idea that all taxpayers had the right to serve in agencies that were funded by all taxpayers, whether the government or the armed forces, and in those occupations they should have equal opportunities and serve alongside other citizens.

Serving alongside others raised another question: Can government power be used to change social relationships? Recall that in 1896 the Supreme Court ruled in the *Plessy* case that man-made laws were "powerless to eradicate social instincts or to abolish distinctions based upon physical differences." Yet combat experiences in World War II and integrated foxholes in Korea challenged traditional thought. Perhaps governmental laws and policies could change opinions and social behavior, an idea that resurfaced again in the 1960s.

The Roosevelt and Truman administrations also demonstrated that the federal government could open some doors of opportunity for citizens. That included many young African Americans who began careers with the government or with the military, men such as Frank Peterson, the first black marine pilot who flew in Korea and who later became the corps' first general officer, and numerous others, including Colin Powell. He entered the army ten years after Truman's executive order, "that historic turning point," Powell wrote. "Beginning in the fifties less discrimination, a truer merit system, and leveler playing fields existed inside the gates of our military posts than in any Southern city hall or Northern corporation." For Powell, Truman's action, and the resulting change in the army, "made it easier for me to love my country, with all its flaws, and to serve her with all my heart."[25]

During national emergencies, a depression and two wars, the concept of fairness began to change in America. Many citizens started to realize that the predominate Jim Crow ideas of the era were in conflict with the ideals embodied in the U.S. Constitution. Many began to consider it fair that all taxpayers should have the opportunity to hold jobs supported by their taxes. That concept was the foundation for a policy that eventually became known as affirmative action.

two | Civil Rights Struggle and the Rise of Affirmative Action

In 1958, Lt. Colin Powell was attending Ranger school at Fort Benning, Georgia, where every time he left the base he was "plunged back into the Old South."

> I could go into Woolworth's in Columbus, Georgia, and buy anything I wanted, as long as I did not try to eat there. I could go into a department store and they would take my money, as long as I did not try to use the men's room. I could walk along the street, as long as I did not look at a white woman.

While training in the north Georgia hills Powell wanted to attend church services on Sundays. A simple request, but in order to do that he had to be driven to an African American church some miles away. The army summoned a white corporal to drive the black lieutenant to the closest Baptist church. On one Sunday, the corporal informed Powell that he also would like to attend services. Powell asked the preacher, but the kindly old minister said that he feared the reaction of local white folks. The "reality I wanted to ignore, was forcing its way into my life," wrote Powell, "the lunatic code that made it wrong for two men to sit together in a house of God, or share a meal in a restaurant, or use the same bathroom."

"Racism was not just a black problem," Powell continued. "It was America's problem." During the 1950s southern states continued to restrict black voting rights by gimmicks and various tests, so by 1958 only 9 percent of Alabama blacks were registered to vote; only 4 percent in Mississippi. Most residential areas were segregated by law; concerning education, Southerners saved money at black schools, which often were shacks where teachers earned about a third of white counterparts. In Clarendon County, South Carolina, officials in 1950 spent $179 on every white student and $43 on each black one; 14 years later, in Holly Bluff, Mississippi, those figures were over $190 for a white student and $1.26 for each black. "Separate but equal" public universities were anything but; in Texas, about three-quarters of federal land grant funds were spent at white Texas A&M while the rest went to its black "sister school" Prairie View A&M. Southern racism could be deadly. In 1955 a fourteen-year-old black from Chicago, Emmett Till, visited Mississippi. Unaware of southern customs, he supposedly whistled at a white woman. Shortly thereafter, the woman's husband and another man captured Till, cut off his testicles, shot him in the head, and dumped his mangled body in a local river. Although the killers later confessed, the white jury acquitted them. African Americans had a better life in the North. They could attend public universities, some companies and a few unions had integrated, more blacks were establishing their own businesses, and they did have voting rights. Yet there were limits. City fathers had established de facto residential ordinances, which meant that minorities were segregated into the worst neighborhoods, and students usually attended segregated schools since districts followed discriminatory housing practices—suburbs had white schools and ghettos had black schools. The result often resembled Levittown, Pennsylvania; in 1956 some 60,000 lived in that suburb, and not one was black.

That was considered fair by white Americans, as demonstrated in opinion polls during the 1950s. Three-fourths of southern and half of northern whites opposed having a black neighbor, while 97 percent of southern and 90 percent of northern whites opposed interracial dating. A Gallup poll asked if America should have a national law requiring employers to hire people without regard to color or race and less than a third supported the idea, while almost half thought the matter should be left up to each state.

President Eisenhower held similar views. After his election the administration supported the passage of state but not national antidiscrimination laws, labeling the FEPC a "Federally compulsory thing." Ike continued desegregating the armed forces and federal government, and he established a Government Contract Committee, chaired by Vice President Richard Nixon. The committee conducted surveys of the racial composition of federal employees and of tax-supported contractors but with few results for they left the main responsibility for enforcing desegregation to the contractor. In seven years the committee prompted only two contractors to stop discrimination. The administration urged integration at restaurants, hotels, parks, and swimming pools in Washington, D.C., but not at public facilities in the rest of the nation. The president believed that the states should have the power to control local affairs, and that included race relations.

To advise him on race the president appointed a black assistant, E. Frederic Morrow, who attempted to defend the administration's record, but he had a difficult time; for three years he was not able to convince Ike to meet with African American leaders. The president usually delegated the race issue to Nixon. After years of working with Eisenhower, Morrow concluded that Ike's "viewpoint on civil rights was southern. . . . In my many talks with him in this area, I found him neither intellectually nor emotionally disposed to combat segregation."[1]

But the Supreme Court was ready to contest segregation. During the previous six decades the court had been unwilling to hear cases concerning discrimination, but that began to change as FDR and Truman appointed liberal justices and as black soldiers fought in World War II. That conflict made it clear that limiting education for minorities was a national security issue. America needed literate young men for combat; training 150,000 black recruits to read and write during the war demonstrated that minorities could be educated to take orders and to give them. During the ensuing Cold War the exclusion of minorities from education was no longer tenable, and the Court responded by accepting many more cases that began to chip away at Jim Crow. By the Korean War the Court had ruled against those states that refused to admit African Americans into professional and graduate schools, and it had invalidated a Virginia statute requiring segregation on public buses moving across state lines.

The most important case came just one year after the end of the Korean War, the 1954 landmark decision *Brown v. Board of Education*. The NAACP filed on behalf of a black student, Linda Brown, who was bused out of her white neighborhood to attend a black school in Topeka, Kansas. Chief Justice Earl Warren read the opinion: "Does segregation of children in public schools solely on the basis of race, even though the physical facilities and other tangible factors may be equal, deprive the children of the minority group of equal educational opportunities? We unanimously believe that it does." The Court ruled that separate educational facilities were "inherently unequal" and violated the Fourteenth Amendment. The next year the Court ordered segregated districts to integrate with "all deliberate speed."

The South responded with outrage. Georgia's governor accused the Court of reducing the Constitution to a "mere scrap of paper," while Senator Harry Byrd of Virginia called the decision "the most serious blow that has yet been struck against the rights of the states." Senator James Eastland of Mississippi predicted that federal efforts to integrate southern schools would lead to "great strife and turmoil."

Strife came the next year in Montgomery, Alabama. On December 1, 1955, an African American seamstress and NAACP member, Rosa Parks, boarded a public bus and sat in "no man's land," the few rows in the middle of the bus where blacks could sit until whites filled up the front seats. Eventually, the driver demanded that Parks give up her seat to a white passenger. She refused, violating local law, and was arrested. In response, local black leaders formed the Montgomery Improvement Association and named as its president 26-year-old Martin Luther King Jr. The MIA started a bus boycott that lasted over a year, and the NAACP sued the bus company. The MIA forged a coalition between black organizations and churches, it received financial aid from northern blacks and liberal whites, and it eventually led to the formation of a larger group, the Southern Christian Leadership Conference. Moreover, for the first time many white newspapers placed articles on page one while the nightly news, a new 15-minute program broadcast nationally, covered the boycott and introduced King to the television audience. Most important, the boycott was victorious: it demonstrated that average people could organize what King called nonviolent direct action. While the bus company lost revenue, a federal court ruled against the local ordinance. The buses desegregated, bruising Jim Crow in Montgomery.

For the most part the Montgomery bus boycott was a local affair, but the *Brown* decision had national implications. The South pledged not to abide by *Brown* and attempted to do that by passing more than 450 laws and resolutions to prevent or limit integration. The attorney generals of Louisiana, Alabama, and Texas issued injunctions to prohibit the NAACP from operating in their states, while Louisiana conducted hearings on racial unrest and published their conclusions: the "Communist conspiracy originating with Joseph Stalin . . . is now widely acknowledged as the origin and guiding influence behind the move to integrate the public schools of the South." Opinion polls demonstrated that over 80 percent of white Southerners opposed school desegregation, a quarter felt that using violence was justified to maintain white supremacy.

The Eisenhower administration did not press states to desegregate schools, and so by June 1957 only marginal amounts of integration had occurred in the border states and none at all in North or South Carolina, Alabama, Florida, Georgia, Louisiana, and Mississippi. Although political pressure mounted outside the South to enforce *Brown*, the president stated in July 1957 "I can't imagine any set of circumstances that would ever induce me to send federal troops . . . into any area to enforce the order of a federal court."

Two months later President Eisenhower sent federal troops to Central High School in Little Rock, Arkansas. By 1957 the city had worked out a plan to comply with the *Brown* case. Nine black students who lived in the district would desegregate the high school in September. But public pressure mounted, and Governor Orval Faubus ordered the Arkansas National Guard to surround the school and prevent integration. When one black girl appeared at Central High she was met by an angry white mob screaming, "Lynch her! Lynch her!" The governor's action challenged the federal government. President Eisenhower, who had refused to endorse the *Brown* decision, now reluctantly federalized the state national guard and ordered a thousand U.S. Army troops into Little Rock.

The president integrated one segregated high school, and that provoked a strident southern response. When a soldier nicked one protestor with a bayonet, drawing blood, Faubus claimed on television that the "warm red blood of patriotic American citizens" stained the "cold, naked, unsheathed knives" of the "military occupation." "Thus Spake King Ike," declared one Louisiana newspaper, while another proclaimed that Eisenhower had ended democracy and established a "frightening monster—A MILITARY DICTATORSHIP."

The Little Rock affair demonstrated that federal attempts to integrate southern schools would be met with massive resistance, perhaps even violence. It also demonstrated the potential power of the federal government to force the states to uphold the Constitution, especially if a president had the desire. Eisenhower did not. His assistant Sherman Adams described Little Rock as "a constitutional duty which was the most repugnant to him of all his acts in his eight years at the White House."[2]

Ike was much more interested in the economy, which was booming for most of the 1950s. The gross national product doubled in the decade, inflation remained low, and consumption soared during the massive baby boom. "Rocketing Births: Business Bonanza," *Time* declared. "1955 showed the flowering of American capitalism."

But not for minorities. Most black men were laborers and a third of black working women in New York City were domestic servants. In 1960 the Department of Labor reported that the average black worker made less than 60 percent of white counterparts. "To be a Negro," wrote Michael Harrington, "is to participate in a culture of poverty and fear that goes far deeper than any law for or against discrimination." Since many Mexican Americans worked as migrant laborers, over half lived in poverty, usually working for a dollar a day. Musician Bo Diddley recalled the financial plight of most minorities: "Some of us didn't have the down payment on a Popsicle."

The main reason minorities lagged so far behind was that many employers refused to hire them. To change that, many states and cities passed antidiscrimination laws and established Fair Employment Practices Commissions. New York was the first in 1945, others followed, so by 1964 about half the states had laws or commissions to prevent discrimination in the workplace. Of those, New York's commission was the model. It had power to hold public hearings and issue a "cease and desist" order, which could legally force an employer to stop discriminating. But the threat was rarely used; during its first 20 years the commission received almost 9,000 complaints, finding probable discrimination in about 20 percent. Officials then discussed the issue with the employer and ordered the boss not to hire the individual who had been discriminated against, or pay compensation but to promise not to discriminate again and display a commission poster. In those two decades, the commission held only three dozen hearings and issued only seven cease and desist orders. Supposedly, 99 percent of employers reformed their ways and began hiring regardless of race, to which one expert wrote: "One need not be a misanthrope to wonder at this remarkable rate of reform," adding in 1966 that with the present commission many businesses are "in their third decade as illegal discriminators and . . . can reasonably expect to make it to the end of the century without interference from an anti-discrimination commission."

Businessmen who complained that fair employment commissions would regulate and dictate hiring practices actually had little to fear from most state and local governments. All of these state committees had one thing in common: while they could embarrass an employer with a hearing, they usually had little effect on hiring practices. A survey of 13 state commissions in 1961 revealed that they had received over 19,400 complaints, and that a resounding 99.7 percent were "resolved" without a formal hearing. Those states issued only 26 cease and desist orders and took only 18 companies to court for violating their own laws.

Public pressure, of course, could convince a few employers to hire minorities during the 1950s. In New York, banks and insurance companies began to hire more African Americans, especially in Harlem, and department stores hired more black and Puerto Rican women to sell merchandise. The state also pressured the airlines to integrate their workforce, especially those carriers who provided interstate travel. In 1956 Dorothy Franklin claimed that TWA would not hire her as a stewardess "because she was a Negro." TWA rebuffed the charge, claiming that it was the woman's "appearance." Nevertheless, the state began to pressure the eighteen airlines that flew into New York, and that slowly cracked open the door. New York Airways, in 1957, hired a black pilot; Mohawk Airlines hired Ruth Carol Taylor, a nurse described as "pretty and charming," and she became the "first Negro airline stewardess in the history of commercial aviation in the United States."

In general, though, state FEPCs failed to have much impact on pervasive job discrimination. African Americans were rarely hired, and that included black college graduates. Nationally, black men held only about 1 percent of all white-collar positions; they usually only could get labor and service jobs. In 1959 there were 58,000 workers at 30 oil refineries on the Gulf Coast, but less than 6 percent were African American; five of these plants had no black workers at all. In the Midwest, two Allis-Chalmers farm-implement factories and the Caterpillar assembly plant were almost void of any black employees; in Delaware, the International Latex synthetic rubber plant had 1,700 employees, and not one was African American. Even Ford, which had a good record of hiring minorities in the North, employed only 21 blacks at its large Atlanta plant because, as a manager admitted, "We agreed to abide by local custom and not hire Negroes for production work."

Most unions also refused to train black apprentices. The National Urban League revealed that African Americans were almost completely excluded from printing and plumbers unions. In apprentice programs for the building trades, there was not one black trainee in Atlanta, Baltimore, Milwaukee, Minneapolis, or Washington. *Ebony* magazine reported in 1963 that only "two of 3,500 apprentices in all trades in Newark are Negro and in Chicago, where a quarter of the population is Negro, the apprentice figure is less than 1 percent." Typical was the Sheet Metal Workers of the American Federation of Labor in New York City. Admission to the local was through their apprenticeship program, which required sponsorship from a member, who traditionally supported a friend or relative. "Sometimes being non-Italian or non-Irish," said one observer, "is almost as sufficient cause for exclusion as being Negro."[3]

All the while the federal government continued to spend taxpayers' dollars for construction projects. Since 1941 all of those contracts contained a nondiscrimination clause, which was not enforced. In fact, as late as 1961 the federal government had never terminated a contract because a contractor refused to hire minorities, and although President Truman had ordered the desegregation of the armed forces thirteen years earlier, some states still did not have one black in their reserve units or in their National Guards.

For the African American in 1960, then, the result was a vicious circle. Job discrimination reduced employment opportunity, resulted in low income, and that in turn limited availability of education and training programs, keeping skills low and reducing employment opportunities and income. Consequently, the average white family income that year was more than $5,800 but the black counterpart was just above $3,200. Blacks were concentrated in labor and other menial jobs, and occupational progress during the booming economy of the 1950s was distressingly slow. Between 1950 and 1960 the number of self-employed blacks actually dropped by 10,000, black-owned businesses declined by a third, while their unemployment remained at double the rate for whites. According to one report, if the occupational trends of the 1950s did not change, minorities could not expect jobs proportionate to their percentage of the population—in skilled trades until the year 2005, in the professions until 2017, in sales until 2114, and among business managers and owners until 2730.

Republicans and northern Democrats began to contemplate black political support, and one of those was unlikely, the Texan Democrat and Senate Majority Leader Lyndon Johnson. He began to consider running for the highest office, the presidency, and to do that he had to demonstrate to the nation that he had broken away from traditional southern views on the race issue. Although in his 1948 campaign for the Senate he had agreed with his southern colleagues and called the FEPC "a farce and a sham—an effort to set up a police state," during the next decade he backed off from such denouncements and in 1957 brokered a civil rights act through Congress. The bill established a Civil Rights Commission and Civil Rights Division in the Justice Department. The commission was empowered to investigate allegations that minority citizens were being deprived of their rights, especially the vote. "It can . . . sift out the truth from the fancies," LBJ declared, "and it can return with recommendations which will be of assistance to reasonable men." Characteristically, the Texan boasted that it was "the most important civil rights bill in history," but in fact it was a weak compromise. The commission did collect facts, but it had little power; the states themselves were supposed to hold trials against white officials who had prohibited blacks from voting. As one black critic wrote LBJ, "If a Southern jury would not convict confessed kidnappers of Emmett Till after he was found murdered, why would they convict an election official for refusing to give a Negro his right of suffrage?" The critic was right; the bill did not increase African American voting in the South.

Then, on February 1, 1960, four African American students at North Carolina A & T College walked into the local Woolworth's in Greensboro, North Carolina, and sat down at the lunch counter. A sign on the counter declared: "Whites Only." A waitress approached and one of them ordered, "I'd like a cup of coffee, please." The waitress answered, "I'm sorry. We don't serve Negroes here," and refused service for the remainder of the afternoon. When the store closed at 5:30 P.M., the students left, and one of them said to the waitress, "I'll be back tomorrow with A & T College." They became known as the Greensboro 4, and that evening they spread the word of the sit-in throughout their campus. The next morning about 30 male and female black students walked into

Woolworth's and sat at the lunch counter. Occasionally a student would try to order but was not served. Next day about 50 sat at the counter. This time they were joined by three white students, and by the end of the week hundreds of blacks students from a half-dozen nearby campuses appeared.

Unlike the few sit-ins during the late 1950s this movement spread rapidly across the South. In the weeks after Greensboro, black students started sit-ins at lunch counters in Winston-Salem, Durham, Raleigh, and other cities across North Carolina, and during the spring activists were using the tactic in most southern states, from Nashville to Miami, from Baltimore to San Antonio. Blacks also began read-ins at other public facilities, such as libraries, and paint-ins at art galleries, wade-ins at beaches, and kneel-ins at white churches. By April black students were marching on state capitols and in the cities of South Carolina, Georgia, Louisiana, and Alabama. Throughout 1960 and the next year about 70,000 participated in various protests in thirteen states. "Never before had so many Negroes been in the streets," proclaimed historian Lerone Bennett. "Never before had Negroes demonstrated so much passion and perseverance." A newspaper in Raleigh noted that the "picket line now extends from the dime store to the United States Supreme Court and beyond that to national and world opinion."

The enthusiasm generated by the sit-ins slowly began to appear in another meaningful campaign—the demand for jobs. In Philadelphia, activists began boycotts; four hundred ministers asked their congregations not to shop at businesses that did not hire African Americans. In St. Louis, the Congress of Racial Equality (CORE) chapter held sit-ins at Woolworth's and McCrory's lunch counters, and after winning integration they pressured the stores to change their employment practices. McCrory's agreed to promote a black dishwasher to counter supervisor, promoted two busgirls to waitresses, and reserved the next two sales openings; Woolworth's hired black clerks at several local stores. Success prompted CORE officials to begin to pressure other local companies, and during the year negotiations resulted in 20 white-collar jobs for African Americans, including two at the only financial institution in that city to drop its color bar, the Bank of St. Louis. These were small victories, to be sure, but pressuring companies to change their hiring patterns would become a mainstay of the civil rights movement during the 1960s.

A "Wave of Negro Militancy Spreading Over the South" declared the *New York Times* in May 1960, and during the next years there were a number of factors that came together that encouraged a vigorous civil rights movement. The nation's largest and most influential newspapers now reported these events, informed and educated blacks and whites throughout the country, while television, now in virtually every American home, revealed the repressive and often brutal side of Jim Crow. African nations were winning their independence from their colonial masters and joining the United Nations. The Montgomery boycott had demonstrated that individual blacks could play an active role in the struggle, which was emphasized even more by the sit-ins. By the early 1960s, the profound significance of the *Brown* case, and the South's refusal to accept court-ordered desegregation, had ignited African Americans. "The whole nation put itself on record then as saying that segregation is wrong," declared Martin Luther King Jr., and James T. McCain of CORE added, "the Emancipation Proclamation freed the Negro physically; the Supreme Court decision freed him mentally."

It was during this wave of activity that Democratic Senator John F. Kennedy campaigned for the presidency. JFK endorsed the sit-ins, while Republican opponent Vice President Nixon was silent on the topic. Nixon remained loyal to Eisenhower and opposed establishing a federal FEPC even as he boasted that his administration had sponsored in 1957 the first civil rights act in more than 80 years. Nixon, in fact, was a member of the NAACP and had enjoyed good relations with African Americans, but liberal Democrats were not going to allow blacks to shift their support back to the Party of Lincoln. While sit-ins were being conducted in cities and states across the nation, the Democrats adopted a platform that contained a strong civil rights plank, demanding equal access in "voting booths, schoolrooms, jobs, housing, and public facilities." It called on all southern school districts to submit desegregation plans by 1963, and it advocated a permanent FEPC. Candidate Kennedy criticized President Eisenhower for not ending discrimination in federally supported housing and declared that when he became president, he would do that with a mere "stroke of a pen." Two weeks before the election JFK also acted to help Martin Luther King Jr., who had been jailed for conducting a sit-in at a department store in Atlanta. Kennedy called Mrs. King and expressed his sympathy, and his brother Robert telephoned the Georgia judge who had sentenced King and pleaded for his release, which happened the following day. This news was heavily reported in the black press and at black churches, and on election day in one of the closest elections in U.S. history, African American voters delivered Illinois and Michigan to Kennedy, giving him the presidency.

The new administration had 16 priority matters for Congress—but not one of those was passage of a civil rights bill. The new Congress was more conservative than before, with the Democrats losing two Senate seats and 21 in the House. Kennedy realized that he did not have the necessary votes for civil rights legislation, and if he tried he would lose southern support for his domestic agenda, the New Frontier. This meant that JFK was not going to issue an executive order creating a federal FEPC, nor would he take the "stroke of a pen" ending discrimination in federally assisted housing for almost two more years until after the congressional elections of November 1962. And fearing the response, his eventual order only concerned about 20 percent of the federal housing program.

Political reality meant that Kennedy did as previous presidents—he sidestepped Congress. "I have dedicated my administration to the cause of equal opportunity in employment by the government or its contractors," he declared in a televised news conference in March 1961 as he issued executive order 10925. The order established the President's Committee on Equal Employment Opportunity (PCEEO), chaired by Vice President Lyndon Johnson. The government was to

> consider and recommend additional affirmative steps which should be taken by executive departments and agencies to realize more fully the national policy of nondiscrimination. . . . The contractor will take affirmative action to ensure that applicants are employed, and that employees are treated during employment, without regard to their race, creed, color, or national origin.

This was the first time that the term "affirmative action" had been used concerning race, and its origin had come about a few months earlier during LBJ's inaugural ball in Texas. As the new vice president was shaking hands in the receiving line, he noticed a young black attorney, Hobart Taylor Jr. LBJ knew his father, a Houston businessman, and he asked the young man to meet with his friends Arthur Goldberg and Abe Fortas and to write the executive order, which they did the next day. "I was searching for something that would give a sense of positiveness to performance under that executive order," Taylor recalled, "and I was torn between the words 'positive action' and the words 'affirmative action'. . . . And I took 'affirmative' because it was alliterative."

The two words had the same sound, and although the notion was ambiguous at the time, Democrats and liberals used the term to signify that, compared to Republicans, they intended a more aggressive strategy to pry open employment opportunities for minorities. That included more federal jobs, where the administration used the term "active recruitment." Thus the new Democratic administration began defining affirmative action for the early 1960s—and it called on employers to overcome their pasts and to hire "*without regard* to race, color, or creed."

Kennedy and his liberal supporters were charting new waters, and they themselves did not know the future course of affirmative action. On the one hand they were asking employers to take affirmative action to hire one group, African Americans, yet as we shall see, they were not demanding any special preference or treatment or quotas for minorities. What did that mean? It was a dilemma that would be addressed for the next four decades. In 1961, all the administration seemed to be advocating was racially neutral hiring to end job discrimination. That seemed a rather simple demand then, but implementing this order would bring on a series of questions and issues that would fundamentally change the American workplace.[4]

Whatever the president thought he was doing in 1961, one thing was sure: he sounded characteristically confident. "I have no doubt that the vigorous enforcement of this order will mean the end of such discrimination." The administration was declaring more support for civil rights because a review of business practices revealed "an urgent need for expansion and strengthening of efforts to promote full equality of employment opportunity," a term, which by the following year, was reported as "equal employment opportunity." Like Harry Truman, JFK put his presidential prestige behind the order by stating that it was the "plain and positive obligation of the United States Government to promote and ensure equal opportunity." Thus, contractors were ordered to end discrimination when advertising for jobs or apprentices, training, promoting, paying, transferring, or laying off workers. If Johnson's PCEEO discovered discrimination, then the "contract may be cancelled" and the company "may be declared ineligible for further government contracts."

As one would expect there were many problems with the executive order. The PCEEO had the power only to conduct surveys, receive complaints, hold hearings, and *advise* federal agencies that hired workers and granted contracts; it had a small budget and staff, and was not mandated by Congress. Moreover, Johnson's committee had no authority over labor unions or over federal loans or grants. Those grants were significant, providing $7.5 billion annually to state and local governments to fund some public schools, welfare clinics, and university research, and to help pay for constructing highways, airports, public housing, hospitals, and urban renewal projects. By excluding federal grants and loans, the Kennedy administration was limiting the scope of the executive order to a few hundred defense contractors, while avoiding thousands of projects that would have disrupted and changed employment practices throughout the nation and in the South—an area that Kennedy needed for his reelection in 1964.

The limitations of the executive order were demonstrated by federal aid for local construction projects. In 1946 President Truman signed the Hill-Burton Act, which provided funding to construct hospitals and other public facilities. Virtually no strings were attached to this aid. The result? By 1963, border and southern states had accepted $37 million to build or remodel 89 medical facilities, all of them strictly segregated. African Americans could be treated in only 13, and in the remaining 76 hospitals black doctors were refused privileges to practice. "The evidence conclusively proved that throughout the country Negroes did not enjoy access to health facilities on equal terms with whites," wrote the Civil Rights Commission, "and that the Federal Government itself was directly contributing to this discrimination."

Another problem with Kennedy's order was that, like all previous fair employment orders, there was no attempt to define discrimination. In general, discrimination was described as refusing to hire people because of their race, color, or creed, but how did the government prove that a contractor intentionally denied a job to a black, a Hispanic, or a Jew? Since a citizen is innocent until proven guilty in America, the proof of discrimination rested on the government. Although the government stated that contractors had to be "in compliance" with minimum federal standards of worker safety and pay, JFK's executive order did not stipulate a number or percentage or quota of minorities as being in compliance with equal opportunity. For the time being, Secretary of Labor Willard Wirtz recommended that in apprenticeship programs, qualified minorities should be encouraged to apply for jobs, and that the trades and companies should hire "a significant number" of minorities, one that would constitute "more than a token."

The NAACP was not interested in tokens; they wanted jobs, and the organization immediately went on the attack. One day after the order took effect, NAACP's labor secretary Herbert Hill filed numerous complaints against Lockheed Aircraft Corporation. During the first months of 1961 the company was negotiating with the defense department for the nation's first one-billion-dollar contract for a single item, a ten-year agreement to build jet transports for the U.S. Air Force. Lockheed was heavily dependent on the government; the taxpayers funded about 90 percent of its business. During the 1950s the company had been somewhat progressive at the plant where they planned to build the transport, in Marietta, Georgia. The employment manager had hired blacks and trained them into some clerical, professional, and especially skilled positions; of 280 occupations blacks were employed in more than 50, unusual at that time in the South. In 1961 the enormous facility had a work force of 10,500, of which about 450 were African Americans. As was tradition, the unions and some facilities were segregated; restrooms and drinking fountains had signs, "White," and "Colored," as did the cafeterias, even the time clocks.

Thirty-one black workers charged Lockheed with "overt discrimination," which set off an alarm throughout the defense industry. The one hundred largest defense contractors and subcontractors employed 10 million workers, and these national and multinational companies had many plants in the South. In 1960, for example, the federal government spent about $2.7 billion on military contracts in ten southern states; enforcement of the executive order could then begin to change employment practices and disrupt Jim Crow.

The potential economic consequences for Lockheed were not lost on the corporation's president, who flew from the California headquarters to inspect the Georgia plant. Shortly thereafter he was discussing plans with the government for job training for minorities. One month later the plant and union had integrated, the "White" and "Colored" signs had been removed, and Lockheed's president was en route to Washington D.C. to sign an agreement with Vice President Johnson that pledged the company to "aggressively seek out more qualified minority group candidates" for jobs in engineering, technical and skilled positions, and administration. The corporation agreed to enlist more blacks in training programs and career development, and it agreed to an annual review of progress.

Progress, however, would be difficult to measure, for the last statement of the agreement was, "it is not intended that specific numerical targets or goals shall be set." The intent was to evaluate "increases in the numbers of minority persons hired, promoted, involved in training, and occupying responsible positions within the corporation." Basically the goal was a "respectable proportion" of black workers, whatever that meant.

The Lockheed agreement was the model for what the administration called a "plan for progress," and Johnson and his assistants began pressuring other large contractors to cooperate and sign the voluntary agreements. In July the presidents of Boeing, Douglas Aircraft, Western Electric, General Electric, and RCA visited the White House, and after a photo-op with Kennedy and Johnson they signed plans for progress. In November a dozen more corporate presidents took the pledge, as an administration official announced the aim of having the nation's 50 largest contractors, employing 20 percent of the workforce, sign on by the end of 1961. "We'll help them do what they ought to do," said the official, "take affirmative action."

Civil rights activists continued to take their own action throughout the next year, 1962. Sit-ins were achieving impressive results, integrating lunch counters and theaters in nearly 200 cities across the South, including large metropolises such as Houston and Atlanta. Other activists were conducting "Freedom Rides" to integrate public transportation and terminals in Mississippi and Alabama. The response was vicious. Whites met the buses and beat riders unconscious, and the brutal scenes were reported in newspapers and on the evening news, all of which resulted in pressure on the Kennedy administration to intervene with federal officials.

Kennedy acted cautiously, ordering the Interstate Commerce Commission to issue rules prohibiting discrimination in all interstate facilities, which resulted in desegregating some terminals in the South; others disregarded the order. The administration acted more boldly with the PCEEO. Throughout the year Vice President Johnson pressured the federal government and their contractors to hire minorities, and that was having an impact, especially on the federal workforce. A survey conducted by *U.S. News and World Report* in March 1962 found that there were over 280,000 black federal workers, or 13 percent of the workforce, and that increased to more than 300,000 the next year. The magazine reported that President Kennedy had ordered more and better jobs for African Americans in a policy of "equal employment opportunity." The survey found that close to 20 percent of the post office's workforce was African American, a third of the General Services Administration, and the defense department was "probably the biggest employer of Negroes in the world." Moreover, more high level positions were being opened, such as ambassadorships and federal judges, than during any other previous presidential administration. "Goal," *U.S. News* declared, "Negro in Cabinet."[5]

In the civilian workforce, however, the record was mediocre. The plans for progress were voluntary agreements. Progress was based on surveys of the corporation's workforce that the companies did themselves. The government set no numerical targets, no quotas, and no time limits. While some visible corporations such as Lockheed, RCA, Chrysler, Ford, General Motors, Westinghouse, and IBM did hire and train more African Americans, including white-collar employees, most did not, especially those in the border states and in the South. A survey of 24 defense contractors in Atlanta revealed that only seven showed any evidence of compliance. For the rest, *Business Week* wrote, the "Plans for Progress were ... largely meaningless." Moreover, the PCEEO put pressure on companies—but it never canceled a contract—even for blatant discrimination such as at Comet Rice Mills. With plants in Texas, Arkansas, and Louisiana, Comet segregated their facilities three ways: white, black, and Hispanic employees. As for oil companies in the South, virtually all remained segregated. Four oil refineries at Lake Charles, Louisiana, employed some 3,600 workers, of whom fewer than 300 were blacks, and they excluded blacks from almost all skilled jobs and even had segregated parking lots.

Enforcing JFK's affirmative action order, obviously, was a problem that was not going to be resolved by voluntary plans. The economy was running fine in 1962, but the unemployment rate for blacks remained twice that of whites. There were over 15 million citizens who were employed by government contracts, of which only a small percentage were African Americans. Almost 23 percent of Atlanta's population was black, but government contracts in that area employed only about half of that number, similar to cities such as Chicago, Houston, and New York.[6]

Employment traditions were hard to break, and that certainly was true for another group that faced discrimination—women. In December 1961 the president established a Commission on the Status of Women, contending that "prejudices and outmoded customs" were preventing the "full realization of women's basic rights." JFK charged the commission with examining employment policies and practices of the government and of contractors.

Gender discrimination was blatant. After the Depression, many men held the view that working women would take jobs from men, but during the economic boom of the 1950s that idea was being discarded. Women took the jobs that most men did not want, either as secretaries, factory workers, or in sales. The workplace was segregated by sex. Employment ads listed jobs as "Help Wanted Male" and "Help Wanted Female," meaning that managerial and executive positions were for men, and lower-paying jobs were for women. Most companies would not allow a female employee to apply for management, and many firms required that women quit when they married, which was particularly true for airline stewardesses. Except for nursing and teaching, men dominated the professions. At professional schools, deans had quotas, usually admitting only about 5 percent females, which resulted in white males becoming about 95 percent of attorneys, physicians, and professors. And the federal government still discriminated. In 1959 females made up a quarter of all federal workers, but the median civil service position for them was GS-4; for the men it was GS-9.

The Kennedy era, of course, was before the women's liberation movement and such discrimination was considered fair—even by most women. Traditionally, businesses had felt that they could pay a man and woman different wages since the male was the breadwinner, and the female worked for "pin money," extra cash, or only to support herself before marriage. Moreover, this was the great era of marriage, the baby boom, and expanding suburbs, when the ideal woman was the suburban housewife. She, as Betty Friedan observed, "was the dream image of the young American woman. She was healthy, beautiful, educated, concerned only about her husband, her children, her home. She had found feminine fulfillment." Opinion polls supported Friedan's assumptions; one reported in 1962 that "few people are as happy as a housewife." Of 2,300 housewives interviewed, some 96 percent declared themselves fairly to extremely happy. They agreed with the traditional roles: "being subordinate to men is part of being feminine" and "women who ask for equality fight nature." Such ideas played prime time at the movies, often with Doris Day in the leading role, or on television with June Cleaver in *Leave It To Beaver* or Harriet Nelson in *Ozzie and Harriet*, which was aired from 1952 to 1966. June and Harriet were happy housewives, great moms, always supporting their husbands.

Furthermore, there was an ideological reason to support the traditional family—the Cold War. The Soviet woman worked alongside men in factories and communes to build the state, so most Americans agreed with Labor Undersecretary James O'Connell: "When a woman comes to be viewed first as a source of manpower, second as a mother, . . . we are losing much that supposedly separates us from the Communist world. The highest calling of a woman's sex is the home."

With such opinions pervasive, Democratic candidate Kennedy had not made many comments on women's issues, and he had few female advisers. Margaret Price of Michigan, vice-chair of the Democratic National Committee, observed that the "absence of professional women in any staff capacity in the Kennedy entourage has led to an initial impression that his is an all-male cast." In fact, Kennedy did not name a woman to his cabinet, prompting journalist Doris Fleeson to write, "for women the New Frontiers are the old frontiers."

But JFK did name many prominent women to his President's Commission on the Status of Women, including the elderly Eleanor Roosevelt. At its first meeting in February 1962, the former First Lady declared that unequal wages for comparable work were "contrary to the concept of equality and justice" in America. She was aware, of course, that her husband's administration had paid women and men the same wages in the Works Progress Administration and had ordered war contractors to do the same for "Rosie the Riveters" who performed "comparable quality and quantity of work" as male workers during World War II.

At that meeting, President Kennedy stated that women's "primary obligation" was to their families and homes but a third of the labor force was female, and his administration wanted no "discrimination by law or by implication" against them. Secretary of Labor Arthur Goldberg then took the podium and noted that several million women earned less than a dollar an hour, declaring, "Women have labored under the term 'weaker sex' for so long that it has become a stigma when they go out seeking employment. . . . It is time we evaluate women on merit and fitness alone when they apply for jobs."

The commission soon received help from the chairman of the Civil Service Commission, John Macy. He announced a survey that demonstrated that more than 94 percent of requests from government agencies to fill management jobs *specified* that *men* fill the posts. Macy asked all departments to review their hiring practices and declared that from now on, department administrators would have to state their reasons for requesting a man rather than a woman.

Congress also became interested. Oregon Democrat Edith Green introduced the Equal Pay Act in the House, and Michigan's Democrat Patrick McNamara led the charge in the Senate. Business groups opposed the bill, citing additional "costs of hiring women," while labor unions supported it because it would reduce the probability of employers hiring females at lower wages than union men. Most congressmen, and the public, favored the bill, and it passed easily in 1963. The Equal Pay Act prohibited discrimination in the payment of wages for "equal work on jobs . . . which requires equal skill, effort, and responsibility." The bill exempted differential pay that was based on seniority, merit, or "quality of production," and it did not allow an employer to reduce male wages to equal those of females.

Initially, the Equal Pay Act did not have much impact on most female workers. The law did not apply to the professions, executive or salaried positions, or to domestic or agricultural workers, and given the sexual segregation in the workplace, only about a quarter of female workers benefitted since so few had "male jobs." A year later *U.S. News & World Report* surveyed businesses and found that many employers had "revised jobs or job descriptions so that men and women no longer are assigned to identical tasks." The magazine also reported "so many loopholes in regulations that firms which study the rules will be able to get around the equal pay idea."[7]

Eventually the Equal Pay Act would become very significant, since future amendments strengthened the bill, and especially because the nation witnessed the women's liberation movement throughout the next decade. JFK's signature on the bill made the traditional reasons for the wage differential irrelevant: From now on the federal government began supporting the idea that companies should not discriminate in wages because of gender. Equal pay for equal work would become equal pay for comparable work, and with government backing, that would change the American workplace.

African Americans were not waiting for the government to change the workplace, for during that spring of 1963 King and his SCLC launched a massive demonstration in Birmingham, Alabama. Public facilities, businesses, and virtually everything else were completely segregated, so much that officials had removed a book from the library that featured white and black rabbits. Blacks had no vote, nor as taxpayers could they get municipal jobs—not one was a policeman or fireman. The city was so violent that local blacks called it "Bombingham." Police commissioner Eugene "Bull" Connor vowed to "keep the niggers in their place," and he predicted that "blood would run in the streets of Birmingham before it would be integrated."

King realized the danger but felt that the campaign would reveal southern "brutality openly—in the light of day—with the rest of the world looking on." That would force Kennedy to act. "The key to everything," King said, was "Federal commitment, full, unequivocal, and unremitting."

On April 3, 1963, black activists peacefully began sitting-in and picketing restaurants and businesses. The police arrested and jailed them. Next day, about 50 activists marched on city hall, and they too were arrested. Each day more black citizens joined in, and the stream of marchers became a river and eventually a flood. On April 12 King, Ralph Abernathy, and scores of activists marched and chanted "Freedom has come to Birmingham!" But it had not, as police again arrested and jailed the marchers. The demonstrations continued the next month, which King labeled the "children's crusade." On May 3 thousands of black teens marched toward city hall. This time Bull Connor finally snapped—with television cameras rolling, he ordered his men to charge the peaceful demonstrators. They did, with dogs snapping, nightsticks swinging, clubbing marchers to the ground. Firemen turned on the high-pressure hoses, ripping into the crowd, blasting citizens off their feet. The next day several thousand blacks took to the streets, and the savage scenes again appeared on front pages of newspapers and on national television. *Time* reported, "The blaze of bombs, the flash of blades, the eerie glow of fire, the keening cries of hatred, the wild dance of terror in the night—all this was Birmingham, Ala."

Birmingham prompted sit-ins and demonstrations in nearly two hundred cities across the South, boosted King's reputation as the greatest black leader, and proved to be a turning point in the civil rights struggle. King's strategy worked: again, black activists revealed their plight to the nation and forced federal action. Like most Americans, President Kennedy and his brother and attorney general, Robert, watched the riots on television and were "sickened" by the police brutality. When King was jailed, the Kennedy brothers called Birmingham officials, and Bobby dispatched assistant attorney general Burke Marshall to negotiate a settlement. With the city facing social disintegration and economic collapse, officials and businessmen agreed to talk, and Marshall worked out a compromise, which eventually integrated public facilities and provided jobs for black taxpayers. In response, vengeful whites bombed King's motel headquarters and his brother's home. Riots ensued, 50 people were injured, and Kennedy announced that his administration would not permit the agreement "to be sabotaged by a few extremists on either side." JFK ordered 3,000 federal troops into position near Birmingham.

The president's action was too much for Alabama governor George Wallace. He had been opposed to federal orders aimed at integrating the University of Alabama, and in May when federal officials insisted, the governor declared, "Segregation today, segregation tomorrow, segregation forever." Yet forever was rather short in Alabama. Two weeks later, Kennedy federalized the state national guard; on television the governor moved aside and allowed the admission of two black students.

The events in the Deep South provoked President Kennedy to address the nation. On June 11 he delivered a landmark speech, televised from the White House. He reminded citizens that America was founded "on the principle that all men are created equal" and continued that the nation was now confronted with a moral issue. "The heart of the question is whether all Americans are to be accorded equal rights and equal opportunities." Then he declared, "One hundred years of delay have passed since President Lincoln freed the slaves, yet their heirs, their grandsons, are not fully free. . . . They are not yet freed from social and economic oppression. . . . Now the time has come for his nation to fulfill its promise."

Eight days later, Kennedy addressed Congress and asked its members to begin fulfilling the promise by passing the most comprehensive civil rights act in American history. The president's bill called for desegregation of all public schools, with new authority given to the attorney general to initiate legal action against public educational institutions that did not comply, and for financial assistance for school districts that did desegregate. He advocated enforcing the constitutional right to vote in federal elections and for granting the right of all citizens to be served in public facilities. "No one has been barred on account of his race from fighting or dying for America," said this World War II veteran. "Surely . . . 100 years after Emancipation, it should not be necessary for any American citizen to demonstrate in the streets for the opportunity to stop at a hotel, or to eat at a lunch counter . . . or to enter a motion picture house, on the same terms as any other customer." And the president advocated job training and fair employment. "There is little value in a Negro's obtaining the right to be admitted to hotels and restaurants if he has no cash in his pocket and no job." Then JFK stated a central principle of affirmative action that had been developing since World War II:

> Simple justice requires that public funds, to which all taxpayers of all races contribute, not be spent in any fashion which encourages, entrenches, subsidizes or results in racial discrimination.

The 1963 civil rights act, the president concluded, should be supported not only because it was good for the economy, foreign policy, and for domestic tranquility, "but, above all, because it is right."

Kennedy's dramatic speech and his civil rights proposal split the nation. King wrote the president that the address constituted "one of the most eloquent, profound, and unequivocal pleas for justice and the freedom of all men ever made by any president." But many southern politicians and many conservatives condemned it. Mississippi Senator James Eastland called the proposal a "complete blueprint for a totalitarian state," while Texas Senator John Tower thought "it would take a virtual police state to enforce" the act. Senator Allen Ellender of Louisiana took another approach, declaring that Negroes were "attempting to use their color to camouflage their lack of capability . . . when they cannot qualify to do a job they contend that they are being discriminated against because of their color."

Two weeks later, Kennedy returned to affirmative action. The president issued executive order 11114, which superceded his 1961 mandate. Declaring that it was the "policy of the United States to encourage by affirmative action the elimination of discrimination" in employment, JFK now extended the idea from jobs created by contracts to all federal funds, which included "grants, loans, and other forms of financial assistance" to state and local governments. Moreover, unions and employers who accepted taxpayer funds would have to list advertisements that declared that "all qualified applicants will receive consideration without regard to race, creed, color, or national origin." Contractors would have to give the government access to books and records to check compliance. In the event of noncompliance, federal officials could cancel the contract and declare the company ineligible for further ones.

Kennedy's actions, along with three years of the civil rights movement culminating with the violence in Birmingham, resulted in a new national awareness of the plight of African Americans. For the first time polling organizations took substantial national surveys on racial issues, and it became apparent that the civil rights movement was having an impact. Recall that most whites during World War II felt that blacks were an inferior race, that almost 70 percent favored separate schools, and that only 45 percent thought that blacks should have equal opportunities to obtain jobs. Racial attitudes became a little more tolerant during the 1950s, yet most whites were not concerned about civil rights during the baby-boom era, and in the early 1960s a majority of whites continued to believe in the contemporary stereotypes about African Americans—they had less ambition and looser morals, laughed a lot, and smelled different. But after Birmingham and Kennedy's speech, pollsters found that citizens now listed civil rights as the nation's number one problem, eclipsing the cold war's usual front-runner, foreign policy. They discovered a significant shift on questions concerning race. Public facilities: The response to "Do you think there should be separate sections for Negroes in streetcars and buses?" dropped in half from the 1950s to only 21 percent approving and 79 disapproving; the percentage of northern whites who supported a law "which would give all persons—Negroes as well as whites—the right to be served in public places" rose from 55 percent in June 1963 to over 70 percent in January 1964, a time when Congress was debating the Civil Rights Act. Fairness: "Do you think Negroes should have as good a chance as white people to get any kind of job?" A resounding 85 percent answered "yes" in the summer of 1963. And the civil rights movement had resulted in new awareness: Are blacks being discriminated against? More than 70 percent of white Americans said "yes," even 56 percent of those polled in the South. Did they actually "have as good a chance as white people in your community to get any kind of job for which they are qualified?" Only 43 percent said "yes," while 48 percent replied "not as good." "In the minds and hearts of the majority of Americans," pollsters wrote in 1964, "the principle of integration seems already to have won." Jim Crow was on its deathbed.

"History would mark it," *Newsweek* editorialized, "the summer of 1963 was a time of revolution, the season when 19 million U.S. Negroes demanded payment of the century-old promissory note called the Emancipation Proclamation." In a large Harris survey of African Americans the magazine reported: "The Negro wants no less than an end to discrimination in all its forms. He wants a better job, better pay, a better home. He wants the right to join the white man—to live next door . . . to work beside him, to send the kids to school with his, to eat at his restaurants and stop at his hotels and pray at his churches."[8]

To publicize those aims, and to gain support for Kennedy's Civil Rights Act, Martin Luther King Jr. and other black leaders declared their March on Washington. On August 28, some 200,000 blacks and whites sang as they walked past the Capitol, continuing on to the Lincoln Memorial. After folksingers greeted them with "We Shall Overcome," after Mahalia Jackson led the massive crowd with spirituals, the leaders of the NAACP, CORE, SCLC, SNCC, and the Urban League gave short addresses. A. Philip Randolph was the elder statesman, telling Americans that "we are not a mob. We are the advanced guard of a massive moral revolution for jobs and freedom," and then the youngster of the group, SNCC's new chairman, John Lewis, reminded America that blacks "do not want to be free gradually. We want our freedom and we want it now." But it was King who carried the day, reminding citizens of the "sacred obligation" promised by the Emancipation Proclamation and Declaration of Independence and declaring his hopeful vision for the nation, "I Have A Dream."

"It seemed like the beginning of a new era for America," John Lewis admitted. President Kennedy invited the black leaders to the White House, where A. Philip Randolph said to JFK, "it is going to take nothing less than a crusade to win approval of the civil rights measures . . . a crusade that . . . nobody but you can lead."

Kennedy never would be able to lead the crusade, for on November 22, 1963, the president was assassinated. When the new president, Lyndon B. Johnson, addressed the nation soon after that tragic death, he declared, "We have talked long enough in this country about civil rights. It is now time to write the next chapter and to write it in books of law." That was the "appropriate eulogy," he continued; we must "honor President Kennedy's memory."

Shortly thereafter, LBJ proposed his Civil Rights Act—one more comprehensive and thus more controversial than Kennedy's. Title II aimed to integrate all public facilities, including *private businesses* that sold to the public, such as motels, restaurants, theaters, stores, and gas stations. Title IV would desegregate all public schools, hospitals, libraries, museums, playgrounds, parks, and other public places, while Title VI would write into law JFK's executive order 11114 by prohibiting discrimination in all federally funded programs and by authorizing the government to deny their contracts to businesses that discriminated. Significantly, Title VII aimed to end discrimination in employment in *all firms* with 25 or more employees, a proposal that had so much opposition among conservatives and many businessmen that it was not in the Kennedy bill. Another provision would establish the Equal Employment Opportunity Commission, the EEOC, which would become the agency charged with ending discrimination in the nation's workplace.

The hearings and debates during 1963 and 1964 over what type of act to pass provoked angry exchanges and illuminating testimonies about what was considered fair employment practice in America. Congressional hearings began in summer 1963 and continued into early 1964 when debate began in the House. To stall the vote and its probable passage, congressmen offered more than 120 amendments to the bill; some specified that the act would not protect communists and atheists while other amendments aimed to ban alleged discrimination against white Protestants. The House passed its version of the act in February, and that spring the Senate debated the bill. The opposition there also attempted to amend the bill and stall its passage. During one speech Virginia Senator A. Willis Robertson held the floor for two hours, punctuating his remarks by waving a small Confederate flag, and on another occasion Georgia Senator Richard Russell introduced a plan for the federal government to spend $1.5 billion—to distribute blacks equally among the 50 states. On and on they argued, and eventually southern members conducted a long filibuster. "We are assigning ourselves a unique niche in history," declared New York Senator Jacob Javits, "as the biggest and longest-running slow-motion show to hit Washington."[9]

Yet significantly, this show revealed and accentuated a number of crucial issues concerning race relations in America and the future of affirmative action.

One of the first issues was employment preference. If two applicants were basically equal, which one should get the job?

The idea of preferences, passing laws to help one group, was rather rare but not new in the Republic. The U.S. Constitution of 1789 favored the gentry class, those with wealth and land, some of whom owned slaves. In that sense the Constitution never was "color blind" for it allowed slavery, which was based on race. Most African slaves in 1789 had been born in the United States, but they were not considered citizens until adoption of the Fourteenth Amendment after the Civil War. With slaves emancipated, federal officials soon realized that most of the new freedmen were illiterate, unskilled, and landless. Congress passed the Freedmen's Bureau Act, and along with other programs the federal government tried to help former slaves by providing some land and education, funds for black military personnel, and various charters to support the aged or indigent women and children. Post–Civil War aid was not limited to African Americans, and substantial amounts were given to white veterans, but generally speaking federal help often gave the freedman "preferential treatment" in an attempt to make up for over two centuries of slavery; yet that aid was of short duration and was not particularly successful.

During the twentieth century the federal government passed other preferential bills which granted benefits regardless of race or gender. Social Security's retirement program, established in 1935, granted a monthly check, but only if one was over the age of 65, while the 1944 G.I. Bill of Rights helped only World War II veterans but not those who contributed to the war effort as civilians. With a national population of about 140 million, the 15 million veterans received payments to attend college, federally guaranteed low-interest home loans, and other bonuses that could lead to public jobs. These programs were very popular and considered fair by the vast majority of citizens.

But as the nation discussed the Civil Rights Act, what was considered fair was mired in debate. To some—especially minorities and their liberal allies—some sort of preferential treatment for past injustices and discrimination was fair: to others—many whites and their conservative allies—that was reverse discrimination and unfair.

CORE took the lead on the preference issue. In 1962 the organization demanded that employers hire a specific percentage of blacks and adopt a set of preferential employment guidelines. The national organization urged its local chapters to make "very specific demands which far exceed tokenism" in hiring and to insist that businesses have the responsibility to select and train minorities. We "used to talk simply of merit employment," wrote one official. "Now, National CORE is talking in terms of 'compensatory' hiring. We are approaching employers with the proposition that they have effectively excluded Negroes from their work force for a long time and that they now have a responsibility and obligation to make up for their past sins." The New York CORE began a boycott of the Sealtest Dairy Company, which had only 1 percent of black employees in their 1,400 personnel workforce, and within two months Sealtest agreed to hire ten blacks immediately and to give "initial exclusive priority to all job openings" in 1963 "to Negroes and Spanish-Americans." That year CORE continued boycotting certain businesses and won concessions from a few employers in Denver, Detroit, Seattle, Baltimore, and other cities in New York and California.

Parallel issues to preferential employment were proportional hiring, compensation, and quotas, which appeared soon after JFK called for a civil rights act. Some southern black leaders had advocated hiring public workers such as bus drivers in proportion to their percentage in their community, and a New York civil rights group demanded 25 percent of construction jobs on city contracts. Such ideas aroused interest, and at an August 1963 press conference a reporter asked President Kennedy if there should be "some kind of special dispensation for the pain of second-class citizenship" for blacks, and for his view on "job quotas by race." The president responded that "there is some compensation due for the lost years, particularly in the field of education," hinting that special programs were needed to train minorities for jobs. "I don't think quotas are a good idea," he continued. "I think it is a mistake to begin to assign quotas on the basis of religion, or race, or color, or nationality. I think we'd get into a good deal of trouble." As for hiring workers, the president advocated that employers should give "everyone a fair chance. But not hard and fast quotas."

These issues also appeared during congressional hearings that summer. New Jersey Democrat Peter Rodino asked CORE's James Farmer about quotas. "We are not one of the organizations that believe in a quota," Farmer responded, and then continued. "We do believe, however, in aggressive action to secure the employment of minorities, but not in terms of a quota."

"That is fine," Rodino continued, but he wondered if Farmer felt that employment should be based on the applicant's "education and qualifications."

FARMER: Yes, but if two people apply for a job and are equally qualified and generally or roughly have the same qualifications, one is Negro and one is white, and this is a company which historically has not employed Negroes, I think then that company should give the nod to a Negro to overcome the disadvantages of the past.
RODINO: Well, isn't this then preferential?
FARMER: Well, you could call it preferential, you could call it compensatory....
RODINO: Isn't that discriminating against a white who may have been innocent of any discrimination against anyone else in that time?
FARMER: You see none of us are really innocent because we are caught in a society, the social system which has tolerated segregation. Negroes have received special treatment all of their lives.

They have received special treatment for 350 years. All we are asking for . . . is some special treatment now to overcome the effects of . . . the past. I am not asking that any white person be fired. We do not want Negroes to displace whites.

Farmer concluded that, as the employment system was now, "preferential treatment is being given to whites."[10]

This public exchange between Rodino and Farmer, along with many more like it in the ensuing months during congressional hearings, opened Pandora's box—quotas, preferences, compensation, reverse discrimination—all became hot topics and headlines in the media for the remainder of the Johnson years, and for decades after.

The quota issue reappeared numerous times in hearings on the Civil Rights Act as politicians focused on Title VII, aimed to end discrimination in employment, and it was vigorously debated in the Senate. The conservative argument was simple and direct. The federal government had no right to become involved in regulating business, including mandating who an employer should or could employ. That was regulation of the workforce and was unconstitutional.

Some conservatives, such as Arizona Senator Barry Goldwater, still believed that the passage of the child labor law and the right to collective bargain, both passed thirty years earlier during the New Deal, were unconstitutional and should be repealed. Liberal and moderate Democratic and Republican sponsors, along with the labor unions, disagreed. They maintained that the Civil Rights Act had nothing to do with quotas. AFL-CIO lobbyist Andrew Biemiller insisted that the bill "does not require 'racial balance' on a job," did not "give any race the right of preferential treatment," nor did it "upset seniority rights already obtained by an employer." It was inconceivable to him that the government would approve of "righting ancient wrongs by perpetrating new ones."

The Senate floor manager of the bill, Minnesota Democrat Hubert H. Humphrey, went farther, declaring in the Senate:

Contrary to the allegations of some opponents of this title, there is nothing in it that will give any power to the Commission or to any court to require hiring, firing, or promotion of employees in order to meet a racial "quota" or to achieve a certain racial balance.

That bugaboo has been brought up a dozen times; but it is nonexistent. In fact the very opposite is true. Title VII prohibits discrimination. In effect, it says that race, religion, and national origin are not to be used as the basis for hiring and firing. Title VII is designed to encourage hiring on the basis of ability and qualifications, not race or religion.

In an attempt to appease business, Humphrey later declared that Title VII meant that an employer "must have intended to discriminate."

Title VII eventually included a very significant clause that would be debated in future courts:

It shall be an unlawful employment practice for an employer . . . to limit, segregate, or classify his employees or applicants for employment in any way which would deprive or tend to deprive any individual of employment opportunities or otherwise adversely affect his status as an employee, because of such individual's race, color, religion, sex, or national origin.

Finally, Title VII mandated that employers, employment agencies, and unions end their discriminatory practices, and it gave the courts power to enforce the act. The "remedies" section stated that a judge may order "such affirmative action as may be appropriate," including reinstatement of employment, with or without back pay, or any other equitable relief excluding punitive damages. At the same time, Title VII provided some protections for employers. It allowed them to apply different standards or wages based on seniority or merit, to use various educational or skill tests as a basis for their hiring and promotion, and in certain cases it allowed some exceptions. Indian tribes and nonprofit and private membership organizations (such as country clubs) were excluded from the law, as were small firms with fewer than 25 employees. Defense contractors did not have to hire applicants who could not get security clearances, while businessmen did not have to employ "members of the Communist Party or a Communist-front organization." Companies could employ certain nationalities, religions, or gender if it was a *bona fide* occupational qualification; a French restaurant could advertise to hire a French cook, a Catholic school could stipulate that its teachers be Catholic, and the Girl Scouts could hire only female camp counselors.

Conservatives, naturally, opposed Title VII and the entire Civil Rights Act. As early as 1962, when Vice President Johnson attempted to increase black employment in the federal government, Virginia Representative J. Vaughan Gary declared in the House, "We are getting to the point now where we are bending over so far backward we are discriminating against the majorities and in favor of the minorities." Next year, *U.S. News & World Report* noted protests by white postal clerks in Dallas when three junior African Americans were promoted over more senior white employees. The magazine asked, "Are Whites Being Discriminated Against?" Such headlines in 1963 prompted a reporter to ask President Kennedy in a news conference if there would be a "white backlash against the Democratic party" for supporting civil rights. Kennedy did not think so, but he was wrong. Alabama Governor George Wallace used that message to win more than 30 percent of the vote in the Wisconsin, Indiana, and Maryland Democratic presidential primaries of 1964 and to build his political base for his run for the presidency in 1968.

In 1964 the most important opponent to Title VII and the Civil Rights Act was the Republican who would be his party's nominee in the upcoming presidential election, Senator Barry Goldwater. Explaining why he would vote against the act, Goldwater said that its provisions "fly in the face of the Constitution," that there was "no constitutional basis" for federal regulation of public accommodations or equal employment opportunities, and that to enforce the act the government would need the "creation of a police state of mammoth proportions." Alabama's Senator Ellender agreed, predicting that passing the bill would "bring on more strife than one can contemplate."

Nevertheless, Hubert Humphrey won the debate over Title VII. Realizing that the Democrats never would be able to pass the bill without Republican support, the Minnesotan continually wooed the Republican Senate minority leader from Illinois, Everett Dirksen. "I courted Dirksen," Humphrey explained, "almost as persistently as I did Muriel." Humphrey's pledge that the bill required no quotas, just nondiscrimination, convinced many pro-business Republicans to support Title VII. As Dirksen declared, "Civil rights—here is an idea whose time has come, and it can't be stopped."[11]

Conservatives, however, tried another tactic to stop the act. When the House debated Title VII in February the 80-year-old conservative, Democratic Representative Howard K. Smith of Virginia, interrupted and moved to add the word "sex" to the list of those protected by Title VII. "This bill is so imperfect," he said, "what harm will this little amendment do?" He continued by ridiculing the idea of "rights" and read a constituent's letter contending that since females outnumber males in the nation, women were being deprived of their "right to a husband." Congress, he continued, should attend to this "grave injustice . . . particularly in an election year." Amid laughs, another congressman rose and felt compelled to reveal the secret for his marital harmony, "I usually have the last two words, and those words are 'Yes, dear.'"

While the liberals were not prepared for the levity, they were for Congressman Smith's ploy. Conservatives had tried to add sex discrimination bans to all the titles of the Civil Rights Act, which was an attempt to divide supporters and defeat the bill; an amendment to prohibit age discrimination already had been dropped. Conservatives also noted the supposed consequences of "total equality" for women, which they claimed included compulsory military service, elimination of laws against rape, and destruction of the family. Thus, Justice Department officials had asked for help from Representative Edith Green, a sponsor of the Equal Pay Act. Green stood in opposition to the sex amendment, but Michigan's Democrat Martha Griffiths surprised almost everyone, declaring her staunch support: "It would be incredible that white men would be willing to place white women at such a disadvantage." Without adding this amendment to the act, she continued, "you are going to have white men in one bracket, you are going to try to take colored men and colored women and give them equal employment rights, and down at the bottom of the list is going to be a white women with no rights at all."

Griffiths' argument carried the day. The House passed the amendment in two hours, an incredibly short time for an amendment that eventually would have a profound impact on the American workplace.

Two days later, on February 10, the House passed its version of the Civil Rights Act, approving it by the overwhelming margin of 290 to 130 and sent it on to the Senate, where it was bogged down in the filibuster. Months later, on June 10, senators voted 71 to 29 to end the longest filibuster in the nation's history: 82 working days, or 534 hours, 1 minute, and 51 seconds. On June 19 the Senate passed the act, one year after JFK had proposed it, by a vote of 73 to 27. Six Republicans joined 21 southern and border-state Democrats to oppose the bill.

The Senate version of the bill was returned to the House for final approval, where it was immediately attacked by Representative Howard Smith. Attempting to stall passage he declared that the House had too little time to discuss a bill containing provisions "unmatched in harshness and brutality . . . since the tragic days of Reconstruction." Then he attacked civil rights activists, many of whom that June were northern white college students participating in Freedom Summer, an attempt of a thousand white northern university students to help southern blacks register to vote and learn how to gain their civil rights. "Already the second invasion of the Southland has begun," Smith declared. "Hordes of beatniks, misfits, and agitators from the North, with the admitted aid of the Communists, are streaming into the Southland mischief-bent, backed and defended by other hoards of federal marshals, federal agents, and federal power."

But Smith's obstruction was overcome, and on July 2 the House agreed to the Senate's amendments and passed the final version of the bill. President Johnson signed it a few hours later, declaring it "a major step toward equal opportunities for all Americans—a milestone in America's progress toward full justice for all her citizens."

Democracy had triumphed. A Harris poll that spring showed that 70 percent of citizens supported the act. After almost 250 years of slavery, and a hundred years of Jim Crow, racial discrimination no longer was considered fair in the "Land of the Free."

The Civil Rights Act was of profound significance. It demonstrated that the federal government could begin to change and subsequently alter deeply entrenched prejudices and behaviors, and the new law eventually markedly decreased overt racial discrimination. Politically, it was a knockout punch for the old Civil War alignment. Blacks still in the Party of Lincoln left and became Democrats. As for white Southern Democrats, LBJ was correct when he told an aide after he signed the act: "I think we delivered the South to the Republican Party for your lifetime and mine." That year Democrat Strom Thurmond of South Carolina switched to the Republican Party, and that began the transformation of the Solid South from Democratic to Republican, which was completed during the first term of President Ronald Reagan.

Constitutionally, the act was another nail in the coffin of the "state's rights" doctrine. Economically, Title VII generally outlawed employment discrimination in America.

The Civil Rights Act was a major achievement, yet there were problems. Title VII was phased in slowly, meaning that large businesses with more than 100 employees were affected in 1965, but employers with 25 workers did not have to stop discriminating until 1968. Moreover, less than 10 percent of companies in the nation hired more than 25 workers; those large corporations employed about 40 percent of the workforce, meaning that the act did not affect about 60 percent of the workers. The seniority clause meant that during the first recession the last hired would be the first fired, most of whom were minorities, and the employer's right to hire and promote based on tests hurt all minorities, since their educational skills were generally much weaker than the average white applicant. Title IV, which demanded public school desegregation, often was not enforced by local school boards, nor was Title VI, which banned the use of federal funds for public projects or institutions that discriminated. The Civil Rights Commission discovered that in the South the Agriculture Department had a totally segregated extension program, and that thousands of hospitals, clinics, and welfare programs continued to discriminate, either by placing blacks on separate floors or by refusing to admit African Americans. All these facts increased black frustration: The Civil Rights Act had passed, but for the next four years when blacks applied for many jobs they were turned away, or couldn't pass the skill test, or they remained in segregated schools, all which naturally embittered them—and incited some to riot during those long, hot summers from 1965 to 1968. Finally, and ironically, passage of the act sowed the seeds for the decline of the civil rights movement. Even though it was landmark legislation, its implementation eventually defined the meaning of equal employment opportunity and affirmative action, which raised questions of fairness and divided America.[12]

Before that division happened, and while the national agenda remained focused on civil rights, President Johnson and his allies advocated overturning the gimmicks that restricted the southern black vote, and in spring 1965 they began to press for the passage of the Voting Rights Act.

Then, violence erupted in Selma, Alabama. Selma was a typical town in the Deep South. Although the Civil Rights Act guaranteed integration of public facilities, all remained strictly segregated. Although the Fifteenth Amendment guaranteed the right to vote, only 2 percent of local blacks had been allowed to register. To protest that situation, activists in March 1965 began a 54-mile walk from Selma to the state capital in Montgomery. As 600 walked across the Edmund Pettus Bridge, some 200 state troopers at the other end ordered them to halt. They did. Then the troopers charged: a cloud of tear gas, nightsticks swinging, bullwhips cracking. The officers knocked John Lewis to the ground and beat five women unconscious. "I saw a posse man raise his club," recalled a participant, "and smash it down on a woman's head as if he were splitting a watermelon."

"Bloody Sunday," the marchers called it, and that evening the nation saw it on television. Scores of activists rushed to Selma, and again the response was vicious. Four local whites attacked three civil rights workers, including a white minister from Boston, whom they struck in the head with a club, shattering his skull, killing him.

Across the rest of the nation citizens were appalled by the killing, and that included President Johnson, who soon thereafter addressed a joint session of Congress. With an enormous television audience of about 70 million, LBJ recalled Lexington and Concord, Appomattox— and Selma. He called on Congress to pass a voting rights act, and he beseeched Americans: "It's not just Negroes, really, it's all of us who must overcome the crippling legacy of bigotry and injustice." And then he used the motto of the civil rights movement, "And we *shall* overcome."

Congress rose to a standing ovation. The media and many southern papers hailed the speech, and a few months later Congress passed the Voting Rights Act. It invalidated the use of any test or device to deny the vote, and it meant that federal examiners could register voters in states that had a history of discrimination. The results were dramatic: federal intervention ensured virtually no violence, and by the following summer half of southern adult blacks had registered to vote—and *that* changed politics in the South forever.

During the summer of 1965 Americans applauded Johnson's liberalism. His approval ratings were about 70 percent, and most felt that the nation was moving forward, that LBJ was fulfilling Kennedy's idealism—and more. Johnson had passed more than 80 bills during the first eight months of that year, an unsurpassed record, and many of them concerned his domestic policy, the War on Poverty and the Great Society, which aimed to help the 35 million poor in the nation. The government set a "poverty line," and Congress passed social legislation: educational acts, work-study programs, college loans, Job Corps, Food Stamps, Head Start, Medicaid and Medicare.

These acts targeted certain citizens that the majority felt deserved federal assistance—the poor, hungry, and ill, school children, college students, and the elderly. While these programs helped citizens regardless of race, they also focused on the largest minority, African Americans. Nevertheless, some black leaders began boosting the idea that the nation had an additional obligation to help their race by compensation and preferences, and one of the most intriguing was the Marshall Plan.

After World War II the United States had given about 12 billion dollars to help rebuild Western Europe in a program named after Secretary of State George Marshall. That generosity appealed to some black leaders, and as early as 1962 and throughout 1963 Whitney Young called for "an unprecedented domestic 'Marshall Plan' . . . a massive 'crash' attack on the complete range of economic and social ills" affecting African Americans. Published as *To Be Equal*, his ten-point program urged the "best schools and the best teachers" to educate the underclass, to open housing opportunities, and to place qualified blacks on all public boards and commissions. Young felt that employers should exercise the "same creative zeal and imagination to include Negro workers at all levels that management has used throughout the years in excluding them," including hiring blacks first before whites to redress previous injustices.

While most civil rights leaders felt that such ideas would only turn whites against their movement, Lerone Bennett agreed with Young and supported the Marshall Plan. Writing in 1965 Bennett declared that if "we are to avert a disaster" we need the "immediate cessation of segregation and discrimination and a massive program of national atonement for hundreds of years of soul-destroying oppression, a program that would involve *as a minimum requirement* the expenditure of billions of dollars and the engagement of the energies of all our citizens. Anything less is a lie. Anything less is deceit, fraud, silence."

Just how much should the Marshall Plan cost and how long should it last? In hindsight, these activists were very optimistic. Young declared:

For more than 300 years the white American has received special consideration, or "preferential treatment," if you will, over the Negro. What we now ask is that for a brief period there be a deliberate and massive effort to include the Negro citizen in the mainstream of American life. Furthermore, we are not asking for equal time; a major effort, honestly applied, need last only some 10 years.

Young continued that the "special effort program that we recommend should phase out as needed for it diminishes over the next decade."

A. Philip Randolph was not that optimistic and gave his answer in November 1965 when he called for a "Freedom Budget" of $100 billion. The next year he raised the ante, advocating $18 billion each year for the next decade: "In this, the richest and most productive society ever known to man, the scourge of poverty can and must be abolished—not in some distant future, not in this generation, but within the next ten years!"

During 1965 other African American leaders began speaking out in support for the "freedom budget," including Martin Luther King Jr. Years later, as we shall see, some conservatives declared that King did not support affirmative action, but that does not seem to be the case. The term was not popular before his death in 1968, so he did not use it, and he was very concerned about alienating his white supporters with calls for programs only for African Americans. This was evident in January 1965 when King was asked if he thought it was "fair to request a multi-billion-dollar program of preferential treatment for the Negro?" "I do indeed," he declared, stating that a program would cost "about 50 billion . . . which is less than one year of our present defense spending." He continued that his program "would certainly cost far less than any computation of two centuries of unpaid wages plus accumulated interest" for slavery. He noted precedents for compensatory programs, including benefits for millions of World War II veterans, but then he backtracked, noting that his program "should benefit the disadvantaged of *all* races." In August, King visited Washington D.C., with a new message, "economic freedom," and he called for large public works and job training programs for blacks. A year later, as many cities witnessed race riots, King demanded that Congress pass a $100 billion ten-year Marshall Plan to rid the cities of the conditions that "cause Negro riots and unrest." Such expenditures, he said, were more important than two major efforts of the Johnson administration, escalating the war in Vietnam and the space program: "It is much more important to put men on their own two feet on earth than to put men on the moon." He then began an intensive campaign for a "guaranteed annual income" for *all* the poor, and during summer 1967, as minorities again rioted, King leveled the blame—not on the rioters, but on "a very insensitive, irresponsible Congress." He called on President Johnson to ask Congress "to face up to this emergency; to create a new government agency, similar to the W.P.A. to end the massive unemployment in the Negro community."

The Marshall Plan also was supported by some white liberal politicians. "We are spending $2 billion a month to defend the freedom of 14 million people in South Vietnam," declared Senator Edward Kennedy of Massachusetts. "Why shouldn't we make the same kind of efforts for the 20 million people of the Negro race right here in America," and *New York Times* columnist Tom Wicker editorialized, "Time to Pay the Piper."

But most liberals and the majority of citizens did not support special treatment. Gunnar Myrdal warned that the "demand for a discrimination in reverse, i.e., to the advantage of the Negroes, is misdirected;" it would "create hatred for Negroes." President Johnson agreed that it was not a good idea to help only one race out of poverty, and Congress did not vote on a Marshall Plan.[13]

Yet by the summer of 1965, LBJ had become acutely aware of the plight of African Americans and their special circumstances, and this became apparent on June 4, 1965, when he delivered a commencement address at Howard University. The speech was written by White House aide Richard Goodwin with the help of assistant labor secretary, Daniel Patrick Moynihan. The speech was based on Moynihan's research that had been completed a few months earlier, "The Negro Family: The Case for National Action." The Moynihan Report detailed "the deterioration of the Negro family," marked by illegitimate births, divorces, separations, and unemployment, which "has continued at disaster levels for 35 years." The impact of poverty on "Negro youth has had the predictable outcome in a disastrous delinquency and crime rate. . . . That the Negro American has survived at all is extraordinary." To end this "tangle of pathology," Moynihan called on a national effort of federal programs.

Moynihan's report had an impact on the president, and at Howard University LBJ made one of the most passionate and significant pleas for African Americans during the 1960s. "In far too many ways," he declared, "Negroes have been . . . deprived of freedom, crippled by hatred, the doors of opportunity closed to hope." LBJ was proud that he had signed the Civil Rights Act and declared that the barriers to freedom "are tumbling down. . . . But freedom is not enough. You do not wipe away the scars of centuries by saying:

> Now you are free to go where you want, and do as you desire. . . . You do not take a person who for years has been hobbled by chains and liberate him, bring him up to the starting line of a race and then say, "You are free to compete with all the others," and still justly believe you have been completely fair. Thus it is not enough just to open the gates of opportunity. All our citizens must have the ability to walk through the gates. This is the next and more profound stage of the battle for civil rights. We seek not just freedom but opportunity. We seek not just legal equity but human ability, not just equality as a right and a theory but equality as a fact and equality as a result.

What did Johnson mean, "equality of result?" Years later, opponents of affirmative action would use the term to claim that federal policy was attempting to bring about the same results for all citizens—regardless of an individual's qualifications or merit. In 1965 the president continued his address, elucidating his meaning: "equal opportunity is essential, but not enough, not enough."

> Men and women of all races are born with the same range of abilities. But ability is not just the product of birth. Ability is stretched or stunted by the family that you live with, and the neighborhood you live in—by the school you go to and the poverty or the richness of your surroundings.

The president was making a pitch for his social programs. Later in the speech he declared that American justice embodied the idea that "Each could become whatever his qualities of mind and spirit would permit—to strive, to seek, and, if he could, to find his happiness." And the president called for a chance for African Americans, and for poor whites, to pull themselves out of "gateless poverty." "The Negro," he continued, "will have to rely mostly upon his own efforts." But unlike other minorities and immigrant groups, LBJ added, black citizens "just cannot do it alone" because of the centuries, the "endless years of hatred and hopelessness."

Hence, his administration needed to do more to help the poor, and especially African Americans. "We are trying to attack these evils through our poverty program, through our education program, through our medical care and our other health programs, and a dozen more of the Great Society programs that are aimed at the root causes of this poverty."

Johnson was giving a political speech to a friendly black audience at Howard University. He aimed to increase support for his major policies, many of them being debated that summer a few miles away in Congress. During the address the president massaged his audience by making an incredible admission of guilt, asking the question of who was responsible for the "breakdown of the Negro family structure. For this, most of all white America must accept responsibility."

In a sense, then, the administration's civil rights policies were beginning to shift—Johnson and some other liberals were now beginning to advocate opening the doors of opportunity, and as the *New York Times* editorialized, "translating newly reinforced legal rights into genuine equality." For the first time, equality became a policy of the Johnson administration.

But just what did equality mean? Johnson meant that black citizens had a different past than other minorities, and that being the case they deserved additional help, more social programs to get them to the starting gate so they could start the race equally with other citizens. The president never stated that all runners should end the race the same, in a tie, an equal result. Throughout his life LBJ had been a liberal individualist who passionately believed that all Americans should be given the same opportunities so they could make the best out of their own lives, a feeling that he again stated two months later to a mostly black audience in the White House Rose Garden. Title VII was "the key of hope" for African Americans, but it was only a key. "It will open the gates only for these willing to shoulder the responsibilities." The liberal and business media understood LBJ's remarks. "The task is to give 20 million Negroes the same chance as every other American to learn and grow," wrote the *New Republic,* and *Business Week* penned a special report, explaining that the Howard University address meant "not just freedom, but opportunity" for African Americans. "Business is now giving them training to help them toward that goal." In fact, "many corporations are now giving Negro workers that special consideration."

A few months later the man that President Johnson picked as the first chairman of the Equal Employment Opportunity Commission, the former president's son, Franklin D. Roosevelt Jr., made the same pitch, now using the term and defining "affirmative action" in a letter to *Nation's Business*. The commissioner stated that the EEOC would investigate complaints of discrimination, but that "we regard our other approach—affirmative action—as important as the . . . correction of violations." "We assume that merit employment is morally right and that most companies are living up to the civil rights law," he continued, "but there's room for them to go beyond the law and it will be good for them and for the community." The EEOC's affirmative action program meant "more aggressive leadership and participation by private business in promoting equal employment opportunity . . . more than is required by law," and that translated to "aggressive recruitment" and then training minorities: "we must go out looking for potential employees . . . let them know they are now welcome in places where doors were once closed . . . and give them special training so that they may qualify."

Special consideration defined affirmative action in the mid-1960s, and the challenge was profound. The average educational level of African Americans then was only two-thirds that of whites, while more than half of black men over 25 had less than a grammar school education, and an extraordinary 67 percent failed the armed forces' preinduction test. When white sports announcers began interviewing black athletes on television that decade, many wondered what language they were speaking, and after the Chrysler Corporation instituted a training program, their president lamented that some signed up with an X. "As we registered those who did report, we found that many of them had no social security number, had never been counted in a census, or registered to vote, or belonged to any organization of any kind. In most of the accepted senses, they really didn't even exist."

The Johnson administration knew that the challenge could be met only with the help of the business community. As *Business Week* reported, "the government is constantly looking for fresh approaches," and many joined the new crusade. The Campbell Soup Company and other firms began training programs for black workers. Diamond Alkali's chemical plant near Houston and Western Electric's assembly plant in Chicago started teaching its black laborers basic math and English; if they passed the 20-week course, they were promoted to better jobs. Chase Manhattan Bank established classes in reading, math, and language skills, paid the students while they attended, and after graduation hired them as clerks. Pacific Telephone & Telegraph sent representatives to high schools to persuade students to get their degrees and then come to them for a job. Textron's president lamented the labor shortage during the booming economy and declared, "Today, each of us can afford to go out of our way to train the disadvantaged."[14]

LBJ, of course, was implementing training programs during summer 1965, and for the first time in years African Americans were making legal, economic, social, and political progress. Numerous businesses began their searches for black talent and not just locally—managers began sending recruiters to traditionally black universities. Bill Cosby became the first black TV star by appearing on the popular sitcom, *I Spy*. LBJ appointed the first black to the cabinet, Robert C. Weaver, and the next year Thurgood Marshall to the Supreme Court; Massachusetts voters sent Edward Brooke to the U.S. Senate, and those in Cleveland elected the great-grandson of a slave, Carl Stokes, as the nation's first black mayor of a major city.

The summer of 1965 marked the pinnacle of liberalism during the 1960s, but like all summits the path would eventually lead downhill. In August a black ghetto of Los Angeles, Watts, exploded. The riot raged on, and authorities called in more than 15,000 troops and police. Troops grew tense, shooting wildly. "Several persons were killed by mistake," a presidential commission later reported, and "Many more were injured." Authorities restored law and order after six days, but at a high price: almost 4,000 arrested, over 1,000 injured, and 34 dead.

Watts did incalculable harm to the civil rights movement. Blacks saw an America still filled with discrimination. Passage of civil and voting rights acts did not immediately decrease the racism or open many doors of opportunity, and that was frustrating; the upcoming summers would witness many more urban riots. Watts shocked many white moderate and conservatives, and it boosted the "white backlash." More citizens began to feel that the federal government was concerned only with minorities and not about the white majority. By mid-1966 a Harris poll revealed a large increase of white voters, 75 percent, who thought that blacks were "moving too fast" in their demands for civil rights. Watts confused liberals. They saw an America finally trying to live up to its dream, passing major legislation, and they could not understand why ghettos were burning. "What do they want?" LBJ asked. "I'm giving them boom times and more good legislation than anybody else did, and what do they do—attack and sneer. Could FDR do better? Could anybody do better? What do they want?"

The president responded by asking Congress to pass a Model Cities Act for urban renewal and an Open Housing Act to end residential restrictions, but the first was not effective, and the latter was held up in debates for years in the Senate. A more immediate response came just one month after Watts. In September the president issued executive order 11246. It essentially superceded and abolished all previous orders—and became the standing rule for affirmative action for future decades.

LBJ's order charged the Civil Service Commission to end discrimination in the federal government, the Department of Labor to do that with federal contracts, resulting in the establishment of the Office of Federal Contract Compliance (OFCC). It commanded the Equal Employment Opportunity Commission to investigate and end discrimination in private employment. Johnson's executive order used the exact words as Kennedy had in 1961:

> The contractor will take affirmative action to ensure that applicants are employed, and that employees are treated during employment, without regard to their race, creed, color, or national origin.

That order included recruitment, promotions, salary, transfers, layoffs, and selection for apprenticeships and training. Each contractor was ordered to make "reasonable efforts within a reasonable time" to comply, and if they did not, the government could terminate or suspend the contract and the company "may be declared ineligible for further Government contracts."

Thus, during 1964 and 1965, the Johnson administration signed or ordered the necessary legislation and executive decrees to significantly decrease discrimination in the workplace. The reaction from the black community was to try to get the federal government to uphold the new law. Just days after the EEOC opened for business in July 1965, the NAACP's Herbert Hill delivered the first complaints. They targeted mostly southern companies and unions, such as Southern Bell, Kroger of Memphis, and various department stores in New Orleans, but also Darling Chemical of East St. Louis and its segregated union, part of the AFL–CIO. Hill demanded that chairman Roosevelt invoke the "full power" of the commission. Soon civil rights organizations were flooding the EEOC with complaints; although experts had estimated 2,000 in the first year, there were 5,000 in the first nine months and more than 8,800 by the next July, the commission's first anniversary. Lamented Roosevelt, "We are being overwhelmed."

The flood of complaints was only one problem for the new EEOC. Chairman Roosevelt was not an effective administrator, liked sailing his yacht more than appearing at congressional hearings, and left after only months on the job for a doomed attempt at being elected governor of New York. Leadership remained a problem, and during 1966 the agency had no chairman at all for three months. LBJ named Stephen Shulman, a 33-year-old white lawyer with government experience in labor and civil rights law, who brought in more energy and determination, streamlined the agency, but also left the job after a little more than a year. Johnson then appointed the first African American as chairman, another 33-year-old attorney, Clifford Alexander Jr. In addition, the EEOC was understaffed and underfunded. An agency ordered to enforce nondiscrimination in the nation's workforce was funded less than the Office of Coal Research, preventing it from opening many regional offices and hiring staff to investigate thousands of complaints, some of which were not investigated for over a year, some for two years. Before "an aggrieved person can get a remedy," CORE's James Farmer complained, "he may have found another job or starved to death."

In disarray and swamped with complaints, the immediate question for the EEOC was, how to proceed? Could the federal EEOC be more effective than the state agencies in bringing about more fairness in hiring? How would the commission interpret the new law? Title VII was "replete with good intentions," *Business Week* editorialized. "But its fine print leaves up in the air many questions of just what constitutes illegal discrimination in employment" and what the EEOC "can do about infringements."

That was the case. The five-member commission of two Republicans and three Democrats, two blacks and three whites, came from various ideological backgrounds, held different views on discrimination, and advocated different approaches toward business. Consequently, during the next years the commission held discussions on the meaning and enforcement of Title VII, while the OFCC did the same concerning LBJ's executive order. Facing the agencies, and many employers, during the last years of the Johnson administration were significant questions that became part of the affirmative action debate for future decades:

What is discrimination, and how do you prove it?

How would the government measure compliance with LBJ's executive order and Title VII?

Did the executive order mandate preferences or quotas?

Historically, discrimination had been understood to mean deliberate conduct or hostility based on prejudice, some act treating a person unequally because of his/her race, religion, sex, or national origin. Yet as the government passed major civil rights legislation most companies did not have a written rule stating "do not hire Negroes," or a policy that mandated that only minorities be employed in the lowest jobs. Most businesses simply did not chance breaking tradition and perhaps irritating their white workers. "Take my company," one corporate president admitted. "We have no official policy against hiring Negroes. But, the fact is, we don't have one on the payroll!"

That being custom, some officials and civil rights organizations claimed that a local ratio or statistical approach could be used; that is, if there were 10 percent minorities in a community, and a company only had 2 percent black workers, then that would be proof of discrimination. The Johnson administration rejected that formula, and one of the main reasons was because the level of education and training for minorities was so much lower than that of whites. Thus, it was difficult to measure the qualifications of many black applicants.[15]

Another issue concerned the intent to discriminate. Did a company try to exclude minorities from its workforce? That, too, was difficult to prove, so Congress in Title VII had given the EEOC the right to examine the effects: Did a corporation's hiring policy have a negative impact on certain citizens, such as minority applicants? By the mid-1960s black leaders and some of the media were using a new term, "institutional racism," which connoted that racism was so embedded in society that businesses were not particularly aware that they discriminated in their hiring and promotion practices.

Institutional racism, of course, concerned not only African Americans. In 1964 the American Jewish Committee accused 50 utility companies of discrimination. The committee noted that Jews made up 5 percent of the population, 8 percent of all college graduates, but of more than 6,300 executives in those utility companies, less than 1 percent were Jews. At Chrysler, a corporation with 18,000 white collar employees, only 100 were Jews. The explanation for that, stated a spokesman, was that corporations "select a type that represents conformity to themselves." That being the case, some minorities began to declare that the government should intervene and mandate hiring programs.

The selection alarmed the business community. As early as 1963 *U.S. News & World Report* published the shocking headline: FORCED HIRING OF NEGROES—HOW IT WOULD WORK." Once Congress passed the Civil Rights Act, the magazine claimed, the government might be ordering the "hiring of Negroes instead of white applicants. It could require an employer to pay back wages to a Negro who had not been hired, given a raise, or promoted." If the businessman failed to comply with the government, then he would be penalized, "including a fine and jail sentence."

A second question also disturbed many executives: How would the government enforce the executive order and Title VII and get states and businesses to end discriminating?

As mentioned, previous presidents had relied on force. They had sent federal marshals or the military to Little Rock's Central High School or to the University of Alabama. Those actions upheld the law and resulted in desegregation of those institutions, but it had been unpopular in the South and it was not appropriate or possible to integrate each business and school in the nation. In 1963 the Civil Rights Commission had proposed another idea. It issued a report on Mississippi and startled most politicians by suggesting that the president and Congress should consider not appropriating federal funds to any state that continued to refuse to abide by U.S. laws and the Constitution. A few citizens agreed.

The Louisville *Courier-Journal* editorialized that American taxpayers were entitled to be assured that their funds were "not being used to perpetuate Mississippi's brand of apartheid." Yet most papers and politicians disagreed. *U.S. News* called the idea "cruel and unusual punishment," and the *New York Times* wrote that such ideas would not "cool the inflamed passions." JFK did not support the idea, calling it "unwise."

LBJ also thought it unwise, and as he became more involved in pressing domestic and foreign policy issues, he left discrimination investigation to the EEOC and enforcement to the Justice Department. The commission could examine a complaint against a company and mediate a compromise, which it began to do, but significantly it could not issue a "cease and desist" order, which would legally force compliance. Nor could the EEOC file a suit, and so critics called the commission a "toothless tiger." Suits were left to the complainant or to the Justice Department, and during the next years Justice looked for carefully selected complaints that would become test cases. The federal bureaucracy and the courts would be left with establishing a new legal foundation for affirmative action.

Another part of this enforcement dilemma was measurement. At that time the government and many businesses did not keep a count of minority workers. With the exception of southern companies who had no black workers, many corporations did not know if they were bigots or responsible employers. A national database did not exist, and some civil rights leaders opposed such a list because southern states and many employers had used racial identity on application forms as a way to bar blacks from jobs. Yet without these statistics, how could the government measure if a corporation was hiring all citizens and complying with Title VII? A similar problem at that time was school desegregation. Without a count of white and black students in a district, and at each school, how could the government know that schools were integrating? And there was another measurement problem: What was the appropriate number or ratio of minorities at a plant that would be in compliance with the new law? Was the business supposed to hire a certain percentage, and if so, based on what? The proportion of minorities in the locale, state, nation?

Added to this confusion was the fact that various titles of the Civil Rights Act barred the EEOC from demanding that companies adopt compensatory hiring for past discriminatory practices. "Nothing contained in this title shall be interpreted to require any employer to grant preferential treatment to any individual or to any group" because of their "race, color, religion, sex, or national origin." Thus, the Civil Right Act that forbid discrimination in the workplace also barred preferential treatment to any group who had suffered discrimination.

Title VII was colorblind and so was LBJ's executive order. It simply demanded that contractors "will take affirmative action to ensure that applicants are employed, and that employees are treated during employment, *without regard* to their race, creed, color, or national origin." Neither law nor regulation demanded that employers hire people because of their race; on the contrary, the aim was to *end* employment practices that discriminated. But then the next question: If the government had outlawed discrimination against African Americans, how could it encourage, even demand, that employers *begin* hiring a race that traditionally had suffered discrimination?

This contradiction was what scholar John David Skrentny labeled the irony of affirmative action. If businesses continued to hire the most skilled person for a job, almost always a white applicant in that era of segregated schools, then that company apparently was not in violation of Title VII. Management was simply following tradition and hiring based on merit. That being the case, how could the federal government open up the doors of opportunity to African Americans? Affirmative action, the Johnson administration answered, since that executive order called on contractors to integrate the workplace, which meant that most companies would have to give hiring preference to minorities. Moreover, if the government was to measure "progress," how could they do that without counting the number of blacks on the job, and if necessary demanding that a contractor hire more minorities, even if that meant some form of de facto quota on the factory line? The irony of affirmative action resulted in confusion for the rest of the 1960s and until 1971, when the Supreme Court ruled on *Griggs v. Duke Power Co.*[16]

The Johnson administration attempted to address the irony of affirmative action during the booming economy of the mid-1960s, and it scored an early victory in March 1966 against the Newport News Shipbuilding Company. The shipbuilder received 75 percent of its business from the taxpayers and was the largest employer in Virginia. Some

5,000 of its 22,000 employees were black, and 40 of them filed charges against the company with the EEOC. Blacks were doing the same work as whites and paid less, were not allowed to transfer to white departments, were passed over for promotion, and were not admitted to apprenticeship school. Moreover, the company had segregated toilet, shower, and locker facilities while at the same time it was building a nuclear submarine named after a famous African American, George Washington Carver. The EEOC formed a coalition with OFCC and the Justice and Defense departments, and they attacked Newport News, who quickly capitulated. The company agreed to end its policies and promote almost 4,000 black workers and to designate 75 to become supervisors.

Like other defense contractors, Newport News was vulnerable because it depended on the government for most of its business; the EEOC's other efforts were not very successful in 1966 and 1967. Yet most citizens and their political leaders then were not interested in employment issues. They were becoming increasingly concerned about other problems: campus demonstrations, cries for black power, hippies flaunting their new culture, the long, hot summers of urban race riots— and always the war in Vietnam.

It was not the war as much as the urban riots that had an impact on affirmative action. During the summer of 1966 ghetto dwellers rioted in Cleveland, Dayton, Milwaukee, and San Francisco, resulting in 400 injured and at least seven dead. The next summer was worse. From Boston to Tampa fires burned in the streets. Then Newark exploded. The governor declared an "open rebellion," ordered in the National Guard, and what remained days later was a burned out city and 25 dead. And then Detroit. LBJ had to call on the U.S. Army, who arrived with machine guns, tanks, and helicopters: 2,000 injured and 43 dead. "Detroit," declared *Newsweek*, was "An American Tragedy."

The summer riots fragmented the civil rights movement, bolstered white resentment, and stimulated federal action. The Johnson administration earmarked additional War on Poverty funds for ghettos, and in 1967 the president charged Illinois governor Otto Kerner to lead a commission to study the disturbances while he ordered his subordinates to come up with proposals. The subsequent Kerner Report was blunt and significant, selling more than a million copies in three months. The commission placed the blame for the upheavals, not on black rioters but on whites; their "racism is essentially responsible for the explosive mixture which has been accumulating in our cities." White "society is deeply implicated in the ghetto." Moreover, the report reiterated "institutional racism." White employers did not necessarily discriminate consciously, but they had hired their own for so long that it had become tradition. Discrimination, apparently, could be eradicated only by changing the system. The commission and presidential advisers urged local officials to increase the number of black employees, especially police officers. Half of Newark's population was black, but only 10 percent of that population were police. As for the National Guard, composed of only about 1 percent African Americans, Attorney General Ramsey Clark advised the president that "steps should be taken immediately to correct the racial imbalance" by enlisting black soldiers, which would have "a general moderating effect on the residents" in the ghetto. The message was clear: Hire blacks. In an attempt to prevent additional riots many companies did that, and they tossed out their traditional hiring standards based on merit. "This is discrimination in reverse," one company official explained, "but such steps are required to convince the Negroes that we are serious and want them to apply for work with us."

Ghettos were burning, and employing more black residents seemed a pragmatic response, for as one economist remarked, "The more educated, the more experienced, and the more integrated the Negro labor force becomes, the less tension and the fewer problems we'll have in this country." Fires in the streets contributed to a shift in the Johnson administration's policy. It began to abandon what it had fought for in 1964, the "colorblind" criteria of Title VII, and to promote affirmative action—by getting more minorities into the workforce. In 1966 the EEOC required 60,000 employers with over 100 workers to file EEO-1 reports, listing the gender and race of their employees; minorities included "Negro, Oriental, American Indian, and Spanish Americans." The subsequent reports gave the government the necessary statistics to begin measuring and analyzing the workforce. As the EEOC began processing this information, citizens continued to bombard the agency with complaints.[17]

Surprisingly, over a third of those complaints came from women charging sex discrimination, referring specifically to unequal benefits, discriminatory seniority lines, and unfair restrictions because of state protective labor laws. Yet an EEOC official recommended to the director that "less time be devoted to sex cases since the legislative history would indicate that they deserve a lower priority than discrimination because of race." The only female commissioner on the five-member EEOC was African American and union director Aileen Hernandez. "The message came through clearly that the Commission's priority was race discrimination," she recalled, "and apparently only as it related to Black *men*."

Hernandez was only stating the usual response of the American society in the era before the women's liberation movement. At that time race discrimination was the national issue, not gender, and the idea that Title VII had something to do with a worker's gender disturbed corporate bosses. "We're not worried about the racial discrimination ban," an airline executive told the *Wall Street Journal*, "what's unnerving us is the section on sex. . . . What are we going to do now when a gal walks into our office, demands a job as an airline pilot and has the credentials to qualify? Or what will we do when some guy comes in and wants to be a stewardess?" An electronics businessman stated that he only hired women with small fingers to assemble fragile electronic components, and now he wondered sarcastically if he would have to "hire the first male midget with unusual dexterity."

"De-Sexing the Job Market" was picked up by the *New York Times*, which whimsically labeled this issue the "Bunny Problem," referring to the popular Playboy Clubs. What would happen, asked the paper, if a man applied to become a Playboy Bunny, or a women to be an attendant in a male bathhouse? Ads that had begun many careers, "Boy Wanted" were over, for want ads should no longer be categorized by gender. And the language has to be neuterized: "Handyman must disappear . . . he was pretty much a goner anyway, if you ever started looking for one in desperation. No more milkman, iceman, serviceman, foreman. . . . Girl Friday is an intolerable offense. Saleslady is forbidden. The Rockettes may become bi-sexual, and a pity, too." It might be better, the paper added, if Congress "just abolished sex itself. . . . Bunny problem, indeed! This is revolution, chaos. You can't even safely advertise for a wife anymore."

Something seemed funny, at least to many men. At EEOC meetings the male commissioners refused to take women's complaints seriously, joked about the issue, laughing about a "flat-chested cocktail waitress who filed a Title VII complaint." They refused to condemn segregating job want ads by gender, declaring that "for the convenience of readers" papers could maintain separate sections, "Jobs of Interest—Male," and "Jobs of Interest—Female." As a male commissioner explained, "There are people on this commission who think that no man should be required to have a male secretary—and I am one of them."[18]

Thus, in the first two years the EEOC was more cautious enforcing gender than race discrimination. It did not rule on the so-called "protective" labor laws that states had erected decades earlier, leaving the issue up to the states. Utah, for example, had a law that prevented women from lifting 15 pounds on the job, while Ohio had laws specifying 19 jobs that women were not allowed to hold, from metal molder to electric meter reader. Texas forbade female employees in places of "immoral conditions." "If it's a good law," one Texan woman declared, then "it should protect men also"; other critics complained that 15 pounds was the average weight of a one-year-old baby, and that such protections really restricted women from good jobs in the buildings trades and the construction industry. Nevertheless, the EEOC was not listening. The sex provision to Title VII, the EEOC director said, was "a fluke . . . conceived out of wedlock."

That provoked Representative Martha Griffiths into action. She attacked from the House, labeling the director's remark a "slur on Congress" and declaring that the agency was "shilly-shallying and wringing its hands about the sex provision" instead of enforcing the law. The congresswoman wrote United Air Lines and complained about its practice of firing female airline flight attendants when they married or reached the age of 32 but not firing male stewards. "You are asking," Griffiths declared, "that a stewardess be young, attractive, and single. What are you running, an airline or a whorehouse?"

Other women joined the cause. Betty Friedan, whose book *The Feminine Mystique* had become a best seller, began meeting with professional women and came to believe that a new organization was needed, a group that would fight for women's rights as civil rights organizations had done for African Americans. Pauli Murray, a black professor of law at Yale University, and Mary Eastwood of the Justice Department published "Jane Crow and the Law: Sex Discrimination and Title VII." The article not only introduced a significant term with troubling connotations but declared "the rights of women and the rights of Negroes are only different phases of the fundamental and indivisible issue of human rights." To get the EEOC to uphold the law, Murray suggested a women's march on Washington.

Many activists marched throughout 1966, but those demonstrations concerned race, war, and student issues, not women's rights. Instead, the federal government held a national conference on the status of women in Washington. Included in the delegation were a number of females who had met in Friedan's hotel room the evening before the conference, including Kathryn Clarenbach of Wisconsin, who told her colleagues that they must "stop being afraid to rock the boat." Next day, during a session on sex discrimination, some delegates attempted to present a resolution but were told that they were not permitted to recommend policy, a rebuke that made them "fighting mad." Shortly thereafter, Friedan, Murray, Eastwood, and Clarenback formed NOW, the National Organization for Women, with the purpose "to bring women into full participation in the mainstream of American society *now,* assuming all the privileges and responsibilities thereof in truly equal partnership with men." They picked Friedan to be the first president and Aileen Hernandez as executive vice president, who then resigned from the EEOC.

Although this was the nascent phase of the women's liberation movement, a few officials began to listen, including President Johnson. His wife, Lady Bird, had quietly let key congressmen know in 1964 that she supported the addition of the word "sex" to Title VII, and she discreetly supported the emerging women's movement. Now, as the federal government failed to enforce the ban on sex discrimination in Title VII, these feminists urged presidential leadership. That was not much of a problem, for as early as 1964 Johnson had told his cabinet to start looking for females, "this untapped resource," for executive positions in the federal government, continuing that "the day is over when the top jobs are reserved for men." He publicly supported having female employees protected by Title VII and promised to place at least fifty women in policy-making positions, marking the beginning of the end of what he called "stag government."

It was not much of a surprise, then, in October 1967 when LBJ signed executive order 11375, which amended his 1965 order on affirmative action to include sex discrimination and then charged enforcement to the Labor Department. The new policy also was more specific, "to provide equal opportunity in Federal employment and in employment by Federal contractors on the basis of merit without discrimination because of race, color, religion, sex or national origin." Thus, gender assumed its place in affirmative action, and in subsequent years it would become significant, for this was a declaration that equal employment for women was not a "fluke" but an illegal practice like racial discrimination.[19]

Meanwhile, the Johnson administration stumbled forward in 1967 attempting to develop policies on enforcement and compliance. The EEOC compiled the first national census of minority group participation in apprenticeship programs, which pinpointed targets for future antidiscrimination efforts. The OFCC began to withhold federal grants, which began forcing contractors and unions to open up some jobs for minorities. The Justice Department initiated scores of lawsuits against unions that barred black workers. And with these sticks there was a carrot: the Labor Department offered grants to recruit and train African Americans. The department awarded Chrysler almost $6 million to hire and train 3,000 unemployed blacks in 50 cities. Graduates of the 12-week course became mechanics at dealerships or were given jobs on the assembly lines.

These efforts also revealed the administration's evolving definition of affirmative action. Attorney General Clark wrote a memorandum concerning possible presidential decrees or legal changes that might cut employment discrimination. His department listed 15 proposals—not one suggested erecting racial quotas for hiring to reach some percentages or goals. Affirmative action meant opening the doors of opportunity and encouraging the business community to hire and train minorities, especially African American men. Clark's first proposal concerned enforcement: give the EEOC the power "to hear cases and issue cease and desist orders enforceable in the courts."

Affirmative action was vague, to be sure, and the government that year attempted to enlist the business community to help further define the term. OFCC Director Edward C. Sylvester Jr. issued a statement to businessmen: "Affirmative action is going to vary from time to time, from day to day, from place to place. . . . There is no fixed and firm definition of affirmative action. I would say in a general way, affirmative action is anything that you have to do to get results. But this does not necessarily include preferential treatment. The key word here is 'results.'"

To get results the administration developed new policies for the workplace. EEOC ruled that airlines could not hire only female flight attendants, that businesses could not set different retirement ages for the sexes, and that separate male-female want ads were illegal. The agency also decreed that segregated seniority lines, promotion lists, or local unions violated Title VII, as did failing to hire or promote women because they were married. The OFCC established a "pre-award approach." Businesses interested in bidding on contracts over $1 million had to submit employment plans that demonstrated that they had hired some minorities and were in compliance with affirmative action. The office also began temporary "special area programs" to get construction industry contractors in St. Louis, San Francisco, Cleveland, and Philadelphia to "assure minority group representation in all trades and in all phases of the work."

Naturally, there were problems with these special area programs. Most contractors had agreements with unions that stipulated that they would employ only unionized labor for a project, but the contractors themselves had little influence over who the union sent to the job. The unions guaranteed the highest quality work, but locals had apprentice programs that kept out minorities. In St. Louis, for example, the plumbers, pipefitters, electrical, and sheet metal workers locals had more than 5,000 members—but only three were black. The first two special area programs were failures. The St. Louis project was to build the Gateway Arch, and it resulted in union boycotts and a long legal battle. In San Francisco the project was BART, the Bay Area Rapid Transit, and contractors wrote affirmative action plans but successfully avoided hiring more than a token of minorities.

The administration had more success in Cleveland, where the people had elected an African American mayor, Carl Stokes. With only about a dozen blacks in the skilled construction unions in that city, the OFCC invited bids with plans that had a "manning table," which would have "the result of assuring" minority group representation. One NASA contractor there, eager to win the contract, decided on a novel approach. He made a proposal to the OFCC, which for the first time stated a number or "goal" of how many minorities he would hire if the government granted him the contract. Impressed, the OFCC adopted the idea for all federal construction in the region, and, significantly, withheld funds totaling some $80 million until contractors submitted suitable plans. Accordingly, between June and November 1967 contractors committed themselves to hire 110 minorities out of a total of 475 workers—thus achieving results.

With some success in Cleveland, the federal government and local officials developed a plan for Philadelphia. The "Philadelphia Plan" demanded that contractors' bids "must have the *result of producing minority group representation* in all trades and in all phases of the construction project." The administration was going to withhold funding until contractors submitted appropriate plans. In May 1968 the Labor Department issued a significant new regulation—for the first time contractors and unions doing federally financed work had to have affirmative action programs that had *schedules* and *target dates* or "specific goals and timetables" for correcting deficiencies in their minority employment and promotion practices.

Surprisingly, the government did not mandate the goals: the contractors themselves had to devise their own plans. To these businessmen the plan's regulations were too vague, and some asked the government if there was some number or ratio of minorities that were supposed to be on the job—an issue pregnant with peril.

The administration was slowly prying open the doors of opportunity, which LBJ continued to do during 1968. In January the president reached out to the business community, summoning 15 titans of industry to the White House, first for a scrumptious steak lunch, and then for a "no bullshit meeting." "We've looked at every kind of job program," he told the corporate leaders of Ford, Coca-Cola, Mobile Oil, Safeway Stores, Aluminum Company of America, and McDonnell-Douglas. "What works best is what you do best: on-the-job training." LBJ pledged federal funds to those companies that would teach and train the "hardcore unemployed," those who live in the ghetto and have never had a job. "You can put these people to work and you won't have a revolution because they've been left behind. If they're working, they won't be throwing bombs in your homes and plants. Keep them busy and they won't have time to burn your cars." LBJ pleaded "Don't tell me how you can't do it. All I want to know is how you can do it. . . . I need you, each of you. I need your commitment to make taxpayers out of these tax-eaters."

"I commit! Mr. President, I commit!" interrupted James McDonnell, chairman of McDonnell-Douglas. LBJ looked down the table at him, stared, and declared, "Mr. McDonnell, you committed when you ate the first bite of my steak."

After laughter and dessert, the men began forming the National Alliance of Businessmen. LBJ named a northerner, Henry Ford II, CEO of his automobile company, as chairman of the NAB, and for vice chair a southerner, J. Paul Austin, president of Coca-Cola. The next month the president announced the campaign, asking Congress for a $2 billion manpower program, "the largest in the nation's history," to help train and find jobs for people living in the slums of the 50 largest cities. While the president noted that unemployment was the lowest in 15 years and that one million blacks had been hired since 1961, "Our past efforts, vital as they are, have not yet effectively reached the hard-core unemployed."

Henry Ford went to work, helping to created the National Alliance of Businessmen in those 50 major cities while asking CEOs to revise their hiring rules, to overlook prison records, excuse inferior work, and forgive tardiness. "We Americans have reached the point in our history where we must at last put up or shut up about equality," Ford told his corporate colleagues, "and the price of silence is much greater than this richest of all nations can afford." He asked businesses to take a train-and-hire pledge, with a goal of 500,000 permanent jobs by 1971. In general, the response was positive. A survey of 15 cities that had witnessed riots found that 86 percent of businesses that year accepted the idea that they had "social responsibility to make strong efforts to provide employment to Negroes and other minority groups." The presidents of Levi Strauss and ITT joined the campaign, civil rights organizations worked with businesses, and when the Labor Department pledged education and training grants, more than 600 companies applied. "Will it work?" asked *Newsweek*. "Can business make the massive—and permanent—contribution it must if ghetto breadwinners are to gain self-sufficiency and self-respect?" The magazine answered, "The returns, of course, aren't yet in."[20]

The returns would not be in for many years, but throughout 1968 few were concerned about employment issues. The administration was overwhelmed by events and was no longer focused on discriminatory practices, even neglecting to replace EEOC commissioners, sometimes for many months. Instead, Americans were transfixed on incredible scenes in one of the most eventful years in history: North Korea captured the USS *Pueblo* in international waters; the Vietcong launched the

Tet Offensive in Vietnam; an obscure Minnesota Democratic Senator, Eugene McCarthy, almost beat LBJ in the New Hampshire primary; Senator Robert Kennedy entered the Democratic primaries; President Johnson announced he would not run for another term; assassins gunned down Martin Luther King Jr. and Bobby Kennedy; violence erupted at the Democratic convention; African American sprinters proudly gave the black power salute at the Olympics; the first uniformed soldiers marched against the war; and females proclaiming "women's liberation" demonstrated against the Miss America Pageant.

All that before the final days of the presidential election, which slated Democrat Hubert Humphrey against Republican Richard Nixon and independent candidate George Wallace running on the American Party ticket, championing the "white backlash" and winning 13 percent of the vote. The close election that placed Richard Nixon in office, most pundits believed, meant that domestically, civil rights issues would be replaced by one of his campaign promises, "Law and Order."

LBJ left office in January 1969, and by then it was obvious that the meaning of fairness had changed considerably during that tumultuous decade. Unlike the 1950s most citizens now felt that all minorities deserved political equality and equal opportunities on the job. Most supported Johnson's attempts to level the playing field, to educate the poor and train the unskilled, and that included many corporations who instituted their own job training programs.

Yet even as affirmative action was being developed, it became obvious that there were limits to the pursuit of fairness. Citizens overwhelmingly felt that social programs should be aimed to help *all* the poor. Few accepted the idea of preferences or special programs for only one group of Americans, regardless of past discrimination. Congress never considered a bill that would have instituted a "crash program," a domestic Marshall Plan, even if this preferential treatment were in return for centuries of slavery and discrimination, and even if it were to last for only one decade.

Neither Kennedy nor Johnson favored a Marshall Plan for just one race, but their administrations did aim to make equal employment opportunity and affirmative action federal policies. JFK continued Truman's legacy in an attempt to end two traditions, hiring practices that excluded or discouraged minority applicants, and paying women lower wages for the same work. Johnson took a more active role, signing the Civil Rights and Voting Rights acts, funding various poverty and manpower training programs, and urging the business community to hire and train African Americans. LBJ's aim, as he said, was to open the door of opportunity and give blacks special consideration, a "hand up." That was the definition of affirmative action when he left office.

Generally speaking, the OFCC and EEOC began to enforce the first national nondiscrimination employment policy, yet the task was complicated and ineffective. OFCC made demands on contractors, but as late as January 1969 the office had not taken away one major contract from a company that had discriminated or failed to live up to its plans. Enforcement also revealed a contradiction. The irony of affirmative action was that it clashed with the original intent of Title VII, which only demanded employment *without regard* to race, color, creed, sex, and national origin, not that employers take action to hire a certain group of Americans. There was yet another variable during the Great Society and Vietnam War: all taxpayers were funding building projects and the defense industry, but because many unions and some corporations resisted hiring minorities and women, not all taxpayers were being hired to build those projects.

What was the answer? For the Democrats there was no alternative; they relied on black votes in key states and by 1963 had accepted civil rights as their political agenda. Given the dire economic and social status of African Americans during a booming economy, given the movement's legitimate demands that America live up to its creed, the Kennedy and Johnson administrations felt compelled to try to end discrimination in employment. Both administrations urged employers, and demanded federal agencies and contractors, to get "results," that is, to begin hiring African Americans and eventually women, even if that meant hiring *with regard* to race and gender.

Given the historical circumstances the Democratic response was logical, although there were unforeseen consequences, and ending employment discrimination in that decade was not successful. Most likely that was because it would take years to end traditions and, in the late 1960s, the nation was deluged with urban riots, demonstrations, and the Vietnam war. The Johnson administration never really established a clear vision of affirmative action, and at the same time critics declared that special area plans with "goals and timetables" violated the usual bidding practices. Some in the federal bureaucracy agreed, such as the U.S. Comptroller General Elmer Staats, who in November 1968 declared the Philadelphia Plan in violation of Title VII. That set the stage for a future debate: what was the definition of affirmative action?

A weary LBJ left that question to the courts, and especially to his successor, Richard Nixon—and *that* Republican president surprised almost everyone.

three | Zenith of Affirmative Action

"Bring Us Together" was Richard Nixon's campaign slogan, and after his inauguration in January 1969 most Americans desired just that: a time of national healing and unity.

But that was not to be. Urban riots, campus demonstrations, the Vietnam war, and what *Time* called the counterculture "youthquake" had ended political and social consensus and divided the nation. On one side was a vocal minority who opposed the president and the establishment, the sixties culture; on the other were those who supported it and who Nixon eventually labeled the "great silent majority." By June 1970, a month after the Kent State tragedy, a government commission wrote that division in the nation was "as deep as any since the Civil War."

The division was exemplified in two powerful social currents during the late 1960s and throughout the 1970s—empowerment and liberation. Since the mid-1960s many young blacks had become tired of asking whites for their rights, listening to liberals talk about gradual change, and they became more militant, shouting for "Black Power." The war was another factor, for many young black men could not understand why they were drafted to fight 12,000 miles away in Vietnam when they were beaten by white cops in the South. Activist Stokely Carmichael blasted selective service as nothing more than "white people sending black people to make war on yellow people to defend the land they stole from red people." Such ideas were gaining currency within the black community as Nixon took office in 1969. On the assembly line, African Americans formed organizations such as DRUM, Dodge Revolutionary Union Movement, and shut down a Chrysler plant. On campuses that year, younger brothers and sisters began making demands for black studies programs at more than 200 universities across the nation. Riots erupted at San Francisco State University, and at Cornell the Afro-American Society took over one building, demanding more black students and faculty. After the administration agreed, the society's members marched out of the building—armed with shotguns and rifles.

Such events had an impact on mainstream African Americans. "The Black Mood: More Militant, More Hopeful, More Determined," proclaimed *Time*. A survey in spring 1970 found that 85 percent of blacks supported high school and college courses on what now was being called "Afro-American studies." The term "Negro" was being dropped by the mainstream press. "For black Americans," *Time* continued, "pride in themselves and their culture, so long smothered in a predominately white society, is now a pervasive reality." The future aim, the survey found, was that "Blacks must keep pushing and fighting for equality." And while two-thirds of respondents agreed that life in America had improved in the last five years, they felt that next phase of progress should be educational and employment opportunities.

The expansion of black empowerment had a national impact. Cesar Chavez mobilized "Brown Power" in the Southwest. "The Chicano Rebellion," announced *The Nation*. "Now it's the Mexican-Americans—Chicanos, they are called in California—who are appearing on the scene of protest." Native Americans invaded and occupied Alcatraz Island, proclaiming "Red Power," and gay men, tired of police harassment, went on a rampage in Greenwich Village outside of the Stonewall Inn. As the police made arrests the angry crowd chanted "Gay Power!"

Along with almost daily examples of empowerment there was personal liberation, which had been spreading across the nation since young hippies appeared on magazine covers during the 1967 "Summer of Love" in San Francisco. By 1970 some three million hippies were liberating themselves from their parents' mainstream values, forming various types of communes and collectives, or were hitchhiking around America and the world—from Marrakech to Kabul to Kathmandu—challenging the status quo and developing their own lifestyles.

Women, too, were challenging American values and culture, and more than any other group they successfully merged empowerment and liberation. Since the mid-1960s some women had been questioning the male-dominated society, demanding that the EEOC enforce the discrimination laws concerning them. By 1970 women's liberation was taking the nation by storm, dominating media reports and headlining numerous TV specials. The media programs and "consciousness-raising" group sessions exposed not only stereotypes and sexism but also legal, educational, and economic discrimination, what activist Mary King labeled the "caste system for women."

Thus, as Nixon assumed the presidency and during his first two years in office, many vocal minorities and women were calling for their personal liberation from the past and their empowerment in the future. To them the most pressing problems had become ending discrimination and opening employment and educational opportunities, and those issues would be affected by the position the Nixon administration took on affirmative action.[1]

Richard Nixon was a complex man, and one aide said that he had a "light and a dark side." The private man was suspicious of virtually anyone who criticized his policies, and this trait would eventually be his downfall. The public Nixon appeared as a statesman who had run for office on three themes: the New Federalism, an attempt to give states more power after LBJ's Great Society; law and order; and what he labeled "peace with honor" in Vietnam.

After years of civil rights demonstrations and campus turmoil, law and order was popular with the suburban silent majority, the urban and rural white backlash, and with most Southerners. To these citizens, civil rights programs had gone too far, as had violence, and Nixon called for a "war on crime," doubling funds for local police forces. More importantly, the president and his attorney general, John Mitchell, felt that, for the first time since the Democratic party captured the South in the 1870s, the Republicans now had a chance to dominate that region. George Wallace had won 13 percent of the vote in 1968, and Nixon was determined to capture that vote in 1972.

The Mitchell-Nixon idea became known as the "southern strategy," which appeared in the first year of his presidency. Two Supreme Court justices retired, including Chief Justice Earl Warren, which allowed Nixon to make nominations. To avoid a fight over the chief's coveted position in a Senate dominated by Democrats, Nixon nominated a moderate federal judge, Warren Burger, who was confirmed easily. Shortly thereafter, Justice Abe Fortas resigned, and the president began his strategy, nominating Clement Haynesworth of South Carolina, a federal judge whose rulings had not supported civil rights or labor. Civil rights organizations were appalled that Haynesworth had opposed a court ruling that hospitals accepting federal funds had to integrate their facilities. AFL-CIO president George Meany declared that Haynesworth had made seven decisions on labor cases, had opposed unions each time, and so his nomination was "a declaration of war." For the first time in 40 years, the Senate rejected a Court nomination, with 17 Republicans voting against their president. Nixon then turned to Judge G. Harrold Carswell of Florida, who years before had publicly declared his "firm, vigorous belief in . . . white supremacy." Moreover, 60 percent of his rulings had been reversed by higher courts, raising questions of competency. Again the Senate rejected the nominee, this time with 13 Republicans voting against Nixon. Furious, Nixon proclaimed that the Senate had made "vicious assaults" on his nominees because of "regional discrimination . . . they had the misfortune of being born in the South." That stance won political support in Dixie but not in the Senate, so Nixon nominated moderate Harry Blackmun of Minnesota, who easily won confirmation, as did his subsequent nominees Lewis Powell of Virginia and William Rehnquist of Arizona.

The Nixon administration continued its southern strategy by opposing the extension of the 1965 Voting Rights Act with an attempt to amend it, and this was rejected by Congress, who extended the act. Attorney General Mitchell supported the state of Mississippi in arguing against integrating its school districts and the administration opposed busing students to achieve school desegregation. A "new evil," Nixon called busing, "disrupting communities and imposing hardship on children—both black and white." The Supreme Court ruled busing constitutional and mandated school integration "at once." Like Eisenhower at Little Rock, Nixon grudgingly enforced the law, writing to assistant John Ehrlichman, "do what the law requires and not *one bit* more."

During his first months in office Nixon's civil rights policies were inconsistent. At his inaugural address Nixon referred to the Kerner Report when he called on the nation "to go forward together. This means black and white together, as one nation, not two." Then his Justice Department went to court to force the largest single school district in the South, Houston, to integrate, took action against Cannon Mills to end discrimination in their company housing, and filed a suit to stop real estate agents from selling property at higher rates to blacks than to whites in Chicago. "The Administration," *Time* declared in April, "seems to be suffering from a mild case of schizophrenia."

That was apparent when the administration began considering affirmative action. Recall that in the waning years of the Johnson administration, the OFCC was conducting temporary affirmative action "special area programs" to get construction builders and unions who accepted federal contracts to assure minority group representation on their job sites, and that in May 1968 the Labor Department issued regulations that required them to establish *schedules* and *target dates* for correcting deficiencies. Also recall that during 1968 the administration began using the threat of cutting off funds if contractors did not establish affirmative action programs. By 1969 that threat had considerable leverage, since taxes were paying to construct an interstate freeway system, funding numerous Great Society programs, and waging a war in Vietnam; in other words federal funds were supplying 225,000 contractors with $30 billion in annual construction, giving the federal government a direct economic impact on 20 million workers, or almost a third of the entire labor force. Finally, remember that in November the U.S. Comptroller ruled the Philadelphia Plan in violation of Title VII.

The Comptroller gave the new Republican administration an easy excuse to abandon the Democrat's Philadelphia Plan. Would Nixon abandon or abolish affirmative action, and if not, then how would these Republicans define the policy?

Naturally, the administration's first dealings with affirmative action were inherited from the Johnson administration and concerned Philadelphia, the "City of Brotherly Love," which had demonstrated little such love and suffered race riots during the 1960s. Approximately 30 percent of Philadelphia's population was black, and the federal government was planning to fund a new hospital, some university buildings, and construct a new U.S. Mint, at a cost of $550 million. Would all taxpayers be hired? Probably not. JFK had promulgated affirmative action eight years earlier, and while there were some African Americans in the unions and in apprentice programs in the city, many of the local unions continued tradition and resisted integration. The ironworkers union had 850 members, 12 were minorities; plumbers and pipefitters had over 560, with only three blacks. Locals in the sheet metal trade with 1,400 members, elevator constructors with more

Unions is culpable as businesses.

than 600 members, and stone masons with more than 400—none had minority workers.

The nation's "skilled building trades unions," claimed *Newsweek*, "are nearly as lily-white as the snootiest country club." One union leader in Detroit surveyed the pace of integration in the local building trades and declared, "at the present pace it will be somewhere around 2168 before Negroes achieve their full equality." That being the case, a labor law expert predicted, unions had better make "a quick move" to integrate or the government would intervene. But, he lamented, "only a small number of trade unionists seem interested in that kind of argument."[2]

The unions stalled, and that was unacceptable to the new Secretary of Labor, George Shultz. He was a moderate Republican who hired an assistant secretary, African American Arthur Fletcher, and put him in charge of revising the Johnson administration's plan. Fletcher was a lifelong Republican, a successful businessman who had heard, and supported, Nixon's campaign call for more "black capitalism." He was not interested in calls for compensation, Marshall Plans, or "a fruitless debate about slavery and its debilitating legacy." Philadelphia's construction union workers had Polish, Italian, or Irish surnames. "In essence," he wrote, "public taxes were being used to take care of a family clan called a union. So I asked the question, Are we in the business of taking care of the Kawaski family?" Fletcher found in Philadelphia that "Italians with green cards who couldn't speak English . . . were working on federal contracts" while "those same unions and contractors were saying they couldn't find qualified blacks."

Fletcher and Shultz presented their ideas about affirmative action at a cabinet meeting just weeks after the inauguration. The labor secretary outlined his new plan, stressing that it would demonstrate that the administration was helping blacks "gain the opportunity for economic advancement, now far more important than new laws or more welfare." Fletcher agreed, pleading a "case for black economic advancement." Both men declared that their plan was appropriate for Republican ideology. Shultz claimed that it was "consistent with a spirit of self-reliance," and Fletcher argued that implementation would demonstrate the administration's commitment to "helping people help themselves."

Faced with many more pressing issues, the president allowed Shultz and Fletcher to devise their new employment policy, which Fletcher announced in June in the City of Brotherly Love, simply called the

Philadelphia Plan. Sounding very much like previous Democratic officials, Fletcher declared that years of segregation and discrimination meant that specific "goals or standards for percentages of minority employees" were necessary. He admitted that it would be better if goals were not required, but in fact the long history of discrimination meant, "Visible, measurable goals to correct obvious imbalances are essential." Later he revealed that the administration's primary civil rights aim was to alleviate economic problems for African Americans. "I won the right to go to the hotel, and I won the right to go to school, and I won the right to buy a house," Fletcher declared on behalf of the average black man, "now I need the money."

Contractors and unions, of course, wanted to know how this plan would be implemented. Fletcher clarified that later at hearings in Philadelphia. Minorities included African Americans, obviously, and also "Orientals, American Indians and persons with Spanish surnames." He did not mention women. The OFCC would establish not specific numbers but a flexible "target range" for contractors and unions, which was related to a percentage of workers in a certain area. That percentage naturally could be translated into a number of workers that should be hired during the upcoming five years. Philadelphia was 30 percent African American, so if those locals wanted to win contracts they would have to hire a "minority goal" which would increase annually and could result in approximately 20 percent of the workforce by 1973. Sheet metal workers, for example, had 1 percent minorities in 1969; because of retirements and attrition it hired about 10 percent new workers annually. That union could qualify for a contract if it made "a good faith effort" to have between 4 and 8 percent minorities by the end of 1970, escalating to between 19 to 23 percent by the end of 1973. Thus, the union was "in compliance." If it did not comply, the contractor would trigger an investigation and in the future might not be eligible for federal funds. "We must set goals, targets and timetables," Fletcher told reporters a month after the lunar landing in July 1969. "The way we put a man on the moon in less than ten years was with goals, targets and timetables."[3]

Goals and timetables, of course, fulfilled the aim of affirmative action to hire more minorities, but to critics it violated Title VII, for it would mean the preferential hiring with regard to race: The irony of affirmative action.

Was this fair? There are two ways to look at this plan. One is to argue that 4 to 8 percent, even 19 to 23 percent, was an improvement over 1 percent but low because 30 percent of the city was black and since unionized labor was one of the fastest jobs to learn and quickest way to begin the climb into the middle class. A second way was to say that these goals were illegal, a violation of Title VII, and in fact established quotas. Whatever terms the reader decides today, it is interesting to note that, first in 1968 and then again in 1969, both Democratic and Republican administrations adopted basically the same plan.

Why? The national aim was to increase minority employment, change traditional hiring practices, reduce the chances of more urban riots, open federal contract work to all taxpayers. Both administrations decided that the only way to achieve those goals was to use the economic power of the federal government, and that meant establishing some sort of Philadelphia Plan. For the Democrats, who had become the party of civil rights during the 1960s, this way seemed obvious, but not for the Republicans, whose standard-bearer in the previous 1964 election, Barry Goldwater, had supported states rights and voted against the Civil Rights Act. The Republicans were not wed to the civil rights agenda, exemplified by Nixon's southern strategy, so why did this new adminis-tration approve the Philadelphia Plan?

The answer remains somewhat of a mystery. Twenty years later, when historian Hugh Davis Graham asked George Shultz that question, the former labor secretary could not recall the reasons for reviving the plan. Some years later Shultz told historian Dean Kotlowski that in the con-struction industry, "We found a quota system" for black workers. "It was there. It was zero." In 1969 the labor secretary wanted to move beyond the race relations of the past and felt that the key was employment. "I am deeply interested in civil rights matters," Shultz declared on ABC's *Issues and Answers*, "and feel the Department of Labor can—and should—play a significant role in assuring equal opportunities to all Americans." Nixon agreed. Although preoccupied with the nation's other pressing issues, the new president was interested in curbing infla-tion in the housing industry, which he blamed on union wages, encour-aging African American employment, boosting black capitalism, even giving minorities some compensation. Sounding a little like LBJ at Howard University in 1965 and demonstrating that civil rights moral-ity had captured mainstream America, Nixon promised "everybody an equal chance at the line and then giving those who haven't had their chance, who've had it denied for a hundred years, that little extra start that they need so that it is in truth an equal chance." Nixon's "little extra start" was the Philadelphia Plan.

Nixon later wrote in his memoirs that the Philadelphia Plan was "both necessary and right. We would not fix quotas, but would require federal contractors to show 'affirmative action' to meet the goals of increasing minority employment."

Promoting affirmative action was another demonstration that the president flirted with liberalism during his first two years in office. He signed an executive order establishing the Office of Minority Business Enterprise and another order directed the Small Business Administration to "consider the needs and interests of . . . members of minority groups seeking entry into the business community." This action led to the 8(a) program, which slowly and inconsistently granted "set-asides" and contracts to "socially disadvantaged" firms, at first in the ghettos and later throughout the nation. Nixon proposed a Family Assistance Plan, guaranteeing an annual wage, which horrified conservatives who helped defeat it in Congress. He signed Democratic bills that increased federal regulations and expanded the bureaucracy, establishing the Occupational Safety and Health Administration, Drug Enforcement Agency, Office of Management and Budget, and the Environmental Protection Agency. He reformed the selective service system into a fairer lottery and eventually abolished the draft, and he supported the bill that resulted in reducing the voting age to 18 and which became the Twentieth-sixth Amendment to the Constitution.

There was a political reason why this Republican president signed so many Democratic proposals. Nixon was a realist, or as biographer Joan Hoff wrote, an "aprincipled pragmatist." In 1968 Nixon was elected with the smallest plurality since the 1912 election, only 43 percent, and he had no political coattails the first president elected since 1848 in which the opposition party controlled both the House and the Senate. Thus, Nixon knew that in domestic policy he would have to compromise with the liberals while he focused on his primary interest, foreign policy. Moreover, before the June announcement of the Philadelphia Plan, liberal Democrats attacked the administration's employment policies. The new secretary of transportation proclaimed that highway builders would no longer have to meet federal antidiscrimination standards when bidding on contracts. Although that statement was retracted, the outgoing chairman of the EEOC, Clifford Alexander, fired a salvo: "The public conclusion is inescapable. Vigorous efforts to enforce the laws on employment are not among the goals of this Administration." On Capitol Hill, Senator Edward Kennedy charged that the administration was easing enforcement of rules on equal employment: the administration had awarded a $9 million contract to three southern textile firms who had no affirmative action programs. Some companies who are not in compliance with EEOC regulations, he claimed, were "making millions" off the taxpayers.

Such attacks provoked heated denials from the administration and encouraged Shultz and Nixon to adopt the Philadelphia Plan. Moreover, the plan also provided a political dilemma for the Democrats since it affected two of their main constituents—labor and African Americans. Nixon's aide, John Ehrlichman, explained, "The NAACP wanted a tougher requirement; the unions hated the whole thing. Before long, the AFL-CIO and the NAACP were locked in combat over one of the passionate issues of the day and the Nixon Administration was located in the sweet and reasonable middle."[4]

Actually, there was no sweet middle to affirmative action, which the administration soon learned as opposition mounted. Labor was outraged. "We are 100 percent opposed to a quota system," declared one union leader, "whether it be called the Philadelphia plan or whatever." AFL-CIO's George Meany agreed, carping that Nixon had nominated Haynesworth to the Supreme Court and now his labor secretary was dictating "quotas." He announced at a union meeting that he was disgusted, amazed by Nixon's attack:

> when you figure how small participation of Negroes and other minorities is in . . . the banks of this country, the press, on the payroll for newspapers and communications media. . . . I don't think that when President Nixon looks around his cabinet . . . he sees any black faces in there either. But we in the Building Trades are singled out as 'the last bastion of discrimination.' . . . I resent the action of government officials . . . who are trying to make a whipping boy out of the Building Trades.

The new regulations provoked unrest that autumn. At construction sites across the nation African Americans chanted, "If black men don't work, nobody works." Protests ensued as all-white union crews worked on federal projects in all-black neighborhoods, and demonstrations flared as black men attempted to shut down federally funded construction at the University of Washington, Tuffs University, and the State University of New York at Buffalo.

Confrontations also increased the white backlash. When Pittsburgh's mayor advocated that unions hire more blacks, more than 4,000 angry white workers marched to City Hall with signs, "Wallace in '72" and "We Are the Majority." Violence erupted, resulting in some 50 injuries and over 200 arrested. When Assistant Secretary Fletcher appeared at a meeting in Chicago, 500 white union men jammed into the room, jeering and catcalling, postponing the meeting. The next day, 2,000 construction workers "created havoc" in the downtown area, reported the *Chicago Tribune*, as "hundreds slugged it out with 400 policemen." "I had to wait my turn," complained a white union man, "why should these guys be given special consideration, just because they happen to be black?"

Back in Washington, Comptroller General Staats for the second time in two years ruled that the Philadelphia Plan violated Title VII, again pitting the executive branch against Congress. The Labor and Justice Departments quickly disagreed. Attorney General Mitchell, in a dubious legal maneuver, simply overruled the comptroller, declared the new plan legal since it only set goals, not quotas. The plan "governs only those employers who enter into contracts with the United States, construction contracts financed with Federal assistance." That being the case the executive had the power to ensure that contractors were not discriminating against some citizens. In essence, then, the Nixon administration made the claim that it was not violating Title VII, but in fact upholding the law.[5]

Opposition also appeared in Congress, and one of the most powerful critics showed up in the president's own party, Senator Everett Dirksen. He sent letters to Nixon, Shultz, and Mitchell complaining that the regulations violated Title VII and he was alarmed that a Republican administration would force additional regulations on business. "I myself will not be able to support you on this ill-conceived scheme," Dirksen told the president, and Republicans would fight the plan in the Senate where it "is about as popular as a crab in a whorehouse."

The administration would outlast Dirksen. The senator died of cancer a month later, and Shultz went on the offensive, meeting the press and explaining that the plan only required goals. A "quota is a system which keeps people out," he said. "What we are seeking are objectives to get people in." But in where? At the same time the administration was trying to stall school busing and integration, so obviously they did not mean "in school," nor did they mean "in all jobs," as became apparent in September when the president revealed his target: It "is essential that black Americans, all Americans, have equal opportunity to get into the construction unions," for "in the long run we cannot have construction unions which deny the right of all Americans to have those positions."

While the president attacked unions, Congress attacked the administration. In October North Carolina's Democratic Senator Sam Ervin held hearings, and part of those proceedings concerned various riders to appropriations bills. The riders were complex and were a way to circumvent a direct vote on affirmative action—not wanted by the Nixon administration or by Congress. A rider to help victims of Hurricane Camille asserted that the U.S. comptroller, not the executive branch, should determine who could receive federal aid, grants, or contracts, while another rider sought to make Title VII the nation's only employment law, which was an attack on the Philadelphia Plan.

The congressional hearings were not illuminating. Critics claimed that the "range" of minority workers on a job site was an illegal quota. No it was not, responded an administration official, it was an attempt to get contractors to make a "good faith" effort to hire minorities. Percentages were not quotas, but "goals, targets, ranges." This made no sense to Senator Ervin, who picked up a dictionary and read the definitions of "quota," "goal," and "range," and then said, "I think you have made it as clear as the noonday sun in a cloudless sky that the Philadelphia Plan requires contractors actively to take the race of people into consideration when they employ them." Not to Secretary Shultz, who testified that the administration *did not* intend that contractors hire "on the basis of race but to take affirmative steps to see to it that you expose yourself to people of various races, and you give them an equal chance of employment." Looking straight at Ervin, Schultz then declared, "I quite agree with you that this means that you pay attention to race."

SENATOR ERVIN: In other words, an affirmative action program . . . of the Philadelphia Plan is that in order to achieve hiring without regard to matters of race, a contractor must take into considerations of race in hiring.

SECRETARY SHULTZ: You take them into consideration in that you must provide yourself with a reasonable range of choice in the hiring process. However, that is not the same thing as saying that when it comes to hiring people, you have to decide between A and B on the basis of race. . .

Perplexed, Senator Ervin then moved to the definitions of range, quota, and goal, declaring that in the new Philadelphia Plan he did not see "any difference between those three things." "Well," Secretary Shultz assured him, "I certainly respect that opinion."

Well and good, but what was a quota? The secretary defined it as "a limitation . . . holding something down." What the administration was trying to do, he continued, was "opening of opportunity by getting people to aspire to get out and give a greater crack at these jobs to people in minority groups."

Nothing was clarified by this exchange and little wonder that many Americans have been confused about affirmative action ever since. The Senate responded to the subterfuge on December 18 by passing a rider, 52–37, that imperiled the Philadelphia Plan and mobilized the administration. The next day the Labor Department and White House issued press releases. Shultz declared that the "country's long established commitment to affirmative action for equal job opportunity has been gravely jeopardized by the United States Senate." To him, the "rider is part of an effort by some unions . . . to block affirmative steps to open skilled and high-paying jobs to blacks and other minority groups." Nixon was just as blunt as he stated his definition of affirmative action: "Nothing is more unfair than that the same Americans who pay taxes should by any pattern of discriminatory practices be deprived of an equal opportunity to work on federal construction contracts." The Philadelphia Plan, he continued, "does not set quotas, it points to goals."

The issue then was debated in the House. The administration called on its allies, and House Minority Leader Gerald Ford of Michigan led the charge, declaring that approving the rider meant "you vote to perpetuate job discrimination in Federal contracts," while rejecting it "means that individuals will have the protection of the Federal Government in getting jobs." Others disagreed. Some saw the vote as a separation of powers issue between the comptroller and Congress and the chief executive. Others wondered why the plan concerned only a single industry, construction, when the administration had awarded large contracts to textile firms, which the EEOC had judged as discriminatory employers. A California Democrat was suspicious of Nixon's entire civil rights program, and he read a letter from the NAACP: "It is amazing that the same administration which has sought to destroy the voting rights bill, . . . which has been guilty of outrageous footdragging in school desegregation, now suddenly is on the great crusade to save the Philadelphia Plan."

Nixon came to the rescue. On December 22, as the holiday break approached, the president threatened to keep the House in session if they passed the rider and defeated his policy. The tactic paid dividends—the next day a coalition of moderate Republicans and liberal Democrats defeated the rider, 208 to 156, and then the Senate reversed itself, 39 to 29. Congress went home for the holidays, giving the president his Christmas present—the Philadelphia Plan.

This bizarre vote was significant. It was the first time the U.S. Congress voted on affirmative action. American politicians in Washington had debated the policy in various forms but had not had the courage for a straightforward vote on this crucial public policy: Should the federal government have or not have affirmative action in all contract employment? Instead, the first time the issue was raised it was mired in politics, an indirect vote on a rider over aid for damage caused by a hurricane, and it was demanded by a president who earlier had lost the battle for a Supreme Court justice and who now desperately wanted a victory in Congress. The result was incredible: most House Republicans voted against business to side with their president 3 to 1, while the majority of Democrats voted against civil rights organizations and a policy first proposed by one of their own presidents. By the end of 1969 Americans had forgotten Nixon's promise to "Bring Us Together."

And so it was: The Philadelphia Plan eclipsed Title VII and became the official policy of the U.S. Government. The Nixon administration defined affirmative action as racial goals and timetables, not quotas, and in February 1970 Shultz signed Order No. 4, which expanded the Philadelphia Plan. *All businesses*, not just the construction industry and those unions who accepted a $50,000 federal contract and who hired more than 50 employees, were to have affirmative action plans. This meant that these businesses were to have hiring goals and timetables based on "the percentage of the minority workforce" in their city with the aim of correcting any "underutilization" of minorities "at all levels" of employment. That affected a quarter-million contractors throughout the nation, employing 20 million workers, a third of the labor force.

Order No. 4 was of profound significance. It directly linked the ratio of minorities in a locale with those working on contracted employment, which subsequently established proportional hiring as a way to prove compliance with affirmative action. It protected four minority groups who could receive affirmative action remedies: "Negro, Oriental, American Indian, and Spanish Surnamed Americans." Labor Department employees did all of this with virtually no public discussion on which groups should receive federal protection, no questioning about expanding the original intent of affirmative action—to help African Americans—and no precise definition of terms. Just what were "Spanish surnamed Americans," and did that category include citizens who originated from Spain or Portugal, or was it aimed only at those from Puerto Rico, Mexico, and all of Latin America? Why were Orientals included? Did Japanese and Chinese Americans, who had suffered past discrimination but who in 1970 had higher incomes than the average citizen, need this protection, especially compared to poor whites? In fact, what was a "minority" in this nation of people with ethnically and racially mixed ancestry? These were profound questions—all left unanswered—that later would ignite debates dividing the nation.[6]

Thus, in its first year the Nixon administration greatly extended affirmative action, but it did not have immediate results at the construction site. The government had to impose minority hiring plans on Philadelphia, St. Louis, Atlanta, San Francisco, and Washington D.C., while allowing some three dozen other cities to establish alternate "hometown" plans, which permitted voluntary hiring goals. Throughout 1970 actual results were disappointing. In Philadelphia, the administration aimed at 1,000 new construction jobs for blacks, but by the end of building season in August contractors had hired only 60. In Chicago, where the Labor Department granted almost $500,000 to train minorities with an aim of 4,000 jobs, only 75 were recruited. Hometown plans in Atlanta, Buffalo, New York, and other cities flopped, and the NAACP berated the administration for weak enforcement. Assistant Secretary Fletcher lamented, "Neither the Philadelphia Plan nor the various home-town plans have accomplished a darn thing yet."

A main reason was that unions and some businesses had sued the federal government and were waiting for the courts to rule on affirmative action. The suits challenged the plan as a violation of Title VII, as exceeding the secretary of labor's and president's authority, and as a violation of the Fifth and Fourteenth Amendments. The first significant case began in Ohio as a response to the Johnson administration's plan for Cleveland. There, the federal government was funding a project for Cuyahoga Community College. Breaking with tradition, college authorities rejected the lowest bid, because the contractor, Hyman R. Weiner, did not follow federal guidelines by submitting a bid with goals and timetables stating the approximate number of minorities that would be working on the project. Instead, the bid contained the caveat that Weiner's obligation to hire minorities depended on availability of those workers in local unions. Since there were almost no black union members in the Cleveland locals, Weiner really had no obligation to enforce affirmative action, so college authorities rejected the lower bid, accepted the second, higher bid that would result in black men working on the project.

Weiner sued Cuyahoga Community College, but he failed to persuade the local Ohio court that goals and timetables broke the standard rules of competitive bidding or constituted a "ratio quota system," which violated Title VII and required "preferential treatment ... for the purpose of achieving racial balance." He appealed and in July 1969 *Weiner v. Cuyahoga Community College* was decided by the Ohio Supreme Court, which ruled against Weiner. He appealed again, and the next year the U.S. Supreme Court declined to review the case, allowing it to stand as law.

Federal courts in 1969 also began to define a "quota." In *United States v. Montgomery Board of Education* the court defined it as a system "which restricts or requires participation of a fixed inflexible number or ratio of minorities." That definition supported the administration and its claim that the Philadelphia Plan was a flexible system of goals.

In 1970 federal courts began ruling more directly on the Nixon administration's Philadelphia Plan. The Contractors Association of

Eastern Pennsylvania sued Secretary Shultz, charging that the plan violated Title VII's ban on preferential treatment and the association's collective bargaining agreements with unions and that it was an unconstitutional executive action. The association complained that they were being attacked for their history of discrimination. The case arrived in federal court in March, and the judge ruled that the plan was needed to end an employment practice that "has fostered and perpetuated a system that has effectively maintained a segregated class. That concept, if I may use the strong language it deserves, is repugnant, unworthy, and contrary to present national policy. The Philadelphia Plan will provide an unpolluted breath of fresh air to ventilate this unpalatable situation."

The contractors appealed, and in 1971 Federal Judge John J. Gibbons denied the appeal with a revealing decision that confirmed the irony of affirmative action. Writing for a unanimous bench, he noted that the Philadelphia Plan was merely a more specific version of affirmative action obligations that had been in effect since Kennedy's executive order of 1961. The federal government, he continued, had a legitimate interest in equal employment opportunity because it would result in what Congress had intended in Title VII, nondiscrimination in employment. If Congress meant otherwise, the judge continued, then the legislative branch had the power to pass a law revising Title VII. "Clearly the Philadelphia Plan is color-conscious," the court admitted, and that was inherent in affirmative action but also necessary to expand minority employment in the workforce. Moreover, the Philadelphia plan "merely invited" contractors "to bid . . . with terms imposed." Thus, the "affirmative action covenant is no different in kind than other covenants specified in the invitation to bid." The Philadelphia Plan did not punish "for past misconduct. It exacts a covenant for present performance."

Later in 1971 the Supreme Court ruled for the first time on Title VII of the 1964 Civil Rights Act in *Griggs v. Duke Power Co.* Thirteen black workers at the company's Dan River station in North Carolina brought a class-action suit against their employer, who had admitted employing minorities only as laborers prior to the passage of the 1964 act. After passage, the African Americans asked to be promoted to coal miners, but the company confronted them with a new requirement. To improve the quality of its workforce, Duke now demanded that both black and white miners either have high school degrees or pass an aptitude test. The test was devised by another company who had developed these instruments for many businesses. The exam was welcomed by the white workers, but not by the blacks, for none of them had finished high school; as late as 1960 only 12 percent of black males had graduated from secondary school in North Carolina. They took the test and were confronted with questions such as "does B.C. mean before Christ?" and do "adopt" and "adept" have similar meanings? All of the black laborers failed, and a dozen co-workers filed the suit. Their NAACP lawyers claimed violation of Title VII.

A lower court held that the test did not violate the Civil Rights Act because the tests were professionally developed, given to both black and white employees, and used without intent to discriminate. But the Supreme Court reversed that ruling, 8 to 0, and it supported the interpretation of the law advocated by the EEOC, which was the "disparate impact" theory of discrimination. For years that commission had argued that tests were permitted only if they examined the applicants ability to do the required work. The plaintiffs naturally agreed, for given the history of a segregated school system in the state, tests were "potent tools for substantially reducing Negro opportunities," which operated as "thinly veiled racial discrimination." In fact, the test used by the company screened out nine times as many black as white workers and so had a fundamentally different or disparate impact on minorities. Chief Justice Burger declared that "if an employment practice which operates to exclude Negroes cannot be shown to be related to job performance, the practice is prohibited."

In *Griggs* the Court began to interpret Title VII and they favored the administration's stance on affirmative action. Burger stated that the "objective of Congress in the enactment of Title VII is plain. . . . It was to achieve equality of employment opportunities and remove barriers that have operated in the past." The Civil Rights Act did not order that a person be hired "because he was formerly the subject of discrimination or because he is a member of a minority group." But, he continued, the Court must take into account "the posture and condition of the job-seeker." That sounded like LBJ at Howard University and Nixon in January 1969. In words that resembled a previous federal court ruling on seniority, *Quarles v. Philip Morris*, the chief justice stated that "practices, procedures, or tests neutral on their face, and even neutral in terms of intent, cannot be maintained if they operate to 'freeze' the status quo of prior discriminatory employment practices." To Burger, "Congress directed the thrust of the Act to the consequences of employment practices."

That meant *results*, which validated Johnson and now the Nixon administration's tactic to obtain them—goals and timetables—which the Court did not consider were quotas. In 1971 this definition of affirmative action became the law of the land.

Griggs defined affirmative action for the next two decades. Like the executive branch, the Court showed less concern about the words of Title VII, hiring *without* regard to race, and more interest in minority employment, hiring *with* regard to race. In effect, *Griggs* eliminated the irony of affirmative action: LBJ's 1965 executive order and Title VII became one. The Court basically made fair employment more of a group than an individual right, and it no longer mandated that an employee had to prove that an employer had intended to discriminate; from now on businesses would have to prove that their hiring practices did not discriminate against a group, in this case African Americans, and later, all minorities and women. Burger defined discrimination as "the consequences of employment practices, not simply the motivation." What was the *effect* of a hiring practice or a test, and did that have a disparate impact on one group of citizens? The Court was suspicious of any test that would maintain the status quo or act as "built-in headwinds" for minorities, "and are unrelated to measuring job capability." Both Democratic and Republican administrations realized that forcing contractors to comply by withholding funds was the most efficient, and in some regions the only, way to change traditional employment practices and to open the doors of opportunities for minorities.[7]

Yet changing tradition and hiring more minorities on federally funded projects was difficult, as exemplified by Washington, D.C. The metropolitan area was about 25 percent black, and the district itself about 70 percent. The federal government had appropriated $3 billion to build a quality subway system, the Metro. The Labor Department established the "Washington Plan," which set minimum levels of minority employment in 11 crafts working on the project. To administration officials, this would also encourage another Nixon goal: boosting black capitalism and business growth. But by the summer of 1971, threats and incrimination had deeply divided the city. The Rev. Jerry Moore Jr., a black member of the D.C. City Council, charged the Metro staff with "open hostility" to black construction firms, that the only jobs for minorities were unskilled "pick and shovel work." Metro Chairman Carlton Sickles was outraged, declaring that such charges did "nothing to further the cause and a great deal to harm it." A coalition of prominent African Americans then demanded a fourth of the $3 billion, $750 million in construction work for black firms. That was unrealistic, Sickles responded, for while he supported more minority workers, black contractors would "all fall on their faces" because they did not have the necessary experience to build such a large project. By the end of the year very few black contractors had bid on the Metro, and only $2 million had gone to those firms out of the $300 million spent. While some African Americans declared that they would hold demonstrations at Metro construction sites, Sickles lamented, "We have a tremendous communications problem with the black community."

These were difficult years in America. Everyone seemed angry, as many new groups were demanding empowerment. In 1971 Hispanics launched their first national campaign against inequality, filing a suit against the federal government. About 7 percent of citizens had Spanish surnames, but Latinos comprised less than 3 percent of federal workers, mostly concentrated in menial jobs. California congressman Edward Roybal declared that the government "has acted immorally and illegally" and "has perpetuated this caste system and turned the ideal of equal employment into another American myth." The plaintiffs demanded freezing all federal hiring and promotions for 90 days while the government developed a plan to eliminate discrimination against them. Again for the first time, the American Civil Liberties Union filed a class-action suit against the federal government on behalf of four employees who claimed that they had been dismissed only because "they were either homosexuals, reputed to be homosexuals or had associated publicly with persons known to be homosexuals." The ACLU charged "no compelling governmental interest" in the sexual practices of federal employees and demanded reinstatement of the plaintiffs.

Yet no group was making more demands to end discrimination than were women. In August 1970 they formed a massive coalition and held a major demonstration, the Women's Strike for Equality. With the slogan "Don't Iron While the Strike is Hot," hundreds of thousands boycotted work, invaded offices, deposited children at husbands' desks, and marched down main streets in the first major feminist demonstration in half a century. They demanded equal pay, education, and job opportunities, along with child-care centers and the right to an abortion. The message was clear, as Kate Millett declared to a crowd of 40,000 in New York City: "Today is the beginning of a new movement."

It was, for studies demonstrated widespread discrimination. Protective labor laws mandated that in 17 states women could not work in mines, in 10 they could not tend bar, while in others they could not work at night unless they were nurses or telephone operators. When baby-boomer females graduated from college and searched for jobs, they realized that professional and management positions were reserved for men and that their future was limited to the Ts—Teach, Type, and Take Temperatures. A Harvard Business School survey of one thousand male executives found that only a third would give females management opportunities. The same was true for law firms. Ruth Bader Ginsburg, who graduated first in her class at Columbia University, could not get a job offer nor a judicial clerkship. "Does she wear skirts?" inquired Supreme Court Justice Felix Frankfurter when he was asked to consider Ginsburg. He refused, saying, "I can't stand girls in pants!" This attitude was not much more enlightened at the nation's universities. Funded by male and female taxpayers directly or in grants, both public and private institutions still advertized for "male professors," with the result that UCLA had only 7 percent female professors, only 2 percent at Columbia, although their graduate schools awarded 25 percent of doctorates to women. Blocked from most professions, women took home lower paychecks. Female workers in the 1950s earned about 64 cents for every dollar earned by a male, but during the 1960s that figure declined to about 58 cents. As *Time* noted, "the status of American women is, in many ways, deteriorating."

"What is women's liberation?" Marilyn Salzman Webb asked. "It is simply organized rage against real oppression," and those feelings appeared forcefully in courts across the nation as women's organizations attacked with scores of lawsuits. Women's Equity Action League, WEAL, sued 350 universities for sex discrimination, including the entire state college systems in California, Florida, New Jersey, and New York, and all of the nation's medical and law schools. All received taxpayer's funding and federal contracts, but WEAL claimed that they did not treat female taxpayers equally in admissions, financial assistance, hiring practices, salaries, or promotions. NOW agreed, and it filed a class-action suit against all public schools on the grounds that they discriminated in salaries, promotion, and maternity benefits. Feminists filed complaints against 1,300 major corporations that received federal funds or contracts, demanding goals and timetables for equal employment, and they sued many unions and companies, such as Southern Pacific, General Motors, Colgate-Palmolive, and American Airlines.

Rage also reached the halls of Congress. In March 1971 the House of Representatives held the first hearings in more than twenty years on the Equal Rights Amendment to the U.S. Constitution. The ERA aimed to eliminate state laws and some federal practices that activists claimed were discriminatory, at the same time sexual equality was being written into the Constitution. Manhattan Democrat Bella Abzug led the crusade, declaring "real outrage" that congresswomen were excluded from positions of power in the House. "And as a last straw it is absolutely indefensible that the committee which considers the questions of equal rights for women—the Judiciary Committee—has not a single woman member to represent our interest." Martha Griffiths listed a number of examples of federal discrimination, such as the Air Force setting higher standards for female than for male volunteers, the FBI refusing to hire women to be trained as agents, or the government guaranteeing home loans for banks that discriminated against female buyers.

Naturally there was resistance to the ERA. Senator Sam Ervin declared that amending the Constitution to get rid of such "minor examples" of discrimination was "about as wise as using an atom bomb to exterminate a few mice." But most politicians agreed with the *Los Angeles Times* that equality was "long overdue" and with the *New York Times* that the ERA was an "idea whose time has come." It had, and it passed overwhelmingly in the House that spring and the next year 84 to 8 in the Senate, whereupon it was sent out to the states for ratification.[8]

President Nixon, realizing the overwhelming congressional support for the ERA, wrote a letter that he had supported it since he was a senator in 1951 and again when he ran for the presidency in 1968. While he was busy with more pressing issues, his administration was taking action. The EEOC had issued guidelines in 1969 that declared that state protective labor laws conflicted with Title VII, and in June 1970 the OFCC published its new guidelines on sex discrimination. The EEOC demanded equal treatment for both sexes, single or married, in advertising, recruitment, job opportunities, pay, seniority, and benefits, and banned employer penalties for pregnancy and having children. A contractor could be out of compliance if he employed "fewer minorities or women than would reasonably be expected by their availability," and the new secretary of labor, James Hodgson, ordered all federal contractors to take action to end the "under-utilization of women." The administration began hiring women in all careers in the government, from air traffic controllers to narcotics agents to park rangers, and it began holding up grants and contracts to universities while conducting investigations of 40 institutions, including Harvard, Chicago, and Michigan.

The Justice Department also filed its first sex discrimination case. In 1969 some 7,500 women filed sex discrimination charges with the EEOC, prompting a large review against Libby Owen and its AFL-CIO union. The women charged that the company hired them in only one of five plants in Toledo, Ohio, and that they were assigned to lower paying jobs, violating Title VII. The company defended itself by claiming that Ohio law required special treatment for women in the number of hours they could work and the weight that they could lift, so it was the state that prevented the company from being in compliance with federal law. Such notions were "romantic paternalism," a federal court had declared earlier in *Weeks v. Southern Bell Telephone and Telegraph*; Title VII had vested "women with the power to decide whether or not to take on unromantic tasks." The die was cast. When the case reached the courts in 1970 Libby Owen quickly settled with the Justice Department, agreeing to open jobs to females and to promote women to management positions immediately. That set off alarms in corporate headquarters.

As women marched for the ERA, the Labor Department was quietly becoming more serious about another issue, equal employment opportunities. On a Saturday in early December 1971, the department issued Revised Order 4. The new order was not noticed by the press, but it became what historians later called the "women's employment Magna Carta" because it declared the female majority an "affected class." Revised Order 4 mandated that with the exception of the construction industry, all other businesses holding federal contracts over $50,000 had to submit affirmative action plans—with goals and timetables—for hiring minorities and *women*. Moreover, contractors now had to establish a "utilization analysis" to ensure that the company was employing a reasonable number of women and minorities at all job levels. Specific numbers or goals were not mentioned, not "rigid and inflexible quotas" but "targets reasonably attainable" through a "good faith effort," or the company could face cancellation of its contracts. Thus, the feminist steamroller relatively quickly and quietly won the same affirmative action guidelines that had taken years for African Americans.

To make such orders effective the government needed tougher enforcement, and that issue was addressed a month later in January 1972 as Congress debated amending Title VII of the Civil Rights Act. Commonly called the Equal Employment Opportunity Act, the idea behind the amendment had been floating around liberal circles since Harry Truman proposed it in 1948, the Kerner Commission recommended it in 1967, and the Johnson administration urged Congress to pass it in 1968: giving "cease and desist" power to the Equal Employment Opportunity Commission. "If there is one thing that is clear," declared liberal Joseph Rauh at hearings, "it is that everybody who has been for civil rights has been for cease-and-desist powers, and everybody who has opposed . . . civil rights has been against cease-and-desist powers." In addition, the new bill would close what advocates called the loopholes of the 1964 Act: the exemptions for more than 4 million employees of educational institutions and over 10 million workers of state and local governments. Because of this latter loophole, many southern states still refused to hire their black citizens. The new bill would also expand coverage from businesses employing 25 workers to 8, extending coverage to about 10 million employees, and it would shift responsibility for the federal government's 2.5 million workers from the Civil Service Commission to the EEOC.

The Democrats and the Nixon administration had introduced different bills in 1969, but the nation was focused on law and order and Vietnam. Opponents conducted stalling tactics, and the act did not have a chance of passage until January 1972. Liberal Democrats and some northern Republicans continued pushing for their original bill, but Nixon was opposed to cease and desist powers for the EEOC. A new, powerful regulatory agency that might attack business was a nightmare for Republicans, and the president told his assistant H. R. Halderman, "I will veto the EEOC. Not appealable. Won't discuss it." The administration proposed that the EEOC, instead of merely negotiating with accused contractors, now be given the power to take them to court. Conservatives and southern Democrats opposed any new powers for the agency, and in the Senate they were led by Sam Ervin. Not immune to hyperbole, the senator declared that the "ridiculous" act would "rob all American citizens of basic liberties" and was the "greatest threat of tyrannical power ever presented to the American Congress throughout the history of this Nation." Ervin later offered some amendments to the bill, one of which was a significant attack on affirmative action: "No department, agency, or officer of the United States shall require an employer to practice discrimination in reverse by employing persons of a particular race, or a particular religion, or a particular national origin, or a particular sex in either fixed or variable numbers, proportions, percentages, quotas, goals, or ranges."

The Senate rejected Ervin's amendment 44 to 22. Some proponents cheered, claiming that senators had upheld affirmative action and had granted it congressional approval. But like the hurricane rider in 1969, this was another indirect vote. A third of the Senate was absent, and the amendment was drawn up so quickly and was so confusing that many would not vote for it anyway. Just what was "discrimination in reverse" and was an "officer of the United States" a cabinet member, judge, or any employee, such as a postman?

Again, Congress avoided a direct vote on affirmative action as it passed Nixon's version of the Equal Employment Opportunity Act. The EEOC did not gain cease and desist powers, but now it could file discrimination charges, and that left the courts to decide if an employer had discriminated and violated the law. Both sides compromised on other issues. The bill now covered all businesses and unions with 15 workers (not 25 or 8), state and local government employees (but not elected officials and their advisers), and those working at educational (but not religious) institutions.

In general, this compromise bill left the EEOC supporting goals and timetables for work on government contracts, but not fixed and rigid quotas, which pleased Nixon during the election year 1972. As the president privately wrote, he supported "numerical goals . . . as tools to measure progress which remedies the effect of past discrimination," but they "must not be allowed to be applied in such a fashion as to, in fact, result in the imposition of quotas." That was a very fine line, which was not clarified by Congress.[9]

In 1972, then, the EEOC was receiving an enlarged budget, an expanding staff including scores of attorneys, and was armed with the new power to initiate lawsuits against employers: the tiger now had teeth, and it began to bite. The chairman, African American Republican William H. Brown III, stated that his agency "ought to be filing perhaps 10 or 15 cases every two weeks," and it did. The EEOC charged trade unions in Miami and Detroit and a transport company in Atlanta with race discrimination, and the agency issued new guidelines, which *Business Week* proclaimed, "narrow, almost to a vanishing point, a company's legal grounds for keeping women out of jobs traditionally categorized as 'for men only,' or for barring men from jobs traditionally held by women."

To prove that point, the EEOC charged that General Motors discriminated against women at its St. Louis plant, but the most significant case was against the nation's largest private employer, American Telephone and Telegraph, AT&T, commonly called the Bell system. Bell was an appropriate target. The giant corporation employed 800,000; with retirements and attrition Bell hired 200,000 workers annually, meaning that it would be relatively easy for the company to establish a diverse workforce. The case began when AT&T filed a request with the government for a rate increase. During subsequent hearings the EEOC intervened, since the agency discovered that 5 percent of its growing number of complaints had been filed by the company's workers. Many of those employees were disgruntled, and in summer 1971 a half million workers declared a strike against Bell. Reflecting that the women's liberation movement was sweeping into the rank and file, feminists in Madison, Wisconsin, declared that "women are relegated to the dullest jobs, paid sub-standard wages, and are treated like both small children and slaves. . . . Ma Bell Is a Cheap Mother!"

During summer 1972 the EEOC declared that Bell engaged in "pervasive, systemwide, and blatantly unlawful discrimination in employment against women, blacks, Spanish-surnamed Americans, and other minorities." Presenting 5,000 pages of testimony and statistics, the agency declared that while over half of the corporation's employees were females, women held only 1 percent of career management positions. In unusually tough language the EEOC proclaimed that AT&T was the "largest oppressor of women workers in the U.S."

The corporation responded by presenting 10,000 pages of facts and figures, contending that it had been hiring more women in better positions for years. But eventually the company gave in and in January 1973 signed the first major "consent decree" with the EEOC, which up to that time mandated the largest back-pay settlement in U.S. history. While AT&T did not admit discrimination, it agreed to pay $15 million to 13,000 females and 2,000 minority males, and wage adjustments of another $23 million to be paid annually to 36,000 employees. Those women included some 1,500 college graduates who joined AT&T after Title VII but were barred from management training programs. *Newsweek* declared the payments "reparations."

"Suddenly, a single sweeping settlement," *Newsweek* continued, "gave the back-pay issue unprecedented thrust—and sent corporate executives scurrying for legal advice." As an AT&T vice president lamented, "the rules of the game have been changed."[10]

The administration was beginning to have an impact on the workplace, but the president was moving in the opposite direction. Nixon's support for affirmation action and civil rights always had been tenuous and temporary, and was melting away long before the 1972 election. A man who wrote a thousand-page memoir devoted only about two pages to affirmative action, and the president realized that civil rights leaders distrusted his administration. A 1970 poll published in *Time* declared that Nixon had "almost totally alienated blacks from government." While about two-thirds of blacks had looked to the federal government for leadership in racial affairs under JFK and LBJ, only 3 percent said the same about the Nixon administration.

The president was preoccupied in 1970, not on race issues, but with the Vietnam War. On April 30, 1970, after 16 months of claiming to be "winding down" the war and seeking "peace with honor," Nixon expanded the conflict by ordering the invasion of Cambodia. Activists took to the streets, blocking traffic and holding sit-ins at federal buildings, and students at 60 colleges went on strike. Then—Kent State. Ohio national guardsmen fired more than 60 rounds into a group of students, wounding nine and killing four. That sparked protests across the nation, resulting in demonstrations and strikes that closed 500 campuses, 50 for the remainder of spring semester. To quell the rioting, governors of 16 states had to activate their National Guards: In other words, the government was forced to employ the military to occupy the campuses to curb the insurrection of its own youth.

Nixon called the protesters "bums." Conservatives and a surprising number of union men agreed. Many of these workers were World War II veterans, and they were outraged by the behavior of young college students protesting against their own country. AFL-CIO president George Meany cheered the Cambodian invasion, and on May 20 some 100,000 marched in support of the president, many union men wearing hard hats, including the president of the AFL-CIO New York construction unions, Peter J. Brennan. Workers marched in New York City from Broadway to Wall Street, while on sidewalks antiwar demonstrators held signs; the event quickly degenerated into chaos. Union men charged, injuring 70 antiwar activists and prompting one observer to note that the workers "went through those demonstrators like Sherman went through Atlanta." That impressed Nixon, and he invited construction workers to the White House. With cameras clicking, Nixon donned a hard hat and congratulated the men for their support.

With increasing union support, and none from African Americans, Nixon moved away from his own affirmative action policy. As aide William Safire recalled of the Philadelphia Plan, "the zip went out of that integration effort after the hard hats marched in support of Nixon on the war." The administration decreased pressure on unions and gave more support to voluntary hometown plans. "The Nixon administration is destroying the Philadelphia Plan," declared the NAACP's Herbert Hill, which was a "pay-off to the building-trades unions for their support of the war in Indochina." The plans were a fraud, he continued, "a meaningless hodgepodge of quackery and deception, of doubletalk and doublethink." The administration now shifted personnel, including the most effective advocate of the Philadelphia Plan, Arthur Fletcher. After the president held a meeting with Brennan, Fletcher was forced out of the Labor Department. Nixon and his officials quietly promised union leaders that they would relax nondiscrimination efforts after the presidential election, which they did, and George Meany refused to support Democratic presidential candidate Senator George McGovern.

During the 1972 election campaign Nixon totally abandoned his own policy, and in a curious twist he now began labeling the Democrats the "quota party." The president was fortunate, for Senator McGovern claimed that he did not endorse quotas but repeatedly told blacks and other minority groups that they should receive appointment to federal jobs based on their proportion in the population. Nixon pounced, labeling McGovern the "quota candidate," claiming quotas were "alien" to the American way of life and embracing the "merit system" at the Republican Convention:

> Every man, woman, and child should be free to rise as far as his talents, and energy, and ambitions will take him. That is the American dream. But into that dream there has entered a specter, the specter of a quota democracy—where men and women are advanced not on the basis of merit or ability, but solely on the basis of race, or sex, or color, or creed. . . . You do not correct an ancient injustice by committing a new one.

Nixon also signed an order on August 17 prohibiting the use of quotas in minority hiring for federal contracts, which bewildered everyone. At the White House, adviser William Safire wondered about a "clear definition" of the Philadelphia Plan "and how different this all is from the quota system we oppose?" The *Washington Post* was more direct, asking the sobering questions: If quotas were not being used, then "why was the President's directive issued at all?" Why did the Justice Department earlier in March ask a "federal court to order Mississippi to fill half of its State Highway Patrol vacancies with members of minority groups?" Why in July 1971 did the "federal government impose a racial quota system on the St. Louis construction industry," along with Washington, D.C., and the Philadelphia Plan? And why did the Office of Economic Opportunity agree "to employ at least 37 percent women and 38 percent total minority workers at all levels in its offices nationwide within a year?"

In September the administration continued running away from its own past. An official said the Labor Department was "considering a major restructuring" of 55 hometown plans—and the "controversial" Philadelphia Plan—and Labor Secretary Hodgson wrote a memorandum stating that previous goals might have been "misinterpreted or misapplied" by contractors, that goals now were merely "targets" and that failure to reach them would not be regarded as a violation. "All that remained," wrote John David Skrentny, "was for America to forget that it was the Republican Nixon who pushed racial quotas through a formerly reluctant Congress."[11]

Forgetting was not difficult in the heat of the campaign, for the voters were much more concerned about other topics. The economy was in a tailspin, with rising inflation and mounting unemployment. Women were calling for liberation and demanding equality, pushing for job opportunities and the ERA. Candidate McGovern was charging the administration's complicity in the strange break-in of Democratic headquarters at the Watergate complex, which few believed, while almost everyone hoped for the end of the endless war in Vietnam. Two weeks before the election, Nixon's national security adviser, Henry Kissinger, returned from negotiations in Paris and declared, "Peace is at hand." It was not, just a campaign stunt, but it was the message that citizens had wanted to hear for years. At the polls, Nixon overwhelmed McGovern. A few months later Nixon named a new secretary of labor— Peter J. Brennan.

The taste of victory, however, was not lasting; early in 1973 the Senate began conducting hearings on the break-in at Watergate, chaired by Senator Sam Ervin. Those investigations would devour the remainder of the presidency of Richard Nixon.

Watergate would torment Nixon and the nation, but it had a more subtle impact on affirmative action. Armed with the power to bring corporations to court, buoyed by increased funding and more attorneys, optimistic after the success against AT&T, and now without a chief executive to curtail its actions, the EEOC began the most aggressive enforcement policy in its history. With a massive backlog of cases, the agency consolidated hundreds of individual complaints, and in April and May 1973 it filed ninety discriminations suits. In September the agency charged many major unions with discrimination, including the United Auto Workers, and leveled the same charges against Sears, General Electric, General Motors, and even a company that had boasted about its fair employment practices, the Ford Motor Company. The following year there were more suits, including a major one against Goodyear Tire and Rubber and Uniroyal. "The pace of litigation appears relentless," declared a law professor, who predicted a continuation of "systematic litigation against major, visible corporations." Job discrimination will end, one EEOC official stated, "when companies learn that it is going to cost them more money in back pay and litigation . . . than it is worth to continue current practices."

That was the case. The EEOC ordered Bethlehem Steel's plant in Sparrows Point, Maryland, to end the effects of years of discriminatory practices. Three years after passage of Title VII over 80 percent of African American workers at the plant still were employed in the lowest-paid segregated labor units. The company agreed to open all jobs, but black workers who transferred lost their seniority, prompting threats from the Labor Department that the corporation would be cut from government contracts. This opened the steel industry to scrutiny, involving some 700,000 employees, and in 1974 nine steel companies and the United Steelworkers paid almost $31 million in back pay to 40,000 female and minority workers at 225 facilities. "It's the first industry-wide agreement," declared a department lawyer, "and it's the largest." The accord also set timetables in which half the openings in trade and craft positions would be filled by minorities and women, and those workers would eventually be selected for 25 percent of management training.

The Labor Department also went after the trucking industry, suing more than 250 companies. Combined with the AT&T case, the Justice Department and EEOC quickly obtained consent decrees that included goals, timetables, and back pay against companies that had over two million workers. That shocked the business community, and many began reviewing their employment procedures. Companies understood one thing, noted *Business Week*, "The cash deterrent to discrimination."

These rulings and consent decrees, *Newsweek* declared, were "working very radical changes in American business," and that was the result of the Equal Employment Opportunity Act, the new Age Discrimination in Employment Act, protecting workers ages 40 to 65, and the Rehabilitation Act, which outlawed discrimination against the handicapped. Previously, antidiscrimination action had usually concerned a small proportion of society, often African American and Hispanic men, but by the mid-1970s the government was investigating thousands of complaints from all minorities, women, and older citizens, especially drivers and pilots complaining about mandatory retirement—and that increased the pool to a majority of Americans. A White House official stated that the rulings were having "absolutely thunderous implications for our society."

Indeed, for by the mid-1970s minorities and women were winning significant victories, which could been seen on construction sites, exemplified by the building of the Metro in Washington, D.C. Mayor Walter E. Washington took a dramatic step, mandating a strong affirmative action program in which all private companies doing business or having contracts with city hall would have to submit plans with goals "to advance the hiring of minorities *and* women." By 1974 minority firms had won few contracts to build the subway, distressing many District of Columbia members who sat on the Metro board, and they began to veto contracts for new construction. That jeopardized the construction of many important Metro stops—Capitol South, Union Station, Smithsonian, L'Enfant Plaza, Pentagon—which the federal government wanted completed by the celebrations planned for the 1976 Bicentennial. After intense negotiations, city officials unanimously adopted a program that set goals of 10 percent minority participation for building the larger structural construction projects for the subway, and 20 percent for the less skilled finishing work, a plan that encouraged partnerships and joint ventures between white and minority firms. The *Washington Post* hailed the breakthrough as "a landmark program . . . that will test Metro's determination to change its approach to the issue of building black economic capability as it builds the subway."

Empowerment surged on. More than twenty states quickly ratified the Equal Rights Amendment, the Supreme Court ruled in *Roe v. Wade*, legalizing abortion, and voted for the first time on the 1963 Equal Pay Act, upholding it and ruling that employers must pay men and women equal wages for essentially the same work, a decision that cost Corning Glass Works $1 million in back pay. Congress passed and the president signed Title IX, which prohibited sex discrimination in educational programs and led to the growth of female sports at universities. AT&T made a surprise announcement in 1974 that from now on it would not discriminate against homosexuals in hiring and employment, that a worker's "sexual tendencies or preferences are strictly personal," which the Gay Task Force hailed as the first significant strike against gay employment discrimination.[12]

The federal government was also scrutinizing employment practices at colleges and professional schools. "The universities haven't even grasped the upheaval they face," declared a government official. Prompted by discrimination suits filed by women's organizations, the

Department of Health, Education, and Welfare issued new rules that universities that accepted federal funds, except military and some religious institutions, could no longer have "sex based quotas" or discriminate against women in admissions, course offerings, facilities, or other services. HEW also demanded that those institutions advertise faculty positions publicly (attacking the "old boy" tradition of job placement), allow husbands and wives to teach at the same college, and begin affirmative action programs with goals for hiring both women and minority faculty members. HEW had power. Federal contracts to the University of Michigan alone amounted to $60 million and more than $70 million for the University of California, and it startled academe by delaying over $20 million in research funds to a dozen universities until they established appropriate "equal employment opportunity" plans.

"Faculty Backlash," *Newsweek* declared. Alarmed, male professors organized, and some 500 joined the Committee on Academic Nondiscrimination and Integrity, which was led by scholars such as Sidney Hook of New York University, Eugene Rostow of Yale Law School, Nathan Glazer of Harvard, and Paul Seabury of the University of California, Berkeley. "To comply with HEW orders," declared Berkeley political scientist Seabury, "every department must come up not with the *best* candidate, but with the best-qualified *woman* or *non-white* candidate." Because of this order "large numbers of highly qualified scholars will pay with their careers simply because they are male and white."

Jewish organizations and professors were particularly alarmed and had become increasingly concerned about affirmative action. During the 1972 election campaign, the American Jewish Committee wrote both candidates urging them not to support "timetable programs and goals for minority hiring," which they felt were really quota systems. Columbia's president William J. McGill stated that many of his Jewish faculty members remembered the 1930s "when America's best colleges were rampant with anti-Semitism," including quotas to limit their admission and hiring. The situation had improved markedly, he continued, and had now reversed so that "Jews are represented on university faculties far out of proportion with their representation in the population. Affirmative action goals or quotas or whatever your call them ... can only convince Jewish faculty that an effort is afoot once more to exclude them from universities and that simple excellence no longer counts in matters of university appointments."

"Nonsense," answered Bernice Sandler, who had been denied a job at the University of Maryland because she "came on too strong as a woman." Colette Seiple of Berkeley agreed: "The white male has not had to compete with anybody and now he suddenly has to compete with blacks and women. He views that as reverse discrimination." Sandler added, "I wish those Jewish men who are so concerned about affirmative action would become concerned about Jewish women."

The battle was on for the Ivory Tower. Seabury complained that it was ridiculous to recruit faculty based, not on scholarship but on "statistically under-represented" groups: "Blacks, Irish, Italians, Greeks, Poles, and all other Slavic groups (including Slovaks, Slovenes, Serbs, Czechs, and Croatians) are under-represented," he declared, and so are Catholics, and even Republicans. His department had only "two Republicans in a department of thirty-eight . . . . Yet I doubt that even Nixon's HEW crusaders for equality of results would tread into this minefield of blatant inequality." Others added that only 1 percent of Ph.D's were black at that time and only 13 percent were women, meaning that it was difficult or impossible to conform to HEW's demands and hire quality faculty from the pool of female and minority applicants. "To put it shortly but accurately," Irving Kristol declared, "a discriminatory quota system—based on race, color, religion, sex, and national origin—has been imposed upon college faculties." HEW bureaucrats were the culprits, Kristol continued, for they claim "that a 'goal' plus a 'timetable' does not add up to a 'quota.' Of all the lies to emanate from Washington in recent years, this is . . . the most dispiriting—it is such a blatant lie, perceived by everyone involved to be a lie, in elementary logic a lie, on the record a lie."

"Balderdash," responded HEW's J. Stanley Pottinger. "That is the biggest crock I have ever heard." There are no quotas, he declared, just goals, and Labor Department guidelines state that goals "may not be rigid and inflexible quotas that must be met." City College of New York exemplified the problem; the English Department had 104 faculty members, but just 15 were females, and only one was tenured. Ann Scott of NOW declared that resistance on campus was just "a move to consolidate the 'old boy' system of male superiority," and HEW's Mary M. Leeper added, "If one-tenth of the energy spent by the academic community on criticizing the affirmative action program were devoted to helping us solve our problems, we would be much, much farther ahead."

A. Philip Randolph and others picket outside the Democratic National Convention, July 1948. *Bettman/CORBIS*

President Truman, the first president to address the NAACP, on the steps of the Lincoln Memorial. *Harry S. Truman Presidential Library*

President Kennedy discussing equal employment at a press conference two days after signing the affirmative action executive order, March 1961. Behind him is his assistant press secretary, Andrew J. Hatcher. *Abbie Rowe, White House, John F. Kennedy Library, Boston*

Congresswoman Martha Griffiths, who added "sex" to the 1964 Civil Rights Act. *Library of Congress, Prints and Photographs Division, photo by Warren K. Leffler for U.S. News & World Report*

President Johnson walking into the crowd after his important affirmative action speech at Howard University, June 1965. *Lyndon B. Johnson Library, photo by Yoichi Okamoto*

President Johnson meeting with corporate leaders to enlist their support for affirmative action hiring and job training, January 1968. *Lyndon B. Johnson Library, photo by Mike Geissinger*

Civil rights demonstrators demanding union jobs for African Americans near a construction site in Pittsburgh, August 1969. *AP/WIDE WORLD PHOTOS*

Arthur Fletcher, with George Shultz, defending the Philadelphia Plan at a news conference, December 1969. *National Archives/Nixon Library 2672–22*

Eleanor Holmes Norton, the first woman to head the EEOC, at her Senate confirmation hearing, 1977. *Historical Picture Collection, Equal Employment Opportunity Commission*

Allan Bakke leaving his first day of class at U.C. Davis Medical School with plainclothes security officers helping him through a crowd of reporters, September 1978. *Bettman/CORBIS*

The Anti-Affirmative Action team in the 1980s. From left: John Svahn, Edwin Meese, President Reagan, William French Smith, and William Bradford Reynolds. *Courtesy of the Ronald Reagan Library*

EEOC Chairman Clarence Thomas with President Reagan, 1985. *Courtesy of the Ronald Reagan Library*

After President Bush labeled the 1990 Civil Rights
Legislation a "quota bill," he signed the 1991 Civil Rights Act.
George Bush Presidential Library

UCLA students rally for affirmative
action admission preferences, April 1995.
Los Angeles Times, photo by Paul Morse, 1995

Ward Connerly and Pete Wilson at the
University of California Board of Regents
meeting where the regents eliminated
affirmative action, July 1995. *Jim Wilson/The
New York Times*

ADMISSIONS

IT'S HIS FAULT!

DAUGHTER of ALUM   SON of BIG DONOR   SOCCER PLAYER   RAISED in DISTANT STATE   MINORITY   DIDN'T GET IN

The Washington Post Writers Group. Reprinted with permission

Barbara Grutter and Jennifer Gratz, two of the plaintiffs in the University of Michigan cases, on that campus in 2003. *AP/WIDE WORLD PHOTOS*

A nation divided. U.C. Berkeley student Louis Alberto Barocio-Uribe and University of Michigan student Adam Dancy react to the Supreme Court rulings in the University of Michigan cases, June 2003. *Alex Wong/Getty Images*

Many scholars agreed and subsequently formed the Committee for Affirmative Action in Universities.[13]

As academics bickered over employment policies, Richard Nixon resigned in disgrace, and Vice President Gerald Ford moved into the White House. Unfortunately for the new president, he inherited the worst economic downturn since the Great Depression, with rising unemployment, stagnant production, and almost 14 percent inflation, what economists dubbed "Stagflation." "The state of the union," Ford admitted too optimistically, "is not good."

During the brief Ford administration, affirmative action took a back seat, while enforcement stumbled along. When HEW released regulations on increasing opportunities for women and minorities at the nation's colleges, critics pounced, claiming that the plan was ridiculous. Over the next 30 years at Berkeley, for example, the university was supposed to hire 100 new women and minority faculty, including "1.38 blacks in the social welfare department, 0.19 women in the engineering department, 0.05 American Indians in the dramatic arts department, and 1.40 Orientals in the architecture department." HEW retracted the regulations and allowed numerous universities to collect federal funds without approved affirmative action plans. As a Harvard personnel official said, "there is clearly a retreat in Washington from affirmative action."

That was the case during the Ford administration. EEOC had a backlog of 124,000 cases, and the agency was attempting to locate some 12,000 complainants to see if they were still interested, if they had moved or found other jobs—even if they were still alive. The Office of Federal Contract Compliance did not even have a director for six months, and the regulations overlapped and created confusion. The government had 1,800 compliance officers, but they were spread out in 18 agencies. Thus the Defense Department policed some industries, HEW supervised universities, and the Treasury Department regulated bank hiring and promotions. The new director of the OFCC confessed, "We don't even know how many employers we cover."

Affirmative action "chugged along in low gear," declared *Business Week,* and the main reason was the slumping economy and the nation's focus having shifted to the 1976 presidential campaign. President Ford won his party's nomination, but only after a bruising battle with former California Governor Ronald Reagan. Confronted by conservatives in his own party, Ford ran against "big government," declaring that "a government big enough to give us everything we want is a government big enough to take from us everything we have." That surprised many, since earlier he had named as his vice president one of the most liberal Republicans in the nation, former New York Governor Nelson Rockefeller. For the 1976 election he dropped Rockefeller altogether and picked a more conservative running mate, Senator Bob Dole of Kansas.

The Democratic nominee was the former Georgia governor, Jimmy Carter. "Jimmy Who?" pundits asked when he began his campaign, but soon Carter was well known, for he had many valuable assets. He was not involved in Watergate and was not from "that mess in Washington." As a governor he had promoted integration and racial tolerance in the South, and this self-proclaimed "peanut farmer," Mr. Everyman, continually talked of old-fashioned virtues. "Trust me," he said, "I would not tell a lie," which seemed refreshing after Nixon. Moreover, he was a perceptive politician who demonstrated a keen ability to appeal to all sides of the political spectrum, shrewdly sidestepping the most controversial issues of the campaign—abortion, busing, amnesty for Vietnam draft dodgers, and the economy. Thus, a poll showed that liberal voters thought that he was a liberal, moderates believed him a moderate, and conservatives viewed him a conservative. "Who is Jimmy Carter?" one of his rivals asked while a writer joked, "He has more positions than the *Kama Sutra*."[14]

It was a close election. Carter won 52 percent and a main reason for his victory was that he captured a stunning 94 percent of the black vote. That made the difference in Ohio, Pennsylvania, Texas, and also delivered him every southern state except Virginia. "Black people have a claim on Jimmy Carter—a strong one," declared National Urban League's Vernon Jordan. With a black unemployment rate double that of whites, 25 percent in some cities, Jordan demanded jobs and also a "massive attempt to solve the problems of older, slum-ridden cities through a domestic Marshall plan."

There would be no plan, for the time had passed and the economic recession was too deep, partly caused by oil embargos, which in turn resulted in soaring prices and long lines at gas stations. The new president had inherited a budget with large deficits, and he was too conservative for any massive spending projects. Moreover, he would become preoccupied with the economic and energy crises, with diplomatic issues concerning human rights, Vietnamese refugees, recognition of China, the Panama Canal treaty, and the Middle East and subsequent Camp David Accords. Carter did name more minorities and women to his administration than any previous president, including 37 black federal judges—more than all previous administrations combined—the first African American woman to the cabinet: Patricia Harris, and heading the EEOC, Eleanor Holmes Norton. The president eventually proposed a national urban plan, but it was very limited and failed to pass through Congress.

More successful was the administration's 1977 Public Works Act, which Carter signed into law to pump $4 billion into the flagging economy. It included a "set-aside" provision that attracted little attention but would later become controversial: 10 percent of the federal grants spent each year for public works would be allocated for "minority business enterprises" if they were available in the local area. Such companies had to be at least 50 percent owned or controlled by "Negroes, Spanish-speaking, Orientals, Indians, Eskimos, and Aleuts." Also important, the following year the president signed the Pregnancy Discrimination Act, codifying the ban issued by the EEOC, and he issued executive order 12067. It reorganized the OFCC into the Office of Federal Contract Compliance Programs and, more significantly, mandated the EEOC to provide leadership and coordinate efforts of all federal policies and regulations that "require equal employment opportunity without regard to race, color, religion, sex, national origin" and which now included "age or handicap."

The Carter administration's initial stance on affirmative action was cautious and somewhat confusing. In one of his first appearances in June 1977, the new Secretary of Health, Education, and Welfare, Joseph Califano Jr., used the term "quota"; after the uproar Califano apologized, stating that he had made a mistake using the "nerve-jangling word." "Arbitrary quotas will not be part of our enforcement program," he declared later. "We want to rely on the good faith and special effort of all who join in the final march against discrimination. But we will also rely—because we must rely—on numerical goals as benchmarks of progress." Carter did not clarify the situation. He surprised many liberal supporters, and dismayed blacks, when he was asked his views in a press conference: "I hate to endorse the proposition of quotas for minority groups, for women or for anyone else that contravenes the concept of merit selection." While he felt that the government, business, and colleges should compensate for past discrimination, he stated later that he also felt that racial quotas for jobs or education were "unconstitutional." That statement resulted in a spirited debate within the administration between Carter and Patricia Harris, Andrew Young, and Califano, all of whom supported "goals," "benchmarks," or "numerical measures" in college admissions and employment. In a cabinet meeting that June, Attorney General Griffin Bell agreed with Califano, adding that the nation would "not be able to eliminate past discrimination unless we have goals." By August Harris informed the cabinet that minorities were "nervous and uncomfortable" about the administration's commitment to civil rights, and Young urged the president to hold a White House conference with black leaders to "discuss our future directions and priorities." During the confusion a HEW official stated, "We're negotiating hundreds and hundreds of affirmative action plans. Any chink in that armor—any statement casting doubt on affirmative action—would set us back tremendously." Eventually, and like Nixon and Johnson before him, Carter called for goals.

"It was dues-collection time for blacks," noted the *Nation* six months into the new administration. "But Jimmy Carter was not paying up." One reason was that just four months after he moved into the White House, pollster George Gallup asked citizens a very significant question: "Some people say that to make up for past discrimination, women and members of minority groups should be given preferential treatment in getting jobs and places in college. Others say that ability, as determined by test scores, should be the main consideration." The poll's results were reported nationally and were surprising. While 53 percent supported federal programs to provide free education or vocational courses that would enable minorities to improve their test scores, Americans favored tests over preferential treatment 8 to 1. That included 82 percent of women and 64 percent of nonwhites. As Gallup concluded, "Not a single population group supports affirmative action."[15]

One major reason for that response was that respondents often misunderstood a question on a controversial topic, which had not been clearly defined for the public—as social scientists later discovered—but in 1977 the Gallup Poll was reported nationally and inspired more debate over affirmative action, which now took on a more ominous tone. "Reverse Discrimination," declared *U.S. News*, "Has It Gone Too Far?" "We have no openings for you now," a Chicago newspaper told a white woman, "We're hiring only Latinos and blacks."

As newspapers and magazines printed many such articles, academics joined the fray. Benjamin Ringer of Hunter College penned "Affirmative Action, Quotas, and Meritocracy"; Allan Ornstein of Loyola University of Chicago called for "Quality, Not Quotas." Others published books. Alan Goldman pondered *Justice and Reverse Discrimination*, and Barry Gross questioned *Discrimination in Reverse: Is Turnabout Fair Play?* Nathan Glazer labeled the government's policy *Affirmative Discrimination*.

"Is Equal Opportunity Turning into a Witch Hunt?" asked *Forbes*, and others wondered if the program was getting a little out of hand. "Now, a Drive to End Discrimination Against 'Ugly' People," wrote *U.S. News* followed by "Short People—Are They Being Discriminated Against?" Then there was the "Weighty Problem," in *Newsweek*, and the result, according to *U.S. News*, "Fat People Fight Back."

"Anti-Discrimination Run Amuck," declared one magazine editor, and *Time* called for "Sensible Limits of Non-Discrimination." And so did the *Washington Post* after Robert Edward Lee, a retired Navy captain, changed his name to Roberto Eduardo Leon and then demanded preferential treatment from his employer, Montgomery County, Virginia. The county refused, and the newspaper found it "heartening to learn that some portion of the world's idiocy has been exposed or removed."

Even some African Americans began to question affirmative action. Conservative economics professor Thomas Sowell opposed what he called "compensatory education" and asked, "Are Quotas Good for Blacks?" Not to him, and the *Washington Post* columnist William Raspberry wondered about the difference between goals and quotas, asking, "Affirmative Action: How Much Is Enough?"[16]

Such questions would be left to the Supreme Court, which continued to refine its definition of affirmative action. In 1976 the Court ruled on *Runyon v. McCrary*, 7 to 2, which gave African Americans the right to use a section of the Civil Rights Act of 1866 to sue employers—and to collect damages. All other plaintiffs could sue under Title VII, and, if successful, would receive back pay only. In *Runyon* the Court in effect elevated blacks to a special status in front of the bench, but that was not its position concerning another topic, which affected many more citizens during the recession, that of seniority, or as *Time* asked, "Who Gets the Pink Slip?" The rule had been "last hired, first fired," but minorities and women had made tremendous gains since the 1960s and did not want to see those advances wiped out in one economic slump—which would happen if traditional work rules were enforced. The NAACP argued for "racial ratios" in which a plant would maintain the same proportion of black workers after a layoff as it had before, an idea which naturally angered senior white male workers. A number of cases were filed during the mid-1970s, such as *Watkins v. Local No. 2369, Dawkins v. Nabisco, Bales v. General Motors*, as businesses and their unions lined up against women and minorities. In June 1977 a divided Supreme Court ruled in a complicated truck-driver case, *Teamsters v. United States*: "Although a seniority system inevitably tends to perpetuate the effects of . . . discrimination," wrote Justice Potter Stewart for the majority, "the Congressional judgement was that Title VII should not outlaw the use of existing seniority lists and thereby destroy or water down the vested seniority rights of employees."

Seniority was upheld in the workforce, which some liberals and civil rights advocates felt was a setback. A year later the Court ruled on another part of affirmative action, how it affected college admissions, in a case that concerned an engineer who wanted to become a medical doctor—Allan Bakke.

The Bakke case resulted from the desire to create a much larger black professional and middle class, and from African American, Chicano, Native American, Asian, and women students who demanded classes on their own culture, literature, and history taught by professors who looked like them. The faculty search was on, and it would take many years to train those graduate students, for in 1970 only 1 percent of all Ph.D.'s in the nation were African American. Other deans aimed to attract black and brown students to professional schools in an attempt to create more minority doctors, dentists, and lawyers. Some universities had developed flexible admission plans, which considered the applicant's race, along with grades, test scores, personal characteristics, geographical origin, parents' alumni status, and such talents as the ability to compose a sonata, write a play, or pass a football. Such a policy had resulted in Harvard's all-white-male classes in the 1950s becoming over 40 percent female, 8 percent black, 6 percent Asian, and 5 percent Hispanic by the late 1970s. Other universities established admission programs that had strict numerical targets for minority enrollments.

One such program was at the medical school of the University of California at Davis. Medical and legal societies had called on educators to increase the percentage of blacks attending those programs from about 3 percent in 1970 to a more representative ratio of the population. In that year, for example, there were only about a dozen black doctors in Arkansas and about the same number of Native American attorneys in the entire nation. Like many professional schools, Davis responded by establishing its own affirmative action admission program. California's population was more than a quarter minority, and each year the medical school accepted 100 students, of which they reserved 16 places for "disadvantaged" applicants, meaning minorities. Without such special preference programs, the Educational Testing Service reported, only about a third of minority students enrolled in professional schools would qualify and be admitted. But with such programs the percentage of black students in medical schools reached 9 percent nationally in 1977 and 8 percent in law schools. While there were problems with a higher minority dropout rate, even conservative college administrators supported such programs during the 1970s, most agreeing with an Ohio State dean who declared, "A university doesn't deserve to call itself a university if it's not diverse."

Diversity was becoming vogue, but Allan Bakke was not diverse. In fact he was rather typical for an American of Norwegian ancestry growing up in Minnesota. Blond and blue-eyed, almost six feet tall, he earned an engineering degree from the University of Minnesota and then served his country, rising to U.S. Marine captain on his tour of duty in Vietnam. After the service he moved to California and worked as an engineer for a NASA laboratory. His real interest, however, was medicine, and he attended night classes and took the chemistry and biology prerequisites for medical school. In 1972, at age 32, he applied to eleven medical schools, including Davis, writing on his application, "More than anything else in the world, I want to study medicine."

So did more than 2,400 other applicants that year who applied to Davis. Bakke's grades were good, 3.45 grade point average on a 4.0 scale, and he scored better than the average applicant on the Medical College Admission Test, but he applied later than most, and almost all of the 84 positions had been taken. Bakke was rejected at all eleven medical schools. He applied earlier the next year, when there were more than 3,700 applicants and was again rejected at Davis.

With the help of a sympathetic admissions officer, and throughout the long trial, Bakke learned some significant facts about the 1972 application process. Medical schools did not like to admit applicants over the age of 30, feeling that they would have a shorter career, for as Davis wrote, "an older applicant must be unusually highly qualified." In the regular competition for places, no blacks, two Hispanics, and thirteen Asian Americans could be admitted, while the special admissions for disadvantaged students admitted six blacks, eight Hispanics, and two Asians. This latter group had a grade point average of 2.88 versus 3.49 for the regular competition. All whites with a GPA of 2.5 or below were automatically rejected, and while there was no minimum for the special group, at least one minority was admitted with a 2.1 GPA. Bakke's MCAT scores were 359; the average regular admission was 309; and the average special was 138. Moreover, the medical dean had another "special admissions" program, one in which he reserved as many as five places every year for the children of important state politicians or of substantial financial contributors to the university. The regular odds were 29 to 1 against admission, but the minorities faced ratios of 10 to 1.

Bakke sued the University of California. "I am convinced," he wrote to the admissions committee, that some applicants are "judged by a separate criteria. I am referring to quotas, open or covert, for racial minorities. I realize that the rationale for these quotas is that they attempt to atone for past racial discrimination, but insisting on a new racial bias in favor of minorities is not a just situation." To Bakke and his attorney, the affirmative action policy denied him of equal protection guaranteed by the Fourteenth Amendment. Unlike previous individuals in the civil rights era who sued, Bakke was white, and soon his grievance was labeled the "reverse discrimination" case. The county court agreed and ruled in favor of Bakke, discovering that the special disadvantaged program had never admitted a white, and so ruled that it discriminated against Caucasians. The case went to the California Supreme Court, and they also ruled for Bakke. The 6 to 1 majority argued that the university could not discriminate for or against anyone, and since no white had been admitted in the disadvantaged program, then that had become a quota based on race. The "lofty purpose" of the Fourteenth Amendment, the California Supreme Court declared, "is incompatible with the premise that some races may be afforded a higher degree of protection against unequal treatment than others." Race could not be used in the admission process. The University of California Regents appealed the case to the Supreme Court.[17]

The Court accepted the case and heard the oral arguments on October 12, 1977. Hundreds of spectators lined up outside the Supreme Court building. "They carried placards and banners and cheered as their lines grew and wound down the marble steps and around the corner," reported the *Washington Post*. "All for an old reason, and an emotional cause—race." Inside the building the 400 seats were quickly taken, and outside more spectators chanted, "Defend, Extend Affirmative Action!" The media was in full attendance, more than 90 reporters, which was the largest number there since the Court ruled against Richard Nixon, ordering him to hand over the Watergate tapes in 1974. CBS reporter Eric Severeid told a television audience that *Bakke* was "as significant as the school desegregation cases of the early 1950s," and NBC's anchor John Chancellor predicted that it might enter "the Hall of Fame of great cases which changed the interpretation of the Constitution."

The *Bakke* case divided the nation, and almost 150 interest groups submitted a record 58 briefs before the Court heard the case. *Merit v. Equality*, it could have been called, or perhaps *Scores v. Social Justice*. Many whites felt that they had never discriminated, nor had Davis, so why should they have to pay the consequences of past discrimination? "Once you institute preferential treatment along racial lines," wrote the president of the American Federation of Teachers, "you are again opening the door to discrimination along those same lines." Ethnic organizations joined the fray, such as the Italian-American Foundation, the Polish-American Affairs, and several Jewish groups. A lawyer for B'nai B'rith Anti-Defamation League condemned the idea that "a society trying to rid itself of racial discrimination" should "achieve equality in the professions . . . by practicing still more racial discrimination."

The University of California disagreed, naturally, and it was supported by scores of other universities and by a roll call of liberal organizations: the National Council of Churches, the American Bar Association, the Association of American Medical Colleges, and the NAACP. Such policies were necessary to overcome centuries of discrimination and create a black middle class, and it argued that while minority applicants might not have the highest test scores, they certainly are sufficient to enter such programs, graduate and become professionals. After extensive debate the Carter administration filed an *amicus* brief supporting the University of California. While opposed to quotas, "we believe it is permissible to make minority-sensitive decisions." Newspapers like the *New York Times* editorialized against Bakke, labeling the California system "Reparation, American Style," but admitted that letters to the editor disagreed with their stance 15 to 1. "Both sides are right," declared the *Times*, "But it is in the national interest that Mr. Bakke should lose the case."

Anticipation mounted, and finally the decision came eight months later on a warm, muggy June morning in 1978. The nine justices took their places in their black leather chairs, quickly disposed of two other cases, and Chief Justice Warren Burger announced that Justice Lewis Powell would deliver the judgment on *Regents of the University of California v. Allan Bakke.* "I will now try to explain how we divided on this issue," Powell said with a smile, "It may not be self-evident."

It wasn't, for like the nation, the Supreme Court was deeply divided. Four justices, including Burger and William Rehnquist, felt that allotting a precise number of places for minorities in a university program violated the Fourteenth Amendment and Title VI of the 1964 Civil Rights Act, which barred racial discrimination by any institution receiving federal funds. Bakke had been excluded from a public medical program only "because of his race," and that was unconstitutional. Four others, including Harry Blackmun and the only African American on the court, Thurgood Marshall, felt that the university's program was acceptable to overcome the effects of past discrimination. Blackmun hoped for the time when affirmative action was unnecessary, but for now, "To get beyond racism, we must first take account of race. And in order to treat some persons equally, we must treat them differently." Marshall agreed, calling for "greater protection under the Fourteenth Amendment" for blacks. "After several hundred years of class-based discrimination against Negroes," he wrote, "a class-based remedy is permissible."

In the middle was Lewis Powell, a Virginian nominated by Nixon, who believed that the law had to serve social justice and stability. In his majority opinion the southern gentleman admitted that California had a legitimate interest in eliminating "the disabling effects of identified discrimination," and that the "attainment of a diverse student body . . . clearly is a constitutionally permissible goal for an institution of higher education." But he continued that the "guarantee of equal protection cannot mean one thing when applied to one individual and something else when applied to a person of another color. . . . This the Constitution forbids." Powell then switched sides and favored admissions in which "race or ethnic background is simply one element—to be weighed fairly against other elements—in the selection process."

"Preference yes, quotas no," declared *Newsweek*. By a vote of 5 to 4 the Court held that quotas were unconstitutional and, by the same margin, that race could be used as one of the many considerations in the university's admission process. "Mr. Bakke won," wrote columnist Anthony Lewis, "but so did the general principle of affirmative action." The court ordered Bakke admitted the next semester at Davis, and universities with strict quotas for admission would have to establish flexible "goals" or "targets," which, since LBJ, conformed with federal policy. "The bottom line was to confirm what we thought the law was," said Attorney General Bell. As for compensation, the justices answered that demand with a decision that "gave almost everyone—Bakke, the government, civil rights groups, and most universities—a victory, if a small one," wrote the *Washington Post*, as long as admissions were flexible. *Bakke* was very significant: the case defined affirmative action in college admissions and would become the law of the land.[18]

But not the law concerning employment. One year later, in June 1979, the Supreme Court ruled on a suit by another white man; as one journalist penned, "The Bakke Case Moves to the Factory." Brian Weber was a white worker at the Kaiser Aluminum and Chemical Company plant in Gramercy, Louisiana. In the past the company had discriminated in hiring skilled positions, so in 1974 only five of 290 such jobs were filled by African Americans. In order to avoid potential litigation and remedy the situation, the company entered an agreement with the United Steelworkers of America that established an affirmative action program to train blacks for skilled positions. Weber applied, and he was denied. He was surprised to discover that the union had reserved 50 percent of the training slots for black employees. Of the 13 openings seven were filled by blacks and six by whites, and two of the blacks had less seniority than Weber. He claimed the company and union had devised a quota. "I was being discriminated against because I was white."

Weber sued, charging reverse discrimination. To him, Kaiser's policy violated Title VII of the Civil Rights Act, and he won in two lower federal courts but not in the Supreme Court. Writing for the majority, Justice William Brennan declared that nothing in Title VII "forbid all voluntary race-conscious affirmative action." The company's plan was a temporary measure that would end when the percentage of black skilled workers in the plant resembled the ratio of blacks in the local labor force. It did not bar any worker from training, nor did it "trammel the interest of white employees." The company's aim was "simply to eliminate a manifest racial balance" at a previously discriminatory plant. "It would be ironic indeed," Brennan continued, "if a law triggered by a nation's concern over centuries of racial injustices and intended to improve the lot of those who had been excluded from the American dream for so long constituted the first legislative prohibition of all voluntary, private, race-conscious efforts to abolish traditional patterns of racial segregation."

"I'm very disappointed," said Weber, and the Anti-Defamation League of B'nai B'rith hoped that employers didn't read the decision "as sanctioning racial quotas." But Benjamin Hooks of the NAACP took a different view, stating that if the Court had sided with Weber the "cause of affirmative action would have been set back 10 years." A Mexican American group added that the decision could "open doors that have been closed . . . too long," and a leader for the National Women's Political Caucus was "thrilled. With this decision women and minorities come closer to making equal opportunity in employment a reality instead of a dream."

Thus, the Court ruled that businesses could establish voluntary affirmative action policies that give preferences, even temporary quotas, to minorities and women. But a related question soon appeared: Could the federal government mandate a 10 percent set-aside on all local public works contracts, as it had done in the 1977 Public Works Act? "We see no evidence to indicate that the 10 percent standard . . . is anything but a quota," declared a spokesman for the Association of General Contractors. One of their members, H. Earl Fullilove, a white New York contractor, challenged the act, which raised the question in *Fullilove v. Klutznick*: Did Congress have the power to establish a set-aside for contract funds or was that a violation of the equal protection clause of the Fourteenth Amendment?

The Court ruled 6 to 3 upholding the Public Works Act. Chief Justice Warren Burger wrote that eliminating the effects of past discrimination was a proper function of Congress. The set-asides in the law were not an inflexible quota because they could be waived when qualified minority firms did not exist in the area or did not submit a competitive bid. Justice Marshall argued more broadly. "By upholding this race-conscious remedy, the Court accords Congress the authority necessary to undertake the task of moving our society toward a state of meaningful equality of opportunity." *Fullilove* demonstrated that in the Supreme Court there were "six Justices who will uphold almost any congressionally mandated affirmative action program," The *Nation* editorialized, it "is now clear that seven of nine Justices think that race-conscious programs to overcome the effects of past discrimination are constitutional."[19]

Fullilove, Weber, and *Bakke* exemplified the zenith of affirmative action. Between 1969 and 1980 all three branches of government lined up and supported the policy. With the exception of set-asides, Congress avoided a direct vote on affirmative action. That left the executive and judicial branches to define the policy and give it what one journalist called a "bureaucratic virgin birth." Presidents Nixon and Carter had faced the same dilemma as Johnson: How to increase black employment, hiring with regard to race, while subscribing to Title VII, hiring without regard to race. Since there were few alternatives, since the inequality of minorities was so obvious, and since the majority of citizens favored opening the doors of opportunity, those administrations accepted the same basic policy—some form of compensation. Whether civil rights leaders realized it or not, during the 1970s they were winning their final demand, compensation, and the next questions then became "how much?" and for "how long?" Johnson had begun compensation with the Philadelphia Plan, Nixon had revised and nationalized it, universities and many businesses had established their own programs, and Carter signed set-asides into law with the 1977 Public Works Act, all upheld by federal courts.

Along the way the definition of affirmative action had changed considerably since President Kennedy's 1961 executive order, from simply ending discrimination and opening jobs to all citizens to "results" in employment, college admissions, and minority-owned businesses. The government first supported race and eventually gender-conscious remedies to overcome past discrimination, even if that included establishing goals and timetables for government contractors, consent decrees with temporary quotas for employers who had discriminated, set-asides for minority owned companies, and special consideration in admission to university programs.

"Ultimately," *Newsweek* wrote about the *Bakke* case, "the issue forces Americans to look inside themselves and ask: What is fair?" Should white males be penalized in order to make up for past discrimination against women and minorities, and if so, then what type of preferences?

The question was partly answered in a 1979 opinion poll, which again surprised the nation. "The findings by the Harris organization contrast greatly with the 1977 finding by a Gallup poll," wrote the *New York Times*. The *Bakke* decision had been a "critical threshold event in changing white attitudes toward affirmative action." The poll found whites felt by 71 to 21 percent that "as long as there are no rigid quotas" they agreed that "after years of discrimination it is only fair to set up special programs to make sure that women and minorities are given every chance to have equal opportunities in employment and education." As for affirmative action, 67 percent of whites favored such programs on the job and in higher education, and another survey of 300 corporate executives found that over 70 percent of them felt positive about affirmative action, and they claimed that it did not hamper productivity. Moreover, polls found that other racial attitudes had changed dramatically. Between 1963 and 1979 the ratio of whites worried about a black family moving in next door had dropped in half to 27 percent, and feeling that blacks were an inferior race to 15 percent. Although large majorities of whites remained opposed to busing, the ratio of whites and blacks satisfied with the busing experience for their children had climbed to about 60 percent. Integration was having an impact, as 90 percent of the whites reported that the contacts with blacks were "pleasant and easy" socially and on the job. Blacks did not necessarily agree, citing continued discrimination and lack of good jobs. Nevertheless, the National Conference of Christians and Jews declared "a period of real progress is now imminent."

The statement might have been too positive, especially during a recession, but during the 1970s affirmative action was having an impact. "Face it," said the personnel director at Lockheed, "affirmative action has done its job. Without government surveillance we certainly wouldn't have gone this much out of our way" to hire women and minorities. Studies by the Potomac Institute and the OFCCP supported that contention, both finding "substantial employment gains," especially in the 77,000 businesses and construction unions that held contracts with the federal government. Jobs were opening up. Between 1970 and 1980 the percentages of black union workers and apprentices had doubled; African American officials and managers, professionals, and skilled workers increased 70 percent, twice the national rate of growth for those positions. The case was even more positive for white women. The *Washington Post* labeled females the "biggest winners" as they quickly advanced into technical and skilled positions.

Enforcement reached new levels. During the Carter years the EEOC received about 75,000 discrimination complaints that warranted investigation, some 5,000 suits were filed annually, naming almost half of the nation's largest corporations. By the end of the decade, commissioner Eleanor Holmes Norton announced that the agency had reduced its backlog of cases by 40 percent and that companies had settled discrimination claims worth $30 million in compensation and benefits.

Affirmative action also was having an impact on campuses. "We're encouraged," declared Norton. "Finally we're winning some cases" as many universities—Brown, Rutgers, Minnesota, the City University of New York—settled claims and joined the national trend of hiring and granting tenure to more female professors, who along with minorities were teaching a new curriculum in women's and ethnic studies. All the while, women were opening professional doors; during the decade female enrollment in dental schools increased from 2 to 19 percent, from 11 to 28 percent in medical schools, and from 9 to 35 percent in law schools. Education was changing in primary and secondary schools as book publishers, such as Houghton Mifflin, issued new guidelines to textbook writers and editors: "achieve a 20 percent minority representation and a 50 percent male, 50 percent female balance." Women's roles must include "doctors, lawyers, accountants" as well as chefs and bus drivers, and men should be included as elementary school teachers, nurses, and "as employees of women."

By the end of the Carter years affirmative action had reached its zenith, yet its public support was always tenuous. Political pronouncements often had been contradictory, definitions slippery, too many suits were filed, some ludicrous—all of which confused citizens, stumped pollsters, and encouraged critics who charged "reverse discrimination." Moreover, the agencies empowered to enforce the policy had not always set the best examples. In 1980 the OFCCP demanded that a Firestone plant conform to guidelines by hiring "at least nine-tenths of a woman chemical engineer, five and five-tenths minority foremen and two-tenths of a minority craftsman," prompting a suit from the company and giving conservatives ammunition in their fight against government regulations. Meanwhile, the EEOC began urging government officials to hire their employees not according to merit but to the ratio of minorities in the locale, and when the agency attempted to construct a perfect employment model within itself, the result was embarrassment. In fact, the ratio of minorities in America had little relation to the EEOC's workforce: 49 percent black, 44 percent female, 11 percent Hispanic, and only 20 percent white male. In 1979 the agency decided to reorganize, selecting 19 district directors from 89 male and 15 female applicants and appointing only 11 men, which led the men to sue the "sex blind" selection process. The judge sided with the men, stating that the EEOC was standing the noble goal of Title VII on its head. "In plain language, this is a case of the cow stepping into the bucket."[20]

By the end of the decade many citizens felt that the nation also was stepping into the bucket, or as President Carter admitted in a national speech, sinking into "national malaise." "It's clear that the true problems of our Nation are much deeper—deeper than gasoline lines or energy shortages, deeper even than inflation or recession. . . . It is a crisis of confidence." And then the president asked, "What can we do? First of all, we must face the truth, and then we can change our course."

Many agreed, including a Californian who during 1980 was running an aggressive campaign to change the course of the nation—Ronald Reagan.

four | Backlash

"The Reagan Revolution," declared *U.S. News & World Report* after the Republican nominee's victory in the 1980 election. As the tall, handsome Californian rode into Washington, he and his supporters aimed to end the pessimism of the late 1970s and bring about a rebirth, sunshine, what Reagan called "Morning in America."

The campaign had been focused on the stagflation economy, which in 1980 suffered over 7 percent unemployment, 12 percent inflation, and a prime interest rate of 15 percent. Reagan promised to "move boldly, decisively, and quickly to control the runaway growth of Federal spending, to remove the tax disincentives that are throttling the economy, and to reform the regulatory web that is smothering it." He pledged to rescue the nation from "economic chaos." His campaign battle cry was effective: "Are you better off today than you were four years ago?"

The Republican also pledged to "restore our defenses," which most citizens felt was necessary. In November 1979 Iranian radicals took 53 Americans hostage at the U.S. Embassy in Tehran. While the Islamic militants burned Old Glory in front of television cameras, the Soviet Union invaded Afghanistan in an attempt to keep a friendly communist regime in power on their southern border. During the election year Carter responded to the hostage crisis with a helicopter rescue mission, which ended in disaster: television showed scenes of burning choppers in the desert. He responded to the Soviet invasion by reviving draft registration, which sent fears across campuses; embargoing grain sales to Russia, which cut prices for American farmers; and by boycotting the summer Moscow Olympics, which outraged sport fans.

Reagan beat Carter, winning 44 states and 51 percent of the vote, including every southern state except Georgia. His strongest supporters were white males and a surprising number of working class voters who abandoned Carter and were known as "Reagan Democrats." Moreover, the telegenic Californian had coattails. For the first time since the 1952 election the GOP won control of the Senate and paired with southern Democrats, conservatives now were a majority in the House.

Republicans won on a platform that advocated curbing social programs to "restore individual freedom" from the liberal social policies of Lyndon Johnson and Franklin Roosevelt. "Government is not the solution to our problem," Reagan maintained. "Government is the problem." He promised to "get the government off our backs" by cutting regulations and abolishing some 80 programs, including the Department of Education and the Environmental Protection Agency. Supported by a growing legion of Christian fundamentalists who were appalled by the gay, sexual, and women's liberation movements of the 1970s, Reagan's moral agenda called for a return to "true American values," which included Constitutional amendments to ban abortion and to "take sex out of school and put prayer back in."

Reagan was fortunate, for on the morning of his inauguration Iran released the hostages. They had been in captivity for 444 days, and the release solved the most immediate issue. But on that day what seemed important to most citizens was hope, and in his address he did not waver, standing tall and telling the nation that it was now time to move forward, "we are too great a nation to limit ourselves to small dreams. . . . Let us renew our determination, our courage, and our strength. And let us renew our faith and our hope. We have every right to dream heroic dreams."

Reagan's new cabinet was a mix of conservatives and moderates, many of whom had served him in California or had worked for presidents Nixon and Ford. Caspar Weinberger became Secretary of Defense, David Stockman directed the Office of Management and Budget, Donald Regan became Treasury Secretary, and William French Smith took over at Justice. Raymond J. Donovan became Labor Secretary, and a close friend of Vice President George H. W. Bush, James A. Baker III, became White House Chief of Staff. The president named only one black to his cabinet, Samuel Pierce Jr., who became Secretary of Housing and Urban Development. Except for Pierce, the new administration did not appoint any blacks to the top 100 positions, and only 19 to the most significant 400 jobs. Nor did Reagan appoint a woman to the cabinet, but to placate critics he named Jeanne Kirkpatrick as Ambassador to the United Nations.

During the spring the administration presented its program for economic recovery, "America's New Beginning." The president demanded that individual and business taxes be cut 30 percent over three years, called waste and fraud in the federal government a "national scandal," and asked for reductions on agencies that regulated business and the environment. He urged slashing $40 billion from social programs, including cutting food stamps, school lunches, health care, housing assistance, and welfare, and shifting those services to the states.

Congress began to review the proposals when, suddenly, a gunman almost ended the Reagan presidency. John Hinckley, who had a history of mental problems, stepped from a crowd outside a Washington, D.C., hotel and fired point blank at the president. One bullet lodged near his heart, missing the aorta by an inch, and another seriously wounded press secretary James Brady. As Americans held their breath, the president was rushed to the hospital emergency room, where he winked at his wife, Nancy, "Honey, I forgot to duck." Then he turned to the surgical staff and asked if they were Republicans. They replied, "We're all Republicans today."

Reagan recovered quickly, and his warm sense of humor and confidence won over many Americans, not just for his first year but throughout most of his presidency. His personal appeal was a result of his movie-star looks, his optimistic vision for the future, and his ability to deliver a sterling speech. Reagan, as biographer Lou Cannon noted, was not believable because he was the Great Communicator. He was a "Great Communicator because he was believable."[1]

Riding a wave of popular support, Congress soon passed the president's two immediate objectives, enlarging defense spending and decreasing tax rates, and his administration announced that it was reviewing plans to eliminate federal agencies and cut regulations.

That made some citizens leery of the Reagan Revolution, especially those who felt that they were benefitting from government programs such as affirmative action. Carter won 93 percent of the black vote, and he won a majority of the female vote mainly because Reagan opposed abortion and the Equal Rights Amendment. Thus, for the first time the electorate witnessed a "gender gap" where a sizable percentage of white men voted differently from women in the same social and economic status.

During the presidential campaign the two main parties divided sharply over racial issues. The Democrats supported busing and the Republicans opposed it to bring about integrated school districts and the use of racial considerations in redistricting congressional districts, which was mandated after the 1980 census. Naturally, civil rights groups were interested in hearing Reagan's views, for during the 1960s he had opposed all civil rights acts. During the summer campaign the NAACP asked Reagan to address its convention, but the communicator begged off, claiming a calendar conflict and that his staff had "misplaced the invitation." This only increased pressure on the Californian, so in August he devoted a week courting African Americans. He spent a day politicking in a minority neighborhood in the South Bronx, held a discussion with Jesse Jackson, and gave a speech to the Urban League. Yet the performance was unconvincing, for Reagan gave a speech in Philadelphia, Mississippi—where three civil rights workers had been murdered in 1964—and proclaimed his support for states' rights. He also refused to take a tough stand against the repressive apartheid regime in South Africa. It "will take more than a whirlwind week," *Newsweek* wrote, "to change many black minds about Ronald Reagan."

The same was true concerning another contentious issue that separated the parties: affirmative action. "An effective affirmative action program is an essential component of our commitment to expanding civil rights," declared the Democratic platform, while the Republicans had been moving to the right since Nixon abandoned his support before the 1972 election. By 1980 conservatives had captured the G.O.P. and their platform criticized "bureaucratic regulations and decisions which rely on quotas, ratios, and numerical requirements to exclude some individuals in favor of others." Reagan added, "We must not allow the noble concept of equal opportunity to be distorted into federal guidelines or quotas which require race, ethnicity, or sex—rather than ability and qualifications—to be the principal factor in hiring or education."

Such views meant that the new Reagan administration began with little support from African Americans, and the outgoing Carter administration made the predicament even more difficult as it left Washington. On his last day in office, Associate Attorney General John Shenefield signed an agreement with minority federal workers who had sued the government in 1979. They alleged cultural bias in the test for mid-level governmental positions, the Professional and Administrative Career Examination. Accordingly, over the next three years the agreement would scrap PACE, and, in its place, agencies would be required to construct new exams that aimed to pass and promote a higher proportion of blacks and Hispanics. In fact, the new guidelines were aimed at results; they assured that the number of minorities getting better jobs would be almost proportional to the number taking the new tests. Thus, if 50 percent who took the exams were minorities, then 50 and no less than 40 percent of the jobs would be given to minorities until each agency had 20 percent blacks and Latinos. If the new exams did not produce more minority promotions, then agencies could scrap the new tests and recruit minorities without PACE or at least demonstrate that the test contained no hidden biases. Some government attorneys declared that the agreement was a quota, as did B'nai B'rith, but Shenefield responded that the current exam did not test knowledge needed for the jobs and that the new plan did not impose a strict numerical requirement, which he defined as a quota.

Shenefield's response was not good enough for the Reagan transition team, who had first asked the Carter administration not to implement the plan and leave the issue to the next administration. A federal judge gave tentative approval to the agreement, commenting that it was "fair, just, equitable, and appropriate under the law."

The new administration moved to Washington and shortly thereafter began to define its stand on affirmative action. During his first news conference the president was asked if there would be a retreat on affirmative action. "No, there will be no retreat," Reagan responded. "This administration is going to be committed to equality." Then he added:

> I think that there are some things, however, that may not be as useful as they once were, or that may even be distorted in practice, such as some affirmative action programs becoming quota systems. And I'm old enough to remember when quotas existed in the U.S. for the purpose of discrimination. And I don't want to see that happen again.

Reagan's statement was the beginning of the backlash; now, for the first time, a presidential administration joined other critics in opposition to affirmative action. Shortly thereafter a White House official stated that getting back to "colorblind" hiring was the "ultimate goal," and later that spring the administration indicated that affirmative action rules would be one of the first targets for "regulatory relief."

To the new administration, government regulations were hurting the economy, decreasing efficiency, and burdening business, and these "anticompetitive" rules were choking the individualism and free enterprise necessary for recovery. Armed with these ideas the administration began attacking regulations, which happened to be many of the same liberal policies they had opposed for years—federal regulations that mandated worker and consumer safety, environmental protection and conservation, and rules that forced employers to demonstrate that they did not discriminate—in other words, affirmative action.

That alarmed proponents. Reagan was practicing "Doublespeak on Affirmative Action," declared *Black Enterprise* and many agreed with the *Washington Post*, "opponents of affirmative action may finally have won, not in court, but at the ballot box . . . when Ronald Reagan was elected president."[2]

The idea received more credence as the Reagan Revolution appeared in Congress. In the House, Pennsylvania's Republican Representative Robert Walker proposed an amendment to the 1964 Civil Rights Act that would prohibit federal rules requiring employers to hire workers or colleges to admit students on the basis of race or sex, as well as barring the use of quotas, goals, or timetables. In the Senate, Utah's Republican Orrin Hatch had introduced a constitutional amendment to forbid state and federal governments from making "distinctions on account of race, color, or national origin," both attempts to bring about what conservatives were calling a "colorblind society." During the year Hatch held hearings in the judicial subcommittee on many constitutional topics, and especially on affirmative action. As the chair, his purpose was clear, since he had declared "affirmative action is an assault upon America, conceived in lies." At the hearings in May, the senator stated that it was remarkable that the policy "should have begun to take root within our system almost totally in the absence of legislative sanction . . . developed solely through judicial and executive branch decisions." It was time for some dialogue on the contentious topic, he continued: "The thing that bothers me is that so many people in our society are terrified to even discuss this issue for fear of being called racist."

Hatch called witnesses. Morris Abram, a New York lawyer who had won many civil rights cases, now concluded that affirmative action was leading to a dangerous "Balkanization" of ethnic groups, that a "color-conscious interpretation" of the Constitution was a "loaded weapon," while another witness contended that the policy was stamping women and minorities with a "badge of inferiority." The only black to testify was Harvard professor Martin Kilson. He agreed with Hatch that there could be stigmas associated with affirmative action but those were relative: "Italian contractors in Massachusetts" who win lucrative contracts because of political patronage "are willing to accept the stigma." Then turning on Hatch, Kilson demanded, "if affirmative action is going down the drain then give us a Marshall Plan. . . . I have no doubt you're going to shave off something, from that smile on your face."

"Never interpret my smiles," Hatch responded with a faint smile, but he was more serious during the July hearings, which concerned government regulations and local officials. During the Carter administration the Justice Department had filed a suit against Fairfax County, Virginia, where the population was one-fourth black, but less than 6 percent of the county's 7,000 workers were African American. Hatch called on the county board chairman, who decried federal officials employing a "battering ram of punitive action" against the county, and who called on the Reagan administration to fulfill its campaign promise: get the government off our backs. Hatch sympathized that federal actions could be examples of "burdensome, governmental repression."

The burdening agency often was the EEOC. Some businessmen complained that they were wasting too much time on paperwork and spending too much money defending themselves against discrimination charges. One research organization estimated that a contract compliance review cost a contractor over $20,000, and that such appraisals were costing the Fortune 500 companies $1 billion annually. It cited one example in which a Hispanic employee filed a discrimination case against Union Camp in Michigan. Eleven different supervisors at the paper company had disciplined the employee 22 times, leading to suspension and eventual dismissal. The worker charged the company with racial discrimination, which he lost in five arbitration attempts—three times at the Michigan Civil Rights Commission. Nevertheless, with no new evidence the EEOC accepted his case and filed a suit. The discovery and case lasted 19 months. The employee and the EEOC lost, and the judge issued a blistering attack on the agency. The EEOC "tries the case poorly, loses, and hopes a lesson has been taught. A better case of an award of attorney's fees could not be made."

Even within the government some officials began to speak out against regulations. These were not conservatives but liberals who had supported affirmative action in the 1970s and now felt that administering the program had become seriously flawed. "Affirmative action has overwhelmed consideration of fairness and efficiency" stated one high-ranking federal manager. "You are constantly on the defensive, it's on everybody's mind, and when the subject comes up you feel compelled to cite how many women you've hired, how many minorities you've promoted. Any second thoughts, any questioning . . . marks you as a dinosaur, someone whose future is behind him." Another problem was the landslide of complaints filed *within* the federal government. Many of them were frivolous, consuming an incredible amount of time. One employee filed an age-discrimination complaint after his boss referred to him as "old-fashioned"; another claimed race discrimination after he deliberately disobeyed his supervisor's instructions and she was forced to criticize him. Another claimed sex discrimination because her boss refused to allow her to take a course at government expense that was not related to her position; in fact, it was a prerequisite for her future plans after she left government. A middle-aged male filed more than 30 complaints in one year, about one every eight working days. When an office colleague threatened to strike him, he claimed prejudice, although the other person was of the same ethnic background. He also invited himself to the apartment of two female college interns in his department, where he made improper advances; after his supervisor told him not to see the women again socially, he filed a complaint for sex harassment.

During the first months of the Reagan Revolution, then, the backlash slowly emerged, but the administration's actions were not a coordinated effort; instead, they were an awkward and even contradictory skirmish with affirmative action. Just four weeks after inauguration day Attorney General Smith announced that the new administration would abide by, rather than contest, the agreement Carter had made to jettison the

PACE examination. To business supporters this suggested that the administration was ducking its stated platform of boosting merit over preferential treatment. Later that spring Labor Secretary Donovan surprised many by announcing that the "president and I are firmly behind affirmative action," and that the issue was not so much ability and merit but excessive reports and pushy bureaucrats. He aimed "to cut down on the damn paperwork" and to take enforcement "out of the arena of push-pull-slap-punch." Such statements dismayed many conservative supporters. The Heritage Foundation called Reagan's civil rights agenda "patch-work" and a conservative author called it "fitful and uneven. . . . The most ideological administration in recent history seems not to have its ideas sorted out."

Many of those ideas would be left to the administration's appointments in charge of enforcing civil rights laws. Carter's EEOC director, Eleanor Holmes Norton, resigned to accept a professorship. The president nominated William Bell, an African American, to run the agency with its more than 3,000 employees. Bell had no law degree, and his only experience was supervising four people at his consulting firm. Civil rights groups were outraged, aggressively opposing Bell. The president withdrew the nomination, leaving the agency without leadership for months; he eventually named a 33-year-old African American attorney in his Education Department to head the post, Clarence Thomas, who had spoken out against racial preferences. For director of the Office of Federal Contract Compliance Programs, the administration hired a 34-year-old businesswoman, Ellen M. Shong, who pledged her office would mediate or "open doors and not close contracts" for businesses that discriminated. And for the Assistant Attorney General for Civil Rights, the administration named a 38-year-old white Washington, D.C., attorney who had little experience in civil rights law or civil litigation, William Bradford Reynolds. Like his president, Reynolds stated that he was opposed to busing to achieve school integration and that he supported "individual opportunity" and not "group entitlements"; he continually disparaged what he called "race-conscious affirmative action." All of these appointees felt the Carter administration had been too aggressive in enforcing civil rights regulations, and six months into the Reagan administration the *New York Times* reported a "virtual standstill" of enforcement and "virtual paralysis" at the EEOC and OFCCP.

Reagan's appointments did not endear him to African Americans, and in an attempt to improve relations the president accepted an invitation to speak to the NAACP. To African Americans the economic situation was critical. The recession resulted in over 17 percent unemployment for blacks (a postwar record), with 30 percent of them below the poverty line, three times the white rate, just as the administration was proposing to cut social programs that had fed the poor, trained the unskilled, and employed the jobless. Nevertheless, the president began his appearance upbeat, joking to NAACP members about losing the invitation during the campaign. In return Reagan was presented with a gag gift—a jar full of black and brown jelly beans with one lone white one buried within. Then Reagan stepped to the podium, first attacking those who said his policies would hurt the poor as "pure demagoguery," and then declaring that federal programs had enslaved blacks, not helped them. "They've created a new kind of bondage. . . . Just as the Emancipation Proclamation freed black people 118 years ago, today we need to declare an economic emancipation." Such comments won a chilling silence, what the *New York Times* labeled "undoubtedly one of the coolest receptions he has ever received." After the address, NAACP director Benjamin Hooks stated that he welcomed the dialogue but predicted that Reagan's policies would bring "hardship, havoc, despair, pain, and suffering on blacks and other minorities."

Time noted a growing black "antagonism toward the Administration" for there was a firm belief that the president's policy would not bring about "Morning in America" for African Americans. "There is a dark midnight in America today," said the Urban League's Vernon Jordan, and a Gallup poll measuring approval ratings for the president discovered the widest gap between white and black respondents in polling history. Some 65 percent of whites but only 20 percent of blacks approved of Reagan's policies. For some African Americans, *Newsweek* noted, the "feeling of isolation from power is more acute now than at any time since the dawn of the New Deal."[3]

But this was not the case with women, who had mixed feelings about the new administration. They seemed to like the president but wondered about future employment practices and regulations. In April the Senate Labor Committee held hearings on sex harassment on the job. Again chaired by Senator Hatch, he wondered if EEOC guidelines on harassment that had been adopted in 1980 were too restrictive and placed too much burden on employers. Those regulations held an employer responsible if he or his workers engaged in sexual harassment, with the threat that women who were denied raises, promotion, or fired for refusing to grant sexual favors could win remedial action and back pay. Former EEOC director Eleanor Holmes Norton naturally disagreed with Hatch, claiming that demands for sexual favors were too common and degrading and that women were entitled to federal protection. The agency reported that currently there were almost 120 complaints under examination. "Fifty-eight of these cases involve unwelcome physical contact of a sexual nature, such as touching of a person's buttocks or hugging or kissing; 77 involve demands for a person to engage in a sexual act" in return for an employment decision, while the rest concerned derogatory comments or "displaying sexually explicit pictures, photographs, or cartoons."

For that reason, Norton continued, there was a strong need to keep the EEOC regulations, but another outspoken female disagreed. "Sexual harassment on the job is not a problem for the virtuous woman," declared Phyllis Schlafly, "except in the rarest of cases." An attorney by training, Schlafly had become a successful antifeminist organizer; in 1981 the Washington Post labeled her the "grande dame of conservatism in America." "When a woman walks across the room," Schlafly continued, "she speaks with a universal body language that most men intuitively understand. Men hardly ever ask sexual favors of women from whom the certain answer is 'no.'" Schlafly then stated her views of affirmative action. The policy hurt traditional mothers by encouraging women to work, by forcing females into jobs beyond their qualifications, and by giving away the husband's job to women under the quota system, all of which were "obsoleting the role of motherhood."

While Senator Hatch continued the hearings, President Reagan fulfilled a campaign promise and surprised many when he nominated the first woman to the Supreme Court, Arizona judge Sandra Day O'Connor. Justice Potter Stewart retired, and Reagan's nomination received a warm reception, except from the religious right. The Reverend Jerry Falwell of the Moral Majority felt that O'Connor was too moderate on abortion, and he urged "all good Christians" to oppose her confirmation. That outraged Senator Barry Goldwater, who had convinced two Republican presidents to pick nominees from his state, O'Connor and Rehnquist. Before the Senate unanimously confirmed O'Connor,

Goldwater declared that "every good Christian ought to kick Jerry Falwell right in the ass."

That was where many civil rights and labor groups wanted to kick budget director David Stockman, when he hinted that key changes were going to be made to affirmative action. Thirty-seven groups, including the NAACP, NOW, Mexican American Legal Defense and Educational Fund, and even the AFL-CIO, wrote President Reagan that they were "united in our opposition to changes which would sound the death knell for the federal contract compliance program." Nevertheless, Labor Secretary Donovan announced the proposals in August. Previously, all contractors with 50 workers and a $50,000 contract had to submit affirmative action plans with goals and timetables, but the new regulations would exempt all businesses with less than 250 workers and contracts below $1 million. That excused 75 percent of the 30 million employees in some 200,000 companies doing business with the federal government. While large contractors still had to have affirmative action plans, smaller companies would no longer have to write progress reports, and those with under 500 workers could file abbreviated ones. Thus, the number of affirmative action plans federal contractors would have to write would drop from almost 110,000 to less than 24,000. In addition, the new regulations would make it more difficult for employees who felt that they had been discriminated against to collect back pay for jobs or promotions that they did not get. Donovan stated that this policy would keep the "necessary safeguards for protected groups while cutting down the paper work burden for employers," and OFCCP director Shong declared that the changes "will create incentive for voluntary compliance and put an end to mindless confrontation with employers."

"Every Man for Himself," declared *Time*. "And every woman." Apparently the era of governmental protection for women and minorities was coming to an end. The administration began to retreat from affirmative action, labeling it "reverse discrimination." "We really make a mistake," said William Bradford Reynolds, "to try to cure discrimination with discrimination."

Affirmative action proponents fought back. Texas Hispanic leader Raul Castillo claimed that the administration's new regulations would "totally obliterate any kind of gains" made by minorities, and the Women's Equity Action League expressed alarm that higher funding levels in contracts would exempt "some of the largest educational institutions in this country."[4]

Other proponents feared that the White House would now take a more radical approach—to abolish affirmative action. Some in the administration wanted to do that, including Assistant Attorney General Reynolds, who became the main spokesman on racial issues for the Reagan Revolution. During autumn 1981 Reynolds said on many occasions that the Justice Department would no longer go to court to force a business to have goals and timetables, that there might not be "statutory authority" to impose them, and from now on his department would seek remedies on a case-by-case basis. In October he opposed busing, "We are not going to compel children who don't choose to have an integrated education to have one," and before Senate hearings he told chairman Hatch that it was illegal and unconstitutional to give preference to anyone:

We no longer will insist upon or in any respect support the use of quotas or any other numerical or statistical formulae designed to provide to non-victims of discrimination preferential treatment based on race, sex, national origin, or religion. . . . By elevating the rights of groups over the rights of individuals, racial preferences . . . are at war with the American ideal of equal opportunity. . . . This administration is firmly committed to the view that the Constitution and laws protect the rights of every person . . . in an environment of racial and sexual neutrality.

Reynolds stated that the administration opposed the Supreme Court's ruling on the *Weber* case of 1979, which was "wrongly decided," and that his department was looking for a new test case in the attempt to ban all employment preference programs, even voluntary affirmative action. Thus, by its first autumn the Reagan administration was repudiating the legal foundation for affirmative action that had been established since the 1960s.

The backlash did not just concern affirmative action. The Voting Rights Act expired in 1980. Congressional Democrats and Senate Republicans proposed a new bill, which the administration opposed, claiming that it would result in proportional representation by race.

Asked in a press conference about his stance, President Reagan stated that the government should be required to prove "intent" to discriminate in local voting, not just the "effects. . . . You could come down to where all of society had to have an actual quota system." Nevertheless, after Congress demonstrated overwhelming support and the House passed it 389 to 24, the president eventually signed the extension of the Voting Rights Act.

The administration's stance irritated civil rights organizations, and in January 1982 the Treasury and Justice Departments announced that they were reversing an Internal Revenue Service policy that had been in effect since 1970. Henceforth, the administration would allow tax exemptions for racially segregated private schools. Many of these were private Christian schools that had been established to evade integration, one of which was Bob Jones University in South Carolina. Bob Jones accepted a handful of black students, but it prohibited interracial dating and marriage, so the IRS had refused a tax exemption. The administration's new policy ignited a firestorm of protest. "If Richard Nixon was benign neglect," said Julian Bond, Reagan "is malign neglect." Democrats were outraged, and so were many moderate Republicans. Ninety-six hours later the president gave a formal statement, reversing his administration's policy, declaring himself "unalterably opposed to racial discrimination in any form" and proposing a law to bar tax-free status to segregated private schools. The debacle was, admitted a White House official, "our worst public relations and political disaster yet," and *Newsweek* noted that "Reagan's stock in black America, already abysmally low, had probably slipped out of sight."

The fiasco also had another effect, as *Newsweek* wrote, because it "fed the lingering suspicion that Reagan was out of touch" with his own administration's policies. Comparisons with his predecessor were unavoidable. Jimmy Carter knew all the details yet could rarely articulate where he was leading the nation. Reagan had a strong vision for the future, but during his first year in office he demonstrated that he was weak on specifics. When the president came face to face with his Secretary of Housing and Urban Development, his only black cabinet secretary, he surprised onlookers by confusing him with a local official, "Hello, Mr. Mayor." In a radio broadcast he declared that his proposal for student loans would not cut but increase the funding to "the highest level ever," which a Democratic senator called "amazingly confused" and which an administration official contradicted shortly thereafter. When asked in a press conference about the Vietnam war, Reagan quickly made four historical errors, including the one that Kennedy had sent military advisers "in civilian clothes, no weapons." At another news conference a journalist asked the president's opinion of an affirmative action agreement between an aerospace company and a labor union to train and promote minorities. "I can't see any fault with that," he replied. "I'm for that." Yet William Bradford Reynolds had already declared the administration's opposition, and a White House official soon issued a statement that the agreement would be opposed in court. A few months after the Bob Jones controversy, Reagan admitted that he didn't even know that some Christian schools practiced segregation: "Maybe I should have but I didn't." Such misstatements meant that presidential advisers limited the number of press conferences, and in Reagan's first year he held only six, a record low, while some journalists dubbed him the "Teflon president." Even those factual blunders did not stick and make him unpopular. Biographer Lou Cannon, who admired Reagan, concluded that the president's "biggest problem was that he didn't know enough about public policy to participate fully in his presidency—and often didn't know how much he didn't know."[5]

Nevertheless, Reagan and his Justice Department knew that they opposed affirmative action, and by 1982 some conservatives were wondering when the president was going to end the policy. The president had the legal authority either to abolish it in the federal government or change goals and timetables for contractors simply by a stroke of the pen. "Since the Reagan Administration has repeatedly criticized the existing affirmative action setup," journalist Daniel Seligman wrote in *Fortune*, "you might assume the answer to be, obviously, that we're heading toward a phaseout." But after weeks of interviews with administration officials and businessmen, Seligman concluded, "affirmative action is here to stay. . . . The system will clearly survive the Reaganites, which presumably means that it can survive anything." Why? Seligman found that the "affirmative action locomotive has a lot of momentum, and it is plainly easier to make speeches assailing preference than it is to slow down that locomotive." Then, too, business was sending "very mixed signals" to the administration. They wanted less paperwork and a much less confrontational EEOC, of course, but the system was in place, it was working to get more women and minorities on the job, and most corporate leaders now supported the status quo. That was particularly true of big business and large contractors. One survey of the 50 major federal contractors found that not one thought that the program should be weakened. While all opposed quotas, not one felt that goals and timetables required quotas. The survey found that the "affirmative action concept has become an integral part of today's corporate personal management philosophy and practice." Moreover, filling out affirmative action reports provided a way for corporations to show that they were meeting the law, and that kept them out of court. No company wanted to be known as a racist or sexist employer, and so Seligman declared that it was "hard to find business groups asking flatly for an end to goals and timetables."

And so it was. The Reagan Revolution talked tough, but during his first term the president did not pick up the pen and sign the necessary executive order. Labor Secretary Donovan's proposed regulations did not go into effect. The usual 60-day comment period on new federal regulations was extended for additional months and eventually forgotten. Republicans did not want to be labeled a sexist or racist party, especially after the administration dragged its feet on voting rights, opposed busing, and blundered on segregated private schools. There was little political benefit in alienating minorities and possibly women.

Instead of launching a frontal assault, the administration skirmished over affirmative action and other racial issues. The Justice Department continued its efforts to blunt court-ordered school integration in districts across the nation, from Norfolk to Chicago to Seattle, and the administration attacked the U.S. Commission on Civil Rights. In November 1981 the president notified the chair of the commission, Arthur S. Flemming, who supported affirmative action, that he would be replaced. That was the first time since the agency had been established in 1957 that a president had attempted to remove a chair. Reagan nominated conservative African American Clarence Pendleton Jr., who declared, "Quotas don't work." Three months later the president announced that he was nominating the Reverend B. Sam Hart to the commission. A black Republican evangelical Christian, Hart opposed busing, quotas, and stated, "I do not consider homosexuality a civil rights issue." Civil rights groups protested so vigorously that Reagan withdrew the name even before Hart was formally nominated.

The president then sent forward three more names—Robert Destro, a Catholic University law professor, and two former Democrats who had supported the 1964 Civil Rights Act but now opposed busing and affirmative action, John Bunzel of the conservative Hoover Institute, and former Brandeis University president Morris Abram—to replace commissioners Mary Francis Berry, Blandina Cardenas Ramirez, and Murray Saltzman, all known to be critical of administration policies. This was the first time that a president attempted to reshape the commission to reflect his own political views, and many senators were alarmed, proposing a bill that would prohibit the removal of a commissioner except for neglect of duty. As the Senate considered the measure and the nominees, Reagan fired commissioners Flemming, Berry, Ramirez, and Saltzman in 1983, and this resulted in a wave of protest from liberal politicians and almost 200 organizations. Mary Francis Berry responded by initiating a lawsuit against the president, and negotiations quickly began between the administration and Senate. Eventually, a compromise was worked out. The commission was enlarged from six to eight members, each with a six-year staggered term, half of whom would be appointed by the president and the others by Congress. Reagan appointed Clarence Pendleton as chair, and Congress appointed Berry. When critics charged the president with undermining the commission with his appointments, he dismissed the idea as "hogwash." Shortly thereafter the new commission abandoned its position on affirmative action and sided with the administration; it passed a resolution that temporary quotas created "a new class of victims" by denying equal rights for *majority* groups. Outraged, Berry declared that the commission had become "a lapdog for the administration instead of a watchdog" for civil rights.

The skirmish continued. The administration cut the budgets of the EEOC and OFCCP, which reduced their staffs by 12 and 34 percent, and between 1981 and 1983 those cuts contributed to reducing back-pay awards by two-thirds. Enforcement continued to slump. During Carter's last year, the OFCCP had filed complaints against more than 50 companies and barred five from federal contracts, but Reagan's contract office issued only five complaints in 1982 and did not suspend one contractor until 1986—only two were debarred during Reagan's two terms, compared with 13 during Carter's one term, and 26 companies by all previous administrations. EEOC Chairman Thomas opposed goals and timetables, expressed "serious reservations" about using statistical measures to determine discrimination, which had been the standard since the late 1960s. Also standard, the EEOC no longer attempted to identify patterns of bias throughout industries or in companies, and no longer pursued class-action suits. Instead, the agency concentrated on cases of individual discrimination; those suits increased during the decade, but they were much more difficult to prove.[6]

Meanwhile, the Justice Department continued to look for test cases to curtail affirmative action. Many of those concerned consent plans, which had been worked out over the years in cities that aimed to end discrimination in their police and fire departments, such as Detroit, New York, St. Louis, and Seattle. Those cities pledged promotions of black and white officers on a temporary 50–50 ratio until they were more representative of the populations in their communities. New Orleans had such a plan. In 1970 the city was 45 percent African American but only 6 percent of blacks were on the police force, and those cops were confined to patrolling black neighborhoods and using their own restrooms—ones also used by the prisoners—six years *after* passage of the Civil Rights Act. The black cops filed suit in 1973, and by 1981 the sides agreed to a court-ordered "consent decree" or plan; it was to take effect in 1982, a time when the city was more than half African American. There were still only seven black police supervisors of 283 on the force. Before the New Orleans plan, only 20 black policeman had been promoted above the lowest rank. This agreement aimed to increase the number of black sergeants and lieutenants—but not the number of female or Hispanic ones. The EEOC's Clarence Thomas appeared ready to approve the plan, but the Justice Department's Reynolds disapproved. Thomas folded under pressure, and in January 1983 the department asked a federal court to eliminate the plan. "The action," wrote the *Washington Post*, "was the strongest the Reagan administration has taken against an affirmative action program. It marked the first time the federal government has formally challenged a court-approved employment quota aimed at relieving job discrimination." The administration argued that the plan "required innocent non-black police officers to surrender their legitimate promotion expectations to black officers who have no 'rightful place' claim to promotion priority." The New Orleans city attorney called the action "incredible," raising "very serious questions" about the administration's effort to end discrimination, adding that the Justice Department "has no logical nor legal basis for becoming involved in this case."

As the New Orleans case moved through the courts, the administration joined other cases that concerned affirmative action plans, and those came about because the economy continued to slump and unemployment increased. "Last hired, first fired," *U.S. News* reported, "is far from sacred nowadays as employers struggle to apportion layoffs." Should cities layoff minorities and women, many hired recently because of affirmative action programs, or should they be spared while dismissing whites with more seniority? The "race versus seniority" dispute erupted across the country. Memphis officials asked courts to allow layoffs that would result in dismissals of 60 percent of black firefighters, a Cincinnati judge overturned layoffs of 25 female and black police officers because they had been hired under a court approved consent decree, and in Boston police and firefighters were angry about "preferential layoffs" that favored minorities. An appeals panel in that city declared, "There is nothing magical about seniority," which appalled a union leader who complained that some senior white firefighters "lost their homes and were divorced. They were financially shattered."

"What makes the issue excruciating," wrote *Newsweek*, "is that it pits two worthy aims against each other: protection of senior workers versus the need to correct past discrimination." The administration favored seniority. "No person who is innocent of wrongdoing," stated William Bradford Reynolds, "should suffer the sting of rejection solely because of another's race." In his strongest words yet he declared affirmative action "morally wrong."

As usual, the disputes over temporary quotas and seniority were resolved by federal courts in 1984 with two significant cases, *Bratton et al. v. City of Detroit* and *Firefighters Local Union #1784 v. Stotts*.

Detroit's police force was similar to New Orleans's, more than 80 percent white. In 1973 the majority black population elected Colman Young, one of their own, as mayor, and that statistic began to change. A year later the city had in place an affirmative action plan with temporary quotas that hired more African Americans and promoted one black for every white. By 1983, when the city's population was two-thirds black, the percentage of blacks on the force had increased to a third, lieutenants had risen from 5 to 30 percent, and the number of police brutality complaints had declined 75 percent. Hanson Bratton and four other white sergeants challenged the plan and were supported by the Reagan administration, which declared the policy unconstitutional because it violated the equal protection clause of the Fourteenth Amendment. The federal appellate court disagreed and, basing its ruling on the 1979 *Weber* case, declared that voluntary and temporary quotas to overcome past discrimination were constitutional, either in a private business such as in the *Weber* case or in a government such as Detroit. "The purpose of this program is to aid blacks," the judge wrote, "it is not aimed at excluding whites," and it does not "unnecessarily trammel" whites because they too can be promoted. Without dissent, the Supreme Court rejected hearing the case, allowing the decision to stand.

"Perhaps now the Reagan Administration will take a new look at the Constitution," Mayor Colman Young declared, "and cease its attempts to destroy the progress this country has made in recent years in providing basic constitutional guarantees to all American citizens." William Bradford Reynolds disagreed: "The Supreme Court is ultimately going to have to resolve this issue."

The Supreme Court began to do that six months later when they ruled on *Stotts*. The issue was race versus seniority, as it had been in the 1977 *Teamsters* case, but this time it concerned firefighters in Memphis, a city 40 percent African American but holding only 10 percent of jobs at the fire stations. In an attempt to bring about equal employment a federal court in 1980 approved an affirmative action plan: it mandated that qualified minorities fill 50 percent of vacancies until the total minority percentage approached the local minority population, and that they should receive 20 percent of the promotions to better positions. The city hired more African Americans. One year later the recession forced budget cuts, and Carl Stotts, a black firefighter and union leader, asked a local court to ensure that layoffs would be based not on seniority, which would decrease black representation on the force, but on race. A federal judge agreed, and directed the fire department to lay off senior white firemen to maintain a racially diverse department. Three whites sued, and the case went to the Supreme Court in June 1984. The issue had become so explosive that two dozen organizations filed briefs. The Court ruled 6 to 3 in favor of the white firefighters, writing that the city's seniority system was a bona fide program, not intended to discriminate against anyone and so was protected under Title VII of the Civil Rights Act. Most justices limited their comments, but writing for the majority Justice Byron White broached a new topic: Congress intended to provide "relief only to those who have been actually victims of illegal discrimination. . . . Each individual must prove that the discriminatory practice had an impact on him."[7]

Stotts was another victory for seniority, but because of Justice White's comment the Reagan administration put the broadest possible interpretation on the case. The solicitor general hailed the decision as "one of the greatest victories of all time . . . a slam-dunk," while the attorney general declared that from now on federal courts "cannot impose quotas based on racial considerations in employment." Justice White seemed to be retreating from the 1960s idea of institutional racism and the 1970s "disparate impact" theory of discrimination; he appeared to be supporting the administration's claims that remedies for discrimination should be limited to specific individuals and not given to entire groups of people, such as all minorities and women. "I said some time ago that civil rights was at a crossroads," declared William Bradford Reynolds, "that we would either take the path of race conscious remedies . . . or the high road of race neutrality. The Court has moved us off the crossroads and propelled us down the road we have been urging." He immediately advised all federal agencies not to negotiate new affirmative action agreements with "numerical employment quotas." Two months later the Justice Department and Federal Trade Commission informed the EEOC that they would not file affirmative action reports, which all administrations had required since the 1960s.

Reynolds had overstated the ruling. *Stotts* was a narrow judgment that concerned only seniority, not all affirmative action policies, and the Court always had ruled to uphold seniority systems that did not discriminate. Moreover, the case was one of the last concerning race versus seniority—by the mid-1980s blacks had been on jobs long enough to have earned their own seniorities. The federal judiciary rejected Reynold's broad interpretation and did not begin banning affirmative action programs. "The real problem" with the ruling "is not what it said," wrote African American columnist William Raspberry, "but what Brad Reynolds thinks it said. Reynolds is in position to do a good deal of harm before the Court tells him he read it wrong." Yet Justice White's opinion had opened the door: affirmative action *could* be challenged. "One thing is for sure," stated an attorney, "We're going to see an awful lot of litigation on affirmative action plans. . . . All bets are off . . . There's going to be some aggressive battles."

The most aggressive battle for the remainder of 1984 was not about seniority or employment but the upcoming presidential election. For a year the economy had been improving, finally responding to tax cuts and increased federal spending, and this meant that people were going back to work, quickly reviving the president's popularity. Moreover, it was an Olympic year, but unlike 1980 the United States was not boycotting but hosting the games in Los Angeles. In May the president greeted the Olympic torchbearer at the White House. In July he declared, "Our young people are running for their country, running for greatness" and later merged his campaign with the games: "The American ideal is not just winning; it's going as far as you can go."

The Democrats had a long way to go, and this year their campaign had a new twist. Jesse Jackson became the first African American to launch a major run for the nomination. Inspired by black and white voters electing African American mayors in many cities such as Atlanta, Birmingham, Chicago, Cleveland, Detroit, Los Angeles, New York, New Orleans, and Washington, the 43-year-old civil rights activist announced his candidacy in 1983, energizing his Rainbow Coalition of all races and colors to organize and win the nomination. "There is a freedom train a-comin'," he chanted, urging his listeners to register to vote: "Run, Jesse, run!" Yet Jackson had problems, for he had alienated Jews by meeting with Yasir Arafat of the Palestine Liberation Organization, had not repudiated Black Muslim Louis Farrakhan for calling Judaism a "gutter religion," and insulted many by referring to New York City as "Hymie Town." Jesse's most significant problem, however, was the front-runner, former Vice President Walter Mondale, who had gleaned nearly as many black delegates as Jackson and thus easily won nomination. Then Mondale surprised the nation—he picked the first female vice presidential candidate, New York congresswoman Geraldine Ferarro.

The Republican campaign ran on optimism and images, and "Fritz" Mondale never had a chance against Ronald Reagan. The Democrat looked gray on television. "I think you know I've never really warmed up to television," he said. "In fairness to television, it never really warmed up to me." Raised in small-town Minnesota, the son of a

Methodist minister, Mondale's stiffness on the campaign trail had once earned him the nickname "Norwegian Wood." He was honest, telling citizens that taxes would have to be raised to avoid economic disaster, but he sounded like a whiny pessimist when he spoke out against runaway spending, unfair tax cuts, soaring defense expenditures, and environmental catastrophes. In contrast, the colorful Californian was upbeat. Reagan beamed into television cameras and proclaimed, "We see an America where everyday is Independence Day, the Fourth of July." A television ad had the president embracing American Olympic champions as an announcer proclaimed, "America Is Coming Back!" Republicans bombarded the airways with catchy phrases carefully tested in focus groups—"a triumph of hope and faith," "a celebration of the new patriotism"—while the president labeled the Democrats as a party that "sees people only as members of groups." It worked: groups versus One Nation under God. One retired brewery worker stated that Reagan "really isn't like a Republican. He's more like an American, which is what we really need." Mondale was running against America.

Reagan overwhelmed Mondale, carrying all states but Minnesota and 59 percent of the vote. The president won 63 percent of white votes, including a majority of blue-collar workers and women. Yet Reagan's coattails this time were surprisingly short. The Democrats, who had won control of the House in the 1982 election, maintained their domination of that chamber while the Republicans kept their slim majority in the Senate, making for more gridlock in Washington. Mondale captured a majority of the Latino vote, two-thirds of the Jewish vote, and 90 percent of the black vote, even though as early as summer 1983 the administration had attempted to attract African American votes by sending Vice President Bush to justify its civil rights policies to the NAACP convention. Unlike Reagan's appearance in 1981, this time the audience booed Bush. "If Reagan is trying seriously to neutralize black hostility," wrote *Time*, "he has a long way to go."[8]

Correct, especially after the Reagan administration restarted the backlash just weeks after the second inauguration. "Assault on Affirmative Action," declared *Time*. The president appointed a new attorney general, Edwin Meese III, a clear signal that the administration again aimed to either reform or abolish the policy. U.S. Commission on Civil Rights chairman Clarence Pendleton Jr. and vice chairman Morris Abram labeled affirmative action "divisive, unpopular, and immoral" and called hearings for March 1985. All of the civil rights organizations refused to attend since the commission already had made up its mind. Pendleton opened the hearings by stating that preferential treatment for minorities was the "new racism," which prompted African American congressman Parren Mitchell to declare the statement "repugnant," and they "do not deserve a response, nor do they deserve respect." As he stormed out of the session, Mitchell charged that the hearings were "farcical and meaningless."

Not to the administration, who expanded its assault. William Bradford Reynolds declared that affirmative action was "demeaning because it says people are going to get ahead not because of what they can do, but because of their race." The "era of the racial quota has run its course." Attorney General Meese held his first news conference in March and assailed busing; he asked businesses to recruit qualified women and minorities but declared "quotas" improper and illegal. The EEOC's Clarence Thomas announced that his agency would not support the "comparable worth" concept for women as a means of ascertaining job discrimination. The Justice Department sent letters to 53 cities and states demanding that they accept the administration's interpretation of the *Stotts* case—and that they modify or end their affirmative action programs.

On June 15 the president joined in, delivering his most comprehensive statement on civil rights during his weekly radio address:

> There are some today who, in the name of equality, would have us practice discrimination. They have turned our civil rights laws on their head, claiming they mean exactly the opposite of what they say. These people tell us that the government should enforce discrimination in favor of some groups through hiring quotas, under which people get or lose particular jobs or promotions solely because of their race or sex. Some bluntly assert that our civil rights laws only apply to special groups and were never intended to protect every American.

Then the president cleverly reminded citizens that when Congress debated the Civil Rights Act in 1964, Senator Hubert Humphrey declared that he would "start eating the pages of the act if it contained any language which provides that an employer will have to hire on the basis of percentage or quota. . . . I think if Senator Humphrey saw how some people today are interpreting that act, he'd get a severe case of indigestion."

The president concluded his speech by using statements made earlier by Martin Luther King Jr.

Twenty-two years ago Martin Luther King proclaimed his dream of a society rid of discrimination and prejudice, a society where people would be judged on the content of their character, not the color of their skin. That's the vision our entire administration is committed to.

That vision was a colorblind society, one that banned preferences, and that was revealed again in August when administration officials leaked to the press a draft of an executive order that Meese had prepared for President Reagan. The proposed order would ban using "any statistical measures" to determine discrimination. Previously, that had been the only effective way to measure compliance, and it would make bias almost impossible to prove; statistical evidence had been upheld by the Supreme Court. The order also would charge the secretary of labor to "immediately revoke all regulations and guidelines promulgated" by LBJ's 1965 executive order that "require or provide a legal basis for a government contractor . . . to use numerical quotas, goals, ratios, or objectives." That would make affirmative action voluntary. Finally, the order stated that contractors should not "discriminate against, *or grant any preference to*, any individual or group on the basis of race, color, religion, sex, or national origin" in employment.

An "attempt to reverse history," declared Jesse Jackson, one that could result in "an American form of apartheid," but affirmative action critics disagreed. Professor Nathan Glazer labeled the proposal a "step in the right direction," one that "took enormous courage." Whatever the case, most likely the writers at *Fortune* were the most perceptive when they labeled Reagan's proposal either "a rocket or a trial balloon."[9]

It was a balloon which already was leaking in an unlikely venue, the Republican-led city of Indianapolis. The Hoosier capital had agreed to a plan with the Carter administration to establish an affirmative action program to hire more minorities and women into its police and fire departments. Accordingly, if there were qualified applicants, then all future police trainee classes would be 25 percent black and 20 percent female. This had resulted in an increase of African American officers from about 6 to 14 percent of those departments by 1985. The Justice Department asked Indianapolis to end its policy—and white Republican Mayor William Hudnut refused. Conservative ideology versus Midwestern pragmatism. A "lot of progress has been made with affirmative action goals," Hudnut declared, "the white majority has accepted the fact that we're making a special effort for minorities and women. I think it's a great mistake for the Justice Department to ask us to dismantle the program."

The Reagan administration's attempt to dismantle consent decrees and temporary local quotas found itself at odds with cities from California to Indiana to New York. "Does it make sense to risk stirring new divisiveness," asked *U.S. News*, "by reopening antidiscrimination plans arrived at earlier only after much bitterness?" Not to most city officials. "Why stir the mud?" answered Omaha's police chief, while chiefs in Milwaukee and Cincinnati declared that their plans had worked well and would be continued. The deputy mayor of Los Angeles was more blunt: "We're not going to back away one iota." Nor would other cities. A survey of the 53 jurisdictions that the administration had ordered to curtail their policies found that only three supported the Justice Department, while most agreed with the city attorney for Norfolk, Virginia, who refused to change the policy because he did not want "old wounds reopened."

Nor did many congressmen or civil rights organizations who resisted the administration. When the president attempted to promote William Bradford Reynolds from assistant to associate attorney general, the third-highest position at the Justice Department, Senate moderates and liberals blocked the promotion, and others warned Reagan of the possible consequences of signing a new executive order. The director of the Leadership Conference on Civil Rights, Ralph G. Neas, appealed to the White House and sent numerous letters from black politicians and Republicans. "It seems senseless, especially considering the overwhelming bipartisan consensus, to create another *Bob Jones* type firestorm," he wrote, one he predicted would last "not just for a few days or weeks, but for many months."

Nevertheless, the administration fought on that autumn. Reynolds declared his opposition to set-aside programs, charging that those companies that benefited were often those "who have discreetly placed blacks within their corporate structure—often temporarily—in order to be in a position to bid on a job as a minority business enterprise, and ... obtain the preference." Meese surprised many by declaring, "I personally am absolutely committed to affirmative action," and later he declared to faculty and students at Dickinson College that racial preferences really were "a new version of the separate but equal doctrine." Advocates call this reverse discrimination "benign. It is benevolent," Meese continued. "But you should not forget that an earlier generation of Americans heard from some that slavery was good not only for slaves but for society. It was natural, they argued. It was a kind of benevolence."

Comparing supporters of slavery with proponents of affirmative action drew immediate fire. "Unbelievable at best, deceptive at worst," declared the NAACP's Benjamin Hooks, while Ralph Neas was more sarcastic: "His remarks are Orwellian in their inaccuracy. As usual, Mr. Meese ignores history, the facts and the law."

Yet amid all the tough talk the president did not sign the executive order to end affirmative action programs in the government and with federal contractors. "This administration has a history of barking loudly," wrote *Fortune*, "and then failing to bite."

Why? Cities and most businesses aimed to keep affirmative action. While the policy was not supported by the Chamber of Commerce and some unions, it was endorsed by many corporate bosses and by the National Association of Manufacturers. "We will continue goals and timetables no matter what the government does," stated the CEO of Merck. "They are part of our culture and corporate procedures." A survey of more than 120 large corporations found that more than 95 percent of those CEOs agreed; they would continue the "use of numerical objectives to track the progress of women and minorities" in their companies "regardless of government requirements." Businessmen also feared what the states would do if the federal government ended affirmative action. The director of equal opportunity at Monsanto stated that no company wanted to face "a situation where 50 states pass 50 different laws and we'd be subject to compliance reviews in 50 different areas." As in 1981, businesses found that a diverse workforce was a stimulant to research, development, and customer relations, and they wanted to avoid appearing as discriminatory employers, which could result in costly law suits. Moreover, noted one corporate attorney, the next administration might reject Reagan's affirmative action stance, "and then business would be the scapegoat, facing a big back-pay liability."[10]

There also were political reasons. Most congressmen opposed any changes in affirmative action; eventually that included some 200 representatives and 70 senators who went on record, including two important Republicans, Senate Majority Leader Bob Dole and House Minority Leader Bob Michel. "When it works," said Michel, "you don't fix it." There also was the threat that if Reagan did issue a new executive order, Congress would try to pass a law mandating affirmative action, which would confront the president with unwanted publicity concerning racial issues, and, if passed, would present him with a no-win situation—a controversial choice of vetoing or signing the bill. Either way, this would divide the Republican Party. In fact, the second Reagan administration was publicly split over revising the policy. While the Justice Department led the charge, the new White House chief of staff, Donald Regan, and new secretary of labor, William Brock, did not support a new executive order; in fact, seven cabinet members eventually opposed any revisions in affirmative action, including Transportation Secretary Elizabeth Dole and the man who had implemented goals and timetables 16 years earlier, the now current secretary of state, George Schultz. Brock had addressed the NAACP convention that summer and declared that while opposed to strict quotas, "the country would have to have some form of affirmative action for the foreseeable future." And the director of the Office of Federal Contract Compliance Programs, African American Joseph Cooper, openly disagreed with Attorney General Meese over the idea that goals and timetables really were quotas. "Nobody's ever put any cases before me that involve quotas," he flatly declared, continuing that all his office wanted from contractors was "a good faith effort" to hire women and minorities. Moreover, if cities and corporations were going to continue their programs anyway, then what was the point? "Why rock the boat?" said one presidential aide, and after the plan was leaked to the press the White House spokesman dismissed the proposal as "simply a matter that is being discussed."

It was discussed for the next six months. The cabinet debated the executive order in an October meeting, without resolution, as administration conservatives went on the offensive. William Bradford Reynolds declared that he was "pretty much in lock step" with the civil rights movement. The president then gave a series of speeches in January 1986 as the nation celebrated the first national holiday named for Martin Luther King Jr. Reagan promoted a "truly colorblind America," and restated that his administration was:

> committed to a society in which all men and women have equal opportunities to succeed, and so we oppose the use of quotas. We want a colorblind society, a society that, in the words of Dr. King, judges people "not by the color of their skin, but by the content of their character."

On that January day Attorney General Meese declared that he was "trying to carry out the original intent of the civil rights movement" in proposing to eliminate "the use of quotas to discriminate or other subterfuges for quotas." That approach, he continued, was "very consistent with what Dr. King had in mind."

Thus, the president and his attorney general linked King's desire for a colorblind society with their own opposition to affirmative action. In future years other conservatives would follow suit. It was clever, but as we have seen, King had supported preferences for African Americans, and in 1967 he had lashed out against LBJ for not creating "a new government agency, similar to the WPA" for his people. King died before affirmative action developed, before the Philadelphia Plan, set-asides, and Court-approved temporary quotas.

The administration's rhetoric did not fool civil rights organizations. "It is especially scandalous on Martin Luther King's birthday to associate him with those who are attempting to gut the executive order," declared Ralph Neas. "There is no question that if Martin were alive today, he would be a leader of the extraordinary bipartisan consensus that is fighting to save the executive order." An opinion poll that month found that less than a quarter of African Americans approved of the president's performance, and a remarkable 56 percent of them agreed with the thought that Ronald Reagan was "a racist."

And so it was again. During the second Reagan term, like in the first one, the president talked tough but did not sign an executive order curbing or ending affirmative action. We were "expending a lot of political capital on this issue," Reynolds recalled, and it was "getting in the way of other things that are more important. The less problem for Reagan the better." Instead, the president and his Justice Department hoped that the job would be accomplished by the Supreme Court.[11]

The Court dashed the administration's hopes during the next year in four significant cases: one in Michigan that concerned teachers; another in Cleveland about firefighters; one in New York that pertained to sheet metal workers; and still another in Alabama about state police officers.

In an attempt to keep a balance of white and black teachers, the school board in Jackson, Michigan, laid off three senior white teachers in 1981 for every black one. Kindergarten teacher Wendy Wygant received the pink slip, and she and seven others sued the district. They did not claim that affirmative action policies were unconstitutional, but that officials had violated their Fourteenth Amendment guarantees of equal protection—they were laid off only because they were white. There were no findings of discrimination against black teachers, but the district defended its plan "to enhance the racial and ethnic diversity of its faculty following years of serious minority under-representation of its staff, caused by a history of past discrimination."

The Supreme Court ruled for Wendy Wygant, 5 to 4, and against the Jackson School Board. In her first opinion on affirmative action, Justice Sandra Day O'Connor refuted the Reagan administration's argument that such plans had to be limited to "actual victims of discrimination," a view that would sharply curtail policies throughout the nation. "The Court is in agreement," she wrote, that "remedying past or present racial discrimination by a state" warrants the "remedial use of a carefully constructed affirmative action program." The majority could not agree on reasoning for its decision, but Justice Lewis Powell's assertion supposedly won the day: Affirmative action plans had to be "narrowly tailored" to achieve appropriate ends. Plans that *hire* one race over another are constitutional but *laying off* based on race was too harsh for innocent people and thus unconstitutional.

Wygant settled little about affirmative action since the Court consistently had ruled in favor of seniority, but that was not true of three other cases—all strongly repudiated the Reagan administration. In Cleveland, the courts had sanctioned a four-year affirmative action plan that promoted one white for every minority firefighter with the goal of increasing the number of black officers to certain percentages in each rank. White firemen sued, and in *Local 93 of the International*

Association of Firefighters v. City of Cleveland they contended the plan was reverse discrimination and unconstitutional. In New York, the sheet metal workers union had refused to admit blacks since the state ordered it to do so in 1964. The courts twice held the union in contempt, and in 1983 the federal judiciary ordered it to increase its minority membership to at least 29 percent by 1987. The union sued and was joined by the Justice Department, which declared the percentage an illegal quota, resulting in *Local 28 v. Equal Employment Opportunity Commission*. In Alabama, which had about 40 percent black taxpayers, the state police had resisted desegregation. Eight years after the Civil Rights Act the force still was all white, resulting in a court order to integrate. Yet 12 years later only four of the 200 officers were black and none was above the rank of corporal. Thus, the courts ordered a "one-black-for-one-white" hiring and promotion plan, which resulted in whites suing and the Justice Department siding with them in *United States v. Paradise.*

In the Cleveland case the Court ruled 6 to 3 and in New York and Alabama 5 to 4. In all cases Justice William Brennan wrote the majority decision. "In most cases," he wrote about the New York case, "the Court need only order the employer or union to cease engaging in discriminatory practices" and then award compensation to the victims. Yet with "particularly longstanding or egregious discrimination," it "may be necessary to require . . . affirmative steps to end discrimination effectively," and that can mean "to hire and to admit qualified minorities roughly in proportion to the number of qualified minorities in the workforce." That may be the "only effective way to ensure the full enjoyment of the rights protected by Title VII." That stand was upheld in *Paradise*, where Brennan declared that the "one-for-one requirement" was proper because of the state's "long and shameful record of delay and resistance."

Taken together, the court refuted the Reagan administration's contention that Title VII prohibited the use of goals and timetables in hiring, and that only individual victims of discrimination could benefit from affirmative action. Brennan called the administration's views "misguided." Such an interpretation would "deprive the courts of an important means" of guaranteeing equal employment opportunity. Affirmative action plans mandating goals and timetables were constitutional if they were:

- limited in duration,
- "carefully tailored" to remedy the precise discrimination in each case,
- had flexible goals, and
- did not "unnecessarily trammel" the rights of whites.

Quotas could be used only in rare cases of "egregious discrimination" or when an agency had a "shameful record of delay," as in the New York and Alabama cases. Then, temporary quotas or one-for-one plans could be mandated as the only way to enforce Title VII. The rulings were, as *Time* wrote: "A Solid Yes to Affirmative Action."

Proponents cheered while the administration sought a silver lining to the defeat. A "great victory," declared the NAACP's Benjamin Hooks. It was a "significant rebuke to the Reagan administration's pernicious efforts to destroy affirmative action"; the executive director of the National League of Cities added that the decision "puts to rest efforts by the federal government . . . to open old wounds by seeking to characterize voluntary agreed-to hiring targets . . . as a form of reverse discrimination." Meese admitted that the Court "ruled against us," but then curiously stated that the justices had "accepted the general position of this administration that racial preferences are not a good thing." Reynolds stated his disappointment with the decisions but contended that they were "extremely limited," and so there would not be "any change at all" in the Justice Department's enforcement of civil rights laws.

The next month, however, the Justice Department quietly began dropping its lawsuits against cities and states. When a journalist asked a White House official about administration discussions on revising or ending affirmative action, he responded: "It is on the top of nobody's list. There is certainly no need to get into it."

After the bang, a whimper, for that statement marked the end of the backlash for the remainder of the Reagan administration.[12]

But not the end of Reagan's conservative agenda. Congress passed a law that barred American trade or investment with the apartheid regime in South Africa. The president vetoed the bill: Congress overrode the veto and it became law. Closer to home, Congress confronted the president with the Civil Rights Restoration Act. The act was a result of a lawsuit against Grove City College, a conservative Christian college in Pennsylvania, on which the Supreme Court had ruled in 1984. Previously, the Civil Rights Act of 1964, Title IX of the 1972 educational amendments, the Rehabilitation Act of 1973, and the Age Discrimination Act of 1975 had been interpreted to mean that if a public or private institution received federal funding, they could not discriminate on the basis of race, gender, disability, or age. Yet in *Grove City* the Court ruled that if a college did receive funds, then only the recipient program—not the entire institution—was banned from discriminating against women. The administration hailed the ruling, but women's and civil rights organizations, along with most congressmen, thought that it narrowed the previous civil rights acts. Congress wrote a bill to restore the original intent. It passed the House but stalled in the Senate until the Democrats regained that chamber after the 1986 elections. Then Congress passed the restoration act, 75 to 14 in the Senate and 315 to 98 in the House. In the Senate 27 Republicans joined the majority and 73 in the House. The votes were veto proof, but Reagan went on the attack, declaring that the bill would "vastly and unjustifiably expand the power of the federal government over the decisions and affairs of private organizations, such as churches and synagogues, farms, businesses and state and local governments." He vetoed the act. Congress easily overrode the veto and it became law.

The president counterattacked with nominations to the Supreme Court. In the Court's previous session, seven justices had rejected the administration's interpretation of Title VII and affirmative action, yet in all cases it had been upheld in minority briefs by Associate Justice William Rehnquist. Warren Burger announced his retirement in June 1986, and the president nominated Rehnquist to lead his colleagues as Chief Justice, and to fill that vacancy, Reagan nominated a 50-year old energetic conservative federal judge, Antonin Scalia, to become the new associate justice. "The ideological balance of the Supreme Court is likely to shift perceptibly to the right," the *New York Times* warned, "if the Senate confirms" Rehnquist and Scalia.

Yet before the Senate elevated Rehnquist and confirmed Scalia, the Court ruled for the first time on sexual harassment in employment, *Meritor Savings Bank v. Vinson.* Mechelle Vinson, a former employee of the bank, claimed that the manager had fondled her and other female employees and forced her to have sexual relations with him, even raping her. The supervisor denied the charges, citing Vinson's "sexual fantasies," and stating the relationship was voluntary; the courts never could clarify the dispute. The Justice Department supported the bank and the view written by an appellate court judge, Robert H. Bork, who narrowly interpreted Title VII. "Congress was not thinking of individual harassment at all but of discrimination in conditions of employment because of gender." A unanimous Supreme Court rejected that interpretation, Justice Rehnquist writing, "when a supervisor sexually harasses a subordinate because of the subordinate's sex, that supervisor 'discriminates' on the basis of sex."

On-the-job sexual harassment violated Title VII and was illegal, another defeat for the Justice Department and a victory for women's organizations. That happened again in March 1987 with Scalia now sitting on the Supreme Court. In *Johnson v. Santa Clara County Transportation Agency* the question was: Could a public employer voluntarily give a woman an edge in promotions to rectify the fact that while females might not have been discriminated against they had been *under-represented* in the agency's workforce?

Paul Johnson and Diane Joyce worked for the public transportation agency of Santa Clara County, California. When the job of road dispatcher became available in 1979, both applied, as did ten others. The county deemed seven applicants qualified for the job, including Johnson and Joyce, and all were given competitive interviews. Johnson was tied for second, receiving a score of 75, and Joyce was third at 73, with five other applicants above the minimum of 70. Three agency supervisors conducted second interviews, thought Johnson the most appropriate, but before the decision, Joyce informed the county's affirmative action officer that no woman had ever been a dispatcher. Eventually, the director gave the promotion to Diane Joyce.

Paul Johnson sued, claiming that the county had violated Title VII, which banned race and sex discrimination, and he was supported by the Justice Department. In the ensuing case, it was revealed that in 1978 the county had adopted the usual voluntary affirmative action plan with the aim of hiring a workforce in all positions that eventually reflected the ratio of minorities and women in the county. Where jobs had been traditionally segregated by gender, the county would consider sex as one factor in the hiring or promotion process. Nevertheless, not one woman was employed in any of the transportation agency's 238 skilled craft positions, one of which was road dispatcher. Thus, the agency director felt that since both applicants were qualified for the position, he chose Joyce, later admitting that her gender had been the "determining factor" in her selection.

The Supreme Court supported the policy 6 to 3. *Johnson* was the first ruling giving job preferences to women over men, and it marked the first time the Court held that without any proof of past discrimination an employer could use race and *gender* preferences in hiring or promotion to bring its workforce in line with the local population. Writing for the majority, Justice William Brennan declared that the county's policy was in line with *Weber*, declared nine years earlier. The "obvious imbalance" in the skilled craft positions meant that it was reasonable for the agency "to consider as one factor the sex of Ms. Joyce in making its decision." The agency's policy did not trammel "the rights of male employees" or create "an absolute bar to their advancement," and the agency had "no intention of establishing a work force whose permanent composition is dictated by rigid numerical standards." This "moderate, flexible, case-by-case approach" to increase the number of women and minorities in the workforce, Justice Brennan declared, was "fully consistent with Title VII."

"This case will have an impact on all women," declared Diane Joyce. The ruling was a victory for female employees as *Weber* had been for African Americans. Justice Blackmun's concurrence made that clear. The Court had approved an agency or business establishing a voluntary plan giving preference to women and minorities; it need only to point out a "conspicuous imbalance in traditionally segregated job categories."

The Reagan administration was "disappointed," but a more scathing assessment came from Justice Scalia. He ridiculed the idea that women were "eager to shoulder the pick and shovel" on road crews and thus deserved representation on those jobs; "it has not been regarded by women themselves as desirable work," and so it is "patently false" that the ruling corrects a "manifest imbalance" in a "traditionally segregated" job category. Instead, the Court had converted Title VII from a "guarantee that race or sex will not be the basis for employment determination to a guarantee that it often will." Thus, "we effectively replace the goal of a discrimination free society with the quite incompatible goal of proportionate representation by race and by sex in the workplace." The Court's "enormous expansion" of affirmative action was converting the

1964 Civil Rights Act into a "powerful engine of racism and sexism" against white men.

"I dissent," Scalia declared, but to no avail. For the fifth time in two years the Court had rejected the Reagan administration's interpretation of affirmative action and Title VII. The Court again denied pleas of reverse discrimination, first made by Allen Bakke, then Brian Weber, and now Paul Johnson, and that rejected the administration's aim to end preferences and establish a colorblind society. Significantly, the Court upheld affirmative action *and* expanded its meaning: Race and gender preferences were legal, even to benefit nonvictims, in hiring, promotion, university admission, and government contracting, including consent decrees and court-ordered plans for states and cities, and for both public agencies and private businesses. The set-aside program was not mentioned, naturally, but for other affirmative action programs from now on, white males were apparently protected on the job only if they had seniority.[13]

Johnson was not popular, and a Gallup poll asking a question about the decision found that two to one disapproved, but it was a relief for thousands of corporations, which, since the 1970s, had established policies that gave women and minorities preference on the job. Such plans, for example, had resulted in General Motor's white-collar workforce growing to almost 25 percent female and more than 13 percent minority. "It is basically a win for business," said a lawyer for the Chamber of Commerce, "since it gives them the freedom to voluntarily implement their own affirmative action plans, without fear of a reverse discrimination suit."

"The great affirmative action debate of the 1980s is over," declared *Business Week*, and that was true. The Court's spring 1987 session marked the limits of judicial expansion for affirmative action.

This tolerance would only last for the next two years, because that summer the president again nominated another conservative to the Supreme Court. The main author of *Bakke*, Justice Lewis Powell, retired, and the administration nominated Robert Bork. A federal judge and former law professor at Yale (where two of his students had been Bill Clinton and Hillary Rodham), Bork had given numerous speeches and written many decisions that revealed his condemnation of the "liberal drift" of the Court and his conservative notions about the Constitution. He had opposed all civil rights legislation and denounced the *Bakke* decision, calling its supporters "the hard-core racists of reverse discrimination." He stated that "privacy rights," a term that the Court had used to uphold birth control and abortion, was suspect because it was not mentioned in the Constitution. *Roe v. Wade*, he declared, was an "unconstitutional decision, a serious and wholly unjustifiable usurpation of state legislative authority," and he supported easing separation between church and state and the procedural protections for defendants gained because of the *Miranda* case. Such views alarmed civil rights and feminist organizations, liberals, and many moderates, and threatened Bork's nomination, and so did the fact that the president's esteem was faltering. The administration was in damage control mode over the Iran-Contra affair, Wedtech, Pentagon, and Savings and Loan scandals. The Senate rejected Bork 58 to 42, the largest margin of defeat ever for a nominee, and so Reynolds convinced the president to nominate Douglas H. Ginsburg, judge of the appeals court in Washington, D.C. Reynolds knew him personally and thought that he could count on the judge to uphold the administration's views on affirmative action, abortion, and antitrust cases. Reynolds rallied Meese and Reagan to support Ginsburg, which they did, but soon the nomination became a disaster. Ginsburg's wife, a doctor, had performed abortions, and during the 1970s he had smoked marijuana at parties when he was a law professor at Harvard. The nomination fiasco lasted only ten days. The administration withdrew his name and nominated Anthony M. Kennedy, who had never written his views on abortion and who seemed to be a moderately conservative federal judge in California. Liberals felt that he was the best nominee they could get from the Reagan administration, and Kennedy was unanimously confirmed by the Senate.

Thus, President Reagan's civil rights legacy was the appointment of three Supreme Court justices, and that would begin the shift to a more conservative Court. During his eight years in office Reagan appointed more than 370 federal judges, more than any other president in history up to that time, and about half of the total judgeships; that would shift the bench to the right. Supporters hailed Reagan for his attempt to bring about a colorblind nation while civil rights critics assailed him. As for affirmative action, the president stood up in opposition at the beginning of each term, but he lost, not only to liberal organizations but the Great Communicator could not persuade his own party. Republicans remained divided over affirmative action.[14]

Reagan retired to the California sun, leaving civil rights issues to his successor, George H. W. Bush. As early as 1986 the vice president had been quietly distancing himself from the conservative side of the Reagan administration as he prepared his run for the White House. That year he accepted an invitation to speak to the NAACP, and unlike his previous meeting, this time Bush appealed to the audience, calling for change in South Africa, "Restrictions on a free press and free expression must go. Apartheid must end." Digressing from his prepared text, he declared that he supported affirmative action programs that used goals but not quotas in hiring and promoting, winning applause.

Nevertheless, it would be a long campaign for the vice president, for the scandals and the stock market crash of 1987 and subsequent recession had taken a toll on the Republicans. Pollsters announced that most voters were ready for a change, and the Democrats were optimistic about their chances. A large number took to the campaign trail. Jesse Jackson made a second run, and for the first time so did Missouri congressman Richard Gephardt, and senators Paul Simon of Illinois and Al Gore Jr. of Tennessee. But the eventual nominee was Governor Michael Dukakis of Massachusetts. In that state his supporters gave him credit for improving the economy, what they dubbed the "Massachusetts Miracle." For his running mate he picked the popular senator from Texas, Lloyd Bentsen.

Dukakis led in opinion polls throughout the summer as the Republicans nominated the vice president as their standard bearer, and then Bush picked his running mate, the junior senator from Indiana, Dan Quayle. That surprised everyone, including Bush's staff and Quayle himself, who bungled his first statements. To make matters worse, a convention speaker called the junior senator the "electrifying young Giant from Indiana," which resulted in snickers from the delegates. Soon, the new vice presidential nominee was the butt of jokes on the late night shows. Johnny Carson: "Do you get the feeling that Dan Quayle's golf bag doesn't have a full set of irons?" It may have been unfair, but the point was that the vice presidential nominee, not the presidential, had become the story, resulting in an awkward start to the Bush campaign.

The 1988 campaign was a dismal affair, and virtually all commentators charged that most of the time the issues were not addressed. Bush and his campaign manager, Lee Atwater, went on the attack to win votes from the red-blooded Reagan supporters. The Republican used the American Flag as his campaign symbol, and he charged that Dukakis had vetoed a bill in his state that would have required teachers to lead their classes in the Pledge of Allegiance. "What is it about the Pledge of Allegiance that upsets him so?" asked Bush, and then declared that the Democrat was a "card carrying member" of the American Civil Liberties Union. Bush pledged low taxes and said that his liberal opponent had increased taxes in his home state so much that its name should be changed to "Taxachusetts."

The campaign became one of symbols and the most enduring one was Willie Horton. An African American from Massachusetts whose real name was William, he had been jailed with two others in 1974 for a robbery in which the victim had been stabbed to death; prosecutors never proved who held the knife. The federal government and many states, including California when Reagan was governor, then allowed prisoners a furlough for good behavior. Massachusetts had granted Horton nine of these furloughs without incident. In 1987, however, he did not return. Horton traveled to Maryland, broke into a home, knifed the white owner, and raped his fiancee. Campaign manager Atwater ran an ad titled, "Revolving Door," with prisoners walking though a turnstile, and changed "William" to the more racially charged "Willie," although Horton had never used it. The ad's imagery not only conjured up white fears of black crime but reinforced the perception that the Democrats were too tolerant of criminals and favored minorities. The effort worked; citizens forgot the stock market crash and all the Republican scandals. By late October more than 90 voters in focus groups were asked about Horton; all but five mentioned his race, and all but 12 noted that the victim was white. Another survey found that "helping blacks" was the issue that they most identified with Dukakis.

Thus, the race card helped propel Bush to the presidency; he won 66 percent of the white male vote. But it proved costly: most people were offended by the campaign, and the turnout on election day was the lowest since 1924. Opinion polls showed that less than 10 percent of the voters felt that the candidates had addressed the issues, and a remarkable two-thirds wished that two different candidates had been running. Only 43 percent had a favorable opinion of Bush, and that was translated at the polls as the Democrats easily won control of both the House and the Senate, resulting in more gridlock in Washington, D.C.

The new president moved to 1600 Pennsylvania Avenue and quickly named his team, which included seven former Reagan cabinet members. Many of those remained in the same job, such as Richard Thornburgh as attorney general, while others took different positions, such as Elizabeth Dole at the Labor Department. He named two women and two Hispanics, Lauren Cavasos (Education) and Manuel Lujan (Interior), and one African American, Louis Sullivan, as Secretary of Health and Human Services. The appointments sent a clear signal that Bush was moving away from many Reagan policies and toward what he referred to as a "kinder, gentler" nation, and this included civil rights issues. Within months the president stated that he favored affirmative action and outreach programs aimed at hiring minorities. His administration leaked the news that it was not interested in challenging existing affirmative action consent decrees nor in issuing an executive order that would overturn policies for federal contractors.[15]

The new administration would not have to, since during the first half of 1989 the former administration's tactic of appointing conservatives to the federal bench began to pay dividends. The Supreme Court issued five rulings that began the judicial backlash against affirmative action.

The first case concerned set-asides established during the Nixon years and legalized by the 1977 Public Works Act. During the next dozen years 36 states and 190 local governments had established these programs. That, along with the massive expansion of federal loans and grants to, and purchases from, minority-owned businesses was significant in quadrupling these companies from 320,000 to 1.2 million between 1969 and 1989.

Yet by the late 1980s there were many critics of set-aside programs. Governmental regulations during the decade had proscribed that 5 percent of defense procurement, 8 percent of NASA contracts, and 10 percent of transportation projects were to be awarded to minority-owned businesses—if they could be found. Problems developed. "Minority owned" never had been carefully defined nor stringently enforced. Recent immigrants, many of them Hispanics, often went into the construction trades, decreasing the probability that contracts would be granted to African Americans. The largest contracts went to only a few large firms, meaning that in 1990 only 50 firms, just 2 percent of those eligible, received 40 percent of the $4 billion awarded. Moreover, lucrative contracts mixed with vague guidelines and lax enforcement resulted in phony claims and fraud, which was most notoriously revealed in 1987 during the Wedtech scandal.

John Mariotta claimed two-thirds ownership of Wedtech, and because of his Puerto Rican ancestry his Bronx factory qualified for defense contracts to build engines for the U.S. Army. Mariotta became a poster boy for the Reagan administration in the early 1980s, and presidential assistants Ed Meese and Lyn Nofzinger interceded for Wedtech at the Pentagon. Yet during Reagan's second term, Wedtech filed for bankruptcy. When New York U.S. Attorney Rudolph Giuliani investigated, he discovered that Mariotta was a front man. Two immigrants really owned the company—one was not a minority, and the other did not qualify as an owner. Congressional hearings revealed fraud, bribery, and influence peddling, resulting in the indictment of Nofzinger, resignation of then Attorney General Meese, and imprisonment of a Bronx congressman and John Mariotta.

Thus by the late 1980s set-aside programs were becoming suspect, as was confirmed in Richmond, Virginia. The city had more than 50 percent black citizens but in the past minority contractors had received less than 1 percent of municipal contracts. Thus, in 1983, when the city council was dominated by African Americans, they passed a policy establishing a 30 percent set-aside, unusually high compared to other urban areas throughout the nation, which usually followed the 10 percent proportion. The council's plan was based on the federal law, yet it was sloppy, for the wording even included natives of the Aleutian Islands, a group obviously not present in Richmond. Eventually the city advertised for bids to install stainless steel fixtures in jails, and the J. A. Croson Company asked five minority firms if they would subcontract 30 percent of the work, but none replied, so Croson submitted a bid. Without minority participation, the city rejected Croson's bid, even though it was the lowest. Croson sued.

Appeals court Judge J. Harvie Wilkinson ruled in *City of Richmond v. J. A. Croson* that the 30 percent set-aside was not narrowly tailored but the figure had "simply emerged from the mists." Moreover, the figure was "spurious" because less than 5 percent of all construction companies in the nation were minority owned, and over 40 percent of those were in just five states, and that excluded Virginia.

The Supreme Court rejected Wilkinson's idea that a city must limit preferences, and it exempted minority programs approved by Congress, thus upholding the Public Works Act. Then, it rejected Richmond's argument 6 to 3 that cities or states enjoyed sweeping discretion to define their set-aside programs. An important difference between this case and *Santa Clara* was that Paul Johnson declared that he was being discriminated against based on Title VII, while Croson proclaimed that he deserved equal protection because of the Fourteenth Amendment to the Constitution, and this was upheld by the Court. Writing for the majority Sandra Day O'Connor held that the equal protection clause protected individual rights of all citizens, and that the only legitimate reason for racial preferences was to remedy past discrimination. "The 30 percent quota cannot in any realistic sense be tied to any injury suffered by anyone," she wrote. "There is *absolutely no evidence* of past discrimination against Spanish-speaking, Oriental, Indian, Eskimos, or Aleut persons in any aspect of the Richmond construction industry. . . . It may well be that Richmond has never had an Aleut or Eskimo citizen." Any preferences based on race must pass a test of "*strict scrutiny*," a legal term meaning the issue is on dubious constitutional ground and must meet the toughest judicial standard. Preferences could be justified only if they served "compelling state interest" of redressing "identified discrimination." To her, any "rigid numerical quota" was suspect.

In *Richmond*, all of Reagan's appointments voted with the majority. Less than two years after *Santa Clara*, the case began the shift away from racial and gender preferences—but only in contracting and only if there had been no prior discrimination. The adoption of strict scrutiny raised questions if affirmative action plans could survive such a test, and it battered the idea that a policy could be based on the ratio of minorities in a city. O'Connor's opinion cited not just the number but the "number of minorities *qualified* to undertake a particular task."

A "full scale retreat," wrote Justice Marshall, "from the Court's long standing solicitude to race-conscious remedial efforts" to bring about equal economic opportunity. It was a "giant step backward," but not to critics of affirmative action. Charles Krauthammer wrote that the Court was "drawing a narrower and narrower circle—a noose—around any government action that is race-conscious," and George Will praised the ruling for rolling back the "racial spoils system that exists for certain government-favored minorities."

Actually, *Richmond* was too narrow. While cities and states reviewed their set-aside programs, they also kept them because too many questions were left unanswered. What constituted a "minority-owned" business, and if local taxes are used for the construction then do federal or local set-aside rules apply? "The decision is not exactly . . . crystal clear," said the city attorney for Pensacola, Florida. "We have a lot of questions to answer before we find out what the impact of it is."[16]

The questions only became more numerous that summer as the Court ruled on a series of narrow cases, which continued to tighten the noose around affirmative action. In *Martin v. Wilks*, the Court ruled that whites on the Birmingham (Alabama) Fire Department could bring a reverse discrimination suit against the city's 1979 consent decree and subsequent affirmative action plan. In *Patterson v. McLean Credit Union*, the Court upheld a section of an 1866 law used to challenge discrimination but refused to allow Brenda Patterson to use the law to sue and collect damages for racial harassment on the job, which appeared to reverse the practice that had been used since the *Runyon v. McCrary* decision of 1976.

More significant was *Wards Cove Packing Co. v. Atonio*, which involved a suit filed 15 years earlier by Filipino and Native American workers at a salmon cannery in Alaska. The workers claimed that the hiring and promotion practices, including keeping mess halls and bunkhouses segregated, kept them on the cannery line and left the better jobs for whites. The minorities claimed that those policies, while not necessarily racially motivated, had a "disparate impact" on their chances for advancement and thus violated Title VII as the Court had decided in the *Griggs* case of 1971. The company rebutted the charge, stating that the percentage of whites in the skilled positions reflected the available pool of qualified applicants. A trial judge ruled for the company, but an appeals court reversed, saying that the statistical imbalance of workers shifted the burden to the company to show that its policies were justified by business necessity. Supreme Court Justice John Paul Stevens agreed, writing that the Alaska salmon industry bears an "unsettling resemblance to aspects of a plantation economy."

Yet the majority of the Court ruled for the company, 5 to 4, as all Reagan appointees lined up against *Griggs*. If the appeals court opinion stood, Justice Byron White wrote, then that "would almost inexorably lead to the use of numerical quotas in the workplace, a result that Congress and this Court have rejected repeatedly in the past." Supporting the contention Justice O'Connor made in *Richmond* six months earlier,

White continued, "If the absence of minorities holding such skilled positions is due to a dearth" of qualified applicants, then the company's "selection methods or employment practices cannot be said to have had a 'disparate impact' on minorities."

From now on it would take more than just showing that minorities or women were *under-represented* in a company, as had been the issue two years earlier in *Johnson v. Santa Clara*. Employees now must prove that their employers had a hiring or promotion process that actually discriminated against them—which became the law of the land.

The dissent was sharp. Justice Blackmun wondered "whether the majority still believes that race discrimination—or, more accurately, race discrimination against nonwhites—is a problem in our society, or even remembers that it ever was." An "outrage," declared the American Civil Liberties Union. *Wards Cove* had "reversed two decades of precedent" and "effectively read Title VII off the books," while the *Washington Post* editorialized that *Griggs* obviously had just been "An 18-Year Misunderstanding."

During the 1989 session the Court essentially reversed *Griggs*. From now on it would be easier for a white male to sue for reverse discrimination and more difficult for a woman or minority to win a case. Using statistics to prove under-representation, and thus discrimination, was suspect, and the cases reversed the burden of proof: Employees would have to show a discriminatory cause and effect, basically ending the old notion of disparate impact. Moreover, the Court now seemed to be looking for ways to limit discrimination cases. In *Patterson*, for example, the Court took the extraordinary step of deciding to review the rights of minorities to sue under *Runyon*; the parties in *Patterson* had not asked for a reconsideration, so five conservative members had taken the initiative on their own. "When it comes to civil rights," penned the *Nation*, "it is now clear that Reagan's Court has arrived."

That alarmed women and civil rights groups. The "1989 session dealt a devastating array of defeats for women and minority men," declared *Ms.* magazine. The NAACP's Benjamin Hooks stated that the Court had become "more dangerous to this nation than any Bull Connor with a fire hose," for it was "stripping us . . . of the precious hard-won victories." He called on Congress to write a new civil rights law that would restore rights, threatening that if it did not then "the only recourse left to us is civil disobedience, on a scale which has never been seen in this country before."[17]

Congress responded quickly. Senator Edward Kennedy and California Democratic Representative Augustus Hawkins sponsored what became the Civil Rights Act of 1990. Congress "should simply pass a law saying that *Wards Cove* was overruled," Kennedy wrote to the president's chief of staff John Sununu, "and that *Griggs* is the law." The bill aimed to limit lawsuits that challenge court-approved affirmative action programs and strengthen federal protection against harassment on the job by allowing plaintiffs to demonstrate discrimination by using statistics, or disparate impact. It would shift the burden of proof from workers back to bosses. Moreover, for the first time it would give *all* victims of intentional job discrimination a chance to win financial compensation and punitive damages. Previously, only minorities could win such awards; all others could seek only back pay and legal fees. Thus, Mary Ann Vance, a black employee of a Florida telephone company, had won $1 million in compensatory and punitive damages after proving to a jury that her co-workers had twice hung a noose over her desk, while Carol Zabkowicz, a white warehouse worker in Wisconsin, won less than $3,000 in back pay after male co-workers during a five year period pulled on her bra, exposed their genitals, and posted drawings of her having sex with animals, which a federal judge labeled "sustained, vicious and brutal" sexual harassment.

The Bush administration's response was bold—they labeled the Civil Rights Act the "quota bill." Most business groups, of course, opposed the act since it would allow employees to argue discrimination with little more than statistics to prove an imbalance in a company's workforce; critics wanted the weaker standard set in *Wards Cove*, which required only that a practice served an employer's "legitimate business goals." The new bill would increase the probability of more law suits and expensive punitive damages. "Quota systems will be the only way an employer can protect himself," declared a spokesman for the U.S. Chamber of Commerce. Attorney General Thornburgh recommended that his boss veto "any legislation that would encourage quota systems or otherwise divide our society along racial lines."

"Quotas, schmotas," responded Senator Kennedy, a "phony" argument, but quotas and affirmative action became issues during the political campaigns of 1990. As early as 1985, in the wake of the Reagan reelection landslide, Michigan Democrats commissioned pollster Stanley Greenberg to study "Democratic defection" in their state. He went to Macomb County, a white working-class suburb of Detroit, where in 1964 residents gave Lyndon Johnson a remarkable 74 percent of the vote; in 1984 Ronald Reagan won an extraordinary 67 percent. What happened? Unemployment in the "rust belt" and racial issues like busing and affirmative action. Greenberg and others discovered that the white working class now perceived the Democratic party as favoring African Americans. When they asked the workers, "Who do you think gets the raw deal?" the answer was immediate: "We do. The middle-class white guy. The working middle class. 'Cause women get advantages, the Hispanics get advantages, Orientals get advantages. Everybody but the white male race gets advantages now." Preferences were viewed "by almost all of these individuals as a serious obstacle to their personal advancement." Discrimination against whites had become an explanation of their status, vulnerability, and failures. Hence, they had become "Reagan Democrats" for the 1984 election, and during the ensuing years this perception hurt the Democrats who were losing votes from one of their most important constituencies. "When we hold focus groups," stated a Democratic pollster in 1990, "if the issue of affirmative action comes up, you can forget the rest of the session. That's all that's . . . talked about." During the fall campaign the president was winning the fight to define the Civil Rights Act, for as one pollster wrote, "Any bill he signs will be a civil rights bill and any bill he vetoes will be a quota bill."

The Senate passed the Civil Rights Act in October and days later Bush vetoed it, employing the word "quota" seven times in his announcement, declaring the act would "introduce the destructive force of quotas into our Nation's employment system." That tactic was picked up by Republicans across the country who were in tight races. California GOP gubernatorial candidate Pete Wilson ran ads charging that his Democratic opponent, Dianne Feinstein, "favored job quotas," and he squeaked out a victory. In Louisiana, former Ku Klux Klansman David Duke lost his bid for a state senate seat but won 60 percent of the white vote in his district by playing the quota card, and in North Carolina, Senator Jesse Helms hammered his Democratic opponent, African American Harvey Gantt, with a TV ad campaign that showed a white man ripping up a job rejection letter as a voice announced: "You needed that job and you were the best qualified, but they had to give it to a minority because of a racial quota. Is that really fair?"

Fairness became a campaign issue. "The Democrats are about to discover the dark side of the fairness issue," *Business Week* noted, warning that "it should be no surprise to Democrats in '92 if George Bush takes off the gloves and starts bashing the opposition for supporting quotas." Republican Party chairman William Bennet did just that as he endorsed the tactics of Jesse Helms and challenged Democrats to a national debate on affirmative action. Quotas "could be political dynamite in the '92 campaign," wrote *Newsweek*. "Republicans may have found the sequel to Willie Horton."

By the end of the year *Newsweek* predicted of the 1992 election, "To talk quotas will be the polite way to talk race and class. . . . By attacking quotas George Bush will be able to say . . . in essence: if you don't get a job, promotion or a place in the freshman class, blame the Democrats. They are the ones mugging the middle class and giving the spoils to their minority friends."[18]

Yet before the presidential elections the nation turned its attention away from domestic policy and toward war in the Persian Gulf. Iraqi forces had invaded neighboring Kuwait, and President Bush rallied an allied force to liberate the small oil-soaked nation. In January 1991 the coalition forces began Operation Desert Storm, Iraq's dictator Saddam Hussein called on his countrymen to fight the "mother of all wars," but the Allies quickly crushed Iraq's army and liberated Kuwait. As American troops came home heroes, the president's approval rating soared to 90 percent.

Domestic problems and policies would bring the president's approval rating back to reality. In July the civil rights pioneer and ailing Justice Thurgood Marshall announced his retirement from the Supreme Court. This was Bush's second opportunity to nominate a justice; the first one had been a year earlier after the resignation of William Brennan, who had been confirmed during the Eisenhower administration. Brennan had often sided with the liberal side of the bench concerning affirmative action, but Bush was not in a mood for a bruising fight with the Democratic Senate; he nominated moderate conservative David Souter, a federal judge, who won easy confirmation. The retirement of Marshall, however, opened up the possibility of shifting the Court more to the right since the president's postwar approval ratings remained high.

Accordingly, Bush nominated Clarence Thomas, a 43-year old conservative African American. A Yale Law School graduate and former EEOC chairman, Thomas had been a federal appeals court judge for only eight months. Nevertheless, when the president introduced Thomas from his summer home in Kennebunkport, Maine, he professed that his nominee had pulled himself out of poverty and segregation in Georgia, and that the nomination was based entirely on merit. "Judge Thomas's life is a model for all Americans," said the president, he's the "best man" for the job.

The nomination caused an immediate controversy. Unlike liberal Marshall, who was a hero to civil rights organizations, Thomas had given a speech "Why Black Americans Should Look to Conservative Politics," declaring that he had become a success "not only without the active assistance of government but with its active opposition." He opposed all varieties of racial preferences and had attacked goals and timetables, usually labeling them "quotas," stating that they had the insidious effect of promoting the notion that blacks could not compete with whites on equal footing. To him, affirmative action was "social engineering."

The fact that Thomas "is an African American," a NAACP spokesman said, "should not be a basis for avoiding very careful scrutiny of his civil rights record," which began during long hearings that autumn in the Senate. Thomas had been admitted to Yale Law School under that university's affirmative action program, yet he now opposed preferences for other minorities. William Bradford Reynolds held that Thomas represented "the epitome of the right kind of affirmative action," while Jesse Jackson labeled him the "most sponsored black man in American history." Liberal congressmen charged that when Thomas was EEOC chairman he had a "questionable enforcement record" and had been "insensitive to the injustice" of those who have suffered job discrimination. He had criticized the Court's decision in *Roe v. Wade* and opposed *Johnson v. Santa Clara*, stating that the bench was "standing the legislative history of Title VII on its head." Nevertheless, the Judicial Committee sent his nomination forward for a debate and vote in the Senate.

Then came Anita Hill. During the FBI's background check, a former employee of EEOC, African American attorney Hill, charged that Thomas had harassed her at the agency. As TV cameras rolled she detailed his penchant for discussing his sexual prowess with female aides, even his fancy for a pornographic movie, "Long Dong Silver." Suddenly, the nomination was in jeopardy. Senator Orrin Hatch came to the rescue, criticizing the broad nature of harassment laws, declaring that anyone could defame the reputation of an innocent man. Hill was called to defend her statements, and as women's and civil rights organizations lined up in support she told the nation of "the most difficult experience of my life." The media focused in, broadcasting the issue— sexual harassment. Thomas defended himself, condemning the confirmation process as a "lynching" and denying the charges as "the most bigoted racist stereotypes that any black man will face." As politicians yelled at each other on the Senate floor, a Republican aide claimed that Hill wanted to write a book, make a movie, where she would be the "Rosa Parks of sexual harassment." While the circus continued, the president stood by his man: "This decent and honorable man has been smeared."

Eventually the Senate confirmed Thomas by the thin margin of 52 to 48, but the hearings and confirmation hurt the Bush administration. Many conservatives felt that the president should have withdrawn the nomination after Hill's charges. Many women felt the president was insensitive to sexual harassment, and his advisers feared a "sexual backlash" in the 1992 election. Nor did the nomination help Bush with the black community, which was not enthusiastic about Thomas.[19]

During the confirmation hearings Bush also fought Congress over the shape of the Civil Rights Act of 1991. Early in the year Democrats introduced the bill, which like the previous year was aimed at restoring affirmative action law. Sponsors of the new measure emphasized that the bill would shift the burden of proof back to the employer; the boss would have to prove "business necessity," such as a high school degree for certain positions, in order to justify hiring patterns that appeared discriminatory. The bill would amend Title VII of the 1964 Civil Rights Act, allowing not only minorities but also religious minorities, the disabled, and significantly, all women, to sue their employers in a jury trial for discrimination or sexual harassment, and if victorious, to collect back pay and punitive damages.

With sexual harassment a hot topic, the Democrats pursued the women's vote, and the administration countered with its own bill. The Republican measure would make it easier for employers to prove that their hiring practices were based on "legitimate business objectives" and did not discriminate. It supported the idea that white females should be allowed to sue for damages for sexual harassment, but in a trial without a jury, and potential damages would be limited to $150,000. Without such limits, the administration maintained, there was risk of turning the bill into "some lawyer's bonanza." Strangely, the Justice Department distributed its bill in the evening after Congressional offices were closed.

"I know why they didn't show this to you until the evening," stated Ralph Neas of the Leadership Conference on Civil Rights. "It wouldn't stand up in the light of day." Some Republicans agreed; the one leading the fight for a new bill, Senator John C. Danforth of Missouri, wrote to the White House: "The present position of the Administration is truly a turning back of the clock on civil rights," but other Republicans disagreed, and House Republican leader Robert Michel labeled the Democrats' bill "de facto quotas."

"Tossing Around the 'Quota' Bomb," editorialized the *New York Times*, but actually the issue was not quotas: it was business necessity and it was money. What was business necessity and how much could a white woman win if she proved discrimination? That became clear as congressmen discussed the bill and as members of the Business Roundtable, a group of CEOs representing 200 large corporations, held talks with civil rights leaders in an attempt to come up with a compromise. To the chagrin of the administration, the Roundtable stated that quotas were a "non-issue."

In fact, the administration had failed to offer any proof that in the 18 years between *Griggs* and *Wards Cove* businesses had been forced to adopt quota hiring, and that information was discovered in a large survey by *Business Week*. During the spring of 1991 the magazine interviewed and questioned over 400 senior executives at top corporations. Does your company set "numerical goals but not quotas" for hiring minorities and women? Forty percent said yes to goals, 48 said no, meaning that few if any of these businesses had established quota employment practices. Almost 80 percent declared that they were making "special efforts to recruit" minorities, while just 5 percent stated that they had "lower hiring standards for them." When asked how much trouble affirmative action had caused their corporations, only 6 percent answered "a lot." The rest said "some" or "not much," and two-thirds of them felt that they already were hiring women and minorities without government regulations; they did not need equal employment laws. Thus, as Reagan discovered in the early 1980s, affirmative action had become an integral part of doing business in America.

To most corporate leaders the quota issue was bogus, but a more realistic problem at public agencies was called by its supporters "within-group score conversion" and by its critics "race norming." The Carter administration had implemented the practice as it was leaving office in 1980. Recall that those officials had signed an agreement with minority federal workers that scrapped the Professional and Administrative Career Examination (PACE) and established guidelines, which assured that the number of minorities getting better jobs would be almost proportional to the number taking the new tests, thereby guaranteeing professional advancement based on race. Many cities and almost 40 states had adopted such policies since, on average, minorities scored lower on valid job-related tests. To get around this hurdle, agencies, including the Reagan's and Bush's Labor Department, began to rank workers only against other members of their own ethnic group, not against all applicants. For example, if a black, brown, and white each took a test with 500 possible points and they all scored the same raw number, the Labor Department's Employment Service would report a group score, meaning that the same test score would place the black candidate in the top 20th percentile of all African Americans who took the test, the Hispanic in the top 25 percent, and the white applicant in the top 40th percentile. In other words, to be ranked in the 99th percentile a white applicant would have to score 405, a Hispanic 382, and a black 355, which alarmed critics. "If they want to abandon testing, that's one thing," declared Illinois Republican Representative Henry Hyde. "But if you are going to use the test, don't cook the books."

Such views won the day, and the testing issue did not hold up the passage of a new civil rights act; after months of bickering key politicians hammered out a compromise that had sufficient Congressional support to override a possible presidential veto. Republican Senator Danforth and Democrat Kennedy negotiated with White House Counsel C. Boyden Gray and Chief of Staff John Sununu. Just weeks before, Danforth had gone to the mat guiding the controversial Thomas nomination through the Senate, so the president decided to support his bill. "I can say to the American people, this is not a quota bill," declared Bush. It was a "civil rights bill," and it passed overwhelmingly in both the House and the Senate.

In November the president signed the 1991 Civil Rights Act. It amended Title VII and the Americans with Disabilities Act of 1990, which gave more employment protection to the disabled. The new law outlawed race norming, and it made it more difficult to challenge court-ordered consent decrees. It mandated that *all* victims of intentional job discrimination, not just minorities, had the right to a jury trial and if victorious could collect punitive and compensatory damages from businesses with 15 or more employees. Congress set caps on the damages for each plaintiff: $50,000 for firms with 15 to 100 employees; $100,000 for up to 200 workers; $200,000 for up to 500; and $300,000 for corporations with more employees. The bill returned the burden of proof to employers. It wrote the concept of disparate impact into law for the first time, stating that employers must show that a practice is "job-related for the position in question and consistent with business necessity." Yet the term "business necessity" was not firmly defined, leaving its meaning to the courts. Senator Bob Dole felt that since Reagan and Bush had appointed so many federal judges they would support the narrow standard set in *Wards Cove*, but Kennedy declared the bill mandated the disparate impact rules set by *Griggs*.

The 1991 Civil Rights Act was significant but confusing. It rejected the Reagan administration's views on affirmative action, along with those of the conservative majority of the Supreme Court; it reversed the 1989 rulings. It provided some support to court-ordered consensus plans and extended punitive damages to victims of discrimination and sexual harassment. Title II, "The Glass Ceiling Act of 1991," established a commission to examine why women and minorities were under-represented in management. Yet since both political parties needed a bill to present to their different constituents the subsequent act was perplexing. It declared that an "unlawful employment practice" was "when the complaining party demonstrates that race, color, religion, sex, or national origin was a motivating factor for any employment," which seemed to outlaw preferences; another clause stated, "Nothing in the amendments made by this title shall be construed to affect court-ordered remedies, affirmative action, or conciliation agreements, that are in accordance with the law."

For the first time Congress voted on and supported affirmative action but did not define the policy, confounding many. "It took two years to pass this law and it will take 10 years of litigation before there is any full understanding of what Congress meant," declared a Washington lawyer who was the chief negotiator for the Business Roundtable. Most legal experts agreed, saying that political attempts to paper over deep philosophical divisions in Congress led to a bill riddled with ambiguous provisions, leaving the task of clarification to the federal judiciary.

The Bush administration added to the confusion. The president had vetoed the 1990 act claiming that it would establish quotas and encourage hiring based on race but permitted his Department of Education to continue university scholarship programs that were based on race. He declared his opposition to reverse discrimination at the same time his administration supported set-asides. He opposed the idea that the government considered a woman or minority a member of a "protected class" even as his EEOC began to toughen enforcement against sexual harassment and while he supported and signed the 1991 American with Disabilities Act, which expanded that status to the disabled. On the day before Bush signed the civil rights bill his White House counsel, C. Boyden Gray, issued a directive ordering termination of any regulation that mandates or encourages the "use of quotas, preferences, set-asides, or other similar devices on the basis of race, color, religion, sex, or national origin"—essentially the same executive order that Reagan had threatened to sign to abolish affirmative action. The next morning press secretary Marlin Fitzwater stated that Gray had acted without the president's knowledge, and the directive was dropped before Bush signed the act and declared his support for "the government's affirmative action program." As reporters questioned the administration, Fitzwater tried to clarify. "Let me be clear. The president supports affirmative action, preferences, and minority set-asides as long as they are consistent with the new civil rights law, period."

It was the "latest flip flop flap" wrote one journalist while another noted that the "Bush administration still displays no consistent philosophy or clear voice on issues of race and civil rights."

Others noticed this confusion as the 1992 election approached. In 1990 observers had predicted that the president would use quotas in the 1992 elections as an issue to attack the Democrats, but that was not to be. Republicans David Duke and Patrick Buchanan were filling the airwaves with radical rhetoric during an economic downturn, blaming the loss of white jobs on quotas and minorities, immigrants, and anything foreign. With Duke's racial statements staining the Republican party, Bush declared that the candidate had an "ugly record of racism," called him a "charlatan," and urged Louisianians to vote against him. The president also dropped any plans to use quotas as an issue in the 1992 campaign. "Duke," said a Democratic pol, "blows another Willie Horton gambit out—entirely." Moreover, the president had signed his civil rights act and backed away from issuing Gray's executive order, making him a moderate Republican, which irritated many of his conservative supporters. The *National Review* complained that the president "signed into law something we all on principle had once opposed as a quota bill." The editors praised Gray, and hoped that the administration "will recover its nerve" on civil rights issues.[20]

Civil rights would not be the hot-button topic of the presidential race. "The Economy, Stupid," was the sign at the headquarters of the Democratic nominee, former Arkansas governor Bill Clinton. The recession arrived and was in full swing. America's automobile manufactures were losing money, shutting down plants; General Motors cut 74,000 jobs and announced plans to close more than twenty factories. Corporations were laying off management, now labeled "downsizing," as IBM eliminated 100,000 employees. From June 1990 to January 1992 over four million jobs were lost. In 1991 the unemployment rate reached an eight-year high at almost 8 percent and by spring 1992 a Bush aide admitted, "Our whole political problem is the recession," which by then had lasted 20 months. Moreover, annual federal deficits were exploding, and that year saw the highest on record, $290 billion, which meant that the president had to go back on his 1988 pledge, "Read my lips. No new taxes," and sign a tax hike. That, and the deficits, irritated his conservative base and resulted in evaporating popular support. By the summer before the election the president's overall job-performance rankings had sunk to only 29 percent, and only 15 percent approved of his handling of the economy.

The economy opened the door for Bill Clinton and for a third-party challenge from Dallas billionaire H. Ross Perot. Both hammered the president. The Bush campaign floundered and seemed rudderless, while Clinton campaigned tirelessly and acted as the master of ceremony at the Democratic Convention, which bounced him into the lead position of the three-way race. Perot bought chunks of television time and with a library of charts convinced many voters that the nation was headed for ruin. In 1988 almost 60 percent thought America was moving in the right direction, but only 16 percent did by fall 1992. The result was disaster for Bush, who received only 38 percent of the vote, the lowest reelection attempt of any sitting president since William Howard Taft in 1912, another three-way race. Perot won 19 percent of the vote, and Clinton easily won the electoral vote as he picked up over a quarter of Republican votes and two-thirds of the independents. That propelled him into the White House and ended the conservative era of Reagan and Bush.

The Reagan and Bush backlash had an impact on affirmative action. The two presidents appointed scores of federal judges, many of them opposed to preferences. In contrast to Carter, whose appointments to the federal bench were over 16 percent African American, less than 2 percent of Reagan's were black, just six judges. More significantly, the Republican presidents appointed five to the Supreme Court, moving it from being the protector of civil rights—one of its roles since the 1954 *Brown* decision—to adopting what its proponents called a more color-blind approach, as demonstrated by its 1989 and later decisions. Also during the Republican years, civil rights and equal employment laws were not as toughly enforced as during the Carter years. While that is difficult to measure, the EEOC and the OFCCP shifted enforcement away from the class-action lawsuits used in the 1970s to those of conciliation and cases seeking relief only for individual victims of discrimination; relief for groups was seen as "reverse discrimination," which was a shift in the perspective the federal government had held between 1965 and 1980. While no changes were made officially in the agencies' guidelines, both of them informally reduced the pressure on companies and contractors to maintain plans with goals and timetables, another standard throughout the 1970s.

Perhaps that was somewhat natural, in the sense that the first era of enforcement normally would be in the decade after the 1969 Philadelphia Plan and 1971 *Griggs* case, with less needed after businesses had established programs. Yet the Reagan administration went on the attack, attempting to convince businesses, cities, and states to end their affirmative action programs; the Bush administration shied away from that tough stance and never developed a consistent policy, except on sexual harassment where it increased enforcement.

The two Republican administrations also took an additional step—they promoted the idea that affirmative action meant quotas, and that transformed the argument. While quotas had been mentioned since the 1960s, the debate generally centered on colorblind merit versus racial and sexual preferences to make up for past discrimination. Reagan supported merit, so did Bush, but they changed the argument to a simplistic choice that was easy for whites to understand: quotas versus fairness.

Fairness again became the issue. "If civil rights is defined as quotas, it's a losing hand," wrote a pollster. "If it's defined as protection against discrimination and efforts to promote opportunity, then it will remain a mainstream value in American life." Another pollster put it this way: "Only about 10 percent of the people in the country are for quotas, but only about 10 percent are against civil rights." Quota pronouncements during the Reagan–Bush years contributed to declining public support for affirmative action programs. When respondents were asked in May 1985 if they favored preference in hiring or promotion for blacks in areas where there had been past discrimination, 42 percent said yes and 46 percent said no; when asked the same question in December 1990, only 42 percent said yes and 52 percent said no. Depending on how the question has been phrased, and since the last half of the 1980s, usually less than one-quarter of white respondents have supported preferential admissions into college and less than 20 percent approve of preference on the job. In this sense, then, conservatives during the Republican years successfully delineated two competing visions of America: individual merit and open competition for opportunity versus special preferences and quotas.[21]

Thus, the conservative backlash planted the seed in the minds of many citizens that affirmative action equaled quotas. That seed would sprout by the 1994 Republican victory in Congress and bloom later as states passed referendums and the Supreme Court issued decisions—all of which diminished affirmative action—a policy that fewer and fewer Americans still believed was fair.

five | Demise of Affirmative Action in the Age of Diversity

"The Man from Hope," declared one of Bill Clinton's campaign slogans. Hope, Arkansas, was his birthplace, where his mother raised him, where he went to high school, and where he left for Georgetown University, then Oxford, and eventually Yale Law School. He returned to Arkansas with his wife, Hillary, and enough drive to be elected governor at age 33. Six years later he was stunned by Ronald Reagan's overwhelming reelection in 1984, and along with other moderate Democrats, such as Sam Nunn of Georgia and Al Gore Jr. of Tennessee, he began to think that his party would be doomed to more defeats unless it changed its focus from the left to the middle and made a strenuous effort to woo white voters back to the party. A year later Clinton was one of the founders of the Democratic Leadership Council, a group of centrists, and the DLC began advocating welfare reform, a tougher stance on crime, smaller government, a middle-class tax cut, and a strong defense. Clinton embraced those themes in 1991 when he declared his nomination and presented himself during the campaign as a "New Democrat." He was an energetic campaigner, a smooth speaker, and he fought off challenges from Nebraska Senator Bob Kerrey, former Massachusetts Senator Paul Tsongas, and former California Governor Jerry Brown. The South's primary, "Super Tuesday," in March 1992 catapulted Clinton into the lead. He won his party's nomination easily, picked Al Gore as his running mate, and began his march to the White House.

The Clinton-Bush-Perot run of 1992 concerned mainly the economy, with civil rights issues taking a back seat. The Democratic platform supported affirmative action and pledged that the party "will continue to lead the fight to ensure that no Americans suffer discrimination," not only because of their race and gender but now including "sexual orientation." The Republican platform gave only a general statement supporting equal opportunities and civil rights for all citizens. Candidate Clinton avoided speaking on such issues, knowing that it could be a wedge between white male workers and minorities. The New Democrat opposed "racial quotas," called for more "personal responsibility," and proposed a "two years and out" welfare plan, which countered attempts to label the Democrats the party of "handouts" for minorities. Giving a speech to Jesse Jackson's Rainbow Coalition, Clinton condemned rap singer Sister Souljah for insensitive remarks and Ice-T's recording of "Cop Killer"; he would be tough on black criminals, and he declared support for capital punishment, which resulted in a feud with Jackson but won cheers from blue-collar whites. "The day he told off that fucking Jackson," said one white worker, "is the day he got my vote." Bush also supported the death penalty, avoided civil rights issues, and promised a better economy, while Perot showed charts and convinced voters that it was necessary to balance the budget. Bush tried to appear as the commander in chief who had won the cold war and the Gulf War, and the conservatives hammered away at Clinton's so-called character flaws—philandering and avoiding military service during the Vietnam War. At the Republican convention pundit Patrick Buchanan declared war on the cultural left, including "homosexual lifestyles"; the vice president's wife, Marilyn Quayle, attacked the permissive 1960s and what she labeled the subsequent results—unwed mothers and drugs. Most voters were not concerned about the past or Clinton's character, but they were alarmed about the hapless economy. Giving Bush four more years to run the economy, Clinton quipped, would be "like hiring General Sherman for fire commissioner in Georgia."

Clinton won just 43 percent of the vote but easily won the electoral votes, carrying prize states such as California, New York, Ohio, and Illinois. Importantly for the Democrats, he split the South, winning Louisiana, Tennessee, Georgia, and Arkansas. He won a surprising 57 percent of the women's vote and about 90 percent of African Americans', who turned out in lower numbers than in 1988 but still gave him the edge in Illinois, Michigan, Ohio, and New Jersey. Clinton won almost the same percentage of the white vote as Bush, 39 to 40 percent, yet the Arkansan had no coattails. The Democrats maintained a slim majority but lost seats in the House and gained none, but still controlled the Senate. Thus, for the first time since 1980 the Democrats were in the White House and held a slim majority in Congress. Now all they had to do was fix the economy. "My God," remarked Democratic Senator Daniel Patrick Moynihan, "now it's our deficit."[1]

During the campaign Clinton had pledged to make his appointments and cabinet "look more like America," meaning his appointments would be more diverse than the two previous Republican administrations. In his inaugural address it was clear that the decade was becoming the age of diversity, sometimes called multiculturalism, which conservative critics charged was led by a movement they mockingly called "political correctness" or PC.

PC had been emerging in the late 1980s. Conservatives coined political correctness as a label for a broad range of liberals who generally supported expanded rights for women, gays, minorities, along with affirmative action. On campuses it often became a movement to abandon Western classes and classics in favor of multicultural curriculums that included courses on the works of women, minorities, or non-European cultures. That shift alarmed some traditional faculty, who viewed PC as "a new kind of intolerance: a McCarthyism of the left." PC on campus also was an appeal to curb racial slurs and hate speech. After a racial incident at Stanford in 1989, the university adopted a code prohibiting offensive speech, and during the next two years 100 colleges and universities followed suit. Critics complained that the code often restricted freedom of speech and was really a form of leftist censorship. In 1990 and the next year, for example, Brown University expelled a student for shouting racial slurs, the City College of New York rebuked two professors for making comments about racial superiority, and the University of Connecticut ordered an Asian-American student to move off campus after she put up a sign on her dorm door listing who would be shot on sight" if they knocked: "preppies, bimbos, men without chest hair," and "homos."

"Thought Police," *Newsweek* headlined,"Watch What You Say." By 1991 the PC debate was so newsworthy that President Bush discussed the topic during a commencement address at the University of Michigan.

The notion of political correctness has ignited controversy across the land. And although the movement arises from the laudable desire to sweep away the debris of racism and sexism and hatred, it replaces old prejudice with new ones. It declares certain topics off-limits. . . . Political extremists roam the land, abusing the privilege of free speech, setting citizens against one another on the basis of their class or race. Such bullying is outrageous.

The PC debate would continue for years, of course, as would the discourse about another vogue term of the early 1990s, "diversity." Like PC, diversity did not suddenly emerge in the early 1990s. Before the civil rights movement diversity meant differences in geography, religion, and class. A president might fill his cabinet with a wealthy California Protestant banker, a working-class New York Italian Catholic, a Southern planter of British descent, or a Midwestern manufacturer. Everyone knew a politician's religion, heritage, and background. It was not until 1960 that a Catholic was elected to the presidency, John Kennedy, who filled his cabinet with white World War II veterans, but not a single woman. All that changed with the civil rights and subsequent empowerment movements, and so during the 1970s, as we have seen, corporate employers and college deans were calling for racial, gender, even ethnic diversity in their workforces and student bodies, which, as Justice Powell noted, was constitutional in *Bakke*.

During the 1980s diversity continued to emerge and by the early 1990s had become a powerful social movement. Management consultants, along with corporate human resource and affirmative action officers, increasingly promoted the view that workforce diversity was socially and morally responsible, would increase creativity while it staved off possible discrimination lawsuits, and was good for business in the future global economy. In 1991 the first annual National Diversity Conference was held in San Francisco, attended by more than 50 corporations and over 20 federal government agencies, and shortly thereafter bookstores were filling up with titles such as *Managing a Diverse Workforce, Profiting in America's Multicultural Workforce, The Diversity Advantage, Managing Diversity Survival Guide,* and *The New Leaders.* Meanwhile, editors were publishing scores of articles in business journals and the mass media. "The Diversity Industry," proclaimed *The New Republic* in a piece on the new "diversity management consultants" for business, while *Fortune* told readers "How to make diversity pay." *Working Woman* described "Changing the face of management," and the *National Review* responded with "Workforce diversity: PC's final frontier." The movement also slammed into academia. "How will cultural diversity affect teaching?" asked one scholar, and another answered, "Multiculturalism can be taught only by multicultural people." "The Cult of Multiculturalism" had arrived at the Ivory Tower and was having an influence on educating the public. When the National Endowment for the Humanities commissioned a group of historians to write national standards for teaching U.S. history, some hailed the subsequent book as promoting the "rainbow history" of all races; *U.S. News* declared it was biased, PC "propaganda," the "hijacking of American history." On campus, declared *Time*, the diversity controversy was bringing about "the politics of separation."[2]

Nevertheless, during the 1990s diversity was the winner. Democrats understood that, as a political tactic, supporting diversity was less risky than endorsing affirmative action—it redefined the issue not as a preference for minorities or women but as a public good that supposedly utilized the potential of all citizens. While affirmative action drew heat, diversity drew praise, which made it popular on campus and in business. In 1995 a survey of the top Fortune 50 corporations found that 70 percent had established diversity management programs, 16 percent were developing them, and only 12 percent had no such program. By 1996 the GOP had jumped on the diversity bandwagon. At their convention Governor Christine Todd Whitman of New Jersey declared Republicans the "party of diversity," and on ABC's *Nightline* the Republican speaker of the house, Newt Gingrich, boasted, "Diversity is our strength!" By the end of the decade the federal government was giving out 50,000 permanent resident visas a year for a "diversity lottery" to immigrants with a high school degree or two years of work experience and whose only claim was that they came from countries with underrepresented populations in the United States, which included about 150 countries, from Angola to Uzbekistan and, ironically, Germany, France, and Ireland. "In the '90s, affirmative action recast itself as 'diversity,'" wrote conservative columnist Charles Krauthammer, "the colorless, apparently unassailable euphemism for racial, gender and ethnic preferences."

Within a month of the election Clinton had joined the diversity bandwagon, nominating his cabinet. His economic team was mostly white male: Lloyd Bentsen at Treasury, Robert Reich at Labor, Mickey Kantor as trade negotiator, Leon Panetta as budget director, Robert Rubin as chair of the National Economic Council, with Laura D'Andrea Tyson as chair of the Council of Economic Advisers. African Americans included Ron Brown at Commerce, Jesse Brown at Veteran Affairs, Mike Espy at Agriculture, and Hazel O'Leary, who took over the Department of Energy. Eventually the president named three dozen black subcabinet appointments, including M. Joycelyn Elders and, later, David Satcher as the surgeon general. Clinton nominated numerous women to head departments: Donna Shalala at Human Services, Carol Browner at the EPA, and Zoe Baird at the Justice Department. He picked Madeleine Albright to be United Nations ambassador, and during his second term appointed her the first female secretary of state. The president also named Mexican Americans Federico Pena to head Transportation and Henry Cisneros to lead Housing and Urban Development. Clinton's cabinet included five women, four blacks, and two Hispanics. "Bill Clinton did what he promised," wrote columnist Ellen Goodman. "The class photo of his Cabinet presented a more diverse portrait of Americans than had ever been assembled around a presidential table."

Two of his nominations drew fire—Zoe Baird, a 40-year old corporate lawyer with narrow legal experience, for attorney general, and Lani Guinier. Clinton did not know Baird very well. After it was discovered that she employed an illegal immigrant for her child's nanny without paying social security taxes, she stepped down. The president-elect nominated Janet Reno, single and childless, solving the nanny problem, who became the nation's first female attorney general. More contentious, however, was Lani Guinier, an African American law professor at the University of Pennsylvania, the president's friend from law school, whom he nominated for assistant attorney general for civil rights. She had published "The Triumph of Tokenism" in a law review for academics in which she assailed the 1965 Voting Rights Act and contended that it did not result in a fair share of power for minorities in legislatures. She implied reform of the voting procedures with such schemes as "cumulative voting," "minority veto," and "super majorities," all aimed to increase minority political power. None of her writings had anything to do with affirmative action, but conservatives attacked, labeling her ideas as affirmative action for electoral and legislative outcomes and calling her the "quota queen," even "Loony Lani." "She represents the most radical view of American government in recent memory," declared one conservative. Some liberals came to her defense. "Getting Guinier," wrote the *Nation*, declaring that conservatives were "salivating at the prospect of a reverse Borking," but to no avail. Clinton let her nomination hang for months and during the summer reluctantly withdrew her name.

According to some press reports, a few of Clinton's original cabinet picks were scrapped because they were the wrong sex or race. Feminists put pressure on the president-elect to nominate women, and in a December press conference Clinton noted his frustration and lashed out at the "bean counters," the people "playing quota games and math games." But the president himself actually boosted that idea. "They come from diverse backgrounds," declared Clinton, "and we will all be better and stronger for that diversity. . . . I believe this Cabinet and these other appointees represent the best in America."[3]

Clinton adopted the safe strategy of appointing minorities and women to his administration, and eventually to federal judgeships, while remaining low-key on civil rights. The new president was popular with African Americans, but his particular strength was attracting women and middle-class white male voters. The president's polling advisor, Stanley Greenberg, had conducted focus groups in 1985 in the working-class suburbs of Detroit, where white residents perceived the Democrats as favoring African Americans, not helping them, so Clinton was well aware that civil rights pronouncements could hurt his tenuous appeal to white males. Instead, he turned his energies on passing the Family Leave Act, the North Atlantic Free Trade Association, the Brady Bill and assault weapons ban, a tax increase for the wealthy and businesses, and a health-care insurance policy.

The president's first foray into civil rights surprised many because it did not concern either race or gender but gays. During the campaign Clinton had reached out to the gay community, promised to work to decrease discrimination, and in response it had supported his election. The gay and lesbian movement had expanded rapidly in America during the previous twenty years; by 1991 *Fortune* proclaimed, "Homosexuality, once a career-destroying secret, is coming out of the closet in corporate America." Gays organized their own employee organizations in many progressive companies, such as Levi Strauss, Xerox, US West, and Lotus Development. These activists wanted workplace tolerance so they would not be taunted, passed over, or fired, and they sought the benefits that heterosexuals enjoyed, mainly health insurance for partners. They weren't demanding jobs. "We don't need affirmative action—we're already here," said one gay professional. "We need the freedom to be visible."

Moreover, AIDS had reached epidemic proportions in the gay community, and employers often fired those ill workers. California and a few other states responded by passing antigay discrimination laws. Hollywood produced an exceptional film about AIDS, *Philadelphia*, and the media focused on gay employees with TV specials and articles. *Business Week* examined how one professional was the "very model of a company man" at Shell until it was discovered that, after hours, he had used the office computer to send invitations to a gay party. The oil company fired him, he sued, and under California law he won, the judge finding Shell's behavior "outrageous." *Fortune* penned an article quoting a lesbian declaring that in the "company closet is a big, talented, and scared group of men and women. They want out—and are making the workplace the next frontier for gay rights."

In fact, there was no federal law that prohibited discrimination against gays, lesbians, or transsexuals, and many experts considered that this unprotected class was about 10 percent of the workforce; in almost every state discrimination against them was legal. For years gay activists had lobbied for a "sexual orientation" amendment to the 1964 Civil Rights Act, which would protect them nationally, as it did for race, color, religion, sex, national origin, later amended to include age and the disabled.

Congress was not interested, but a few officials in the Defense Department were because they had commissioned experts to conduct studies concerning gays in the military. The studies suggested that gays and lesbians in uniform were not more likely to be security risks than heterosexual troops, that training and then discharging them was an expensive waste of manpower, and that many field commanders were not particularly concerned about gay sex; in a military with many more women, they wanted *all* sex banned in the foxholes.

Only a week after assuming office the new commander in chief announced that he was ending the armed forces' policy of discriminating against gays. That prompted a vociferous response, not only from social conservatives, talk show hosts, and televangelists who had been attacking the "gay lifestyle" for years, but also from such powerful politicians as the chairman of the Senate Armed Services Committee, Georgia Democrat Sam Nunn, influential generals like the chairman of the Joint Chiefs of Staff, General Colin Powell, and many more at the Pentagon and in Congress.

The president backed down, and after discussions with the military chiefs eventually adopted a compromise policy of "don't ask, don't tell," which disappointed gay supporters and most citizens who opposed gays in the armed forces. After just a month in office his approval ratings began to slide, and by the end of his first hundred days 70 percent of those polled felt that the nation was moving in the wrong direction.

The administration sputtered, and that included civil rights appointments. In June the president considered John Payton, a prominent Washington, D.C., attorney, for assistant attorney general for civil rights, but when it was learned that he had not voted in previous elections, many organizations dropped their support and Clinton did not nominate him. A year later, Clinton still had not named an assistant attorney general—or a chairman of the EEOC. Women's groups and civil rights leaders implored him to fill the posts. Finally, thirteen months into his term, Clinton nominated African American attorney Deval Patrick for assistant attorney general, whom conservative Clint Bolick labeled a "stealth Guinier," but who had no paper trail and easily won congressional approval in June 1994.

The administration also moved with turtle speed to nominate an EEOC chairman. The president's first pick was Alex Rodriguez, former chairman of the Massachusetts Commission against Discrimination, but after it was learned that a female clerk had filed sexual harassment charges against him, the nomination was dropped. Distracted with other pressing issues, the president named a Reagan appointee, Tony Gallegos, to continue as acting chairman. This did not cheer civil rights leaders, for in 1980 he had headed the California Democrats and Independents for Reagan. The vice chairman also was a holdover from Reagan. A year and a half into his term the president finally announced his nomination of Gilbert Casellas, a 41-year-old labor lawyer from Philadelphia. He took office in October, almost two years after Clinton had been elected.

By the time Casellas took the helm, the EEOC was overwhelmed with complaints, some 97,000, or 24,000 more than a year earlier and more than double the number in 1990. While Casellas increased enforcement, his agency's budget had been cut because of the nation's economic problems. A complaint might wait 19 months before an investigator would pick up the file, almost twice the time as it took in 1990. The result, according to Casellas: "The agency has essentially lost credibility with the public. . . . Justice delayed, justice denied."

Meanwhile, the administration struggled on with civil rights. During 1993 the Justice Department opposed the Bush administration's stance and supported the idea the 1991 Civil Rights Act should be applied retroactively to all discrimination cases, which the Supreme Court ruled against 8 to 1. Eventually, the administration provided women and minorities preference in bidding for Federal Communication Commission licenses, and the Department of Education supported scholarships for minority students but only if they were given to "remedy past discrimination." During 1994 the administration finally began to demonstrate a policy on discrimination and affirmative action, one that *Business Week* labeled the "Quiet Crackdown." The U.S. Commission on Civil Rights held hearings on the dismal minority employment record of firms on Wall Street. The Justice Department stepped up its policing of biased lending by banks. The EEOC issued guidelines on what constituted being "disabled," and it increased its attempts to use independent mediators to resolve bias disputes, which often resulted in quicker resolutions. The Labor Department scrutinized the civil rights records of federal contractors, eventually reaching a settlement with Honeywell for sexual discrimination, while the EPA began a new program of "environmental justice" to ensure that companies would not pollute more in poor minority neighborhoods than in other areas.

More newsworthy, however, was the case of Sharon Taxman. A white teacher in Piscataway, New Jersey, she was dismissed by the school board in 1989 instead of a black colleague of equal evaluations and seniority in order to maintain "diversity" in the faculty. The school had 50 percent minority students and a faculty of ten in the business department, and only one African American. Taxman claimed reverse discrimination, violation of Title VII, and sued. With the support of the Bush administration she won in U.S. District Court, but on appeal the new Clinton administration reversed federal support, arguing that employers can use affirmative action to justify retaining minorities over equally qualified whites. Although Taxman was later rehired, the Clinton administration's actions cheered advocates but alarmed critics, and one conservative professor claimed the "Administration is giving top management a machine gun to go after expensive, middle-aged white males."

That was an overstatement, for the Clinton administration's stance was to shy away from controversy. In a press conference in October 1994 a reporter asked the president about Taxman. He called it a "very narrow case" that would foster diversity, carefully avoiding a policy statement on affirmative action.[4]

Clinton had good reason to be shy on the topic before the congressional elections. It was becoming increasingly clear that some white males were disappointed with the administration and again held the view that the Democrats were supporting gays and minorities over them. Moreover, with the economy still sputtering and high unemployment, many felt like victims. "Something extraordinary is happening in American society," wrote Charles Sykes. "American life is increasingly characterized by the plaintive insistence, *I am a victim.*"

Such views were boosted by the prime-time media with a splurge of stories about employment complaints and lawsuits. Partly a result of the 1991 Civil Rights Act, the 1990 Americans with Disabilities Act, and the Older Workers Protection Benefits Act, the EEOC's jurisdiction was enlarged and witnessed the largest number of complaints and lawsuits in its history. Many of these suits were serious, but the agency admitted in 1994 that 60 percent of complaints were rejected for lack of sufficient evidence and that 25 percent were closed because the worker withdrew the complaint, declined to cooperate, or could not be found. About 12 percent were settled in the worker's favor by the agency but without a formal charge of discrimination against the company. Surprisingly, only 3 percent had enough evidence to deserve legal intervention in conciliation or court.

Unfortunately, many complaints were unreasonable and they became headline fodder. Donald Keister, who at 640 pounds, sued Baltimore, claiming that the city unconstitutionally refused to recognize his obesity as a disability, entitling him to preferred status in bidding on city contracts. The Chicago man who complained that McDonald's violated federal law because its restaurants' seats were not large enough for his 60-inch waist and enormous posterior, and the Madison Men's Organization, which filed suit charging gender discrimination when local pubs gave the first beer free to college gals but not guys on "ladies' nights." African American Tracy Walker, an Internal Revenue Service employee,filed suit after she was fired, claiming that her black boss, who had dark skin, dismissed her not for poor performance but because of her light skin. Bryan Drummond, who had a speech impediment, filed a complaint against a Health Maintenance Organization when it did not hire him for a job as a spokesperson. Receptionist Patricia Underwood, a black transsexual, sued her employer for firing her for her "personal appearance" and "masculine traits," and a Virginia woman alleged that she was fired because of her "heavy mustache." A chap working the cosmetics counter in a Dillard's department store filed a complaint with the EEOC, claiming that he was discriminated against in sales contests: the prizes were makeup and perfume. In Chicago a group of men filed a lawsuit claiming that they had been discriminated against by the hiring practices of Hooters, the restaurant chain known for scantily clad waitresses in tight fitting T-shirts and hot pants. When the EEOC agreed to investigate, the company held a press conference and a march with 100 "Hooter's girls," many with signs: "Men as Hooter Guys—What a Drag." And in Boston, eight men made a complaint against the Jenny Craig weight-loss organization, claiming that they were asked to do manual work and bombarded with "girl talk" in the office, "who to marry, who is pregnant, how to get pregnant," which the men claimed was offensive. They hired a public relations firm, filed suit, and the story was reported in the *Wall Street Journal,* followed by appearances on CBS *This Morning, Entertainment Tonight,* and the *Today* show. As the "Jenny Craig Eight" awaited the trial, female journalists took aim. "We are asked to believe that these men having to listen to jokes about push-up bras or being asked to lift a heavy box makes for a winning case," wrote Margaret Carlson in *Time,* "when women have been listening to penis jokes and making coffee for decades."

The "hypersensitive society," declared journalist John Leo, in which a flood of "accusations keep a constituency alive with resentment."

That resentment appeared forcefully in 1994 in the form of the "angry white men." This group had been emerging for years, and in 1990 sociologist Frederick Lynch declared, "One of the sleeper political forces in America is the growing sense of grievance among younger working-class and middle-class white males." Many of these men were not college graduates, the first ones hurt by recessions and anxious over tough competition for good paying jobs in the global economy; they felt that they had been losing economic and political power to women and minorities, even losing family authority to their working wives. Lynch noted that opinion polls, newspaper reports, and sociological research supported his claim that whites felt "frustrated and unfairly victimized by affirmative action."

That feeling had been expanding as these males vented their anger on minorities, immigrants, welfare, and preferences. All the blacks do, said a white builder, is "scream, 'We want, we want'. . . . Our tax dollars go to support people just to have kids. They don't care—they have kids just to get the checks." When columnist Anthony Lewis examined why so many whites in Louisiana voted for David Duke for state legislature and then for governor, he noted that Duke also had some national appeal. A college-educated white male from New York wrote the columnist that he backed Duke because he represented the "deepest anger we have with race quotas and welfare mothers." Labeling affirmative action as "quotas" had taken its toll. *Newsweek* reported a "widespread impression that minorities and white women have hopped on a government-protected, quota-fueled gravy train," and that had resulted in "a deep-seated feeling that affirmative action is no longer a device to eliminate discrimination against minorities but a means of discriminating against white males." Not surprisingly, a 1993 poll found that about half of white males felt that they should "fight against affirmative action"; two years later 57 percent of whites agreed that affirmative action had resulted in "less opportunity for white men." Years before, in 1987, only 16 percent of white men felt that "equal rights have been pushed too far," but by 1994 about half of them felt that way.[5]

On college campuses many white male graduate students and professors held similar feelings, especially as universities openly advertised for "targets of diversity." California State Northridge, for example, announced that it was setting aside faculty positions for "departments that identify well-qualified minority candidates" while California State Sacramento set aside funds for "opportunity appointments," defined as blacks, Asians, Hispanics, or Native Americans. Academe knew that these positions excluded all white men, although they were funded by all the taxpayers and most likely in violation of Title VII of the 1964 Civil Rights Act. Often the result of such policies was what political science professor Robert Weissberg called the "gypsy scholars," white males who "wind up with endless temporary positions at third-rate schools," while "black, Hispanic and female job candidates, many of whom are not very well qualified, are on national tours going from one campus to the next receiving the most outrageous offers." These white men were bewildered, Weissberg continued, for they never had practiced discrimination and now felt that they were being discriminated against. Affirmative action hires, he concluded, were creating a "dangerous pool of highly educated . . . angry young white men."

On campus it was definitely *not* PC to hold and publish such views. Debate over diversity hires, wrote a tenured sociology professor, "so easily become melodramas of moralistic self-presentation and recriminatory denunciation that sweep aside the whisper of reason." Weissberg, who also owned a men's clothing store, had hired black and female managers, Hispanic salespeople, female accountants, and had even given family leave to one employee so he could participate in the Miss Gay USA pageant. "None of this counts with my academic colleagues," Weissberg claimed, for because he did not embrace their ideas about diversity, "I remain the Racist Satan Himself, the Great Insensitive One."

Actually, it was difficult to determine the amount of reverse discrimination throughout the nation. African American Roger Wilkins scoffed at the idea: "The only place in America where blacks have taken jobs in a major way from whites is the National Basketball Association," he fumed. Actually the numbers indicated only a minor problem; the EEOC reported that less than 2 percent of discrimination charges had been made by white males, who were not shy about making most of the age discrimination complaints. One researcher found that in more than 3,000 discrimination opinions by federal courts from 1990 to 1994, fewer than 100 cases concerned reverse discrimination, and that charge was upheld and awarded compensation in only six cases. Many of the complaints were brought by disappointed job seekers whom the courts ruled were less qualified than the women or minorities who were given the jobs.

Nevertheless, the perception of reverse discrimination had been planted in the minds of many white men by 1994, a year when the Clinton administration was sinking into political trouble. He was a minority president whose New Democrat policies had irritated many Old Liberal Democrats—union men who had opposed NAFTA, the poor who did not like his idea to "end welfare as we know it," civil libertarians who were dismayed by his support for capital punishment. Clinton's health-care plan, which would have helped his middle-class constituency, failed in Congress, and the president angered many other supporters when he spoke out for gays in the military but remained quiet on women and minorities in the workforce. And his conservative enemies had been on the attack as soon as he moved into the White House. They claimed that the administration's solicitor general was "soft on child pornography," and they alleged corruption concerning "Whitewater," a land-buying scheme in Arkansas a decade before Clinton became president. In order to inspect the "Whitewater" allegation, a three-judge panel eventually named Kenneth Starr as special prosecutor. Then, in February 1994, the conservative magazine *American Spectator* introduced Paula. Ms. Paula Jones charged that Clinton had made sexual advances to her as late as 1991. He denied it, didn't recall meeting her, and she sued for an apology and $700,000. Pretrial questioning kept the Paula story and character issue in the news for years.

Conservative talk-show hosts such as Rush Limbaugh had a field day and so did late night TV hosts. "President Clinton said that there were powerful forces threatening to bring down his administration," quipped Jay Leno. "I think they are called hormones."

By late summer 1994, as the midterm election loomed, Clinton's approval ratings dropped to 40 percent, opening the door for attacks from Newt Gingrich, the House Republican whip. No stranger to hyperbole, this Ph.D. in history labeled Clinton the most left-wing president of the twentieth century. While that was laughable, Gingrich had a more realistic sense of the electorate in 1994. During the summer he and his colleagues declared their "Contract with America." Wisely avoiding racial issues such as affirmative action or socially divisive ones such as abortion and school prayer, the contract declared core principles of accountability, responsibility, and opportunity, and it proclaimed policies aimed at the angry white men—a Personal Responsibility Act that would limit welfare to unwed mothers, a Take Back Our Streets Act that would boost law enforcement and cut crime in cities, a Family Reinforcement Act that would provide stronger child pornography laws— along with tax cuts on capital gains, term limits, line item vetos, and a balanced budget amendment.

While Clinton seemed to flounder, the opposition had presented a vision for the future and that, along with a low minority turnout, resulted in a Republican sweep. "*Angry white men* is a phrase with a certain ring to it these days," declared the *Washington Post* after the election. "They've changed the political face of America by voting disproportionately GOP. . . . They've had it with Democrats." White men voted in droves, and over 62 percent of them picked Republicans, flooding the House with 74 Republican freshmen and the first Republican Congress since 1952. Gingrich became the new speaker of the house and Bob Dole the Senate majority leader. The Republican sweep also had state implications. In California, voters passed Proposition 187, which aimed to deny welfare and other social benefits to illegal immigrants. In New York the previously popular governor, Mario Cuomo, named by pundits as a possible presidential candidate, went down in defeat, and in Texas, Governor Ann Richards was beaten by a political newcomer, George W. Bush.

One commentator saw the election in historic proportions, labeling the GOP takeover of Congress as, "the completion of what Ronald Reagan began" and "the end of the New Deal." Others felt Clinton was, like Carter and Bush, doomed to be a one-term president. Pundits wondered if Clinton still was "relevant" or if the New Democrat only could be reelected as a "Newt Democrat."[6]

In the wake of the election the new chairman of the Senate Judiciary Committee, Orrin Hatch, said that he would review the administration's civil rights agenda and would require assistant Attorney General Deval Patrick to testify at hearings. "Senator Hatch," Patrick joked, "I haven't even had a chance to congratulate you on your appointment before I read in the paper that you are coming after me." Hatch stated that the administration's policies seemed to be moving in the direction of quotas. Asked about that, Patrick fumed, "There are no quotas. I don't know how many times I have to say that."

Just after the Republicans took their seats in Congress, they announced they would study if it was time to repeal all federal affirmative action policies. In the House, Representative Charles Canady of Florida announced hearings to demonstrate that the administration's civil rights policies exceeded the original intent of the 1964 Civil Rights Act. Representatives Bill Goodling of Pennsylvania and Henry Hyde of

Illinois intended to hold hearings to consider proposals to overhaul or eliminate the EEOC, OFCCP, even the 1964 Civil Rights Act. In the Senate, Majority Leader Dole, who previously had supported such policies, wondered if affirmative action discriminated unfairly against white men, if they should "have to pay" for discrimination practiced by generations "before they were born." "Has it worked?" Dole asked on NBC's *Meet the Press*, "sometimes the best qualified person does not get the job because he or she may be one color. And I'm beginning to believe that may not be the way it should be in America." Other conservatives agreed. "Affirmative action has not brought us what we want—a color-blind society," William Bennett said. "It has brought us an extremely color-conscious society. In our universities we have separate dorms, separate social centers. What's next—water fountains?"

Those were the first shots at affirmative action after the Republican victory, and the barrage continued during the winter and spring of 1995. Two white male professors in California, who claimed "widespread reverse discrimination" at state colleges, began collecting the 700,000 signatures needed for a California Civil Rights Initiative that would ban the use of race, sex, or national origin as a criterion for either discriminating against, or granting preferential treatment to, any individual or group in public employment, education, or contracting. "Count me among those angry men," said Professor Thomas Wood. "I know the sting of affirmative action. I was once passed over for a teaching job because, I was told privately, I was white and male. The worm has turned." Ward Connerly agreed. An African American member of the University of California Board of Regents, Connerly declared that the college admission offices were going too far with affirmative action, perhaps violating the 1978 *Bakke* ruling. "What we're doing is inequitable," he said. "We are relying on race and ethnicity not as one of many factors but as the dominant factor to the exclusion of all others." Cheryl Hopwood also agreed, and, with three other white students, sued the University of Texas Law School, claiming reverse discrimination in admission policies. The Supreme Court agreed to hear *Adarand v. Pena*, a case that concerned the legality of the set-aside program. "For supporters of affirmative action," wrote the *New York Times*, "these are nervous days."

Indeed, conservative Republicans again attempted to exploit this Democratic wedge issue. "It's a winner for us any way you look at it," said Republican strategist Bill Kristol. A *Newsweek* poll found Kristol correct. By a 79 to 14 margin, whites opposed racial preferences in employment or college admissions, and an ABC poll found that between 77 and 81 percent of males *and* females opposed preferences for minorities *and* women. Minority support also was on the wane, only by a 50 to 46 margin. Should qualified blacks receive preference over equally qualified whites in getting into college or getting jobs? No, said 75 percent of respondents. Affirmative action, *Newsweek* proclaimed, "is tearing at the Democratic Party."

Many moderate and conservative Democrats realized that. Senator Joseph Lieberman, the new chairman of the Democratic Leadership Council, declared "preferential policies . . . patently unfair" as concern mounted at the White House. Advisers feared that the California Civil Rights Initiative might be on the ballot during the November 1996 presidential election, which could divide Democrats and hand the electorally rich state to the Republicans. Liberals began advocating recasting the affirmative action debate from helping minorities to assisting women, thereby enlisting "angry white women," or scrapping the traditional approach of helping race and replacing it with aid based on need, the "class-based" alternative, both of which had more popular support. Vice President Gore met with civil rights leaders, while the president called House Democrats to the White House. "We have to outsmart the Republicans," he declared. "We have to help those who deserve help. . . . But we should also be prepared to recommend modifications where there are problems. We cannot walk away from this fight." He ordered an "intense, urgent review" of all federal affirmative action programs.

The Republicans, especially those who declared their candidacy to lead their party in the 1996 presidential election, intensified their attack. William Kristol faxed a memo to GOP contenders stating that once Congress passed some Contract with America bills, then a "major element" of their 1996 effort should be "a rollback of the massive system of racial preferences and set-asides." Texas Senator Phil Gramm joined the race, pledging that if he were elected his first executive order would be to abolish racial and sexual "quotas, preferences and set-asides." Former Tennessee Governor Lamar Alexander declared he would do the same thing and announced his support for the California Civil Rights Initiative, as did California Governor Pete Wilson, who also announced his presidential intentions. Having won reelection in 1994 largely because of his stand in favor of Proposition 187, Wilson declared that he had a duty to seek the White House in the name of "fairness." Although in the past he had supported affirmative action, Wilson's fairness now included a pledge that he would abolish "unfair" racial and gender preferences.

In March of 1995, Bob Dole spoke out. "After nearly thirty years of government-sanctioned quotas, time tables, set-asides, and other racial preferences," he declared, "the American people sense all too clearly that the race-counting game has gone too far." He requested hearings on the set-asides, goals, and timetables, and promised to introduce legislation to ban the government from "granting preferential treatment to any person simply because of his or her membership in a certain favored group."

Liberals fought back. The White House wasted no time reminding Dole that in 1986 he had urged President Reagan not to sign an executive order ending affirmative action, that he had supported set-asides, that he voted in favor of the 1991 Civil Rights Act, and that he and his wife, Elizabeth, were the architects in establishing the Glass Ceiling Commission in 1991, which was currently investigating the status of women in the workforce. Jesse Jackson demanded that the president make a national address giving a "clear and authoritative statement" of support for affirmative action; if not, he threatened to launch a third campaign for president in 1996, while House minority leader Richard Gephardt called Republican efforts to curtail the program "politics of division, of finding scapegoats."

"Race and Rage," declared *Newsweek*, was the mood of the nation during spring 1995. The magazine noted that in the 1970s the hot issue was busing, in 1988 it was crime, in 1994 it was welfare reform, "But the most profound fight—the one tapping deepest into the emotions of everyday American life—is over affirmative action. It's setting the lights blinking on studio consoles, igniting angry rhetoric in state legislatures and focusing new attention on the word 'fairness.' When does fairness become 'reverse discrimination'? When is it fair to discriminate on the basis of race or gender? Louder than before, Americans seem to be saying, 'Never.'"[7]

A reason more Americans were saying "never" was because of the problems that had appeared with affirmative action during the first half of the 1990s, problems that were attracting ample media attention.

The first concerned set-asides. As stated, this policy began as a response to the urban riots in the mid-1960s when federal bureaucrats had stapled together a program to aid "economically or culturally disadvantaged individuals" establish businesses, usually in slums, and it became known as the Small Business Administration 8(a) program. President Nixon supported enlarging "black capitalism," established the Minority Business Enterprise, and in 1973 the SBA published regulations. They defined disadvantaged as not only people of African but also of Hispanic, Asian, and Native American descent. Jimmy Carter signed the Public Works Act, which established a minority set-aside program for "Negroes, Spanish-speaking, Orientals, Indians, Eskimos, and Aleuts." Theoretically, white men and women could participate if they could demonstrate that they had suffered because of some discrimination, or if their net worth did not exceed $250,000, exclusive of home and business investment. During the 1980s federal bureaucrats mandated that disadvantaged businesses should receive 5 percent of defense contract dollars, 8 percent of NASA's, and 10 percent of transportation's, and many states and cities also developed programs, which, of course, led to the 1989 *Richmond* case. The Small Business Administration certified companies as "socially and economically disadvantaged" and supposedly they could stay in the program for nine years contracting with the federal government without competitive bidding on small jobs, usually those for less than $5 million. On most other contracts, these disadvantaged companies received a 10-percent bonus or price break, meaning that if a white and a disadvantaged company bid for a job, and the minority bid was within 10 percent of the other company, then the disadvantaged business would get the contract.

There were problems from the start, especially certifying the appropriate companies. Since investigating hundreds of thousands of businesses in order to make sure they were disadvantaged would have been an enormous task, SBA bureaucrats in 1978 simply assumed that the category included *all* African Americans, Hispanics, and Native Americans. Naturally, others banged at the door. Hasidic Jews in Brooklyn petitioned for inclusion, citing not only their strange appearance but anti-Semitism. While the government refused that request they did accept petitions from Asian Pacific Americans, which included people with ancestors from a dozen countries—from Cambodia and Guam to Samoa and Vietnam. During the 1980s the SBA received eleven petitions for eligibility, accepting ones from citizens from India, Toga, Sri Lanka, and Indonesia, and rejecting ones from Iran and Afghanistan. Thus, bureaucrats made the decision about which groups could benefit from set-asides without political guidance and without any rationale of which groups deserved preferential treatment. The fuzzy criteria resulted in including businesses owned by individuals of Japanese and Chinese descent—people in America who had suffered historic discrimination but who also had the second- and fourth-highest standard of living of any ethnic groups in the nation, higher than English and Irish Americans, making a farce out of the criteria "economically disadvantaged." Many local programs also made little sense. In Dade Country, Florida, for example, Cubans could apply for set-asides, although almost all of them were middle class or professionals who had left during the dictatorship of Fidel Castro.

Many beneficiaries were recent immigrants. Immigration, in fact, was surging, a result of the 1965 immigration act, which mandated that foreigners could enter the United States if they had family ties or professional skills. During the 1980s about 80 percent of the immigrants were from Latin America or Asia, and the 1990s became the decade with the largest immigration in the nation's history, more than a million newcomers a year, exceeding the wave of immigration from 1900 to 1910. The immigration act was changing the complexion of the nation. By 1995 some 25 million people in the United States were foreign born, legal immigrants, most of them "people of color." The SBA reported then that the ethnic heritage of the 6,000 firms participating in the 8(a) program was about 47 percent black, 25 percent Hispanic, 21 percent Asian, and 6 percent Native American. Of those 25 million, 16 million were not citizens—yet they remained eligible for minority preferences under many federal, state, and city programs. While some immigrants were of modest income, many were professionals (engineers, computer programers, businessmen, professors) and others had higher education and incomes than average Americans. At the University of Michigan, for example, administrators admitted that large percentages of faculty recruited under their affirmative action program, and funded by the state's taxpayers, were foreign born: almost 20 percent of blacks, more than that for Latinos, and half of the Asian and Pacific Islander faculty members.

By the mid-1990s, then, the set-aside program was riddled with problems. There was fraud, as was demonstrated as early as the 1986

Wedtech scandal, and there was the ethical question of original intent. Who should the program help? Originally, low-income African Americans, but that had changed considerably, as demonstrated by the Fanjul family of Palm Beach, Florida.

The Fanjuls had built a fortune worth over $500 million, much of it based on 170,000 acres of prime sugarcane property in south Florida. Because of U.S. government sugar quotas, America paid eight cents a pound above the world price for sugar, which resulted in an annual bonus to the family of $65 million. To protect this empire they had contributed hundred of thousands of dollars to both political parties and to the campaigns of George H. W. Bush, Bill Clinton, and Florida's governor Jeb Bush. That was legal, and so was their dealing in Dade County's set-aside program. Two Fanjul brothers owned FAIC Securities of Miami, and when the county announced that $200 million in bonds were to be issued to upgrade and expand Miami International Airport, FAIC wanted the lucrative underwriting contract, writing that it was a "95% Hispanic-owned and controlled firm" and that allowed it the "opportunity to participate in programs available to minority owned firms." Dade county agreed. FAIC was awarded marketing rights to 10 percent of the $200 million, meaning that it would earn between $120,000 and $150,000.

Forbes magazine wrote an exposé on the Fanjul family in March 1995, pointing out the original intent and the ethical issue of "adding to the riches of Florida's Fanjul family," whom other sources called the "Sultans of Sugar." The magazine also wrote that the family was from Cuba, were not U.S. citizens, and carried Spanish passports, which allowed them to avoid estate taxes on their considerable foreign assets. Thus, the taxpayers subsidized a wealthy, politically connected foreign family because the county's program stated "minority," not "economically disadvantaged." Eventually, the Fanjuls received so much negative press that they withdrew from the program.

"The Set-Aside Charade" shouted *Forbes*, as the administration and others examined the program. They discovered that in 1981 African American firms won almost two-thirds of contract funds distributed under 8(a), but by the mid-1990s they received only a third, while Asian contractors won 28 percent and Hispanics received 26 percent; of the top 25 firms receiving those contracts only three were owned by African Americans. Also surprising, of all the government-certified minority firms—80 percent had no employees. These firms had an owner and the boss subcontracted out all the work. This meant that by 1990 many firms that benefitted were not new small businesses, but big ones, and they were not owned by disadvantaged individuals but wealthy ones. In 1994 only 1 percent of companies participating in the 8(a) program received 25 percent of the contracts, many given out without competition, and critics charged that businesses never seemed to "graduate" out of the programs to make room for new contractors. In Washington, D.C., for example, a lawsuit revealed that between 1986 and 1990 there were over 500 firms certified, but 80 percent of the city's road and sewer contracts were given to just four companies. The largest of those firms was owned by José Rodriguez, an immigrant, and another of the four companies was owned by his brother; together the wealthy immigrants received about two-thirds of the city's road and sewer contracts. Set-asides, the *Tampa Tribune* headlined, had become "A Fast Track for Minority Millionaires."

The unintended result could bring about alienation from whites and blacks. "It is hardly surprising that unfavored Americans are increasingly resentful," wrote a white commentator. "The American experience still concerns fairness." When the Ohio governor awarded numerous contracts to businesses owned by Indian immigrants, black politicians and organizations were outraged and protested, which resulted in a counterprotest and hard feelings, while Miami witnessed numerous racial incidents between blacks and recent immigrants from South America and Cuba. "Granting benefits to legal immigrants is sound policy," wrote one professor, "but their inclusion in affirmative action programs is an historical accident for which there is no possible justification."

Economic affirmative action was flawed, declared critics, but was it still needed? Advocates pointed out that the set-aside program had stimulated a dynamic growth of minority businesses and did not cost taxpayers much, compared to other programs such as the SBA's other set-aside program, one for all small businesses. That program allotted contracts to firms with as many as 1,500 employees and sales as high as $21 million—almost all of them owned by white men. In 1994 this program set aside almost $13 billion in contracts for small businesses, twice what it set aside for "disadvantaged" companies. "I'm not sure why it's valid to preserve a 20 percent goal for small businesses contracting," said one SBA official, "while eliminating the 5 percent goal for minorities." No politicians were calling for the end of the small business set-asides in March 1995 when the Glass Ceiling Commission released its report. The commission, composed of both political parties, had been studying employment practices for four years. It found that white men, only 43 percent of the workforce, occupied 97 percent of senior management positions, vice president and above, in the Fortune 1000 industrial corporations and that only 5 percent of the top managers at Fortune 2000 companies were women, virtually all of them white. African, Hispanic, and Asian Americans each held about one-half of 1 percent of those jobs. "The world at the top of the corporate hierarchy still does not look anything like America," said Labor Secretary Robert Reich. White women had made greater inroads into middle management, such as office managers, occupying about 40 percent of those positions, but blacks still were way behind at that level, only 5 percent for African American women and 4 percent for men. The report had an impact on the affirmative action debate. "Before one can even look at the glass ceiling one must get through the front door," wrote the commission. "The fact is large numbers of minorities and women of all races . . . are nowhere near the front door of Corporate America."[8]

The Glass Ceiling report heartened affirmative action supporters, but such feelings quickly evaporated during the spring session and subsequent rulings of the Supreme Court. By that time Clinton had made two appointments to the court. Justice Byron White, a Kennedy appointment, retired, and after a protracted search the president nominated Ruth Bader Ginsburg. Justice Harry Blackmun, a Nixon appointee, also retired; he had been a liberal voice on civil rights. Clinton would not get the opportunity to shift the Court to the left. He nominated Stephen Breyer, who along with Ginsburg was overwhelmingly confirmed.

The issues that faced the Supreme Court made liberals nervous. In April the Court let stand a lower-court ruling that declared that race-based promotions were unfair to white firefighters in Birmingham, Alabama. The original consent plan of the 1970s had achieved the goal of promoting blacks and whites on a one-to-one basis until the number of black lieutenants equaled the black percentage of the county's workforce. No whites lost their jobs, but the Court's action now signaled a negative view of earlier consent plans and apparently supported the strong language used by the circuit court that the program was "outright racial balancing" and "discrimination by the government." The following month the Court let stand a ruling that a scholarship program designed only for African Americans at the University of Maryland was unconstitutional, a program supported by the Clinton administration. Many colleges had special scholarships for various races or groups, but those were funded privately; Maryland and many other universities used public funds. The Court's refusal to consider the case put all race-based scholarships in question.

Then *Adarand Constructors v. Pena*, which concerned federal set-asides for "disadvantaged businesses." Adarand Constructors of Colorado Springs was owned by Randy Pech, a white male, and he underbid a Hispanic company by $1,700 on a $100,000 highway guardrail project for the San Juan National Forest. Adarand lost the bid because the general contractor chose to earn a $10,000 bonus by subcontracting a disadvantaged business, the Gonzales Construction Company. Yet to Pech and his attorney the presumption that firms owned by minority groups and women were disadvantaged was open to challenge: Could Congress remedy discrimination to a group with a set-aside, or did it have to target specific individual victims of bias? Moreover, five companies did most of the guardrail construction and maintenance in Colorado, and Adarand was the only one owned by a white man. The four other companies were owned by a woman and three Hispanics, meaning that if Pech did not bid on a project, the "disadvantaged" firms would be competing against themselves, which made the set-aside program irrelevant. The program helped the disadvantaged companies only because they were competing against a white one. Pech and his attorney challenged the preference as a violation of the equal protection clause of the Fourteenth Amendment, attempting to get the court to reaffirm the *Richmond* case in 1989, which had declared state and local set-aside programs constitutional only if they could withstand "strict scrutiny" and were appropriate only for individual cases of discrimination, not for broad group preferences.

Two lower federal courts ruled against Adarand, but not the Supreme Court. While the justices were as divided as the nation over set-asides, their 5 to 4 decision did send a message: Racial preferences were rarely constitutional, "inherently suspect and presumptively invalid." Writing for the majority, Justice Sandra Day O'Connor noted that equal protection is for "persons, not groups," and that the federal government could "treat people differently because of their race only for the most compelling reasons." Accordingly the Court found that "all racial classifications" imposed by federal, state, or local governments "must be analyzed by a reviewing court under strict scrutiny. In other words, such classifications are constitutional only if they are narrowly tailored." That reaffirmed *Richmond* and expanded strict scrutiny to all federal set-aside programs, and it cast doubt on the 1980 *Fullilove* decision that upheld the 10 percent set-asides in the 1977 Public Works Act.

The Court did not end set-asides, it only demanded review. As Justice O'Connor wrote, the new standard for federal programs had to be "pervasive, systematic, and obstinate discriminatory conduct" against minorities. Moreover, the Court did not mention women, who also had some protection by the program, and stopped short of declaring affirmative action unconstitutional. In fact, O'Connor noted the "unhappy persistence" of racial discrimination in the nation and that "government is not disqualified from acting." She went on to declare, "We wish to dispel the notion that strict scrutiny is 'strict in theory, but fatal in fact.'" The immediate result was to send the case back to lower courts to determine if the subcontractor set-aside could survive strict scrutiny, if there was sufficient proof that minorities had been systematically excluded from the specific market, not just a vague pattern of discrimination against a minority group.

Two concurring justices, Scalia and Thomas, would have gone farther and most likely would have ruled affirmative action unconstitutional. Under "our Constitution there can be no such thing as either a creditor or a debtor race," wrote Scalia. "We are just one race here. It is American." Thomas added, "Government-sponsored racial discrimination based on benign prejudice is just as noxious as discrimination inspired by malicious prejudice. In each instance, it is racial discrimination, plain and simple."

The Court made other conservative rulings that spring session. Besides narrowing affirmative action, it struck down redistricting, which resulted in black majority voting districts in Georgia, declared that the University of Virginia had violated the rights of a Christian group by not subsidizing its campus magazine while doing that for nonreligious groups, negated a congressional ban on guns near local schools, declared that a school district requirement that students take drug testing was not violating their civil rights, and rejected a school desegregation plan for Kansas City. "This is the Supreme Court that Ronald Reagan wanted but didn't get," wrote the *Washington Post,* and Clint Bolick of the conservative Institute for Justice agreed. "It has been one of the finest terms in generations."

That was an overstatement. The Court had not ruled against set-asides; it had stated that the government needed "compelling interest," which it did not define. "It's a set back, but not a disaster," commented an NAACP attorney who claimed that set-asides could survive strict scrutiny, while an administration official said that the case fit in with its review of all affirmative action programs: "We're already asking many of the questions the Court focused on."[9]

One month later, Bill Clinton finally addressed the nation on affirmative action, five months after he commissioned a study of the program and two and a half years into his presidency. Earlier, the president had hinted how he felt, telling an audience of California Democrats, we "don't have to retreat from these affirmative action programs. . . . But, we do have to ask ourselves: Are they all working? Are they all fair? Has there been any kind of reverse discrimination?"

On July 19 the president answered his own questions in a significant address given at an appropriate venue, the National Archives. For the first time a president stood before the American people and devoted an entire speech to examine and explain affirmative action. Clinton began on a high note by issuing a challenge to "bring our country together." To do that "we must openly and honestly deal with the issues that divide us. Today I want to discuss one of these issues: affirmative action." He mentioned the legacies of slavery, segregation, and the national aim to open doors of opportunity to all Americans. He noted that simply declaring discrimination illegal had not been enough to end it, yet "leveling draconian penalties on employers who didn't meet certain imposed, ultimately arbitrary and sometime unachievable quotas . . . was rejected out of a sense of fairness." As for angry white males, he noted that affirmative action had not caused the economic problems of the white middle class, nor could it solve the economic and educational woes of minorities and women. Nevertheless, he added that the administration's study found that "affirmative action remains a useful tool for widening economic and educational opportunity."

When affirmative action is done right, it is flexible, it is fair, and it works. . . . Let me be clear about what affirmative action must not mean and what I won't allow it to be. It does not mean—and I don't favor—the unjustified preference of the unqualified over the qualified of any race or gender. It doesn't mean—and I don't favor—numerical quotas. It doesn't mean—and I don't favor—rejection or selection of any employee or student solely on the basis of race or gender without regard to merit. . . .

Now, there are those who say . . . that even good affirmative action programs are no longer needed. . . . Last year alone, the federal government received more than 90,000 complaints of employment discrimination based on race, ethnicity or gender; less than 3 percent were for reverse discrimination. . . . Now affirmative action has not always been perfect, and affirmative action should not go on forever. . . . I am resolved that that day will come, but the evidence suggests, indeed screams, that that day has not come. The job of ending discrimination in this country is not over. . . . We should reaffirm the principle of affirmative action and fix the practice. We should have a simple slogan: Mend it, but don't end it.

The president discussed the problems with affirmative action, including fraud in set-asides and ensuring that disadvantaged firms benefit only for a period of time, not forever. "We clearly need some reform," he declared. In a nod to the class-based idea, he stated that *all* small companies should get government breaks if they locate in blighted neighborhoods and that the first member of a family who goes to college, regardless of race, should get a scholarship. In an attempt to align the government with the *Adarand* decision, Clinton signed an executive order directing federal departments and agencies to review affirmative action programs to see if they met four tests. Any program must be eliminated or reformed if it resulted in a quota, reverse discrimination, preferences for unqualified individuals, or if it continued after its equal opportunity purposes had been achieved.

Like affirmative action itself, the speech received mixed reviews. Liberals responded warmly. "Mr. Clinton took the high road," declared the *New York Times*. He promised "reform that would improve, not undercut, the crusade for fairness." The speech seemed to have an impact on popular opinion. A Time-CNN poll found that while 65 percent wanted to mend affirmative action, only 24 percent wanted to end it. Some conservatives had different views. "The real issue here isn't preferences for the unqualified, which virtually every American opposes," said Senator Dole, "but preferences for the 'less qualified' versus those who are 'more qualified.'" Governor Wilson added, "He should have said end it. You can't mend it," and Pat Buchanan proclaimed, "affirmative action belongs in the same graveyard as Jim Crow."

A day after the president's speech Congressional Republicans vowed to pass laws to eliminate preferences. Senator Gramm hastily proposed an amendment to a funding bill that aimed to prohibit set-asides. The Senate crushed the amendment 61 to 36, with 19 Republicans joining most Democrats. Although Bob Dole voted for it, he stated that the issue was too important to attack "piecemeal," and House Speaker Gingrich indicated that the GOP should first devise a more comprehensive bill, one that also would increase economic opportunity for the disadvantaged.

That same day California acted. "UC Regents, in Historic Vote," headlined the Los Angeles Times, "Wipe Out Affirmative Action."

The controversial vote, of course, had been brewing for years. In 1988 Governor George Deukmejian signed a bill that established affirmative action hires in community colleges with the aim of making the faculty "culturally balanced and more representative of the state's diversity" by 2005; to achieve that goal 30 percent of all new hires were to be "ethnic minorities." In addition, many liberals were concerned about the chronic low college graduation rates for African Americans. While blacks accounted for 10 percent of students admitted to American universities in 1990, they earned only 6 percent of the bachelor's degrees. "In education," wrote Newsweek's Robert J. Samuelson, "the problem is not that blacks don't get into college; it is that many don't stay." Partly in response, California Assembly Speaker Willie Brown and others sponsored a bill in 1991 that passed the state legislature. The act would have pressured universities to hire minorities and women, to admit minority students at the same proportion as they graduated from high schools, and also to "hold faculty and administrators accountable" to achieve ethnic parity in graduation rates. Governor Pete Wilson vetoed it, and many faculty members became alarmed. The "thing that really got us," said Professor Glynn Custred, "was when the state legislature passed a bill that would have mandated quotas—the same proportion as the population of California—for admission and graduation." Joined by Tom Wood, director of the California branch of the National Association of Scholars, they and some others devised the California Civil Rights Initiative, which gained support after the 1994 election, throughout 1995, and by the following February had garnered the 700,000 signatures necessary to put it on the ballot that November in the form of Proposition 209. California would become the first state to hold a plebiscite on affirmative action.

The summer of 1995 became the defining moment for affirmative action. The *Adarand* decision, Clinton's speech, and the debate in California resulted in a national reexamination of the policy. We "may be hurtling toward the most sensitive moment in American race relations since the 1960s," wrote Joe Kline of *Newsweek*, "*more* sensitive in some ways because a reduction of perceived 'rights' seems inevitable."[10]

What were those rights, or in other words, who "deserved" to be admitted into such elite public universities as Berkeley? The media examined that issue extensively and, as during the *Bakke* case, again revealed some interesting findings.

Admission into universities was the result of merit, grades, and SAT scores, but no university admitted students only on merit. All examined supplemental factors such as the applicant's high school, location, gender, race, artistic talent, and, of course, athletic prowess. There also were other preferences: if the parents were wealthy, had money for tuition and later donations; if they had political influence, and "legacies," meaning that the applicant's parent had attended the college. That preference irked many commentators. Joe Kline called for the elimination of legacies, which he labeled "affirmative action for the academically disadvantaged children of alumni," claiming that those students took up "about 12 percent of all admissions at elite colleges." U.C. regent Ward Connerly agreed, "I think we should do the opposite and give a break to students whose parents *didn't* go to college." While critics often stated that affirmative action "stigmatized" African Americans at elite colleges, few mentioned that stigma for those who had gotten in because of mom or dad. As one director of undergraduate admissions at the University of California noted: "I never have the sense of the legacy students feeling, 'Oh. I don't really belong here.' Or,

'I haven't earned it.' The whole thing is, 'Hell, I'm here. That's what counts.'"

Some preferences avoided controversy, especially at those large state universities that admitted a higher percentage of applicants. In 1994 at Texas A&M, for example, admission officials reversed denials for 17 applicants because of requests from the regents; because of requests from legislators, former students, and campus administrators, the officials reversed another 21 denials. In addition, those four groups sponsored 67 other students, whom the university president admitted "might not have gotten in without the request of the groups. Of the total of 105, six did not even meet minimum entrance criteria." The next year more than 20 denied students were admitted at the request of politicians or regents, the president saying that he didn't have a problem with giving special consideration to students recommended by "a person who's important to our university."

"Affirmative action for the well-connected" a journalist labeled such practices as the question again emerged: Who deserved preferences? "I have grave concerns about a policy that tells a young Asian student from a broken family . . . working through high school," said U.C. regent David Flinn, that he would be "treated differently than an African American son of a doctor . . . who lives in Beverly Hills."

One reason why the question generated so much emotion was that at most elite universities, such as Berkeley, the standards to be admitted had soared since the mid-1960s. At that time, a student with a 3.0 grade point average would be admitted to Berkeley's Boalt Hall School of Law. Men enrolled, became attorneys, married and had children, and they expected the same for their sons and, eventually, for their daughters. But then came the baby boom, the faltering economy of the 1980s and early 1990s, meaning that a new generation of students felt that an elite or professional education was the only way to maintain a comfortable income. The result was an incredible surge of qualified applicants at almost all prestigious colleges. For the 1,600 freshman spaces at Harvard in 1994, 18,000 applied, an increase of 50 percent over 1990, with similar odds at some other Ivy League colleges, and professional schools were deluged. Harvard Medical School received 4,000 applications for its class of 165, and respected professional programs ranked nationally in the top 20, such as the University of Texas Law School, had about eight applicants for one seat.

U.C. Berkeley in 1994 received more than 22,500 applications for 3,500 freshman positions. Of those applicants some 9,000 were straight-A students with 4.0 GPA in their high school grades. Who deserved to be admitted?

During the previous two decades the university had decided to create a student body that reflected the ethnicity of the most diverse state in the union, or, in other words, to make the University of California look more like California. Accordingly, the top 12.5 percent of the state's high school graduates would be admitted to one of the system's eight campuses, but not all would get their first choice. The campuses selected between 40 and 60 percent of their students based solely on academic scores, and about half went to Berkeley. Usually less than 5 percent were admitted because of special skills, musical ability or athletics, people who might not be in the top 12.5 percent academically. All the rest were in the high percentile and judged on both scholastic and supplemental factors. That year Berkeley accepted 8,400 (most of whom applied to many prestigious colleges) to fill the 3,500 freshman places. The competition was brutal. Of those admitted, the ethnic breakdown revealed that Asians had the highest SAT scores and grade point average (1293, 3.95); whites were second (1256, 3.86), then Hispanics (1032, 3.74), and African Americans (994, 3.43).

There was little question of the students' potential. "There's a myth that in the course of diversifying the campus we've lowered our standards," said the director of undergraduate admissions. "The opposite its true." In fact, over ten years all indicators had increased, but it also was true that Berkeley's graduate rates reflected the grades and test scores. In six years, 88 percent of Asians earned degrees, 84 percent of whites, 64 percent of Latinos, and 59 percent of African Americans; of course, a higher proportion of blacks had been recruited for varsity sports.

The policy of diversity had changed the face of Berkeley—and it irritated many Californians. In 1984 just over 60 percent of students were white, 25 percent were Asian, and about 5 percent black and the same percentage Hispanic, but ten years later only a third were white, almost 40 percent Asian, 14 percent Latino, and 6 percent African American. The large number of rejections resulted in resentment throughout the state. "We have a system where we're turning away white and Asian kids with 4.0's on a wholesale basis," said regent Ward Connerly, "and admitting blacks and Chicanos with 3.3's." A professor added, "You've got

9,000 kids with 4.0 averages competing for 3,500 places," and "every one of them who gets turned away believes they got turned away because of affirmative action."

U.C.'s affirmative action program had become "the mother of all wedge issues," declared *U.S. News*, and the debate no longer broke down along racial lines; it had become multicultural. The Chinese American chancellor defended the program, while a Japanese American regent attacked it, siding with the African American regent. White students were divided on the issue, not blacks and browns but Asian students often opposed it, some stating that their race had been discriminated against in the state, that they had achieved so much without preferences, so why were bonuses needed for Hispanics and African Americans. "I'd say that 70 percent of Asians look at affirmative action and see a system in which they get the shaft," said Andrew Wong, the Berkeley student body president. "I believe in a meritocracy, not in preferences, and if that produces a less diverse place, well, that's the social cost you pay."[11]

Governor Wilson agreed, and he began to dismantle California's affirmative action program. "What we owe the people is to fix what's wrong, to cure the unfairness and to set it right," he declared before he signed an executive order in June. It repealed previous orders encouraging affirmative action, dismantled boards that provided advice to state agencies on hiring based on race or gender, and required the state department of transportation to reduce from 20 to 10 percent the amount of money set aside for contracts awarded to companies owned by women and minorities. It prohibited employment discrimination and declared that state hiring "be based on merit." "We must make hard work, self-reliance, individual initiative and merit—not group membership—the basis for success in America." Actually, the order had no effect on local, state, and federal laws previously passed or on court decisions. Many felt it was a campaign stunt for his presidential bid, yet observers felt that the order would be implemented for new hires and promotions. The governor also asked other state officials not under his control to comply with the new standards, and that included public universities.

On July 20 the University of California regents met at their San Francisco campus to consider ending affirmative action. Although student groups and all U.C. campus chancellors and faculty senates had declared their support for the policy, the outcome should not have been in doubt. "Affirmative action is dead," Connerly had declared months earlier.

"We're negotiating the burial rights." He and his conservative allies had the votes since 17 of the 26 regents had been appointed by Republicans, five of them by Pete Wilson, including Connerly. The governor, who had not attended a regent's meeting in three years, presided over this encounter. Some 300 media representatives arrived representing all national networks, the same number of police to keep the peace, more than 1,000 students, one hundred elected officials, along with professors and other community leaders, including many who requested time to address the board—Jesse Jackson, Willie Brown, state senator Tom Hayden, even Berkeley 1964 Free Speech Movement advocate Mario Savio. Governor Wilson began. "Race has played a central role in the admissions practices . . . . Indeed, some students who don't meet minimum academic requirements are admitted solely on the basis of race." Some 40 others spoke before Jesse Jackson. He declared the policy must continue for "the promise of equality in America is unfulfilled" and compared Wilson to previous governors who had failed the equal rights test, Orval Faubus of Arkansas and George Wallace of Alabama. "Stand on right!" Jackson declared, looking straight at Wilson. "You can go forward or you can go backwards." The governor stared back in stony silence. After other speeches, and after almost 12 hours, the members prepared to vote. "You're voting for racism!" a protestor screamed. The regents took two votes. By 15 to 10 they eliminated preferences in employment and contracting as of January 1996, which prompted catcalls from the audience. Jesse Jackson and other ministers began singing "We Shall Overcome." Fearful of a riot, the regents moved away from the crowd to a heavily guarded room and voted 14 to 10 on ending affirmative action in admissions in January 1997. "This is a historic moment," said Wilson. "This is the beginning of the end for racial preferences."

The fallout was heavy. "Regents: Too Much Clout?" asked the *Los Angeles Times*. "What is certain is that the regents' decision . . . made in defiance of every major segment of the UC system . . . will renew questions about their independence and qualifications." In the State Assembly, Willie Brown threatened to cut funds for the university system, while another Democrat condemned the regents, "How dare you . . . join the desperate effort of a presidential candidate to jump-start his nonstart campaign." In Washington, D.C., the Clinton administration called the regents' action a "terrible mistake" and stated that it would review the $2.5 billion in federal research funds that it sent annually to the university, since to qualify for the money, public institutions had to have affirmative action programs. Santa Cruz Chancellor Karl Pister called the vote ridiculous. The regents had given U.C. officials "a blueprint that says, 'Do something different—we don't know what it is, but do something different.'"

Pister had a point, for admission standards remained slippery. Connerly had recommended that U.C. increase the percentage of students it admitted—solely on the basis of academic scores—to between 50 and 75 percent and increase outreach programs to help ethnic groups become eligible. The resolution stated that all incoming students had to be academically eligible and that admission officers would have to stop using "race, religion, sex, color, ethnicity or national origin as a criteria for admission." Significantly, the new supplemental criteria included consideration to individuals who had "suffered disadvantage" because of their economic situation, antisocial influences, or neighborhood, and yet had demonstrated "sufficient character and determination in overcoming obstacles" to warrant admission. That clause led one admission officer to say that he was sure he could find ways to "wriggle around" the new rules, and the chancellor of the Davis campus said that "educational deprivation" could be used as a supplemental criterion for admission to offset lower grades and SAT scores.

Nationally, Wilson jumped in the presidential polls by five points and had his most successful fund raiser, $400,000 at one dinner. One week later on Capitol Hill, Senator Dole and Congressman Canady introduced legislation to abolish federal affirmative action programs, the Equal Opportunity Act of 1995. "Our focus should be protecting the rights of individuals," said Dole, "not the rights of groups through the use of quotas, set-asides, numerical objectives, and other preferences." The bill would go beyond *Adarand* because it would end the use of preferences in federal contracting, hiring, and programs while prohibiting set-asides, goals, and timetables. Dole and Canady announced that hearings would be held, but observers felt that Congress was not interested in acting on the contentious issue before the 1996 election.

Many other Republicans weren't interested either. The retired, and popular, former Chairman of the Joints Chiefs of Staff, General Colin Powell, who was constantly mentioned as a presidential candidate, admitted in his 1995 best-seller, *My American Journey*, that he supported equal opportunity and affirmative action. A *Newsweek* article that summer noted that Powell had benefited from the army's program during the Carter years, resulting in his promotion to general; the following summer the general was speaking out against the California initiative. Republican governors of important states also were rejecting the call to end affirmative action. "There continues to be racial and gender discrimination," said Pennsylvania Governor Tom Ridge; New York Governor George Pataki said he planned no change to affirmative action. New Jersey's Christine Todd Whitman wanted the topic "off the agenda," agreeing with Wisconsin Governor Tommy Thompson who felt that attacking affirmative action was "a divisive issue that is counterproductive." By September, Governor Wilson, who had pegged much of his presidential race on a white backlash against affirmative action, had stepped out of the race for the White House.

Again, affirmative action divided the Republicans, as it did America. That autumn politicians in a dozen states—from Delaware to Texas to Washington—submitted proposals to end affirmative action, but they were not voted on or did not pass. Instead, said one observer, many legislatures began a "big push to keep affirmative action but, at the same time, to fix it, to make it work more fairly" by ending programs that gave preferences based only on race, but also increasing outreach programs that would help minorities prepare for college or employment.

Clinton's "mend it, but don't end it" was having an impact not only on states but also on the federal government as the administration attempted to align programs with the *Adarand* case. While the government announced that less than 10 percent of federal contracts went to minority firms (only about 3 percent of those dollars), they intended to keep the 10 percent bonus, or price advantage, for using disadvantaged firms; the Defense Department announced in October 1995 that it was suspending a contracting rule that resulted in about $1 billion in business for minority firms. Begun in 1987 and known as the "rule of two," this meant that if at least two qualified small, disadvantaged businesses expressed interest in bidding, then only those firms could compete for the contract. All of those companies affected had been minority enterprises. In March 1996 the administration announced a two-year "moratorium" on *new* set-aside programs, and the Justice Department reviewed the Small Business Administration 8(a) program to see if it conformed to strict scrutiny. Two months later the administration announced new guidelines, which would take effect at the end of the year: "Race-conscious" set-asides would be allowed only after a "disparity study" found credible evidence of discrimination. Federal agencies now were required to ascertain the availability of minority businesses in some 70 industries in different regions of the nation to see whether there had been past discrimination. In an attempt to stamp out fraud, the government for the first time established a certification process to ensure that companies seeking 8(a) contracts were really owned by minorities, and the SBA announced in 1997 that it would allow an additional 3,000 companies to compete for those contracts. Most of the new companies were owned by white women who could prove that they were "socially disadvantaged," had small businesses, a net worth of less than $250,000, and could prove previous discrimination.[12]

As the Clinton administration scrutinized affirmative action, a federal court again curtailed the policy: *Hopwood* v. *Texas.* Cheryl Hopwood came from a blue-collar family, was 29 years old, married and with a disabled child, and had LSAT scores placing her in the 83 percentile when she applied in 1992 to the University of Texas Law School. The school had discriminated until the 1970s and since had established an affirmative action program, which made it a leading institution in the education of minority lawyers. Admission officers ranked all applicants on the Texas Index, largely based on grades and the LSAT score, and the application form stated that race and ethnicity "may be one factor in the admissions decision," which made it especially attractive to blacks and Mexican Americans. Every year the law school admitted about 500 and tried to have an incoming class with 7 percent black and 11 percent Mexican American students; black and Hispanic applicants competed only against themselves. That year the Texas Index basic admission score for whites was 199, the deny was 192, and the admit score for minorities was 189. In the entire nation there were only 88 blacks and 52 Mexican Americans who scored at least 199. Hopwood's score was 199, although her GPA was suspect because she had attended many community colleges and graduated with a 3.8 from a mediocre institution, California State University at Sacramento. Hopwood was rejected. Through the state's Open Records Act her attorney discovered that more than 30 white applicants had a better index than the two dozen blacks who were admitted. Hopwood and three others sued, claiming denial of equal protection. The Fifth U.S. Circuit Court of Appeals, made up of a three-judge panel of Reagan and Bush appointees, ruled unanimously that the law school had "presented no compelling justification, under the Fourteenth Amendment or Supreme Court precedent, that allows it to continue to elevate some races over others, even for the wholesome practice" of diversity. The law school "may not use race as a factor" in admissions, which in the court's jurisdiction of Mississippi, Louisiana, and Texas reversed the *Bakke* decision and tossed professional, graduate school, and undergraduate admission standards up in the air. "This is the A-bomb," declared provost Mark Yudof. "Once you say race can't be taken into account, what is the law?"

It was an appropriate question. Texas appealed and was joined by the Clinton administration, which claimed "substantial confusion and upheaval among colleges." In July the Supreme Court refused to hear *Hopwood*, Justice Ruth Bader Ginsburg suggesting that the case now was moot since the university had adopted a more flexible admission policy. Yet that left the status of *Bakke*, allowing race as one factor in college admissions, in limbo, thus bewildering admission officers for the next seven years—until 2003 and the cases against the University of Michigan.

Meanwhile, the nation prepared for the 1996 election. The president got a boost in the polls from an unlikely suspect—Timothy McVeigh. In 1995 McVeigh had planted a bomb that exploded and destroyed the Federal Building in Oklahoma City, killing 168 innocent people, the worst act of domestic terrorism until September 11. Clinton went to the scene, gave speeches against those "who spread hate," and like all presidents after national tragedies, his presence and tough talk resulted in soaring ratings: 84 percent approved of his handling of the catastrophe. Somewhat ironically, his rising popularity also was helped by Newt Gingrich. The Republicans would not compromise over the budget, demanding that Clinton agree to balance it in seven years, sign tax cuts for the wealthy and funding cuts in social programs—even Medicare. The Republicans sent their budget to Clinton declaring it was "the largest domestic decision since 1933." He vetoed it, and they responded by refusing to pass a resolution to keep the government itself funded, resulting in a partial governmental shutdown in November and again in December. During the holiday season tourists saw parks close, national museums shut their doors, as hotels, restaurants and many other businesses suffered. The shutdown continued, and as days became weeks the majority began to view Gingrich and his colleagues as extremists. Popular pressure mounted, and after three weeks the Republicans were forced to accept Clinton's compromise budget. The GOP congressmen were getting battered in the opinion polls.

Clinton again became relevant, and that was fortuitous timing for a man running for reelection. Many pundits had predicted that the big wedge issue during the campaign would be affirmative action. "What you can bet on," said conservative Clint Bolick, "is that 1996 will be the crescendo year for affirmative action."

In Dole's acceptance speech at the Republican convention he declared the Constitution "mandates equal protection under the law. This is not code language for racism, it is plain speaking against it.... And the guiding light of my administration will be that in this country we have not rank order by birth, not claim to favoritism by race."

Dole was fighting an uphill battle. Clinton's economic team could boast that the economy was growing, unemployment was evaporating, and the country had a budget that nearly balanced. The Republican nominee countered with a pledge to cut income taxes 15 percent, halve capital gains taxes, and he offered himself as a proud World War II veteran, labeling Clinton a Vietnam war draft dodger who had "character issues." Since there were fewer and fewer World War II vets still alive, and since not many were concerned about Vietnam a generation earlier, the approach did not galvanize much support. The Republican platform supported "equal rights without quotas or other forms of preferential treatment," the Equal Opportunity Act, and Proposition 209. Yet after his nomination Dole tried to shore up the more moderate side of the party by picking Jack Kemp as his running mate, and Kemp backed away from race issues and informed Californians that although the ticket endorsed the initiative, "we're not going to run on a wedge issue." The moderate approach lasted about a month. Dole realized that he could not narrow Clinton's double-digit lead, and he became more and more desperate, resigned from the Senate, and late in October again assailed affirmative action and endorsed Proposition 209. "The Republican leadership," said Representative Charles Canady, "has been spinning around like a weather vane in a hurricane on this issue."

For his part, Clinton did what he did so well in 1992—he avoided civil rights issues. In the presidential debates he was pressed, and he used the same approach that he had in his 1995 speech, first declaring "I am against quotas," and then adding that "since I still believe that there is some discrimination and that not everybody has an opportunity to prove they're qualified, I favor the right kind of affirmative action. I've done more to eliminate programs—affirmative action programs—I didn't think were fair. And to tighten others up than my predecessors have." Sounding like LBJ and Nixon, he added, "For me affirmative action is making that extra effort" and ended his comment with: "I agree with General Powell."

Clinton scored an easy victory. Third-party candidtate H. Ross Perot won 8 percent, and the president won 49 percent of the vote, 31 of 50 states. Exit polls demonstrated that what counted to voters was peace, the environment, and a surging economy which had created over ten million jobs and near record low unemployment. Republicans, however, maintained control of Congress.[13]

The election also demonstrated the demise of affirmative action. Conservative Paul Gigot described California's Proposition 209 as "the most important election of 1996, the presidency included." In the Golden State the opponents of Proposition 209 ran advertisements either equating unpopular figures such as Newt Gingrich or David Duke with supporters of the civil rights initiative or testimonials of celebrities such as Candice Bergen, Ellen DeGeneres, even New Jersey's Bruce Springsteen. Supporters of the proposition also ran advertisements but with a different twist. A radio ad, "Camarena's story," was about a young mother and widow who supposedly was not allowed into an English class at a public community college because it had been reserved for African Americans; another class was reserved for Mexican Americans. "These programs are based not on merit, or even on need, but on race," claimed the announcer. "Janice Camerena Ingraham is white. Her deceased husband was Mexican American." Camerena's voice added, "Recently our public school asked the race of my children. I said the human race," and the announcer added, "Janice now is one of the many women and men leading the campaign for Proposition 209. Proposition 209 prohibits discrimination and preferential quotas."

Such ads undermined the argument that white women and minorities were unified in opposition to Proposition 209, and in November it passed easily with over 54 percent of the vote. While about 75 percent of African Americans and Latinos opposed it, along with about 60 percent of Asians, white men favored it by 66 percent and white women by 58 percent. It was a defeat for feminist and civil rights organizations; the alliance between minorities and women that had begun in the 1970s, while always tenuous, was in tatters. Pundits had overstated the significance of the wedge issues that had frightened Democrats and encouraged Republicans since the 1994 election: Californians favored Clinton over Dole, 51 to 38 percent, while they ended their state's affirmative action programs.

Liberal groups sued to stop implementation of Proposal 209, and conservatives in Congress again presented legislation to end affirmative action. House Republican Charles Canady and Senators Mitch McConnell of Kentucky and Orrin Hatch of Utah reintroduced legislation that would ban the federal government from using race or gender as factors in hiring and contracting, which again ignited heated debate. One Republican strategy session turned into "a virtual shouting match" between moderates and conservatives, and like the previous Equal Opportunity Act, this one also died in committee. The next year the House considered an amendment to forbid the use of affirmative action in public college admissions, and it failed, with 55 Republicans voting against it. In the Senate an amendment to the Federal Highway Bill, which would have revised the 1977 Public Works Act and ended the set-aside program, also flopped with 15 Republicans joining the Democrats.

As the Republicans bickered, the Clinton administration held public discussions on civil rights issues and eventually reformed affirmative action. "The divide of race has been America's constant curse," the president declared in his second inaugural speech. In June 1997 he called for "a great and unprecedented conversation about race" and appointed a committee to "study race" headed by the distinguished African American historian John Hope Franklin. The committee and the president held town meetings, even debating some opponents of affirmative action such as Ward Connerly and Abigail Thernstrom. More significantly, the following summer Clinton's administration announced the findings of another affirmative action review and the subsequent changes in the set-aside program. To make the program "narrowly tailored," disadvantaged businesses would no longer be given preferences across the board, but only in *areas* and *industries* where they were under-represented and did not have a fair share of the market. Thus, set-asides would continue in trucking but not in food processing where minorities now had obtained a proportional amount of business. The new policy meant that preferences would apply in about 75 percent of industries. The administration ended programs in which a specific sum of money or percentages of contracts were reserved for minority firms only, soon eliminating or altering 17 programs. The Defense Department ended its rule of two; the Energy Department cut set-asides by more than two-thirds; and the Federal Highway Administration, NASA, EPA, and the Commerce Department all scaled back their programs. The administration also reduced programs aimed only at minorities to increase their number of teachers, scientists, and foreign service officers. Yet there was one exception to the cuts. In May 1998, Clinton signed an executive order that amended earlier orders and added "sexual orientation"; for the first time a presidential mandate prohibited "discrimination based on sexual orientation" in the federal civilian workforce. "These reforms," the president declared in June, "continue my promise to mend, not to end affirmative action," and Congress passed legislation that authorized set-asides in the Disadvantaged Business Enterprise Program. Later, Franklin's commission presented their findings, which included continuing affirmative action and outreach programs while upgrading social services for minorities, and the president exclaimed that the nation needed additional "dialogue on race."

Still, Congressmen were no longer interested in that dialogue; they were pressing the president to have a dialogue about sex—his relations with Monica Lewinsky.

While Bill Clinton was preoccupied fighting for his political life, the demise of affirmative action was observed at select venues in the nation. The Supreme Court had refused to hear a lawsuit against California's Proposition 209, making it clear that the future of the policy would be left up to voters, or regents, as the University of California decision and the *Hopwood* case was having an immediate impact. In 1997 the percentage of black, Latino, and Native American undergraduates at Berkeley had been more than 23 percent; the next year it had plummeted to just over 10 percent, while those percentages at UCLA dropped from about 20 to less than 13. Berkeley and UCLA law schools witnessed a more significant decline, as the number of blacks admitted declined over 80 percent, while Hispanic admissions dropped in half. At the University of Texas Law School where African American and Hispanic students had made up about 75 of the 500 incoming students, the number dropped to 30: only four were blacks. "It took us 30 years to get here," said Mexican American student Diana Saldana, "and it took them 24 hours to dismantle any progress we have made."

Texas Hispanic and black politicians responded by getting a bill passed, signed by Texas Governor George Bush, that established the "Top Ten" rule for undergraduate admissions. It scrapped grades and SAT scores and stirred merit into the equation by allowing high school students who had graduated in that top percentile automatic admission to the state university of their choice. The results were mixed. The quality of education in high schools across Texas, and the nation, varied greatly; at the strongest schools half the graduating class could be eligible for admission into the two public flagship institutions, while at the weakest schools no students might be eligible or prepared for the amount of work necessary to pass freshman classes. By 2000 the student populations at Texas A&M shot up to over 46,000 and at the University of Texas to over 50,000, making Austin the largest campus in the nation, straining resources and budgets, and allowing university officials to have no say in the majority of admissions, because those issues were automatically decided by just one criteria—class rank. At Austin, black and Hispanic numbers reached pre-*Hopwood* numbers and percentages by that year, but not at College Station, a relatively small town. Before *Hopwood*, Texas A&M's student body was 77 percent white, but by 2002 it was over 80 percent, and the percentages of minorities attending the two universities were very low compared to percentages of minorities in Texas, more than 45 percent.

Other states scrambled to work out their own admissions policies. The University of Massachusetts reduced the amount of impact that race and ethnicity counted in admissions, and when threatened with a suit the University of Virginia stopped using a point system, remaining vague on race as did Rutgers University. California passed a law allowing the top four percent of high school graduates to attend one of the campuses of the U.C. system if they met eligibility requirements, and by 2000 minority percentages were again at levels not seen since the regents banned affirmative action in admissions—but not at Berkeley or UCLA. There, whites and Asians dominated freshman classes, as minorities were reshuffled to the other campuses in the system, especially to Irvine and Riverside. Eventually, as scholars had projected, the real winners of the affirmative action battles at select public universities were Asian Americans. Nationally, they counted for about 4 percent of all citizens in 1998, but they made up about 20 percent of medical students, while at Berkeley they logged in at 40 percent of incoming freshmen. In Washington, a state where six percent of citizens were Asian Americans, they made up over 20 percent of students at the University of Washington.[14]

After Proposition 209 passed in 1996, Ward Connerly had predicted antipreference initiatives would have momentum "like a freight train," but the next year he was proven wrong in Houston, Texas. Like many cities with large black populations—Atlanta, Detroit, Washington, D.C.—Houston had established successful set-asides in the mid-1980s when minorities won few city contracts. The Minority, Women, and Disadvantaged Business Enterprise Program set a voluntary goal of granting certified firms about 20 percent of city contracts; in 1996 they won 21 percent of the $1 billion allotted. After the passage of Proposition 209, a white contractor got the 20,000 signatures necessary to force a vote to ban the program. The city council had learned from the California experience, rewrote the initiative, and placed it on the ballot as Proposition A. Instead of asking voters if they wanted to ban "preferential treatment" as in the Golden State, Houston's proposition asked if citizens wanted to ban "affirmative action for minorities and women" in contracting and hiring. Advocates got city and business leaders, along with civil rights organizers, on board from the start, including the popular outgoing mayor, Bob Lanier. Their advertisements did not employ pictures of people like David Duke, but Lanier reminded voters that "Anglo male contractors got between 95 and 99 percent of the business before affirmative action" and "today they still get 80 percent. . . . Let's not turn back the clock to the days when guys like me got all the business." On election day the voters defeated Proposition A by ten percentage points, with the highest proportion of blacks showing up at the polls in Houston's history.

The Houston vote demonstrated a lesson of language. California exit polls in November 1996 had asked voters whether they supported affirmative action programs "designed to help women and minorities get better jobs and education." Surprisingly, 54 percent said yes, 46 said no—almost the exact opposite of the vote for Proposition 209. In general, citizens overwhelmingly supported civil rights, a majority supported affirmative action if it was defined as giving qualified women and minorities a hand up, but they opposed preferences and greatly opposed anything called a quota. "It's an easy choice to say you're for civil rights," said Rice University political scientist Bob Stein, "but it's a bigger leap to say that the choice for civil rights leads you to ban affirmative action."

"The fundamental truth that seems to have emerged from the debate" in Houston, wrote a journalist, "is that the future of affirmative action may depend more than anything else on the language in which it is framed." That lesson was not learned the next year in Washington. That state's Initiative 200 declared that it "shall not discriminate against, or grant preferential treatment to, any individual or group on the basis of race, sex, color, ethnicity, or national origin" in hiring, contracting, and admission to public colleges. Washington was, however, an unusual proving ground. The population was 86 percent white. Its largest minority group was six percent Asian, many of whom were not even eligible for the state's affirmative action program, which also extended preferences to whites—veterans, the disabled, and all low income people. Only a tiny proportion of whites in Washington felt that their chances of being hired had been harmed because of their race: they had elected a black mayor of Seattle, Norm Rice, and the nation's first Chinese American governor, Gary Locke. Moreover, many of the state's leading businesses—Boeing, Microsoft, Starbucks coffee, the *Seattle Times*—opposed the initiative, while the No! 200 campaign spent much more on advertisements, many of which insinuated that the real winners of the state's program were not minorities but white women benefiting from set-aside programs. "It's the big lie," said Ward Connerly. "There is no way you can read that and say it's somehow going to disadvantage women." As election day neared polls demonstrated confusion with the wording and the advertisements. When Initiative 200 was read to citizens, most responded yes, and that carried election day in November 1998, as 58 percent of the voters approved the second state initiative to ban affirmative action.

Connerly tried to keep his freight train rolling in Florida, attempting to enlist Republicans to support a petition drive to put a no-preference referendum on the 2000 ballot. But he did not find much support in a state with a 38-percent Hispanic population and a party chairman who was Cuban American. "He wants a war," said Republican Governor Jeb

Bush. "I'm a lover." Perhaps, but in reality the last thing that the governor wanted on the ballot in November 2000 was a nasty fight over affirmative action (which would get out the minority vote) while his brother, George, was running for president as a Republican. Instead, Jeb Bush issued an executive order slashing the state's set-aside program and establishing his One Florida plan, which guaranteed admission to one of the ten state universities for the top 20 percent of high school graduates, provided they had completed the college prep curriculum. The regents approved it in spring 2000, making it the fourth state to curb or end affirmative action programs.

As the decade came to a close Connerly's train was running out of steam. The Washington initiative was the last state plebiscite on affirmative action, and Jeb Bush's executive order and One Florida policy resulted in large demonstrations in Tallahassee. Bills to cut or end affirmative action that had been introduced in a dozen states were either floundering or dropped, and a reason for that was the soaring economy, the strongest and longest growth rate in the nation's history, thus creating four years of budget surpluses and record low unemployment.

With jobs plentiful and a hot stock market, citizens lost interest in the affirmative action debate. This became obvious during the 2000 election where both presidential candidates, Texas Governor George W. Bush and Vice President Al Gore Jr., avoided civil rights issues. There was good reason for that, for opinion polls demonstrated voters were most interested in health-care topics, such as HMOs and prescription drug costs for the elderly, and with such issues as school violence, while they were least concerned about immigration, defense, and affirmative action. Polls also demonstrated that majorities of both blacks and whites felt that race relations were "generally good" in the nation, and more than 80 percent said the same thing about their own neighborhoods. And when asked, "In order to make up for past discrimination, do you favor or oppose programs that make special efforts to help minorities get ahead?" 46 percent of whites favored, 44 percent opposed, meaning that there was little political reason to run a campaign for or against affirmative action, especially since opposition had not helped Bob Dole.

Both candidates were aware of those opinions. Campaigning in California Bush stated, "I support the spirit of no quotas, no preferences," but at the same time he refused to take a position on Proposition 209, in what *U.S. News* labeled "the Texas two-step." The Republican stated that he supported a new concept, "affirmative access," but during the long campaign neither he nor his campaign manager, Karl Rove, took the time to define it, other than saying it was a "merit-based" way to open up access to everyone. Bush promoted the same agenda as his father, "compassionate conservatism," and, after the Clinton sex scandals, talked a lot about family values, trust, and "bringing respect back to the White House." Gore supported affirmative action but, like Clinton, usually avoided the topic, unless speaking in front of a black audience or pressed. One such time was during the final presidential debate in October. An African American rose from the audience and asked a simple question: What were the candidates' positions on affirmative action? Bush said he was "opposed to quotas" and supported "affirmative access," again left undefined. "I don't know what affirmative access means," Gore shot back. "I do know what affirmative action means. I know the governor is against it, and I know I'm for it." The debate continued to another topic as television cameras scanned the puzzled faces in the audience.

Then, the election—one of the most unusual in American history. Gore won two-thirds of the Hispanic vote, over 90 percent of the black vote, and he won 500,000 more popular votes in the election, but not in the electoral college. The counting was feverishly close in Oregon, New Mexico, and Florida. Officials commenced recounts. Oregon and New Mexico fell into the Gore camp, but the work dragged on into December in Florida. There, Green Party candidate Ralph Nader had won 1.6 percent of the vote, which swung the state toward Bush by 537 votes. As the recount dragged on, the Republicans filed a lawsuit to stop it, and it was quickly accepted by the Supreme Court. By a 5 to 4 vote, the five Republican appointees stopped the recount, giving the state—and the presidency—to Republican George W. Bush.[15]

The president-elect nominated his cabinet, which again exemplified the age of diversity. His nominees included only 6 white men in 14 positions, the rest going to African Americans, Hispanics, and five women, including the nation's first black secretary of state, Colin Powell, and first black female national security adviser, Condoleezza Rice. The civil rights team included an Asian American as the secretary of labor, Elaine Chao, and Charles E. James Sr. as the director of OFCCP. The only nominee who had problems with Senate confirmation was John Ashcroft for attorney general; Democrats saw him aligned with the Christian right, but he survived hearings and got the vote. The president nominated Cari M. Dominguez as chair of the EEOC. A former director of the OFCCP and of the Glass Ceiling Initiative, she was unanimously confirmed by the Senate.

The age of diversity became even more apparent that year in the 2000 census. For the first time officials allowed individuals to identify themselves as being of more than one race, and the resulting snapshot of the nation revealed more than ever that race no longer could be measured in black and white, but in living color. The incredible increase of interracial couples since 1970, and their kids, was changing the face of America. In California, mixed parents gave birth to one out of every seven babies. Interracial marriages had soared during the last generation. In 2000, about half of native-born Asians and 40 percent of Hispanics, ages 25 to 34, had married someone of another race. While still small in comparison, the number of black-white marriages increased seven times since 1960; about 8 percent of black husbands had white wives, including such prominent people as Justice Clarence Thomas and Ward Connerly, who was of African, Indian, French, and Irish descent. "Yet," Connerly declared, "I have reporters call me African American! What does that mean?" To confuse matters almost half of all Hispanics checked "white" or "other" as their race on the census form, and during the next two years this fastest-growing population supplanted African Americans as the largest minority group in the nation.

Many commentators noted this trend during the last half of the 1990s. Michael Lind published *The Next American Nation* labeling the future "Transracial America," and Farai Chideya wrote about *The Color of Our Future.* By the new century George Yancey wondered "Who Is White?" Randall Kennedy discussed the "creolization" or "browning" of America, Gregory Rodriguez used the less flattering phrase "Mongrel America," and others labeled it "post-ethnic America." Whatever the name, all agreed that race now meant less than ever before, especially with the younger generation. "My daughter listens to hip-hop," said Tim Cisneros of Houston, "belongs to the Asian engineering society and has a crush on a black guy." Predictions were that the shade of America would continue to tan because of marriage patterns and, according to

Leon Wynter, because "Transracial America sells" in advertisements, showbiz, and TV.

All of this led to racial confusion at best, and at worst irrationality concerning affirmative action. In employment, "Why does Hispanicity include people from Argentina and Spain," asked social scientist Nathan Glazer, "but not from Brazil or Portugal? Are there really so many races in Asia that each country should consist of a single and different race, compared to simply 'white' for all of Europe and the Middle East?" And why should someone from Spain "merit special treatment, as opposed to people from Italy, Poland, or Greece?" Racial lines also were being blurred in college admissions. "It seems that everyone has a story of a friend who is one-eighth Cherokee and was admitted as an American Indian," wrote a journalist covering Berkeley in the mid-1990s, "or one parent who is Mexican American and was admitted while others of similar socio-economic backgrounds and better grades were not." A Texas journalist investigating the *Hopwood* case predicted "a frustrated white person will someday check the Black/African American box on his law school application in order to have a better chance at entry and scholarships. If the perpetrator is challenged, his answer can simply be, 'Prove that I am not black.' There is no legal definition, and to create one would be abhorrent. Those were the kind of laws passed in the days of Jim Crow."

The development of Transracial America resulted in some profound questions about affirmative action: What is diversity, and how is it measured? Who is defined as a minority? Who is protected or preferred? University administrators "first classified me as Latina because of my Cuban roots," said professor Ruth Behar, "then withdrew the identification because of my Jewish roots, and finally designated me as a Latina again when they granted me tenure." "We equate diversity with skin color," a college dean added. "We play these silly games" when in reality there are many forms of diversity, and as the nation moved toward becoming transracial some wondered if race still should be a reason for preference. Who would think, suggested Wynter, that people like Halle Berry, Jennifer Lopez, Beyonce Knowles, Mariah Carey, Jimmy Smits, or Tiger Woods—or their children—deserve preferences?[16]

The results of the 2000 census raised profound questions about affirmative action, but the circumstances of the 2000 election meant difficulties for the new president. Bush received no honeymoon period, had mediocre public support, and struggled during his first eight months—until September 11. Like the Oklahoma City bombing, the shocking terrorist attacks boosted the president's approval ratings. It also refocused his agenda away from domestic to foreign affairs and resulted in the subsequent wars in and occupations of Afghanistan and Iraq. Except for homeland security and tax cuts, domestic issues took a back seat to military action.

Back home on the civil rights front, the administration took a moderate approach. Although the Justice and Labor secretaries had stated their opposition to affirmative action while favoring outreach programs, the administration did not slash enforcement or the budgets of the EEOC or OFCCP. As in the late 1990s the EEOC continued cutting the time of resolution of cases and boosting the use of mediation. The administration surprised some observers by supporting federal set-asides mandated by the Disadvantaged Business Enterprise Program. Officials filed an *amicus* brief in *Adarand v. Mineta,* citing "extensive evidence of public and private discrimination," declaring the program "narrowly tailored," to which the Supreme Court agreed, dismissing the case and allowing federal set-asides to continue. Meanwhile, the president's call for "affirmative access" never materialized, until it resurfaced two years later during discussions about the suits against the University of Michigan. Press secretary Ari Fleischer attempted to define it as seeking "ways to encourage diversity and to do so in a way that does not rely on either quotas or racial preferences . . . which have a tendency to divide people."

Federal courts remained interested in affirmative action and they continued to chip away at various programs. A three-judge panel, Reagan and Bush appointees, unanimously found that the Federal Communications Commission's program to increase job opportunities and ownership for women and minorities in the broadcasting industry "ultimately does not withstand constitutional review." The new rules made clear that a company's record in hiring women and minorities no longer would be a factor in deciding whether to renew a broadcaster's license. Another court ruled the University of Georgia's admission policy, which gave minorities an extra half point in the process, was "naked racial balancing" and unconstitutional. By 2002 Georgia banned affirmative action in college admissions, while most other states continued their programs, leaving the nation with a patchwork quilt of admission practices—until the Michigan cases.

"Many civil rights lawyers agree that the University of Michigan could be the Alamo of affirmative action," wrote *Time*, "the place where they make their last stand."

During spring 2003 the Ann Arbor campus became the epicenter of the national debate. More than 3,000 organizations filed over 60 briefs supporting the university, including briefs from over 110 members of Congress, 70 from Fortune 500 companies, and almost 30 from former military and civilian leaders of the armed forces. U.S. Army General Norman Schwarzkopf, commander in the 1991 Persian Gulf War, even argued that the policy was mandatory at the military academies for recruiting minority officer candidates. Only a few cases in history had seen so many *amicus* briefs, even more than *Bakke*. Leading Democrats running for their party's presidential nomination in 2004, Senator John Kerry, Congressman Dick Gephardt, former Vermont governor Howard Dean, former NATO commander General Wesley Clark, all supported the university.

President Bush took the opposite side, asking the court to declare the admission system unconstitutional, supporting affirmative access and the state percentage plans to guarantee admission. He declared his support for "diversity of all kinds" but stated that Michigan's admission policy was "fundamentally flawed . . . divisive, unfair and impossible to square with our Constitution." That provoked a vicious attack on the president. "It wasn't his SAT scores," wrote Michael Kinsley, "or his C grades, but "bloodlines and connections" that got him into Yale. Bush, who graduated near the bottom of his college class, nevertheless was accepted by Harvard, demonstrating that he "may be the most spectacular affirmative action success story of all time." "When It Comes to Hypocrisy," added a *Newsday* columnist, "He's Brilliant!"

During the firestorm the administration's two most prominent African Americans, Colin Powell and Condoleezza Rice, declared that they supported affirmative action in college admissions: The Bush administration was as divided as the nation.[17]

Both cases concerned reverse discrimination. In 1995 high school senior Jennifer Gratz applied to the University of Michigan. She had a 3.76 GPA, good test scores, had been a student council leader, math tutor, blood drive organizer, cheerleader, and homecoming queen. During the process she learned that some of her minority classmates, who had lower grades, had been accepted, but she had been placed on the waiting list. According to the university, Gratz was evaluated in a group of more than 400 students with similar academic qualifications. The university admitted every qualified minority applicant, in this case 46 of them, and 121 whites, but not Gratz, who eventually attended the Dearborn campus. "I was treated unfairly because of my skin color," she maintained, and in 1997 she and another white applicant, Patrick Hamacher, sued the university and the case became *Gratz v. Bollinger.*

Barbara Grutter, in her 40s and a mother of two, applied to the University of Michigan law school with a 3.8 GPA and 161 on the LSAT, but she was rejected in 1997. "We have always conscientiously taught our children that discrimination is wrong," she said, "morally wrong and illegal. . . . Is what I'm teaching them a platitude, or is it real?" She charged that she was rejected because the law school used race as the "predominant" factor in its selection process and that the school had "no compelling interest to justify their use of race in the admissions process." The case became *Grutter v. Bollinger.*

Both sides based their cases on *Bakke.* The Center for Individual Rights, a nonprofit law group in Washington which had sued for Cheryl Hopwood, filed both lawsuits against U.M. The center claimed that the university's use of racial preferences violated the equal protection clause of the Fourteenth Amendment and Title VI of the 1964 Civil Rights Act. U.M declared that *Bakke* ruled that diversity could be a compelling governmental interest; the university did not claim that it had a history of discrimination and that its policy was a remedy for the past.

Every year about 25,000 apply for a freshman class of about 5,500 at the University of Michigan. To deal with this mass of applicants, the university had established a system with 150 possible points. Almost all students needed 100 for admission, 99 to 90 was admit or postpone, 89 to 75 was delay or postpone. The largest number of points was given for high school grades. Each black, Hispanic, and Native American applicant automatically got 20 points, as did out-of-state minority applicants, all athletes, and those from residents from "economically disadvantaged" backgrounds or predominately minority high schools. Because minorities did not do as well on standardized tests as Asians and whites, SAT scores were discounted and could add up to twelve points; Michigan residents got ten points; from two to ten points on the quality of the high school; four points for parental legacies; up to five points for artistic talent; and a few more points for advanced placement or honors courses in high school and for geographical areas in the state underrepresented in the student body. All things equal, 20 points meant a minority with a 3.0 high school GPA automatically equaled a white applicant with 4.0. In other words, being a minority earned 8 points more than scoring a perfect 1600 on the SAT. The university admitted virtually every "qualified" minority. A white student with a 3.2 GPA and a SAT of 1000 would be rejected; a black or Hispanic would be admitted, even those with even lower grades and scores.

The result was diversity—and disgust. While there were about 8 percent blacks in the student body, 14 percent in the state, there were twice as many Hispanics present than the state's demographics and 10 times more Asian Americans. In a state about 83 percent white, the student body was about 25 percent minority. The University of Michigan did not look like Michigan. That was good, declared the former university president Lee Bollinger, an advocate of diversity. "A classroom that does not have a significant representation from members of different races produces an impoverished discussion," he claimed. Many debated that idea, while some minority students felt isolated, noting little interracial socializing. "One of the reasons I chose to come to U.M. is their boastful reputation on diversity," said a black sophomore. "But . . . this campus is extremely segregated." Many white parents in small towns and working-class Detroit suburbs were irritated because their kids no longer could get accepted to the campus in Ann Arbor. Affirmative action was "the No. 1 economic and social issue" said a state senator representing those Detroit districts. Everyone knew someone "who has suffered a loss due to minority preferences." Various state polls between 1998 and 2002 found that only a quarter of those interviewed supported the university's admission policy, between half and two-thirds were opposed, and the remainder were undecided.

The Michigan law school used a different, more flexible system. It received about 5,000 applicants a year for 350 places, and a committee examined each applicant's GPA, LSAT score, undergraduate college records, personal statement, and recommendations to assess the individual's potential contributions. The policy aimed to achieve "racial and ethnic diversity" by including blacks, Hispanics, and Native Americans, "who without this commitment might not be represented in our student body in meaningful numbers." Admission officers had testified that they used no points, and no numerical targets, for admitting students, while they stated that they felt that it was important to have a "critical mass" or a "meaningful representation" of minority students and not just tokens who felt isolated in the classroom. They stated that the number of minorities in each incoming class varied from year to year, but without the policy only about 4 percent of those students admitted for fall 2000 would have been minorities, instead of the current 14 percent. Surveys demonstrated that there was no significant difference between the races in passing bar examinations.

In *Gratz* and *Grutter* the Sixth U.S. Circuit Court of Appeals supported the university, allowing the affirmative action program—contradicting the Fifth U.S. Circuit Court's ruling in the *Hopwood* decision. That prompted a showdown at the Supreme Court. Accepting the case Justice Sandra Day O'Connor aimed to resolve the judicial disagreement "on a question of national importance.... Whether diversity is a compelling interest that can justify the narrowly tailored use of race in selecting applicants for admission to public universities."

In *Gratz*, Chief Justice Rehnquist wrote for the majority. He noted that the *Adarand* decision established that "all racial classifications ... must be strictly scrutinized" and that meant college admission policies had to be "narrowly tailored measures that further compelling governmental interest." Rehnquist then referred to Justice Powell's opinion in *Bakke* that "race or ethnic background may be deemed a 'plus' in a particular applicant's file," but that such an admission system had to be "flexible enough to consider all pertinent elements of diversity in light of the particular qualifications of each applicant." He pointed out that an applicant with artistic talent that "rivaled that of Monet or Picasso" would "receive, at most, five points," while "every single underrepresented minority applicant ... automatically received 20 points for submitting an application." Moreover, applicants with the same GPA and test scores "were subject to different admissions outcomes based upon their racial or ethnic status. An in-state or out-of-state minority applicant with Gratz's scores" would have been admitted. The Court ruled 6 to 3 against the university's admission policy; it was "not narrowly tailored to achieve ... compelling interest in diversity" and too much like a quota and therefore unconstitutional.

In *Grutter*, Justice O'Connor wrote for the majority. She noted that Justice Powell's opinion in *Bakke* was the "touchstone for constitutional analysis of race-conscious admission policies" at both public and private universities and that he approved the use of race for only one reason: "the attainment of a diverse student body." She wrote that the "critical mass" was not "some specified percentage," a quota. "That would amount to outright racial balancing, which is patently unconstitutional." She continued that the law school used a "highly individualized, holistic review" of each applicant's file with "no mechanical, predetermined diversity 'bonuses' based on race or ethnicity," and that the school frequently accepted white students with grades and test scores lower than minority applicants, demonstrating that its policy considered other diversity factors besides race. To her, the question was whether the admission policy use of race was justified by state interest. "Today," she declared, "we hold that the Law School has a compelling interest in attaining a diverse student body." She concluded:

> It has been 25 years since Justice Powell first approved the use of race to further an interest in student body diversity. . . . Since that time, the number of minority applicants with high grades and test scores has indeed increased. We expect that 25 years from now, the use of racial preferences will no longer be necessary to further the interest approved today.

By one vote, 5 to 4, the court upheld affirmative action for college admissions—and it also upheld *Adarand, Richmond, Bakke,* as it overturned *Hopwood*. Narrowly tailored affirmative action policies were constitutional only if they could withstand strict scrutiny, and in education, only as *one of many* factors to bring about a diverse student body. O'Connor noted that numerous academic studies, along with briefs submitted by corporations and the armed forces, demonstrated that benefits derived from a diverse student body and workforce "are not theoretical but real," including the "military's ability to fulfill its principle mission to provide national security." That statement was written in a post-September 11 environment when U.S. armed forces were engaged in Afghanistan and Iraq.

"This is a wonderful, wonderful day," exclaimed University of Michigan president Mary Sue Coleman. "We're very, very excited and very pleased," as was the civil rights community. Curiously, President Bush praised the decision, stating that the Court struck a "careful balance" between campus diversity and equal protection. Conservative columnist Michelle Malkin described the ruling as, "Go ahead and trample the 14th Amendment's equal protection clause. Just don't make it so damn obvious." Ward Connerly flew to the campus and, flanked by the plaintiffs, pledged to get the necessary signatures to put an antipreference proposition on the Michigan ballot in November 2004. "Our crusade will not end with the state of Michigan," he declared, as his organization considered similar initiatives for Arizona, Colorado, Missouri, Oregon, and Utah.[18]

The Michigan cases closed another chapter—the demise of affirmative action. During the 1990s problems had emerged. Set-asides had too much fraud while the issue of original intent had been complicated by surging immigration. The concept of race itself was becoming increasingly blurry, raising serious questions about who, if anyone, should receive preferences. As for set-asides, the Court mandated strict scrutiny first for cities in *Richmond* and then federally in *Adarand*. After the first decision some 230 state and local authorities suspended their programs, reevaluated them, and by 1995 about 100 remained. In response to *Adarand*, the Clinton administration also decreased the federal program and tightened the criteria for participation. On campus, admission systems that allotted points based on race were tossed out, and colleges revised their processes, but not toward the "class-based" affirmative action. Social scientists had discredited that system because surveys demonstrated that there were not enough poor blacks and Latinos who actually graduated from high school; that policy would eventually result in fewer minorities in college and more poor whites. Voters, governors, or attorneys general in California, Florida, Georgia, Mississippi, Texas, and Washington banned all or part of their state's programs, and some established percentage plans for college admissions.

Yet this was not the end of affirmative action in the nation, most states, college admissions, or the private sector. Some Republicans had tried to end the policy in the first half of 1995, and Bob Dole had run against it in 1996. That stand won Dole few votes and it divided his party. Attempts to place ballot initiatives in more states stalled as citizens lost interest. President Clinton had been right. Giving his landmark speech in 1995, he used a simple phrase, "mend it, don't end it," and that had popular appeal. Before the Michigan decisions, opinion polls found that Americans approved 2 to 1 of "programs designed to increase the number of black and minority students"; the same people disapproved 3 to 1 of "giving preferential treatment" to minorities and that included a *majority* of minority respondents. What 30 years earlier President Lyndon Johnson had called "a hand up," President Nixon had labeled a "little extra start," Justice Powell said was a "plus," and what Justice Sandra Day O'Connor referred to as "some sort of bonus" had become the definition of affirmative action. That type of program had become part of the social fabric—and most Americans considered that fair.[19]

conclusions:
The Pursuit of Fairness

At the beginning of our involvement in World War II, just a year after A. Philip Randolph threatened his march on Washington, Mark Ethridge, the liberal publisher of the *Louisville Courier-Journal* commented at a Fair Employment Practices Commission hearing, "No white Southerner can logically challenge the statement that the Negro is entitled, as an American citizen, to full civil rights and to economic opportunity." But, he continued, Northerners "must recognize that there is no power in the world—not even in all the mechanized armies of the earth, Allied and Axis—which could now force the Southern white people to the abandonment of the principle of social segregation."

In 1942 that outlook was considered realistic, and segregation was considered fair. A poll taken two years later asked, "Do you think Negroes should have as good a chance as white people to get any kind of job, or do you think white people should have the first chance at any kind of job?" Only 44 percent thought that blacks should have equal opportunity.

Fortunately, America has moved light years past those traditional assumptions—and nowhere is that more apparent than in race relations. After the civil rights and women's liberation movements, most citizens began to accept a different interpretation of fairness. An "underlying assumption of the rule of law," wrote Justice Powell in *Bakke*, "is the worthiness of a system of justice based on fairness to the individual," and that meant to every citizen.

This fundamental shift came about because of protests that revealed inequality in American society, a governmental response in the form of civil rights laws and equal employment and affirmative action regulations, and a positive reaction from most universities, local governments, and businesses.

The vast majority of citizens today support the ideals of equal opportunity, and as the nation began the new millennium the federal government, most states, many universities, and the private sector continued various affirmative action programs.

Since Title VII of the 1964 Civil Rights Act it has been illegal to discriminate in employment, and the watchdog has been the EEOC. Its guidelines pertain to all employers—public, private, or nonprofit. The 1964 act concerned employers with more than 25 employees, which the 1972 Equal Employment Opportunity Act reduced to 15 workers. Since the 1991 Civil Rights Act all victims of discrimination and sexual harassment at the hands of such employers have the right to a jury trial and, if victorious, can collect punitive and compensatory damages, which are capped depending on the size of the firm. Almost every year during the 1990s the agency received about 80,000 complaints. During the 2002 budget year, for example, the EEOC received over 84,000 complaints, prompting chairwoman Cari Dominguez to explain that the increase probably was a result of the slow economy, aging baby boomers, and a multinational workforce. Complaints most often alleged discrimination because of age, national origin, and religion, especially against Islam after September 11. The previous year the agency obtained record-breaking monetary benefits of almost $250 million for victims. Clearly, discrimination and harassment remain persistent problems in the American workplace.

The OFCCP oversees more than 400,000 corporations that have federal contracts of more than $50,000, covering about 40 percent of the private sector workforce. Those contractors have to file an affirmative action plan that "commits itself to apply every good faith effort" to "ensure equal employment opportunity," and many states have similar policies. If contractors do not abide by the policy, the federal government can bar them from contracts, which is rare; only five firms were banned during the Clinton years.

Congress legislated set-asides in 1998 with the Disadvantaged Business Enterprise Program, and many cities now have their own programs, which federal courts upheld in *Adarand v. Mineta.*

Tax-supported public institutions and universities must have affirmative action policies, as must private ones if they accept tax funds in allocations or grants, and the Michigan cases decided that they could use race as one of many factors in admissions. At the same time, however, Justice Antonin Scalia's dissent in *Grutter* probably was correct: the decisions will not end "the controversy and the litigation." As one attorney wrote, "The major risk now for higher education is that the yellow light the Supreme Court lit . . . will be mistaken for green."

Private businesses continue many voluntary programs. In fact, most national corporations realized during the civil rights movement that they had an obligation to train and hire African Americans, and so they began instituting their own programs. During the 1970s other businesses feared violation of Title VII and subsequent lawsuits, and during the decade which boosted ethnic awareness and women's liberation, business leaders had no desire to be labeled racist or sexist. By the Reagan backlash, then, corporations had affirmative action programs in place, were declaring them successful, and had no intention of reversing course. The diversity movement, expanding immigration, and the global market during the 1990s solidified business support for affirmative action. In 2003 Procter & Gamble was one of thirty major corporations to file an *amicus* brief supporting the University of Michigan. The Fortune 25 company noted that 2.5 billion people in 75 countries purchase its products every year. "Our success as a global company is a direct result of our diverse and talented workforce," stated the chairman of the board. "Our ability to develop new consumer insights and ideas . . . is the best possible testimony to the power of diversity." Simply put, a Bank One spokesperson stated, "diversity is good business." After the *Grutter* decision, *Business Week* declared, "Corporate America won a big victory."

Yet affirmative action has little or no impact on many citizens, including those employees of small companies that do not contract with government. These businesses, services ranging from cutting hair to mowing lawns or building homes, can hire and promote whomever they wish and do not have to meet any standards for race or gender diversity in their workforces—and they make up about half of all American companies. Moreover, with the exception of the federal workforce, gay and lesbians are not protected. In 1974, at the beginning of the gay liberation movement, some members of Congress submitted a bill aimed to adding the term "sexual orientation" to the 1964 Civil Rights Act. Although a few states did that, the federal government never passed the amendment, meaning that there is no federal law that protects gays and lesbians from employment discrimination.

But generally speaking, affirmative action and equal opportunity practices are followed by most businesses, universities, and public agencies. In 1989 critic Abigail Thernstrom admitted that affirmative action had become "so institutionalized" that court decisions would have little effect. That certainly was the case on most campuses after the Michigan cases. Just weeks after the decision, representatives of almost 50 public and private universities met and discussed ways "to shield race-conscious admissions policies against future legal challenges." Affirmative action in some form has become part of the American way of life and in that sense is fulfilling Martin Luther King's Dream.[1]

Affirmative action has been a national policy for about 40 years, about the length of one person's career. What has been its impact?

Critics have leveled many charges, usually based on anecdotal evidence. African American Shelby Steel claimed the program lowers "standards to increase black representation," offers "entitlements, rather than development," and does nothing to stop "the very real discrimination that blacks may encounter"; in fact, blacks "stand to lose more from it than they gain." Others have claimed affirmative action "stigmatizes" African Americans at elite colleges. The "evil of preferential treatment," wrote Charles Murray, was that it "perpetuates the impression of inferiority."

Perhaps, perhaps not. A better way to measure the impact is to peruse the scholarly record because academics have published numerous studies. The largest, most complete, and most recent one came out in 2000 by economists Harry Holzer and David Neumark, "Assessing Affirmative Action." The review of over 200 academic studies, including findings from William Bowen and Derek Bok's The Shape of the River, concluded that affirmative action had produced tangible benefits for women, minority businessmen, students, and the economy. Employers adopting the policy have increased the number of women and minorities in their workforce between 10 and 15 percent, and the number and amount of federal contracts to minority firms have grown substantially, boosting black and brown capitalism. Female hires usually match the male's credentials and performance, and while blacks and Latinos might not equal the credentials when hired, studies demonstrate that they almost always perform equally on the job.

The result was a very different workplace than when two Democratic presidents declared affirmative action in the 1960s. While unions were almost exclusively white in 1965, 30 years later they were about 15 percent African American, larger than their 12 percent proportion in the society; between 1970 and 1990 the number of black electricians tripled. City programs also altered the public sector. In 1970 there were about 24,000 black policemen; 20 years later there were almost 65,000. The Los Angeles Police Force in 1980 was little more than 2 percent female; in 2000 it was almost 20 percent. Black representation in fire departments rose from just over 2 percent in 1960 to about 12 percent in 2000. Moreover, the number of professionals and college-educated minorities has surged. One in 20 blacks was a professional in 1970; 20 years later it was 1 in 12. During those years the number of African American bank tellers, managers, and health officials quadrupled. The "entry of so many highly educated blacks into the ranks of managers and professionals," wrote Bowen and Bok, "must count as the principal success story for African Americans in the past twenty-five years."

"The Greening of the Black Middle Class" the *New York Times* labeled it in 1995, but women made more impressive gains. Quotas keeping women out of colleges and professional schools have been abolished, resulting in a soaring number of female graduates. In 1960 women earned 39 percent of baccalaureate degrees and 11 percent of Ph.D.s, but by the new millennium they earned a record 57 percent of baccalaureates and about half of doctorates. Between 1970 and 2000 the percentage of female attorneys, professors, physicians, and business managers increased from about 5 percent to over a third, and many first-year professional courses now are more than half female. The result, according to *Ms* magazine in 1989, "was a profound change in workplace demographics—and society as a whole—that amounted to a peaceful revolution unrivaled in this country's history."

Yet how much did this revolution affect profits and white males? Not very much, if at all, according to a number of economists: "There is no evidence that these gains were made at the expense of either firm competitiveness or fair employment practices. It appears that many of the jobs gained by minorities and women were the result of garnering a greater share of new jobs created and not the result of displacing white males."

Affirmative action, along with voluntary outreach and recruitment programs, has resulted in a considerable change in student bodies on college campuses. The percentage of Hispanics over the age of 25 with a college degree more than doubled between 1970 and 2000. Excluding traditional black colleges, the black enrollment as a percentage of the student body at universities between 1960 and 1995 rose from less than 2 to 9 percent, while the percentages of blacks, age 25 to 29, with college degrees rose from just over 5 to more than 17 percent in 2000. More striking was the growth of blacks studying at professional schools over the last 30 years, increasing from 1 to over 7 percent at law schools and from 2 to 8 percent at medical colleges.

In both education and employment, the Holzer and Neumark study concluded, affirmative action had succeeded in "boosting employment of women and minorities, minority enrollment at universities, and government contracts for minority- and women-owned businesses." Bowen and Bok also found that black graduates from elite colleges earn the same proportion of advanced degrees and become more active in civic activities than their white classmates.[2]

Progress has been made, but no one would argue that governmental programs resolved economic or educational inequality. Per capita income for African Americans still lags behind other American ethnic groups—Asian, white, and Hispanic—and twice the percentage of whites are professionals as compared to blacks. Latinos and blacks also lag in education, jobs, and home ownership. "When you look at the data, yes, we have made substantial headway," said the president of the National Urban League in 2002, "but there are still—without a shadow of a doubt—substantial gaps in every category, every vital sign."

Unfortunately, the media has exaggerated the reach of affirmative action, especially concerning education. Few journalists, or citizens, seem to be concerned if a student was admitted into a show-time athletic program at, say the University of Michigan, to play football, basketball, or ice hockey with only the minimum SAT score required by the National Collegiate Athletic Association—as low as 820, depending on the high school GPA. Instead, journalists flood the media with "poor victim with good grades" articles about someone who could not get into an elite public institution like U.C. Berkeley. Affirmative action does have an impact on the students who apply to the most selective colleges—but not on the vast majority of high school graduates heading off to their state universities. For them, affirmative action is a sideshow. Economist Thomas Kane found that policies at elite universities between 1982 and 1992 had resulted giving black applicants "an advantage equivalent to nearly a full point increase in high school grade point average" or "several hundred points on the SAT." But at "the less selective schools that *80 percent* of all four-year college students attend, race seemed to play little, if any, role in admission decisions." That pattern, he reported, "remained largely the same a decade later."

Instead of reminding citizens of that crucial point, the media has tended to focus only on highly competitive institutions denying deserving white students a seat when they could matriculate at many good universities. Recall the initial two cases mentioned in the preface: Jennifer Gratz's co-plaintiff, Patrick Hamacher, did not get into the University of Michigan, but he was accepted, and graduated from, Michigan State; the many who do not get accepted at Berkeley attend other campuses in the fine U.C. system. The 28 private selective colleges who filed *amicus* briefs supporting the University of Michigan had a total of only 15,000 freshmen and only one thousand blacks, a minuscule amount compared to the number of white and minority students attending the top 50 public universities. In reality, increasing the number of black or Latino college graduates really does not depend on the number of them accepted into the Ivy League schools, and the same is true for professional schools. Barbara Grutter, rejected by the University of Michigan Law School, was accepted by Wayne State University Law School. After all, a college graduate can apply to approximately 160 medical and about 170 law schools in the U.S.A.

Most educators agree that the problem is not so much helping minorities—particularly African Americans—into good universities, it is getting them there in the first place. In 1997 the University of Texas president said that in his state there were 36,000 African Americans every year who were of college-entrance age. Just two-thirds completed high school, only 6,000 took college entrance tests, and only 1,000 scored high enough to meet entrance standards at competitive schools. African American Ronald Ferguson surveyed 34,000 seventh to eleventh graders in racially mixed suburbs and found that whites averaged B+ and blacks C+, and that over half of those black kids lived with one or neither parent, compared to 15 percent for the whites. For years Jesse Jackson has been lamenting that there are more black men age 18 to 25 in prison than in college. These depressing facts reveal that so much of college admission is decided not by university officials but by parents, years before their children head off to dormitories. How society addresses such issues is beyond the scope of this book, but the long, hard drive toward educational and subsequent economic equality will take persistent policies, whether governmental, private, or voluntary, to build individual responsibility, strengthen families, improve public schools, and increase outreach programs, all of which are necessary to prepare minority—and all—children for the opportunities in America. If the nation has the will for such heavy lifting, it will not be decided in college admission offices but in the voting booths.

While the educational gap remains a problem, advocates and critics of affirmative action exaggerate the economic gaps between the races, especially between whites and blacks. Liberals overstate lower earnings as proof of discrimination as they call for remedial social programs, while conservatives focus on problems in the ghetto, claiming that lifestyles of crime and drugs will make programs futile. As African American economist Glenn Loury reported in 1995, "It is worth remembering that the so-called 'black underclass' is a relatively small fraction of the total black population—perhaps 3 million to 5 million out of 32 million" people. This group, unfortunately, persists and resides in pockets of poverty throughout the nation and in highly visible media cities where they feed writers with endless plots for televison police series and Hollywood buddy/cop blockbusters. But overall, Loury reported that job discrimination was "not a major factor in accounting for the black–white earnings gap," that preferential hiring has played only a minor role in blacks marching into economic mainstream, and that most of the jobs have become available because of economic and business expansion. According to Loury, the economic status of black workers has risen during the last four decades because of improved education and job skills, "and this transformation has benefited all Americans. As a result, there is now a huge black middle class."

That being the case, is affirmative action still needed? Recall that the program has always been considered temporary, even by its ardent proponents. President Carter's aide, Joseph Califano, wrote that giving "minorities preference was a temporary remedy, not a permanent fixture of America's quest for racial equality, and time would someday run out," and in 1984 the *Washington Post* editorialized, "For a time, remedial laws have been necessary, but a permanent system of racial preferences cannot be justified." The Supreme Court has agreed, most eloquently by Justice Harry Blackmun. Writing an opinion, he expressed his "earnest hope that the time will come when an 'affirmative action' program is unnecessary and is, in truth, only a relic of the past." The nation was going through a regrettable but necessary stage of "transitional inequality," he continued, hoping that "within a decade at the most" American society "must and will reach a stage of maturity where action along this line is no longer necessary."

Blackmun wrote that not a decade, but more than a generation, ago in the *Bakke* case. Has America reached that stage? If not, then who should qualify for affirmative action, who should be preferred, in the new millennium? Most people would probably agree that African Americans should still be included, but what about the child of a black professor? "It is morally unjustified—and to this African American, humiliating," wrote Professor Loury, "that preferential treatment based on race should become institutionalized for those of us now enjoying all of the advantages of middle-class life. The thought that my sons would come to see themselves as . . . disadvantaged because of their race is unbearable to me." And what about others who in the past have had preferences? Should immigrants, who never were the original intent of affirmative action? Should white women, who during the last 30 years have become the majority of college graduates and the main competition for white men at professional schools? Should Asians, who have higher college graduations rates and per capita income than the average white citizens? Should Hispanics, when in Transracial America half of them do not even consider themselves part of that ethnicity on the 2000 census? "As the classification system gets fuzzier and blurrier," said former Census Bureau director Kenneth Prewitt, "we're going to have to re-create ourselves as a society without using a set of social policies which are based on race. That's a pretty big challenge for the twenty-first century."[3]

Indeed, a very big challenge. Affirmative action is a national policy that concerns the way Americans feel about race, past discrimination, preferences, merit—and about themselves. That is why it is an American dilemma, and that is why we must understand how it developed and how its rationale and definition have changed since the 1960s.

Should affirmative action be continued, and if so, in which form, or after four decades would America be better off without the policy? Has the pursuit of fairness reached its goal?

| sources

Affirmative action is a public policy, meaning that the government published volumes of documents while journalists examined all significant court cases or state referendums. Moreover, in the electronic age many governmental papers have been made public on the internet. Below is a select list of documents and books examined for *The Pursuit of Fairness.*

U. S. Government Primary Documents

Civil Rights during the Johnson Administration, 1963–1969. Microfilm collection of primary documents, edited by Steven F. Lawson, Frederick, Md., University Publications of America, 1984.

Civil Rights during the Nixon Administration, 1969–1974. Microfilm collection of primary documents, edited by Hugh Davis Graham, Frederick, Md., University Publications of America, 1989.

Congressional Record, Hearings of the House and Senate.

Congressional Quarterly Service, *Revolution in Civil Rights* (Washington, D.C., third edition, n.d., probably 1967).

Department of Labor, Office of Federal Contract Compliance Programs. Documents, website: dol.gov/esa/ofccp

Equal Employment Opportunity Commission. Documents, history, website: eeoc.gov

———. *EEOC Administrative History,* vol. 1 and 2, housed at Lyndon Baines Johnson Presidential Library.

———. *Legislative History of Titles VII and XI of Civil Rights Act of 1964* (Washington, D.C., Government Printing Office, 1965).

Glass Ceiling Commission, *Good for Business: Making Full Use of the Nation's Human Capital* (Washington, D.C., Government Printing Office, 1995).

Stephanopoulos, George, and Christopher Edley Jr., *Report to the President: Review of Federal Affirmative Action Programs* (Washington, D.C., Government Printing Office, 1995).

United States Commission on Civil Rights, *Federal Enforcement of Equal Employment Requirements* (Clearing House Publication 93, Washington, D.C., 1987).

United States Government, *To Secure These Rights: The Report of the President's Committee on Civil Rights* (Washington, D.C., 1947).

———. White House Press Office, press releases.

U. S. Government Printing Office, *Public Papers of the Presidents.*

———. *Federal Register.*

notes

Most presidential statements, federal regulations, and Supreme Court rulings usually are not in the notes and can be found in the *Public Papers* of the presidents, *Federal Register, Congressional Record*, and in published court documents. Authors and titles are abbreviated in the notes and full citations are in the select bibliography.

Abbreviations for Presidential Libraries:
LBJ: Lyndon Baines Johnson, Austin, Texas
JC: Jimmy Carter, Atlanta, Georgia
RR: Ronald Reagan, Simi Valley, California
GHWB: George H. W. Bush, College Station, Texas

Abbreviations for newspapers and magazines often cited:
HC: Houston Chronicle
LAT: Los Angeles Times
NYT: New York Times
U.S. News: U.S. News & World Report
WP: Washington Post
WSJ: Wall Street Journal

Chapter 1
1. J. Anderson, *Randolph*, 238–39; aircraft in Kesselman, *Social Politics of FEPC*, 6; and labor in Ruchames, *Race, Jobs & Politics*, 12.1.
2. Racial quotes from Litwack, *Trouble in Mind*, 218, 245, 234–36, 221, and Woodward, *Strange Career of Jim Crow*, 96; voting see Cohen, *At Freedom's Edge*, Chapter 8, and Litwack, 224–26.
3. Perman, *Struggle for Mastery*, 91, and Woodward, *Strange Career of Jim Crow*, 98; H.W. Brands, *TR: The Last Romantic*, 422–23; Brinkley, *Rosa Parks*, 24, and Holsey in Litwack, *Trouble in Mind*, 16.

4. Kantrowitz, *Ben Tillman*, 169; Hose in Litwack, *Trouble in Mind*, 281; James M. SoRelle, "The 'Waco Horror': The Lynching of Jesse Washington," *Southwestern Historical Quarterly* 86 (April 1983): 517–36; lynching figures in Cohen, *At Freedom's Edge*, 211–13.

5. Army War College in Daniels, *Not Like Us*, 127–28; Sitkoff, *A New Deal for Blacks*, 20–23; on lynchings in 1919, and see his Chapter 2 on the 1920s; Boulder Dam in Wolters, *Negroes and the Great Depression*, 199; Kirby, *Black Americans in the Roosevelt Era*, Chapter 4; for unemployment figures, see Garfinkel, *When Negroes March*, 17–21.

6. Houston in E. Foner, *American Freedom*, 214; Weaver and Foreman's plan in Wolters, *Negroes and the Great Depression*, 200–03; Ford policy in Myrdal, *American Dilemma*, 1121; quota issue in Moreno, *From Direct Action*, 62, Chapter 2.

7. Hopkins description in Sherwood, *Roosevelt and Hopkins*, 80; on Williams and equal pay, Eleanor and FDR, see Ellis, *A Nation in Torment*, 504, 523–26; female comment and working conditions see Blackwelder, *Now Hiring*, 99–106; affirmative action term is in Graham, *Civil Rights Era*, 6; Rubio, *Affirmative Action*, 35, traces the term to Reconstruction.

8. Kirby, *Black Americans in the Roosevelt Era*, Chapter 4; also see Lash, *Eleanor and Franklin*, Chapter 53, and Hareven, *Eleanor Roosevelt*, 112–29.

9. Nalty, *Strength for the Fight*, 131–33; New Yorker in Polenberg, *War and Society*, 99; Davis and Bethune in Anderson, *Randolph*, 238, 243.

10. Lilienthal is in Polenberg, *America at War*, 76–80; *Crisis*, March 1941, 71; Anderson, *Randolph*, 243–59, is the most dramatic on Randolph-FDR meetings; Dalfiume, *Desegregation of the U.S. Armed Forces*, 115–23, is the most accurate, and see White, *A Man Called White*, Chapter 23; steel president in Garfinkel, *When Negroes March*, 19, and see Pfeffer, *Randolph*, Chapter 2, and Kesselman, *The Social Politics of FEPC*, Chapter 1.

11. Italics added on executive order; Peck in *Crisis*, December 1940, article on warplanes in July and navy in that September, Bennett, *Confrontation Black and White*, 179; White in Garfinkel, *When Negroes March*, 77; FEPC never canceled a defense contract is Ruchames, *Race, Jobs, & Politics*, 142, and so are quotes from teamster and Louisiana 30, 94; Chinaman in Polenberg, *War and Society*, 115; Alabama congressman in *America at War*, 114–15. The debate on the effectiveness of the FEPC is nicely summarized in Reed, *Seedtime for the Modern Civil Rights Movement*, Introduction.

12. FEPC chairman in *To Secure These Rights*, 54–55; refusal to hire other minorities see Reed, *Seedtime for the Modern Civil Rights Movement*, Chapter 8; on West Coast see Broussard, *Black San Francisco*, Chapter 8; Corson, *Manpower*, 135–40; Japanese internee in E. Foner, *Freedom*, 241; Detroit sign in *Time*, 9 March 1942, 14.

13. *Nation* and numerous statements in Peter J. Kellogg, "Civil Rights Consciousness in the 1940s," *The Historian* 42 (November 1979): 30–34; Joseph R. Goeke and Caroline S. Weymar, "Barriers to hiring the blacks," *Harvard Business Review* (September/October 1969): 148; Rosie in Kennedy, *Freedom From Fear*, 776–79, poll in Flynn, *Lewis B. Hershey*, 117; and Gallup Poll, 13 February 1942; War Labor Board in Harrison, *On Account of Sex*, 96.

14. *Crisis* in Garfinkel, *When Negroes March*, 32–33; and "two front" in Sitkoff, *A New Deal for Blacks*, 324; draft issues are in Flynn, *Hershey*, 118–26; Lee, *Employment of Negro Troops*, 88–91, and Dalfiume, *Desegregation of the Armed Forces*, Chapter 3; commandant is in MacGregor, *Integrating the Armed Forces*, 100; governor is Dalfiume, *Desegregation*, 107; Bilbo is in Kennedy, *Freedom From Fear*, 634; and southern fears in Polenberg, *War and Society*, 109–10.

15. Grave implications in Dalfiume, *Desegregation*, 90, and see him on education, 56–58, along with Kennedy, *Freedom From Fear*, 771–73, and Fass, *Outside In*, 141; discrimination in Dalfiume, 92–93, 66–69.

16. Miller, nurses, and fascism in J. Foner, *Blacks and the Military*, 172–75, Chapter 7, 148; Dalfiume, *Desegregation*, 127, 78, 63; other polls in Mershon and Schlossman, *Foxholes & Color Lines*, 88–89, 105, and Schuman et al., *Racial Attitudes*, 10.

17. Negro problem in Dalfiume, *Desegregation*, 94–103; War Department in Franklin and Moss, *Slavery to Freedom*, 485; opinions in Mershon and Schlossman, *Foxholes & Color Lines*,124–26, Nalty, *Strength for the Fight*, 178; test and Jim Crow in J. Foner, *Blacks and the Military*, 178.

18. Tennessee riot is subject of O'Brien, *Color of the Law*; Bilbo in Dalfiume, *Desegregation*, 133; Snipes in Nalty, *Strength for the Fight*, 204–5; Woodard and Truman in Donovan, *Conflict and Crisis*, 244–45.

19. Robert J. Bailey, "Theodore G. Bilbo and the Fair Employment Practices Controversy: A Southern Senator's Reaction to a Changing World," *Journal of Mississippi History* 42 (February 1980), and see Reed, *Seedtime for the Modern Civil Rights Movement*, 155–72; Southern newspaper claims and business response in Kesselman, *Social Politics of FEPC*, 168–73.

20. Pride quotes in Kennedy, *Freedom From Fear*, 776, and Dalfiume, *Desegregation*, 106; Truman in Donovan, *Conflict and Crisis*, 3, 31, 172, and letter in Ferrell, *Off the Record*, 146–47.

21. *To Secure These Rights*, 4, 30–31, 40–49, 162–63; UMT in J. Foner, *Blacks and the Military*, 179–80; Truman in Donovan, *Conflict and Crisis*, 334.

22. Dogcatcher in Donovan, *Conflict and Crisis*, 336; Anderson in *Randolph*, 278–79; white soldiers in J. Foner, *Blacks and the Military*, 181.

23. On campaign see Hamby, *Man of the People*, Chapters 25 and 26; Dono-

van, *Conflict and Crisis*, Chapters 41–42, and Frederickson, *Dixiecrat Revolt*, Chapter 5; the army see Dalfiume, *Desegregation*, 179–84, and J. Foner, *Blacks and the Military*, 187–88.

24. Michaelis in Mershon and Schlossman, *Foxholes & Color Lines*, 225; marine in Nalty, *Strength for the Fight*, 262; infantryman in White, *How Far the Promised Land?*, 93; Korean surveys in Dalfiume, *Desegregation*, 213, and Mershon and Schlossman, 230–40.

25. State FEPC in Skrentny, *Ironies of Affirmative Action*, 28–29, and Moreno, *From Direct Action to Affirmative Action*, Chapter 5; Powell, *My American Journey*, 60–61.

Chapter 2

1. Powell, *My American Journey*, 41–42, and Gallup polls, 16 August 1952 and 7 February 1953; Eisenhower in Burk, *Eisenhower Administration*, 16, 84–87; Morrow, *Way Down South*, 121.

2. Southern response to Brown in Kluger, *Simple Justice*, 897; Stalin and military dictatorship in T. Anderson, *The Movement*, 31, and *The Sixties*, 15; Eisenhower and Faubus in Burk, *Eisenhower Administration*, 172–73. Adams, *First-Hand Report*, 355.

3. Harrington, *Other America*, 4; misanthrope in Sovern, *Legal Restraints*, 48–53; for similar fair employment results in Michigan see Sugrue, *Urban Crisis*, 173–74; a more positive view of New York's commission is Moreno, *From Direct Action*, Chapter 5; little to fear is Ruchames, *Race, Jobs & Politics*, 165; Arthur Earl Bonfield cites 99.7 percent, "The Origins and Development of American Fair Employment Legislation," *Iowa Law Review* (June 1967): 1077; airlines in *NYT*, 10 June and 23 December 1957, and local custom in Burk, *Eisenhower Administration*, 102–8; *Ebony*, May 1963, 28, and non-Italians in Moreno, *From Direct Action*, 151.

4. Minority jobs proportionate in Burk, *Eisenhower Administration*, 107–8; LBJ's farce is Graham, *Civil Rights Era*, 23; reasonable men is Dulles, *Civil Rights Commission*, 14; Till in Burk, *Eisenhower Administration*, 225; Greensboro 4 in T. Anderson, *The Movement*, 43–44; for 1950s sit-ins see Eick, *Dissent in Wichita*; Bennett, *Confrontation Black and White*, 255; Meier and Rudwick, *CORE*, 124; Wave and McCain quotes in *NYT*, 14 May 1960; LBJ: Hobart Taylor Jr., oral history, 12–13; for more on original meaning see Graham, *Civil Rights Era*, 28–35; for different interpretations see Moreno, *From Direct Action*, 189–90, and Belz, *Equality Transformed*, 18; active recruitment is in *NYT*, 6 March 1961.

5. JFK's "equal employment opportunity" and "Negro in Cabinet" in *U.S. News*, 5 March 1962, 83–85; limitations in Dulles, *Civil Rights Commission*, 203–4; Wirtz in Moreno, *From Direct Action*, 193–94; Lockheed from

author's interview and emails with Hugh Gordon, former employment manager, 25–26 September 2003, and *NYT*, 8 April and 14 May 1961; plan in *Monthly Labor Review*, July 1961, 748–49; official in *NYT*, 25 November 1961.

6. *Business Week*, 13 April 1963, 90; LBJ: Hobart Taylor Jr. oral history, 17, labeled most plans "absolutely meaningless documents"; Comet and oil in *NYT*, 18 April and 27 July 1962; Sovern, *Legal Restraints on Racial Discrimination in Employment*, 116–20, 140–42; contractor statistics in *Congressional Record*, 27 June 1963, 1487–88.

7. Federal workers, Price, and Fleeson in Harrison, *On Account of Sex*, 144–45, 74–76; polls and O'Connell in Linden-Ward and Green, *Changing the Future*, x–xi, 5; Zelman, *Women, Work, and National Policy*, Chapter 2; Goldberg and Macy in *WP* and *NYT*, 13 February 1962, and *U.S. News*, 15 June 1964, 91.

8. Birmingham quotes in T. Anderson, *The Movement*, 70–73; southern response to JFK's speech is *NYT*, 7 July 1963; white stereotypes and opinions in Brink and Harris, *Negro Revolution*, Chapter 9; numerous polls and pollsters in Schuman et al., *Racial Attitudes*, 66–67, 27–28, 121, Chapter 3; Harris survey in *Newsweek*, 29 July 1963, 15ff.

9. Randolph in J. Anderson, *Randolph*, 328–31, and JFK in Whalen, *Longest Debate*, 28; for senators' statements on the Civil Rights Act ibid., 146, 20.

10. Preference issue examined in Skrentny, *Ironies of Affirmative Action*, Chapter 3; Meier and Rudwick, *CORE*, 191–92, 235; twenty-five percent in *NYT*, 7 July and 21 August 1963; Farmer-Rodino in Hearings before Subcommittee No.5 of the Committee on the Judiciary, House of Representatives, 88th Congress, 2238–41, 26 July 1963.

11. Biemiller and Humphrey in Graham, *Civil Rights Era*, 140–51; Title VII exceptions see LBJ: Administrative History of the Equal Employment Opportunity Commission, box 1, 12; *U.S. News*, 17 June 1963, 8; Goldwater, Ellender, Dirksen in Congressional Quarterly, *Revolution in Civil Rights*, 70–71, 66; Humphrey in Whalen and Whalen, *Longest Debate*, 204.

12. Zelman, *Women, Work, and National Policy*, 64; Carl M. Brauer, "Women, Activists, Southern Conservatives, and the Prohibition of Sex Discrimination in Title VII of the 1964 Civil Rights Act," *Journal of Southern History* (February 1983): 37–56; longest filibuster in Whalen and Whalen, *Longest Debate*, 203; Smith in Congressional Quarterly, *Revolution in Civil Rights*, 73; LBJ aide is Bill Moyers, reported in Califano, *Triumph and Tragedy*, 55; Title VII problems, Sovern, *Legal Restraints on Racial Discrimination*, 65–73.

13. Selma in Anderson, *The Movement*, 113–20; Young, *To Be Equal*, 26–29, and see *NYT*, 12 September 1962, and *NYT Magazine*, 6 October 1963;

Bennett, *Confrontation Black and White*, 299, and Pfeffer, *Randolph*, 286–88; King's statements in *Playboy* interview, January 1965, 74–76, NYT, 5, 6 August 1965, 2 August 1966, and 27 July 1967; Kennedy and Wicker in *NYT*, 4, 9 August 1966; Myrdal in *New Republic*, 8 February 1964, 15.

14. *NYT* 6 June 1965; LBJ as liberal individualist, see Davies, *From Opportunity to Entitlement*, 32–34; Rose Garden in LBJ: Administrative History of the Equal Employment Opportunity Commission, box 1, 56–57; *New Republic* (10 July 1965): 5–6; *Business Week*, 12 June 1965, 82, 100, 106; *Nation's Business*, December 1965, 10ff; black education level in *WP*, 20 August 1965, test in *Time*, 28 October 1966, 33, and Chrysler in *Newsweek*, 1 July 1968, 21; *Business Week*, 12 June 1965, 82ff; 28 May 1966, 40.

15. Watts in Anderson, *The Movement*, 132–35; EEOC and Roosevelt in Graham, *Civil Rights Era*, 190–203; on the commission's first year, Blumrosen, *Black Employment*, Chapter 2; Farmer in *WSJ*, 28 May 1965; *Business Week*, 12 June 1965, 84; corporate president in *Harvard Business Review* (March 1963): 104.

16. Jews in *Newsweek*, 13 January 1964, 64–66; *U.S. News*, 29 July 1963, 88; other alarms in 11 November 1963 and 29 June 1964; commission proposal in Dulles, *Civil Rights Commission*, 183–86; Skrentny, *Ironies of Affirmative Action*, Chapters 1, 5; Graham, *Civil Rights Era*, 186–201.

17. Newport News in Blumrosen, *Black Employment*, Chapter 8; other early successes in LBJ: Administrative History of the Equal Employment Opportunity Commission, box 1, Chapter 4; impact of riots, Clark, and economist in Skrentny, *Ironies of Affirmative Action*, 87–100; company official in *U.S. News*, 12 February 1968, 61–62, and EEOC in *Business Week*, 18 March 1967, 84ff.

18. Black men in Hernandez, *EEOC and the Women's Movement*, 6–7; EEOC official, electronics businessman, and male secretary in Harrison, *On Account of Sex*, 187–91; Graham, *Civil Rights Era*, 204–18; *WSJ*, 22 June 1965; *NYT* 20, 21 August 1965; flat chested in T. Anderson, *The Movement*, 338.

19. Protective laws in *WSJ*, 22 May 1967; Griffiths, Clarenbach and Friedan, and LBJ in Zelman, *Women, Work, and National Policy*, 100–6, 39–45; Decker, *The Women's Movement*, 323–24; whorehouse in T. Anderson, *The Movement*, 339.

20. Training grants in *WSJ*, 16 October 1967; Clark and Sylvester in Skrentny, *Ironies of Affirmative Action*, 126, 135; special area programs, results, examined in James E. Jones Jr., "The Bugaboo of Employment Quotas," *Wisconsin Law Review* (1970): 341–403; Nathan, *Jobs and Civil Rights*, 106–10; Gould, *Black Workers in White Unions*, Chapter 11; hard-core in

US News, 12 February 1968, 60–62; Labor Department order in *Business Week*, 1 June 1968, 34ff.; LBJ no bullshit meeting from Califano, *Triumph and Tragedy*, 223–26; LBJ: Tom Johnson's Notes of Meetings, box 2, 27 January 1968; survey in *The Labor Month in Review*, December 1968, 42–45; *Newsweek*, 1 July 1968, 21ff.

Chapter 3

1. Quotes from T. Anderson, *The Movement*, 158–59, 300–02, see Chapter 6; *Time*, 6 April 1970, 28–29, and *Nation*, 3 March 1969, 271–74.

2. For Nixon's inconsistent race policy see Skrentny, *Ironies of Affirmative Action*, 178–82; *Time*, 18 April 1969, 19–20; union numbers in James E. Jones, "The Bugaboo of Employment Quotas," *Wisconsin Law Review* (1970): 368; *Newsweek*, 5 January 1970, 49; the 2168 quote and labor expert in *Nation*, 8 September 1969, 203–5; on union stalling see Hill, "Black Workers, Organized Labor, and Title VII . . . ," in Hill and Jones, *Race in America*, 263–344.

3. Fletcher in Curry, ed., *Affirmative Action Debate*, 26–29; Fletcher, *Silent Sellout*, Chapter 7; cabinet meeting in Safire, *Before the Fall*, 585; Skrentny, *Ironies of Affirmative Action*, 194–95; money in NYT, 24 September 1969, and Orientals in *U.S. News*, 18 August 1969, 64; percentages in Jones, Bugaboo article, 371–72; on the moon in Dean J. Kotlowski, "Nixon and the Origins of Affirmative Action," *The Historian* (spring 1998): 532.

4. Graham, *Civil Rights Era*, 325–27 and Chapter 13, 538–39, note 11; Kotlowski, *Nixon's Civil Rights*, 105; Skrentny, *Ironies of Affirmative Action*, Chapter 7; Shultz and Nixon's little extra also in Kotlowski's Nixon article, 529, 534; *WSJ*, 28 March 1969; Nixon, *RN*, 437; Hoff, *Nixon Reconsidered*, 137; for the debate on Nixon's motives see Gareth Davies, "The Great Society after Johnson: The Case of Bilingual Education," *Journal of American History* (March 2002): 1426–29; Kotlowski, *Nixon's Civil Rights*, 6–14, 102–8; Alexander in *Time*, 18 April 1969, 20; Kennedy in *Business Week*, 5 April 1969, 20; Ehrlichman, *Witness to Power*, 228–29.

5. Union leader in *NYT*, 24 September 1969, and Meany in Gould, *Black Workers in White Unions*, 301; confrontations in *NYT*, 28, 30 August 1969; *Chicago Tribune*, 25, 26 September 1969; Kotlowski article, 527–28; Mitchell's letter in Jones, Bugaboo article, 390–91.

6. Whorehouse in Nixon, *RN*, 438; Shultz on quota in NYT, 24 Sept 1969; on the union target, Ervin and Shultz exchange, NAACP, and 1970 rules and Order No. 4, Skrentny, *Ironies of Affirmative Action*, 197–210, 286; Graham, *Civil Rights Era*, 341, 409, and his *Collision Course*, 139–46; for the complexity of designating official minorities, Skrentny, *Minority Rights Revolution*, Chapter 4.

7. On failure of most city plans, see Gould, *Black Workers in White Unions*, 304–15; Fletcher's darn thing in *Time*, 17 August 1970, 62; *Montgomery* case in Jones, Bugaboo article, 378; *Contractors* case in Graham, *Civil Rights Era*, 341; Moreno, *Direct Action to Affirmative Action*, 263–64; *Monthly Labor Review* (September 1971): 65–66; *Griggs* in *NYT*, 9 March 1971; Alfred W. Blumrosen, "Strangers in Paradise: *Griggs v. Duke Power Co.* and the concept of Employment Discrimination"; "Redefining Discrimination," in Burstein, ed., *Equal Employment Opportunity*, 105–19, 121–28; Graham, 382–89, contends that "Burger's interpretation in 1971 of the legislative intent of Congress in the Civil Rights Act would have been greeted with disbelief in 1964"; Moreno in Chapter 10 declared, "For the next twenty years, the development of Title VII law would be based not on what Congress meant in Title VII but on what the Court meant in *Griggs*."; similar views are expressed by Graham, *Collision Course*, 28, and by Herman Belz, Lino A. Graglia, and Paul Craig Roberts; see select bibliography.

8. Metro in *WP*, 2 July and 8 November 1971; Roybal and ACLU in *NYT*, 23 October and 21 December 1971; women's liberation from T. Anderson, *The Movement*, 338–41, 359; Freeman, *Politics of Women's Liberation*, 195–97; Abzug, Griffiths, and Ervin in *NYT*, 25 March 1971.

9. Guidelines for women are in Sobel, *Quotas and Affirmative Action*, 31; Graham, *Civil Rights Era*, 409–13; Kotlowski, *Nixon's Civil Rights*, 243–44; the latter two refer to the Magna Carta, for a detailed account, Skrentny, *Minority Rights Revolution*, 130–41; Libby Owen in Hole and Levine, *Rebirth of Feminism*, 36–40; Virginia in *U.S. News*, 4 October 1971, 96; Rauh in Belz, *Equality Transformed*, 73; Halderman, Ervin, and president privately wrote in Graham, *Civil Rights Era*, 433, 442–46.

10. Brown in *Business Week*, 8 July 1972, 20; cheap mother is in T. Anderson, *The Movement*, 362; Bell case is *U.S. News*, 14 August 1972, 66–68, and 29 January 1973, 69; *Newsweek*, 29 January 1973, 53; Wallace, *AT&T Case*, 1–5, 243–52.

11. *Time*, 6 April 1970, 28; demonstrations in T. Anderson, *The Movement*, 350–51; Safire, *Before the Fall*, 585, 571–72; Hill in Graham, *Civil Rights Era*, 344; "Black Workers, Organized Labor, and Title VII," in Hill and Jones, *Race in America*, 324–25; Brennan and Nixon abandoning Philadelphia Plan documented in Kotlowski, *Nixon's Civil Rights*, 111–15; *WP*, 29 and 25 August and 7 September 1972; Hodgson in Sobel, *Quotas and Affirmative Action*, 104. Nixon's reversal is examined in, and many quotes from, Skrentny, *Ironies of Affirmative Action*, 211–17, 288.

12. Law professor in Antonia Handler Chayes, "Make Your Equal Opportunity Program Court-Proof," *Harvard Business Review* (September–October 1974): 81ff; EEOC official, radical changes, and thunderous

implications in *Newsweek,* 17 June 1974, 75–76; Steel in *Newsweek,* 22 April 1974, 88, and *Business Week,* 20 April 1974, 35; for trucking see David L. Rose, "Twenty-Five Years Later . . . ," in Burlstein, ed., *Equal Employment Opportunity,* 46–47. *WP,* 24 March 1973 and 1 and 9 November 1974; AT&T in *Monthly Labor Review,* October 1974, 78.

13. Government official in *Newsweek,* 17 June 1974, 76; Seabury and Pottinger in "HEW and the Universities," *Commentary,* February 1972, 38–44; for Jews versus HEW see *WP,* 25 August 1972, 5 March 1973; *Newsweek,* 4 December 1972, 127–28; *U.S. News,* 22 July 1974, 54; and Freeman, *Politics of Women's Liberation,* 194–201; Kristol is in *Fortune,* September 1974, 203; CCNY in Gross, *Reverse Discrimination,* 62; Scott in *Newsweek,* 15 July 1974, 78; and Leeper in *U.S. News,* above; for Pottinger and many others in this debate see Gross, *Reverse Discrimination.*

14. Berkeley plan and retreat in *NYT,* 18 August 1975 and 28 December 1975; EEOC in *NYT* 25 November 1976; OFCC in *Business Week,* 10 May 1976, 98; Ford and Carter quotes in Carroll, *Nothing Happened,* 173, 187–89.

15. Jordan in *Newsweek,* 22 November 1976, 15; Califano in *NYT,* 6 June 1977, and his *Governing America,* 232–35; debate and HEW official in *WP,* 14 September 1977; JC: Cabinet Meeting Minutes, 13 June and 1 Aug, 1977, Martha (Bunny) Mitchell collection, box 3; *Nation,* 20 August 1977, 132; Gallup reported in *WP,* 1 May 1977; for the complex issue of misunderstanding questions see Charlotte Steeh and Maria Krysan, "Affirmative Action and the Public, 1970–1995," *Public Opinion Quarterly* (1996): 128–58; Lawrence Bobo, "Race, Interest, and Beliefs about Affirmative Action," in Skrentny, *Color Lines,* Chapter 8.

16. *U.S. News,* 29 March 1976, 26; Ringer, Ornstein and others in *Society,* Jan/February 1976; *Forbes,* 29 May 1978, 29; *U.S. News,* 23 August 1976, 50; 28 March 1977, 68; 29 September 1980, 69; *Newsweek,* 31 March 1975, 64, and magazine editor in *Newsweek,* 17 January 1977, 11; *Time,* 25 July 1977, 52; *WP,* 30 April 1979; Sowell in *Commentary,* June 1978, 39; *NYT,* 14 November 1976; Raspberry in *WP,* 23 February 1976.

17. *Time,* 3 February 1975, 58; on teamsters case see *NYT,* 1 June 1977 and *Monthly Labor Review,* August 1977, 48–48; on "Preferential Admissions: Equalizing the Access of Minority Groups to Higher Education," see Robert M. O'Neil in the *Yale Law Journal* (March 1971): 699–767; Ohio State dean in *NYT,* 25 October 1977; *DeFunis v. Odegaard* was the first preferential admissions case against the University of Washington Law School, but since DeFunis had been admitted and was about to graduate the court declared it moot. Bakke see *NYT,* 19 June, 3 July, 25 October 1977; Ball, *Bakke Case,* 47 and Chapter 3; Wilkinson, *Brown to Bakke,* 254–55; and *Newsweek,* 10 July 1977, 19ff.

18. October 12 scene is in Ball, *Bakke Case*, 1, 88–89; supporters, opponents, and lawyer in *NYT*, 24 August and 15 June 1977; Carter and editorials in *NYT*, 20 September, 3 July and 19 June 1977; *Newsweek*, 10 July 1978, 19ff.; Lewis in *NYT*, 2 July 1978; *WP*, 29 June 1978; Bell in *U.S. News*, 10 July 1978, 14.

19. Factory in *NYT Magazine*, 25 February 1979, 37; for Weber see *WP*, 12 January 1979; *NYT*, 12 December 1978; pro and con opinions in *NYT* and *WP*, 28 June 1979; contractor spokesman in *U.S. News*, 10 July 1978, 17; *Nation*, 19 July 1980, 67–68.

20. Virgin birth in *WP*, 11 April 1982; enforcement numbers in Belz, *Equality Transformed*, 197; *Newsweek*, 26 September 1977, 52; on fairness see, Laurence H. Tribe, "Perspectives on *Bakke*: Equal Protection, Procedural Fairness, or Structural Justice?" *Harvard Law Review* (1979): 864–77; poll in *NYT*, 19 February 1977, and *Newsweek*, 26 February 1979, 48ff; business poll in *WSJ*, 3 April 1979; Lockheed in *Business Week*, 27 January 1975, 98; Potomac and OFCCP is Hammerman, *A Decade of New Opportunity*, 1–9, 42–4; Norton in *NYT*, 18 October 1979 and 15 July 1980; *WP*, 11 April 1982; Houghton in *WP*, 26 November 1976; Firestone in *WP*, 5 May 1981, and EEOC case in *Business Week*, 11 October 1982, 40, and Graham, *Civil Rights Era*, 460.

Chapter 4

1. On the election see Cannon, *President Reagan*, 5–6; for black appointments, *NYT*, 16 July 1981; and all Republicans today, Schaller, *Reckoning*, 43.

2. Reagan and African Americans, see *Newsweek*, 18 August 1980, 33, and *NYT*, 27 October 1980; his views on affirmative action and ultimate goal are in *Fortune*, 19 April 1982, 144; PACE and judge, *WP* 10 and 17 January 1981; colorblind and finally have won in *WP*, 27 March 1981; *Black Enterprise*, May 1981, 20.

3. Hatch hearings in *WP* and *NYT*, 5 May 1981, and *WP*, 17 July 1981; research organization and Hispanic employee in *Fortune*, 19 April 1982, 144; government officials in *Washington Monthly*, January 1981, 18–23, and 24ff; conservative author in *Commentary*, April 1982, 17–28; EEOC standstill in *NYT*, 16 July 1981; Reagan's speech and response *NYT*, 30 June 1981, *Time* and *Newsweek*, 13 July 1981, 11 and 20.

4. Sex harassment hearings in *WP*, 22 April 1981; Goldwater from Schaller, *Reckoning*, 41; thirty-seven groups in *WP*, 7 June 1981; 75 percent from *Time*, 7 September 1981, 8–9; Shong in *WP*, 25 August 1981; every man and Reynolds from *Time*, 7 September 1981, 8–9; WEAL in *Commentary*, April 1982, 23.

5. Reynold's views in *Commentary*, April 1982, 22–26, *WP*, 24 October and 18 December 1981, and for a more positive interpretation see Wolters, *Right Turn*, 1–19 and Chapter 11; Bob Jones in *Newsweek*, 25 January 1982, 24–5, as is Mr. Mayor; misstatements in *WP*, 11 April 1982; on affirmative action, 18 December 1981; Cannon, *President Reagan*, 460–61 and 104.

6. *Fortune*, 19 April 1982, 143ff.; *Business Week*, 25 May 1981, 123–24; contractor survey in 1984 and in Hammerman, *Decade of New Opportunity*, 15; see Franklin and Moss, *Slavery to Freedom*, 565–66 on commission episode, and Hart in *Commentary*, April 1982, 24; hogwash in *WP*, 2 August 1983; majority groups and lapdog in *WP*, 18 January 1984; EEOC and OFCCP in Klinker and Smith, *Unsteady March*, 301; Amaker, *Reagan*, 112–19; Wicker, *Tragic Failure*, 15–16; Blumrosen, *Modern Law*, Chapter 17; EEOC and individual suits, *Federal Enforcement of Equal Employment Requirements*, 20–24, 46; Belz, *Equality Transformed*, 189–90, 295, no. 26.

7. New Orleans see *WP*, 8 January and 6 April 1983; *U.S. News*, 14 March 1983, 70; seniority and Reynolds in *Newsweek*, 25 April 1983, 95; Detroit in *WP*, 10 and 11 January 1984; for *Stotts* see *Congressional Quarterly*, 16 June 1984, and Richard H. Fallon Jr. and Paul C. Weiler, "Firefighters v. Stotts: Conflicting Models of Racial Justice, 1984, *The Supreme Court Review*, 1–69.

8. Reynolds in *WP*, 14 June and 9 August 1984; Raspberry, *WP*, 15 June 1984; response to *Stotts*, *WP*, 14, 15, 17 June 1984; William Bradford Reynolds, "An Equal Opportunity Scorecard," *Georgia Law Review* (summer 1987): 1007–41; for all cases the administration argued on affirmative action during its second term see Charles Fried, *Order and Law*, Chapter 4; election see Schaller, *Reckoning*, 59–62; Cannon, *President Reagan*, 434–36; Edsall, *Chain Reaction*, 177–85; Bush in *Time*, 25 June 1983, 24.

9. *Time*, 25 February 1985, 19–20; Pendleton in *WP*, 1 February 1985; Mitchell in *NYT*, 7 and 10 March 1985; Meese in *NYT*, 16 March 1985; Thomas in *Federal Enforcement of Equal Employment Requirements*, 20; Justice Deptartment letters in *Newsweek*, 13 May 1985, 39; radio address in Laham, *Reagan*, 74–75, and Chapter 4 reveals Meese's role; new order in *NYT*, 15 and 16 August 1985, my italics; for revision and internal debate: RR, Memorandum for Peter J. Wallison from Robert M. Kruger, 13 May 1986, Box 18389, Robert M. Kruger Files; supporters and opponents see *Time*, 26 August 1985, 16; *NYT*, 20 August 1985; *Fortune*, 16 September 1985, 26–30.

10. Hudnut in *U.S. News*, 27 May 1985, 49–50; *Newsweek*, 13 May 1985, 39; *U.S. News*, 15 April 1985, 12; survey see *WP*, 25 May 1985; firestorm from

RR: Ralph G. Neas to Alfred H. Kingon, 12 February 1986, WHORM Subject File case file PQ472595; see Laham, *Reagan*, Chapter 5, for conservative business and union opposition to set-asides and affirmative action; Reynolds in *NYT*, 19 September 1985; Meese in *WP*, 25 August 1985, and *WP* and *NYT*, 18 September 1985; business views and survey see *Fortune*, 16 September 1985, 26–30; *Business Week*, 11 March 1985, 42; *WP*, 10 November 1985 and 23 January 1986.

11. Michel in *WP*, 23 October 1985; Cooper in *WP*, 23 January 1986; spokesman in *Newsweek*, 26 August 1985, 21; Brock, cabinet, and proposed order see Laham, *Reagan*, 27–30, 69, and Chapter 4; Reynolds in *WP*, 15 November 1985; Meese and Neas in *WP*, 16 January 1986; during the California Civil Rights Initiative affirmative action opponent Ward Connerly again used the "I Have a Dream" tactic, *Time*, 3 February 1997, 46; Mrs. King's rebuttal, *NYT*, 3 November 1996; poll in *NYT*, 19 January 1986; Reynolds in *NYT Magazine*, 11 June 1995, 54.

12. For Wygant see *Congressional Quarterly* (19 October 1985): 2105, and 24 May 1986, 1181; *Newsweek* and *Time*, 2 June 1986, 65 and 66; *Paradise* in *NYT* and *WP*, 26 February 1987; *Time*, 14 July 1986, 22; *Congressional Quarterly* (5 July 1986): 1525; Hooks, cities, and officials in *WP*, 3 July 1986; White House official in *WP*, 14 July 1986; 13 August 1986.

13. For Grove City see Cannon, *President Reagan*, 462–63 and Laham, *Reagan*, Chapters 7 and 8; *NYT*, 18 June, and Meritor case in 20 June, both 1986; for Johnson see Urofsky, *Affirmative Action on Trial*, Chapter 1, and *NYT* and *WP*, 26 March 1987; also consult Reynolds, "An Equal Opportunity Scorecard," *Georgia Law Review* (Summer 1987): 1036–41, and Herman Schwartz, "The 1986 and 1987 Affirmative Action Cases: It's All Over But The Shouting," *Michigan Law Review* (December 1987): 524–76.

14. *The Gallup Poll*, 10–13 April 1987, 141; Chamber in *NYT*, 27 March and *WP* 26 March 1987; *Business Week*, 13 April 1987, 37; Bork in Savage, *Turning Right*, 138–43; Ginsburg in Wolters, *Right Turn*, 14; the Ronald Reagan Library cites 371 federal judgeships and for Democrats the Clinton Presidential Materials Project cites 373.

15. NAACP in *NYT*, 4 July 1986; campaign statements and election from Greene, *Bush*, 36–43; Horton, see O'Reilly, *Nixon's Piano*, 378–91; survey from Klinker and Smith, *Unsteady March*, 305; Bush's affirmative action see *MS*. September 1989, 92; *Business Week*, 3 July 1989, 61.

16. For the growth in minority grants and businesses see Kotlowski, *Nixon's Civil Rights*, 150; for Wedtech consult Graham, *Collision Course*, 152–53; Richmond see Wolters, *Right Turn*, 274–76; *Congressional Quarterly* (28 January 1989): 178; *NYT*, 24 January 1989; response in *NYT*, 24 January, 29 January and *WP*, 30 February 1989; Florida in *WP*, 29 January 1989.

17. For *Patterson* and reversal of *Runyon* see *NYT*, 16 June 1989; for *Wards Cove* see *WP*, 6 and editorial 9 June 1989; *Nation*, 3 July 1989, 4; Hooks in *WP*, 10 July 1989.

18. GHWB: Kennedy to Sununu, 29 June 1990, Office of the Chief of Staff, John Sununu Files, box 26; Act and Zabkowicz in *WP*, 8 June 1990; commerce in *U.S. News*, 28 May 1990, 34; Thornburgh in *NYT*, 5 April 1990; Greenberg, *Middle Class Dreams*, 39–49; Edsall and Edsall, *Chain Reaction*, 181–85; quota bill from *WP*, 23 July 1990; really fair from *Business Week*, 3 December, 36; *Newsweek*, 3 December, 26, and 31 December, 28–29, all 1990.

19. Thomas' views and NAACP, *NYT*, 2 July 1991; Reynolds and Jackson in O'Reilly, *Nixon's Piano*, 395–96; Hill in Greene, *Bush*, 156–59, and *NYT*, 14 October 1991; opposition to Thomas in AP article, 4 July 1991.

20. *NYT* for lawyer's bonanza and Neas, 2 March, Michel in 13 March, and quota bomb, 7 April, all 1991; GHWB: Danforth to Sununu, 2 August 1991, Office of the Chief of Staff, John Sununu Files, box 37; *Business Week*, 25 March 1991, 45; Hyde and test in *NYT*, 17 and 19 May 1991; Act in *Congressional Quarterly* (26 October 1991): 3124–25; *NYT*, 26 October 1991; Andrew Dansicker, "A Sheep in Wolf's Clothing: Affirmative Action, Disparate Impact, Quotas and the Civil Rights Act," *Columbia Journal of Law and Social Problems* (1991): 1–50, and "Note: The Civil Rights Act of 1991: The Business Necessity Standard," *Harvard Law Review* (1993): 896–913; the Bush administration's interpretation is bushlibrary.tamu.edu/papers; "statement and remarks on signing the civil rights act of 1991," 21 November 1991; for Gray's views see GHWB: Nelson Lund memo to Gray, 13 November 1991, Counsels Office, C. Boyden Gray Subject File, box 18; quotes, confusion, flip flop discussed by Michael Kinsley in *New Republic*, 16 December 1991, 9–11, and Chester Finn Jr., *Commentary*, November 1991, 17–23; confusion also in *Texas Lawyer*, 11 November 1991, and *Chicago Daily Law Bulletin*, 27 December 1991, which has Washington lawyer quote; Charlatan in *NYT*, 7 November 1991; Horton gambit in O'Reilly, *Nixon's Piano*, 400–01; *National Review*, 16 December 1991, 17–18.

21. Decline of enforcement see Blumrosen, *Modern Law*, Chapter 17, AP article, 4 July 1991, and *Federal Enforcement of Equal Employment Requirements*, 21–24, 45; for the EEOC during the Bush administration on sexual harassment cases see *WP*, 7 April 1991; pollster and survey in *NYT*, 3 April 1991; 10 percent in *Congressional Quarterly* (9 February 1991): 368; opinion analysis in Schuman, et al., *Racial Attitudes*, 178–83; Sniderman and Piazza, *Scar of Race*, 128–35; on competing views see Edsall, *Chain Reaction*, Chapters 9–11.

Chapter 5

1. Told off Jackson in Klinker, *Unsteady March*, 310–11; Sherman in *NYT*, 1 November 1992; Moynihan in Berman, *Center to Edge*, 17.

2. PC in *Newsweek*, 24 December 1990, 48ff.; Bush, *NYT*, 5 May 1991; see Erin Kelly and Frank Dobbin, "How Affirmative Action Became Diversity Management," in Skrentny, *Color Lines*, Chapter 4; Lynch, *Diversity Machine*, Chapter 3; *New Republic*, 5 July 1993, 22–25; *Fortune*, 8 August 1994, 78; *Working Woman*, November 1994, 21; *National Review*, 21 Feb 1994, 32; *U.S. News*, 14 Nov 1994, 36; *Time*, 3 Feb 1992, 44–49, and special issue, fall 1993.

3. Survey in Lynch, *Diversity Machine*, 7, and introduction; diversity Visa see travel.state.gov/DV2004.html; Krauthammer in *WP*, 15 August 1997; Goodman in *Boston Globe*, 31 December 1992; Guinier see *Business Week*, 21 May, 42; *Time*, 14 June, 24, and *Nation*, 31 May, 724, all 1993; Clinton, *NYT*, 23 and 25 December 1992.

4. Gays in business and military see *Fortune*, 16 December 1991, 43ff, and *Business Week*, 26 August 1991, 72; Bolick in *WSJ*, 2 February; Casellas in *NYT*, 26 November, and EEOC numbers in their Press Release, 1 December, all 1994; remedy past discrimination in *Pittsburgh Post-Gazette*, 21 February 1994; *Business Week*, 26 September 1994, 52–54; mediation in *Nation's Business*, June 1995, 38–39; Taxman was awarded a financial settlement before the case reached the Supreme Court, *NYT*, 22 November 1997.

5. Sykes, *Nation of Victims*, 11; Keister in *WP*, 2 October 1990; McDonald's in *Chicago Tribune*, 21 May 1991; skin in *WP*, 22 February 1990; spokesperson in *WP* 21 June 1990; masculine and mustache in *WP*, 10 June 1994; Dillard's in *Fortune*, 3 April 1995, 142–43; Hooters in *WP*, 16 November 1995; Hooters settled out of court, being female was considered a "bona fide occupational qualification," see *Time* 13 October 1997, 65; Jenny Craig in *Time*, 12 December 1994, 62; Leo in *U.S. News*, 4 July 1994, 21; Lynch and William Beer, *Policy Review* (winter 1990): 64–67; Lynch, *Commentary*, August 1990, 44–47; for balance see E. J. Dionne Jr., *WP*, 2 May 1995; scream in *WP*, 22 November 1994; Lewis in *NYT*, 11 November 1991; *Newsweek*, 29 March 1993, 54 for one poll and others in *WP*, 24 March 1995 and *Houston Chronicle*, 15 October 1994.

6. On California's faculty diversity plans see Raza, et al., *Ups and Downs of Affirmative Action*, 93–109; Northridge in Lynch, *Commentary*, August 1990, 47; Weissberg in *Forbes*, 10 May 1993, 138; sociology professor in Lynch, *Invisible Victims*, 124; Wilkins in *NYT*, 3 April 1991; researcher is Alfred Blumrosen, *NYT*, 31 March 1995; Leno, Gingrich, and end of new deal in Berman, *Center to Edge*, 40–42; *WP*, 22 November 1994.

7. Hatch in *NYT*, 18 November and Patrick in *Boston Globe*, 26 November, both 1994; Republican hearings in *Congressional Quarterly* (18 March 1995): 819; Dole in *WP*, 6 February 1995; Bennett in *U.S. News*, 13 February 1995, 35; Wood and Connerly in *NYT*, 16 February and nervous in 7 February, both 1995; Kristol, poll, tearing Democrats, Wilson, and race and rage in *Newsweek*, 3 April 1995, 24–25; other poll in *WP*, 14 April 1995; Lieberman, *NYT*, 10 March, and Clinton and Kristol in *WP*, 24 February and 4 March, 1995; Dole, *NYT*, 16 March and *WP*, 16 and 17 March, 1995; Jackson, *NYT*, 10 March, and Gephardt, 14 March, 1995.

8. Set-aside problems and Rodriguez see Graham, *Civil Rights Era*, 151–54, his *Collision Course*, Chapter 6, his "Affirmative Action for Immigrants?" and George La Noue and John Sullivan, "Deconstructing Affirmative Action Categories," both in Skrentny, *Color Lines*; also see Skrentny, *Minority Rights Revolution*, Chapter 5; *Business Week*, 27 March 1995, 70–72; and *NYT*, 25 June 1998; for an attack on the SBA see Bean, *Big Government and Affirmative Action*; *Forbes*, 13 March 1995, 78–86; *Tampa Tribune*; commentator, 9 April 1995; one professor is Lawrence Fuchs in *WP*, 29 January 1995; no politician is *WP*, 5 April 1995; and glass ceiling quotes in *NYT* and *WP*, 16 March 1995.

9. Racial balancing in *NYT*, 18 April 1995; *Adarand* background, ruling, opinions see *NYT*, 13 and 18 June 1995; Bolick in *WP*, 2 July 1995.

10. Clinton in California, *NYT*, 9 April, and speech and commentary, *NYT* and *WP*, 20 July, poll in *Time*, 31 July, 35, all 1995; *LAT*, 21 July; *Newsweek*, 14 August 1995, 51; background to 209 see Raza, et al., *Ups and Downs of Affirmative Action*, 90–109; Custred and Joe Kline in *Newsweek*, 13 February 1995, 36–37; on 209 see Peter Schrag, *New Republic*, 30 January 1995, 16–19, and Chavez, *Color Bind*, Chapters 1 and 2.

11. Kline, Connerly in *Newsweek*, 13 February 1995, 36–37; undergraduate director in *Newsweek*, 3 April, 34; Texas A&M reported in *Chronicle of Higher Education*, 13 June, 1997, 29ff; well-connected in *San Francisco Chronicle*, 16 March 1996; Flinn in *LAT*, 16 June 1995; competition see Chavez, *Color Blind*, 60–62; SAT scores, opposite is true, Connerly, professor, and Wong in *NYT*, 4 June 1995; *U.S. News*, 5 June 1995, 30.

12. Wilson in *LAT*, 2 June, and *New Republic*, 26 June, both 1995; Connerly in *Newsweek*, 13 February 1995, 36; regents meeting in *LAT*, *NYT*, *WP*, 21 July 1995; Chavez, *Color Bind*, 63–67; clout, democrat, Pister, obstacles in *LAT*, 22 July, and chancellor in *NYT*, 24 July, both 1995; Dole and act in *Congressional Quarterly* (29 July 1995): 2279; Powell, *American Journey*, 592; *Newsweek*, 26 June 1995, 21; governors in *NYT*, 28 July and *WP*, 2 August, both 1995; rule of two, *WP*, 22 October 1995, and administration changes, *NYT*, 9 March, 23 May 1996, and 15 August 1997.

13. Hopwood case background in *Texas Monthly*, July 1994, 5ff and *Houston Chronicle*, 20 March 1996; Yudof in *Newsweek*, 1 April 1996, 54; administration in *NYT*, 25 May 1996; Bolich in *NYT*, 20 November 1995; Kemp in *LAT*, 28 September 1996; Canady in Chavez, *Color Blind*, 109; debate in *NYT*, 17 October 1996.

14. Gigot in *WSJ*, 12 April 1996; Camarena in Chavez, *Color Blind*, 217; shouting in *Congressional Quarterly* (8 November 1997): 2766; new policies, *NYT*, 16 March, 25 June, 1998; minority numbers from *NYT*, 15 May 1997; Byran College Station *Eagle*, 8 December 2002, and *WP*, 20 June 1998; Saldana in *Newsweek*, 12 May, 1997, 58.

15. Houston vote and Lanier see *Nation*, 15 December 1997, 22; for vote, Stein, and fundamental truth see *Houston Chronicle* and *NYT*, 6 November 1997; California exit polls in Chavez, *Color Blind*, 237; Connerly in *NYT*, 20 October 1998; Jeb Bush in *Time*, 2 August 1999, 58; polls in *NYT*, 11 July 2000 and *WP*, 15 November 1999; *U.S. News*, 19 July 1999.

16. Connerly in *WP*, 29 October 1996; Wynter, *American Skin*, 135; Kennedy and Rodriguez in *Atlantic Monthly*, December 2002, 103ff and January–February 2003, 95ff; Glazer in *Public Interest*, fall 2002, 21ff; Cherokee in NYT, 4 June 1995; not black in *Texas Monthly*, July 1994, 92; this became reality in 2003 when the State University of Rio de Janeiro established its affirmative action program: 14 percent of applicants who declared themselves "white" when they took the entrance exams declared themselves black or mixed after the program was established and when they applied, *WP*, Weekly ed., 23–29 June 2003, 17; Behar and silly games from Lynch, *Diversity Machine*, 304.

17. EEOC Combined Annual Reports Fiscal Years 1999–2001, AP article, 7 February 2003; *Adarand* case see WP, 11 August 2001; Fleischer, White House Press Release, 15 January 2003; FCC in NYT, 17 January 2001; U. Georgia in *WP*, 4 December 2002; *Time*, 23 August 1999, 48; background of Michigan case in *Chronicle of Higher Education*, 28 February 2003; Kinsley in *Time*, 27 January 2003, 70; hypocrisy in Newsday, 17 January 2003; Bush's grades in NYT, 18, 19 June 2000.

18. Gratz background in *Time*, 10 November 1997, 52–54; comment in AP article, 1 April 2003; Grutter see NYT, 11 May 1999 and *New Yorker*, 18 December 2000, 46ff.; U.M. 150 point system see *Detroit Free Press*, 23 June 2003, *WP*, 5 December 1997, *Newsweek*, 29 December 1997, 76; for system and Bollinger, state senator see *Chronicle of Higher Education*, 30 October 1998; state polls, 9 July 2003; impact of diversity on education is debated, see Holzer and Neumark, "Assessing Affirmative Action," *Journal of Economic Literature* (September 2000): 553–54, 559; black sophomore in *WP*, 1 April 2003, and bar surveys in *Time*, 23 August 1999, 48;

Rehnquist and O'Connor from their opinions; Coleman in CNN press release, 23 June, Malkin in *Houston Chronicle*, 26 June, and Connerly in *Chronicle of Higher Education*, 9 July, all 2003.

19. Decline of set-aside plans see *U.S. News*, 26 June 1995, 39; for why class-based will not work see Thomas J. Kane, "Misconceptions in the Debate over Affirmative Action in College Admissions," Chapter 2, and Jerome Karabel, "No Alternative," Chapter 3, Orfield, *Chilling Admissions*; polls in *WP*, 24 June, and *New Republic*, 3 February 14, both 2003.

Conclusions

1. Ethridge in Ruchames, *Race, Jobs & Politics*, 29; continuing discrimination see *AP* article, 7 Feb 2003, and EEOC combined annual report fiscal years 1999–2001, 4; Deptartment of Labor, OFCCP, executive order 11246, as amended and see "Federal Laws Prohibiting Job Discrimination, Questions and Answers, eeoc.gov/facts/ganda.html; one attorney and 50 public in *Chronicle of Higher Education*, 17 and 18 July, 2003; half of businesses in *WP*, 2 April 1995; Proctor and Gamble in *amicus* brief A-12; Bank One and big victory in *Business Week*, 27 January and 7 July 2003; Thernstrom in *New Republic*, 31 July 1989, 17ff.

2. Steele, *Content of Our Character*, Chapter 7; Murray in Mills, *Debating Affirmative Action*, 207; Holzer and Neumark in *Journal of Economic Literature* (September 2000): 483–568; black gains see Hartman, *Double Exposure*, 171; Bowen and Bok, *Shape of the River*, 9–11; *NYT*, 18 June 1995; *Ms*, September 1989, 92; Simms, *Economic Perspectives on Affirmative Action*, 6.

3. Kane in Orfield, *Chilling Admissions*, Chapter 2; in 2003 only a third of American colleges considered race as a factor in admissions, see *Chronicle of Higher Education*, 2 October 2003; Grutter chose not to attend Wayne State, see *NYT*, 23 February 2003 on the three plaintiffs; U.T. president in *NYT*, 13 May 1997; Ferguson in *NYT*, 4 June and *Cleveland Plain Dealer*, 12 February, both 2003; Loury in *WP Weekly Edition*, 23–29 October 1995, and in *The Public Interest*, spring 1997, 41–43; Califano, *Governing America*, 235; *WP*, 9 March 1984; Prewitt in *USA Today*, 13 March 2001; for other problems see Graham, *Collision Course*, 168–72.

select bibliography

More books were consulted, but many polemics are not listed because they add little to the historical record. Most of the following books appear in the abbreviated notes, as do documents and articles. For a bibliography of articles in the 1980s and 1990s, see A.M. Babkina, ed., *Affirmative Action: An Annotated Bibliography* (Commack, N.Y., 1998) and Joan Nordquist, *Affirmative Action: A Bibliography* (Santa Cruz, Calif., 1996).

Adams, Sherman. *First-Hand Report: The Story of the Eisenhower Administration* (New York, 1961).

Affirmative Action: The History of an Idea. BJW, Inc. Films for the Humanities & Sciences, 1996. Video.

Altschiller, Donald, ed. *Affirmative Action* (New York, 1991).

Amaker, Norman C. *Civil Rights and the Reagan Administration* (Washington, D.C., 1988).

Anderson, Jervis. *A. Philip Randolph: A Biographical Portrait* (New York, 1973).

Anderson, Terry H. *The Movement and The Sixties* (New York, 1995).

———. *The Sixties* (New York, 1999).

Ball, Howard. *The Bakke Case: Race, Education, and Affirmative Action* (Lawrence, Kans., 2000).

Bean, Jonathan J. *Big Government and Affirmative Action: The Scandalous History of the Small Business Administration* (Lexington, Ky., 2001).

Belz, Herman. *Equality Transformed: A Quarter-Century of Affirmative Action* (New Brunswick, N.J., 1991).

Bennett Jr., Lerone. *Confrontation Black and White* (Chicago, 1965).

Berger, Raoul. *Government by Judiciary: The Transformation of the Fourteenth Amendment* (Cambridge, Mass., 1977).

Bergmann, Barbara. *In Defense of Affirmative Action* (New York, 1996).

Berman, William C. *From the Center to the Edge: The Politics and Policies of the Clinton Presidency* (Lanham, Md., 2001).

Blackwelder, Julia Kirk. *Now Hiring* (College Station, Tex., 1997).

Blumrosen, Alfred W. *Black Employment and the Law* (New Brunswick, N.J., 1971).

———. *Modern Law: The Law Transmission System and Equal Employment Opportunity* (Madison, Wis., 1993).

Bonilla-Silva, Eduardo. *White Supremacy and Racism in the Post-Civil Rights Era* (Boulder, Colo., 2001).

Bowen, William G. and Derek Bok. *The Shape of the River: Long-Term Consequences of Considering Race in College and University Admissions* (Princeton, N.J., 1998).

Brands, H. W. TR: *The Last Romantic* (New York, 1997).

Brink, William, and Louis Harris. *The Negro Revolution in America* (New York, 1964).

Brinkley, Douglas. *Rosa Parks* (New York, 2000).

Broussard, Albert S. *Black San Francisco: The Struggle for Racial Equality in the West, 1900–1954* (Lawrence, Kans., 1993).

Brown, Michael K., et al. *Whitewashing Race: The Myth of a Color-Blind Society* (Berkeley, Calif., 2003).

Burk, Robert Fredrick. *The Eisenhower Administration and Black Civil Rights* (Knoxville, Tenn., 1984).

Burstein, Paul. *Discrimination, Jobs, and Politics: The Struggle for Equal Employment Opportunity in the United States since the New Deal,* (Chicago, 1985).

———, ed. *Equal Employment Opportunity: Labor Market Discrimination and Public Policy* (New York, 1994).

Califano, Joseph. *The Triumph and Tragedy of Lyndon Johnson: The White House Years* (New York 1991).

———. *Governing America: An Insider's Report from the White House and the Cabinet* (New York, 1981).

Cannon, Lou. *President Reagan: The Role of a Lifetime* (New York, 2000 ed.).

Caplan, Lincoln. *Up Against the Law: Affirmative Action and the Supreme Court* (New York, 1997).

Carroll, Peter N. *It Seemed Like Nothing Happened: The Tragedy and Promise of America in the 1970s* (New York, 1982).

Carter, Stephen L. *Reflections of an Affirmative Action Baby* (New York, 1991).

Chavez, Lydia. *The Color Bind: California's Battle to End Affirmative Action* (Berkeley, Calif., 1998).

Chideya, Farai. *The Color of Our Future* (New York, 1999).

Chin, Gabriel, J., ed. *Affirmative Action and the Constitution,* volume 1, *Affirmative Action Before Constitutional Law, 1964–1977* (New York, 1998).

Cohen, William. *At Freedom's Edge: Black Mobility and the Southern White Quest for Racial Control, 1861–1915* (Baton Rouge, La., 1991).

Corson, John J. *Manpower for Victory: Total Mobilization for Total War* (New York, 1943).

Curry, George E., ed. *The Affirmative Action Debate* (Reading, Mass., 1996).

Dalfiume, Richard M. *Desegregation of the U.S. Armed Forces: Fighting on Two Fronts, 1939–1953* (Columbia, Mo., 1969).

Daniels, Roger. *Not Like Us: Immigrants and Minorities in America, 1890–1924* (Chicago, 1997).

Davies, Gareth. *From Opportunity to Entitlement: The Transformation and Decline of Great Society Liberalism* (Lawrence, Kans., 1996).

Davis, Flora. *Moving the Mountain: The Women's Movement in America since 1960* (New York, 1991).

Decker, Barbara Sinclair. *The Women's Movement: Political, Socioeconomic, and Psychological Issues* (New York, 1983 ed.).

D'Emilio, John, William B. Turner, and Urvashi Vaid, eds. *Creating Change: Sexuality, Public Policy, and Civil Rights* (New York, 2000).

Detlefsen, Robert R. *Civil Rights under Reagan* (San Francisco, Calif., 1991).

Devins, Neal, and Davidson M. Douglas, eds. *Redefining Equality* (New York, 1998).

Donovan, Robert J. *Conflict and Crisis: The Presidency of Harry S Truman, 1945–1948* (New York, 1977).

Drake, W. Avon, and Robert D. Holsworth. *Affirmative Action and the Stalled Quest for Black Progress* (Urbana, Ill., 1996).

Drew, Elizabeth. *On the Edge: The Clinton Presidency* (New York, 1994).

Dreyfuss, Joel, and Charles Lawrence III. *The Bakke Case: The Politics of Inequality* (New York, 1979).

Dulles, Foster Rhea. *The Civil Rights Commission: 1957–1965* (East Lansing, Mich., 1968).

Eastland, Terry. *Ending Affirmative Action: The Case for Colorblind Justice* (New York, 1996).

Edley, Christopher. *Not All Black and White: Affirmative Action, Race, and American Values* (New York, 1996).

Edsall, Thomas Byrne, with Mary D. Edsall. *Chain Reaction: The Impact of Race, Rights, and Taxes on American Politics* (New York, 1991).

Ehrlichmann, John. *Witness to Power: The Nixon Years* (New York, 1982).

Eick, Gretchen Cassel. *Dissent in Wichita: The Civil Rights Movement in the Midwest, 1954–72* (Urbana, Ill., 2001).

Eisaguirre, Lynne. *Affirmative Action: A Reference Handbook* (Santa Barbara, Calif., 1999).

Ellis, Edward Robb. *A Nation in Torment: The Great American Depression, 1929–1939* (New York, 1970).

Epstein, Lee, and Thomas G. Walker. *Constitutional Law for a Changing America: Rights, Liberties, and Justice* (Washington, D.C., 1998).

Epstein, Richard A. *Forbidden Grounds: The Case Against Employment Discrimination Laws* (Cambridge, Mass., 1992).

Fass, Paula S. *Outside in: Minorities and the Transformation of American Education* (New York, 1989).

Ferrell, Robert H., ed. *Off the Record: The Private Papers of Harry S. Truman* (New York, 1980).

Fletcher, Arthur. *The Silent Sell-Out: Government Betrayal of Blacks to the Craft Unions* (New York, 1974).

Flynn, George Q. *Lewis B. Hershey, Mr. Selective Service* (Chapel Hill, N.C., 1985).

Foner, Eric. *The Story of American Freedom* (New York, 1998).

Foner, Jack, D. *Blacks and the Military in American History* (New York, 1974).

Franklin, John Hope, and Alfred A. Moss Jr. *From Slavery to Freedom: A History of African Americans* (New York, 2000).

Frederickson, Kari. *The Dixiecrat Revolt and the End of the Solid South, 1932–1968* (Chapel Hill, N.C., 2001).

Freeman, Jo. *The Politics of Women's Liberation* (New York, 1975).

Fried, Charles. *Order and Law: Arguing the Reagan Revolution—A Firsthand Account* (New York, 1991).

Garfinkel, Herbert. *When Negroes March: The March on Washington Movement in the Organizational Politics for FEPC* (New York, 1969).

Glazer, Nathan. *Affirmative Discrimination* (New York, 1975).

———. *We Are All Multiculturalists Now* (Cambridge, Mass., 1997).

Goldman, Alan. *Justice and Reverse Discrimination* (Princeton, N.J., 1979).

Gould, William B. *Black Workers in White Unions: Job Discrimination in the United States* (Ithaca, N.Y., 1977).

Graglia, Lino A. *Disaster by Decree: The Supreme Court Decision on Race and the Schools* (Ithaca, N.Y., 1976).

Graham, Hugh Davis. *The Civil Rights Era: Origins and Development of National Policy, 1960–1972* (New York, 1990).

———. *Collision Course: The Strange Convergence of Affirmative Action and Immigration Policy in America* (New York, 2002).

Greenawalt, Kent. *Discrimination and Reverse Discrimination* (New York, 1983).

Greenberg, Stanley. *Middle Class Dreams: The Politics and Power of the New American Majority* (New York, 1995).

Greene, Kathanne W. *Affirmative Action and Principles of Justice* (New York, 1989).

Grofman, Bernard, ed. *Legacies of the 1964 Civil Rights Act* (Charlottesville, Va., 2000).

Gross, Barry R., ed. *Reverse Discrimination* (New York, 1977).

———. *Discrimination in Reverse: Is Turnabout Fair Play?* (New York, 1978).

Hamby, Alonzo L. *Man of the People: A Life of Harry S Truman* (New York, 1995).

Hammerman, Herbert. *A Decade of New Opportunity: Affirmative Action in the 1970s* (Washington, D.C., 1984).

Hareven, Tamara. *Eleanor Roosevelt: An American Conscience* (Chicago, 1968).

Harrington, Michael. *The Other America: Poverty in the United States* (New York, 1962).

Harrison, Cynthia. *On Account of Sex: The Politics of Women's Issues, 1945–1968* (Berkeley, Calif., 1988).

Hartman, Chester, ed. *Double Exposure: Poverty and Race in America* (Armonk, N.Y., 1997).

Hernandez, Aileen C. *EEOC and the Women's Movement, 1965–1975* (Rutgers University Law School, 1975).

Herrnson, Paul S., and Dilys M. Hill. *The Clinton Presidency: The First Term, 1992–96* (New York, 1999).

Herrnstein, Richard, and Charles Murray. *The Bell Curve: Intelligence and Class Structure in American Life* (New York, 1994).

Hill, Herbert, and James E. Jones Jr., eds. *Race in America: The Struggle for Equality* (Madison, Wis., 1993).

Hoff, Joan. *Nixon Reconsidered* (New York, 1994).

Hohenberg, John. *Reelecting Bill Clinton: Why America Chose a "New" Democrat* (New York, 1997).

Hole, Judith, and Ellen Levine. *Rebirth of Feminism* (New York, 1971).

Hollinger David. *Postethnic America: Beyond Multiculturalism* (New York, 1995).

Hunter, James David. *Culture Wars* (New York, 1991).

Johnson, Haynes. *Divided We Fall: Gambling with History in the Nineties* (New York, 1994).

Kahlenberg, Richard D. *The Remedy: Class, Race, and Affirmative Action* (New York, 1996).

Kantrowitz, Stephen David. *Ben Tillman and the Reconstruction of White Supremacy* (Chapel Hill, N.C., 2000).

Kaufman, Jonathan. *Broken Alliance: The Turbulent Times Between Blacks and Jews in America* (New York, 1988).

Kennedy, David M. *Freedom from Fear: The American People in Depression and War, 1929–1945* (New York, 1999).

Kesselman, Louis C. *The Social Politics of FEPC: A Study in Reform Pressure Movements* (Chapel Hill, N.C., 1948).

Kirby, John B. *Black Americans in the Roosevelt Era* (Knoxville, Tenn., 1980).

Klinker, Philip A., and Rogers M. Smith. *The Unsteady March: The Rise and Decline of Racial Equality in America* (Chicago, 1999).

Kluger, Richard. *Simple Justice: The History of* Brown v. Board of Education *and Black America's Struggle for Equality* (New York, 1975).

Kotlowski, Dean J. *Nixon's Civil Rights: Politics, Principle, and Policy* (Cambridge, Mass., 2001).

Kryder, Daniel. *Divided Arsenal: Race and the American State During World War II* (New York, 2000).

Laham, Nicholas. *The Reagan Presidency and the Politics of Race: In Pursuit of Colorblind Justice and Limited Government* (Westport, Conn., 1998).

Lash, Joseph P. *Eleanor and Franklin* (New York, 1971).

Lee, Ulysses. *The Employment of Negro Troops* (Washington, D.C., 1994 ed.).

Leiter, Samuel, and William M. Leiter. *Affirmative Action in Antidiscrimination Law and Policy: An Overview and Synthesis* (Ithaca, N.Y., 2002).

Lemann, Nicholas. *The Big Test: The Secret History of the American Meritocracy* (New York, 1999).

Lewis, David L. *King: A Biography* (Urbana, Ill., 1978).

Lieberman, Robert C. *Shifting the Color Line: Race and the American Welfare State* (Cambridge, Mass., 1998).

Lind, Michael. *The Next American Nation* (New York, 1995).

Linden-Ward, Blanche, and Carol Hurd Green. *American Women in the 1960s: Changing the Future* (New York, 1993).

Litwack, Leon F. *Trouble in Mind: Black Southerners in the Age of Jim Crow* (New York, 1998).

Loury, Glenn C. *One by One from the Inside Out: Essays and Reviews on Race and Responsibility in America* (New York, 1995).

Lynch, Frederick R. *Invisible Victims: White Males and the Crisis of Affirmative Action* (Westport, Conn., 1989).

———. *The Diversity Machine: The Drive to Change the "White Male Workplace,"* (New York, 1997).

MacGregor, Morris J. *Integrating the Armed Forces, 1940–1965* (Washington, D.C., 1985).

Marable, Manning. *Beyond Black and White: Transforming African-American Politics* (London, 1995).

McCoy, Donald R., and Richard T. Ruetten. *Quest and Response: Minority Rights and the Truman Administration* (Lawrence, Kans., 1973).

McWhirter, Darien A. *The End of Affirmative Action: Where Do We Go from Here?* (New York, 1996).

Meier, August, and Elliott Rudwick. *CORE: A Study in the Civil Rights Movement, 1942–1968* (New York, 1973).

Mershon, Sherie, and Steven Schlossman. *Foxholes & Color Lines: Desegregating the U.S. Armed Forces* (Baltimore, Md., 1998).

Mills, Nicolaus, ed. *Debating Affirmative Action: Race, Gender, Ethnicity, and the Politics of Inclusion* (New York, 1994).

Moen, Ole O. *Race, Color, and Partial Blindness: Affirmative Action under the Law* (Oslo, 2001).

Moreno, Paul D. *From Direct Action to Affirmative Action: Fair Employment Law and Policy in America, 1933–1972* (Baton Rouge, La., 1997).

Morgan, Richard E. *Disabling America: The "Rights Industry" in Our Time* (New York, 1984).

Morrow, E. Frederic. *Way Down South Up North* (Philadelphia, Penn., 1973).

Myrdal, Gunnar. *An American Dilemma: The Negro Problem and Modern Democracy* (New York, 1944).

Nalty, Bernard C. *Strength for the Fight: A History of Black Americans in the Military* (New York, 1986).

Nathan, Richard P. *Jobs and Civil Rights, The Role of the Federal Government in Promoting Equal Opportunity in Employment and Training* (Washington, D.C., 1969).

Nixon, Richard M. *RN: The Memoirs of Richard Nixon* (New York, 1978).

Norgren, Paul H., et al. *Employing the Negro in American Industry: A Study of Management Practices* (New York, 1959).

Northrup, Herbert R. *Organized Labor and the Negro* (New York, 1944).

O'Brien, Gail Williams. *The Color of the Law: Race, Violence, and Justice in the Post-World War II South* (Chapel Hill, N.C., 1999).

O'Reilly, Kenneth. *Nixon's Piano: Presidents and Racial Politics from Washington to Clinton* (New York, 1995).

Orfield, Gary, and Edward Miller, eds. *Chilling Admissions: The Affirmative Action Crisis and the Search for Alternatives* (Cambridge, Mass., 2000).

Orfield, Gary, and Michael Kulanda, eds. *Diversity Challenged: Evidence on the Impact of Affirmative Action* (Cambridge, Mass., 2001).

Perman, Michael. *Struggle for Mastery: Disfranchisement in the South, 1888–1908* (Chapel Hill, N.C., 2001).

Pfeffer, Paula F. *A. Philip Randolph, Pioneer of the Civil Rights Movement* (Baton Rouge, La., 1990).

Polenberg, Richard, ed. *America at War: The Home Front, 1941–1945* (Englewood Cliffs, N.J., 1968).

———. *War and Society: The United States, 1941–1945* (Philadelphia, 1972).

Powell, Colin, with Joseph E. Persico. *My American Journey* (New York, 1996 ed.).

Raza, M. Ali, A. Janell Anderson, and Harry Glynn Custred Jr. *The Ups and Downs of Affirmative Action Preferences* (Westport, Conn., 1999).

Reed, Merl E. *Seedtime for the Modern Civil Rights Movement: The President's Committee on Fair Employment Practice, 1941–1946* (Baton Rouge, La., 1991).

Renshon, Stanley A. *High Hopes: The Clinton Presidency and the Politics of Ambition* (New York, 1996).

Reskin, Barbara F. *The Realities of Affirmative Action in Employment* (Washington, D.C., 1998).

Roberts, Paul Craig, and Lawrence M. Stratton. *The New Color Line: How Quotas and Privilege Destroy Democracy* (Washington, D.C., 1995).

Rosen, Ruth. *The World Split Open: How the Modern Women's Liberation Movement Changed America* (New York, 2000).

Rosenfeld, Michel. *Affirmative Action and Justice: A Philosophical and Constitutional Inquiry* (New Haven, Conn., 1991).

Rubio, Philip F. *A History of Affirmative Action, 1619–2000* (Jackson, Miss., 2001).

Ruchames, Louis. *Race, Jobs & Politics: The Story of FEPC* (New York, 1953).

Safire, William. *Before the Fall: An Inside View of the Pre-Watergate White House* (New York, 1975).

Savage, David G. *Turning Right: The Making of the Rehnquist Supreme Court* (New York, 1992).

Schaller, Michael. *Reckoning with Reagan: America and Its President in the 1980s* (New York, 1992).

Schuck, Peter H. *Diversity in America: Keeping Government at a Safe Distance* (Cambridge, Mass., 2003).

Schuman, Howard, and Charlotte Steeh, Lawrence Bobo, Maria Krysan, *Racial Attitudes in America: Trends and Interpretations* (Cambridge, Mass., 1997).

Schwartz, Bernard. *Behind Bakke: Affirmative Action and the Supreme Court* (New York, 1988).

Sherwood, Robert. *Roosevelt and Hopkins, an Intimate History* (New York, 1948).

Silberman, Charles E. *Crisis in Black and White* (New York, 1964).

Simms, Margaret C., ed. *Economic Perspectives on Affirmative Action* (Washington, D.C., 1995).

Sitkoff, Harvard. *A New Deal for Blacks: The Emergence of Civil Rights as a National Issue* (New York, 1978).

Skrentny, John David. *The Ironies of Affirmative Action: Politics, Culture, and Justice in America* (Chicago, 1996).

———. ed. *Color Lines: Affirmative Action, Immigration, and Civil Rights Options for America* (Chicago, 2001).

———. *The Minority Rights Revolution* (Cambridge, Mass., 2002).

Sniderman, Paul M., and Thomas Piazza. *The Scar of Race* (Cambridge, Mass., 1993).

Sobel, Lester A., ed. *Quotas and Affirmative Action,* (New York, 1980).

Sovern, Michael I. *Legal Restraints on Racial Discrimination in Employment* (New York, 1966).

Spann, Girardeau. *The Law of Affirmative Action: Twenty-Five Years of Supreme Court Decisions on Race and Remedies* (New York, 2000).

Squires, Gregory D. *Affirmative Action: A Guide for the Perplexed* (East Lansing, Mich., 1977).

Steele, Shelby. *The Content of Our Character* (New York, 1990).

Sugrue, Thomas J. *The Origins of the Urban Crisis: Race and Inequality in Postwar Detroit* (Princeton, N.J., 1996).

Sykes, Charles J. *A Nation of Victims: The Decay of the American Character* (New York, 1992).

Tuch, Steven A., and Jack K. Martin, eds. *Racial Attitudes in the 1990s* (Westport, Conn., 1997).

Tucker, Ronnie Bernard. *Affirmative Action, the Supreme Court, and Political Power in the Old Confederacy* (Lanham, Md., 2000).

Urofsky, Melvin I. *Affirmative Action on Trial: Sex Discrimination in* Johnson v. Santa Clara (Lawrence, Kans., 1997).

Wallace, Phylliss A., ed. *Equal Employment Opportunity and the AT&T Case* (Cambridge, Mass., 1976).

Walton, Jr. Hanes, ed. *Black Politics and Black Political Behavior: A Linkage Analysis* (Westport, Conn., 1994).

Wandersee, Winifred D. *On the Move: American Women in the 1970s* (Boston, 1988).

Warren, Earl. *The Memoirs of Earl Warren* (New York, 1977).

Weaver, Robert C. *Negro Labor: A National Problem* (New York, 1946).

Weiss, Robert J. *"We Want Jobs" A History of Affirmative Action* (New York, 1997).

Whalen, Charles, and Barbara Whalen. *The Longest Debate: A Legislative History of the 1964 Civil Rights Act* (New York, 1985 ed.).

White, Walter. *How Far the Promised Land?* (New York, 1955).

———. *A Man Called White* (New York, 1948).

Wicker, Tom. *Tragic Failure: Racial Integration in America* (New York, 1996).

Wickham, DeWayne. *Bill Clinton and Black America* (New York, 2002).

Wilkinson III, J. Harvie. *From Brown to Bakke: The Supreme Court and School Integration: 1954–1978* (New York, 1979).

Williamson, Joel. *A Rage for Order: Black/White Relations in the American South since Emancipation* (New York, 1986).

Wolters, Raymond. *Negroes and the Great Depression: The Problem of Economic Recovery* (Westport, Conn., 1970).

———. *Right Turn: William Bradford Reynolds, the Reagan Administration, and Black Civil Rights* (New Brunswick, N.J., 1996).

Wood, Peter. *Diversity: The Invention of a Concept* (San Francisco, Calif., 2003).

Woodward, C. Vann. *The Strange Career of Jim Crow* (New York, 1974 ed.).

Wynter, Leon E. *American Skin: Pop Culture, Big Business, and the End of White America* (New York, 2002).

Yancey, George. *Who Is White? Latinos, Asians, and the New Black/Nonblack Divide* (Boulder, Colo., 2003).

Yates, Steven. *Civil Wrongs: What Went Wrong with Affirmative Action* (San Francisco, Calif., 1994).

Young Jr., Whitney M. *To Be Equal* (New York, 1964).

Zelman, Patricia G. *Women, Work, and National Policy: The Kennedy-Johnson Years* (Ann Arbor, Mich., 1982).

| index